COGNITION IN
CLOSE RELATIONSHIPS

COGNITION
IN
CLOSE
RELATIONSHIPS

Edited by

GARTH J. O. FLETCHER
University of Canterbury

FRANK D. FINCHAM
University of Illinois at Urbana-Champaign

LEA

LAWRENCE ERLBAUM ASSOCIATES, PUBLISHERS

1991   Hillsdale, New Jersey   Hove and London

Lawrence Erlbaum Associates, Inc., Publishers
365 Broadway
Hillsdale, New Jersey 07642

Library of Congress Cataloging-in-Publication Data

Cognition in close relationship / edited by Garth J. O. Fletcher,
　Frank D. Fincham.
　　　p.　cm.
　Includes bibliographical references and indexes.
　ISBN 0-8058-0568-0
　1. Emotions and cognition.　2. Social perception.
　3. Interpersonal relations.　I. Fletcher, Garth J. O.　II. Fincham,
　Frank D.
　BF311.C54875　1991
　302'.12—dc20　　　　　　　　　　　　　　　　91-14482
　　　　　　　　　　　　　　　　　　　　　　　CIP

Printed in the United States of America
10　9　8　7　6　5　4　3　2　1

Contents

    Relationships: A Knowledge Structure Approach**   69
    Lynn Carol Miller and Stephen J. Read

    Knowledge Structures Useful for Understanding
        Persons and Relationships   *71*
    Developing Models of the Interaction, the Partner, and the
        Relationship   *78*
    Implications   *93*
    References   *97*

4. **Life Tasks, Personal Needs, and Close Relationships**   101
    Nancy Cantor and Janet Malley

    Life Tasks as Motivational Units of Personality   *104*
    Fundamental Personal Needs   *106*
    Analyzing Life Tasks in Close Relationships   *108*
    Integrating Needs and Tasks in Relationships   *113*
    Linking Tasks and Needs to Cognition in Close Relationships   *121*
    References   *122*

5. **A Contextual Model for Advancing the Study of
    Marital Interaction**   127
    Thomas N. Bradbury and Frank D. Fincham

    A Contextual Model of Marital Interaction   *128*
    Research Implications of the Contextual Model   *133*
    Summary and Overview   *143*
    References   *145*

PART II: COGNITION AND AFFECT

6. **Affect and Cognition in Close Relationships**   151
    Joseph P. Forgas

    Affect and Cognition: The Historical Background   *152*
    The Role of Affect in the Cognitive Representations of
        Relationship Scripts   *153*
    The Role of Affect in Cognitive Representations of
        Social Episodes in Relationships   *156*
    Affective Influences on Perceptions and Judgments in
        Close Relationships   *161*
    Affective Influences on Interpersonal Attributions and Decisions   *166*
    Summary and Conclusions   *170*
    References   *172*

Preface

The past decade has witnessed an explosion of interest and research on close relationships and on social cognition. In both areas, handbooks have been published, specialist journals have been established, and numerous textbooks and edited books have appeared. However, it is our impression that although cognitive theories and concepts have filtered through to research dealing with close relationships, much of this research reflects a relatively untutored understanding of the theoretical and empirical work in social cognition. Conversely, the research literature that provides a more sophisticated perspective on the role of cognition in close relationships typically reveals a relatively limited knowledge of the literature on close relationships.

As researchers who have worked in both fields (social cognition and close relationships) we are convinced that each has much to offer the other. Indeed, this book is based on two major postulates: first, that a social cognitive framework offers a valuable resource for developing our understanding of close relationships; and, second, that studying cognition within close relationships has the potential to inform our understanding of basic social cognitive processes.

Our mission for this book, therefore, was to provide a forum that would present an up-to-date account of the theoretical and empirical work concerned with the cognitive structures and processes within close relationships. Accordingly, we have included chapters that deal with established areas of inquiry as well as chapters that cover topics at the cutting edge of work that operates at the interface between social cognition and close relationships. Reflecting the interdisciplinary status of the book, most chapters were written by scholars whose dominant areas of specialization are either in social cognition or in close relationships. Indeed, some multiple-author chapters include scholars from each of these two domains. Thus, this book represents a unique attempt to present material that should be of interest to both scholars of close relationships and to those working in social cognition.

This book is divided into three major sections. In the first section, several chapters present general theoretical accounts dealing with the role of cognition, and related topics, in close relationships. The second section is more research oriented, with chapters that explore the interplay between cognition and affect, and their occurrence in the context of dyadic interaction. The third section contains chapters that examine the role of cognition in the development of close relationships and relationship repair. Finally, the book concludes with an integrative review and critique of all the chapters in the book.

The production of this book has been made possible by the help of many people. In particular, we appreciate the openness of the contributors to our vision and their patience as we worked toward its realization. We also thank Larry Erlbaum for his support and encouragement, and Jean Hammond and Janette Rosanowski for their sterling work in proofreading the manuscripts. To our friends, colleagues, and families, many thanks for your advice, help, and support during the course of this project. Finally, this book is a tribute to the inventors of electronic mail (whoever they are) who made this book possible by enabling two editors living on opposite sides of the world to communicate in a timely and efficient manner.

Garth J. O. Fletcher
Frank D. Fincham

COGNITION IN
CLOSE RELATIONSHIPS

CONCEPTUAL
FOUNDATIONS

This book is concerned with the interface between two areas that have witnessed a burgeoning of attention and interest over recent years: close relationships and social cognition. The chapters in this first section of the book, in part, reflect the historical development of both social cognition and the science of close relationships, and the relations between them. As is made clear in several of these chapters, these two fields have tended to develop in parallel rather than in tandem. Hence, in spite of the common use of cognitive explanations in close relationship research, and the increasing flow of research concerned with cognition in close relationships, there exist very few comprehensive theoretical accounts that focus on cognitive structures and processes as they function within close relationships. The first section in this book is designed to fill this lacuna.

The cognitive perspective in social psychology predates by several decades the cognitive revolution in psychology and its offshoot of social cognition. Moreover, the most influential and imperialistic theory in social psychology to immediately predate the modern social cognitive movement in the 1970s was attribution theory: a *cognitive* theory concerned with the schemata and processes involved when people explain one another's behavior. Indeed, attribution theory has remained popular partly because it has been widely exported to other areas in psychology, including the psychology of close relationships. In fact, research taking an attributional perspective is more voluminous than any other body of work explicitly concerned with the role of cognition in close relationships.

In chapter 1, *Attribution Processes in Close Relationships,* Fletcher and Fincham briefly review this body of research and the underlying standard attribution theory that has been adopted for use in close relationship work. They argue, however, that adherence to this standard model, derived from the classic attribution statements of Heider, Kelley, and others, has saddled the relevant research with various problems and gaps. Accordingly, they co-opt a model that attempts to locate attributional processing within a general, information-processing context. A central feature of this attempt is the use of a dimension that has had considerable currency in cognitive psychology and social cognition: the distinction between *automatic* and *controlled* processing.

In contrast to attribution theory, social cognition is more obviously an outgrowth of modern cognitive psychology with its focus on general features of information processing—a feature that is readily obvious in chapter 2, *Information Processing in Close Relationships.* In this chapter Scott, Fuhrman, and Wyer take one of the most fine-tuned and rigorously tested models of social cognition, developed by Wyer and Srull, and apply it to close relationship settings. As noted by these authors, social cognition theories have not been specifically developed to cope with the complexities of interpersonal communication or dyadic behavior. Hence, in their adroit application of the Wyer and Srull model to close relationships, these authors buttress the Wyer and Srull model with characteristically *social* features including communication norms and the reciprocity of emotional communications.

In chapter 3, *On the Coherence of Mental Models of Persons and Relationships: A Knowledge Structure Approach,* Miller and Read draw on one of the major challenges to the traditional information-processing approach in cognitive science, namely, what have been variously termed connectionist models, neural networks, or parallel distributed processing models. Such models are essentially massive networks of parallel structures, typically thought to be arranged in layers, that operate in terms of simple associative principles. The jury is still out on the validity of such an approach, the main problem being whether such models can adequately account for the sort of higher order cognitive abilities, such as reasoning and language use, that are presumably part and parcel of cognition in close relationships. All the more impressive, therefore, that Miller and Read, have imaginatively grafted a theory of explanatory coherence by Thagard (which in turn is based on a connectionist approach) onto a more traditional knowledge structure approach. Miller and Read's general aim is to understand how people build elaborate cognitive models of personal relationships and the individuals in those relationships. Their attempt is a pioneering one for social cognition, as well as for the science of close relationships.

Cantor and Malley's chapter, *Life Tasks, Personal Needs, and Close Relationships,* shares some features with Miller and Read's chapter, in that it also takes personal and relationship goals to be central elements in individuals' knowledge structures. However, Cantor and Malley move in a novel direction by building a general theory in which goals, personal needs, and what they term *life tasks* are all applied to close relationships. Compared to the other chapters in this section, Cantor and Malley's contribution is most concerned with the long sweeps of time in which close relationships take place, and also with the wider societal structures in which relationships are located.

In the last chapter in this section, *A Contextual Model for Expanding the Study of Marital Interaction,* Bradbury and Fincham provide a compact and updated summary of a general model that has already had an impact on the field of close relationships. Indeed, the pervasiveness of some of the concepts in this book, such as the distinction between proximal and distal contexts or classes of variable, can be traced, in part, to their use in this model. As well as showcasing their own research derived from the Contextual Model, a distinctive feature of Bradbury and Fincham's analysis is the diverse set of research areas they tap into, including the clinical, behavioral, psychophysiological, and social psychological arenas. Although explicitly aimed at marital interaction, their general thesis can be regarded as a wellspring for this entire section, namely, that general theories are desperately needed to interpret and integrate the welter of past research dealing with close relationships as well as to provide theoretical direction for future research endeavors.

1 Attribution Processes in Close Relationships

Garth J. O. Fletcher
University of Canterbury

Frank D. Fincham
University of Illinois

Attribution theory is primarily concerned with describing and explaining the cognitive structures and processes involved in the layperson's causal explanations for human behavior. Over the past decade, interest in attribution processes has been maintained, in part, through the application of attribution theory to a wide range of areas within psychology, including close relationships. Research on close relationships, like other areas of applied attribution research, has derived its theoretical base from assumptions and ideas found in the classic attribution theories of Heider (1958), Jones (Jones & Davis, 1965), Kelley (1967), and Weiner (Weiner et al., 1972).

To better understand the application of attribution theory to close relationship settings, it is important to appreciate that the classic statements of attribution theory and research preceded the emergence of social cognition within social psychology. In contrast to attribution theory, social cognition is more obviously a child of modern cognitive psychology—a pedigree that is clearly evident in social cognition's focus on general features of social information processing (such as encoding, storage, and retrieval of information) and its appropriation of methodologies and concepts from cognitive psychology.

Moreover, the model of human cognition that has informed much social cognitive research stands in stark contrast to that embraced by attribution theory. In the classic attribution models the layperson is assumed to have similar aims to those of the scientist—explanation, understanding, prediction, and control—and attribution processes are conceived of as largely rational and dispassionate. In social cognitive circles the layperson has come to be seen as a cognitive miser whose thinking revolves around simple heuristics or rules that produce endemic bias and error in social judgments. As Fiske and Taylor (1984) note, "Instead of a naive scientist entering the environment in search of the truth, we find the rather unflattering portrait of a charlatan trying to make the data come out in a manner most advantageous to his or her already-held theories" (p. 88).

In this chapter we attempt to reconcile the naive scientist and cognitive miser models, and to outline a model of attributional processing in close relationships that combines the best features of traditional attribution theory with contemporary theorizing from social cognition and cognitive psychology. Toward this end, this chapter is divided into three major sections. First, we provide an overview of research on attributions in close relationships and critically analyze the standard attribution model largely adopted for use in close relationship research. Second, we present a model of attributional processing within close relationships that attempts to locate attributional processes within a general, social, information-processing context. Finally, we discuss the applicability of three different models of social cognition to close relationships: laypeople as naive scientists, as cognitive misers, and as naive lawyers.[1]

ATTRIBUTIONS IN CLOSE RELATIONSHIPS: RESEARCH AND THEORY DERIVED FROM THE CLASSIC ATTRIBUTION ACCOUNTS

The Nature of Attributions

Apparently simple-minded questions often highlight serious conceptual confusions or problems with psychology theories; the question "What are attributions?" is a good example. The term *attribution* has been used in at least three ways that have frequently been confounded: *general* attributions to the person or environment that do not necessarily have causal status, *explicit causal* attributions, and what are sometimes termed *responsibility* attributions (see Hewstone, 1989).

To illustrate these distinctions, an individual might attribute the disposition of aggressiveness to his or her partner not in an attempt to explain the behavior, but merely to describe it. If the individual subsequently uses this attribution to explain the behavior (e.g., yelling at the partner), then the disposition becomes a causal attribution. Perhaps one may also use the attribution of aggressiveness in an attempt to pin the blame on the partner and justify his or her own response (e.g., yelling back). Because this attribution deals with accountability, it would then qualify as a responsibility attribution. These distinctions may be particularly

[1]Our review of the literature is intended to be selected rather than comprehensive. For those who wish to obtain a more detailed description of the research literature dealing with attributions in close relationships, several recent reviews are available (e.g., Bradbury & Fincham, 1990; Fincham, 1985; Harvey, 1987).

important in close relationship contexts, given the wealth of anecdotal evidence from clinical psychologists that attributions of blame or responsibility are common in such relationships.

Attribution research has been criticized for the common use of dependent measures or interpretations that ignore, or are ambiguous with respect to, these distinctions (e.g., Hewstone, 1989; Shaver & Drown, 1986). This problem is probably linked to the fact that these distinctions are also blurred in the classic attribution models. For example, Kelley's famous analysis of variance model of attribution assumes that the process of dispositional inference is equivalent to that of causal inference. Kelley (1973) writes, that "all judgments of the type 'Property X characterizes Entity Y' are viewed as causal attributions" (p. 107). Not surprisingly, studies of attribution in close relationships sometimes overlook the distinction between attributions as descriptive dispositions and as causal attributions (e.g., Fichten, 1984).

However, in close relationship research it is more common for confusion to arise between causal attribution and responsibility attribution. For example, Kyle and Falbo (1985) interpreted the results from a causal attribution measure (a single-item scale ranging from "extreme situational" to "extreme dispositional") as indicating that "people in high-stress marriages gave their spouses less credit for their positive interpersonal behaviors and more blame for their negative interpersonal behaviors than people in low-stress marriages" (p. 349).

We agree with the arguments of Shaver and Drown (1986) and others that researchers should be cognizant of the distinctions, noted above, in devising their dependent measures. One can only wonder, for example, what goes through subjects' heads when answering attributional questions that simply ask to what extent people are responsible for a particular event. Moreover, the research we discuss later is consistent with the proposition that dispositional ascriptions, responsibility attributions, and causal attributions may be represented cognitively in rather different ways. However, we will also argue that accepting such conceptual distinctions does not mean that these conceptualizations do not overlap, and also that exemplars of these categories do not, at times, reside in more than one category in everyday cognition.[2] These issues are not purely conceptual, as we shall see, but have direct implications for our understanding of the cognitive processes involved in causal attribution.

---

[2]A recurrent problem in conceptual and theoretical analyses dealing with this area, in our view, is the failure to recognize an important distinction in relation to the aims of the professional psychologist: *describing* the concepts used by the layperson, and developing an overarching theory that embraces and *explains* the layperson's psychological concepts and theories. For example, it is difficult to determine to what extent Shaver and Drown's (1986) conceptual analysis of attributions offers a description of the layperson's cognition or naive psychological theory, versus a theoretical account of the same phenomena that psychologists should accept as an overarching psychological theory.

Attribution Dimensions

An additional conceptual difficulty, that close relationship research work has inherited from the classic attribution models, concerns the appropriate causal attribution dimensions for use in close relationship settings. The internal–external dimension is pivotal in attribution theory. However, this dimension has various meanings not always differentiated in attribution theory or research. We might mean internal–external in a spatial sense (usually termed *locus*), which entails that everything located inside the person, such as personality dispositions, emotions, intentions, and illnesses, is internal, and everything outside, such as the behavior of other people, is external. Alternately, one might construe the dimension in terms of control. In this sense emotions, some abilities, and personality traits tend to be external (i.e., not under the control of the individual), and plans, beliefs, intentions, and effort are internal (i.e., under the control of the individual). Although there is evidence that these dimensions are psychologically distinct (Ross & Fletcher, 1985; Weiner, 1986), this distinction has almost invariably been interpreted in terms of locus of causality in close relationship research (see Bradbury & Fincham, 1990). Accordingly, when referring to the internal–external dimension we shall mean *locus* of causality, unless otherwise specified.

However, no matter how we interpret the internal–external dimension, it raises problems when applied to close relationship contexts (Fincham, 1985; H. Newman, 1981). At the *individual level,* attributions made to one's partner are external (in terms of locus). At the *relationship level,* however, where the relationship becomes the unit of analysis, factors outside the relationship become external attributions. Moreover, attributions toward oneself or one's partner may be directed at the individual (e.g., I am a bad-tempered person; she is an extrovert) or focus on the interaction between the partners (e.g., we communicate well; he gets uptight when I don't have meals cooked on time). These latter attributions have been dubbed *interpersonal attributions* by H. Newman (1981). The evidence suggests that interpersonal attributions are commonplace in close relationships (Fletcher, Fincham, Cramer, & Heron, 1987; Howe, 1987).

The Association Between Attributions and Relationship Satisfaction

Much of the research concerned with attributions in close relationships has examined differences between satisfied and dissatisfied couples in the way they explain positive and negative partner behaviors. The major findings, with respect to causal attributions, are summarized in Fig. 1.1. The basic idea, represented in the standard attribution model, is that people in happy relationships make attributions that maximize the favorable implications of positive behavior but minimize the implications of negative behaviors. Conversely, the attributions of folk in unhappy relationships, relative to those in happy relationships, deemphasize the

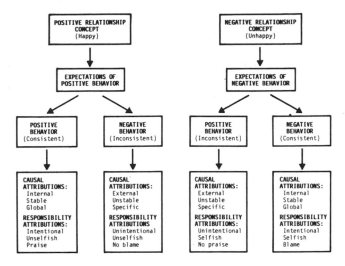

FIG. 1.1.   The relation between relationship satisfaction and attributions for interactive behaviors within close relationships: The standard attribution model.

favorable implications of positive behaviors but accept the unpleasant implications of negative behaviors.

To give an example using causal attributions, a happily married man explains his partner's warm greeting with a stable, internal, and global cause (e.g., she is a warm, wonderful person), but attributes his partner's sharp rebuke to an unstable, externally located, and specific cause (e.g., she must have had a hard day at work). The opposite attributional pattern (the right half of Fig. 1.1) characterizes those in unhappy relationships. Using the same example, an unhappily married man is likely to explain his partner's (unexpected) warm greeting with an unstable, external, and specific cause (e.g., she must have had a gambling win), but to attribute his partner's sharp rebuke to a stable, internal, and global cause (e.g., she is insensitive and bad-tempered). There is a considerable body of correlational evidence that supports the general pattern of attributions shown in Fig. 1.1, with both married couples and unmarried couples in long-term relationships (for reviews see Bradbury & Fincham, 1990; and Harvey, 1987).

Although a number of measurement techniques have been adopted in this area of research, a popular methodology has been to supply subjects with real or hypothetical interpersonal behaviors, ask them to provide the major causes of each behavior, then obtain ratings of these causes on a number of causal or responsibility dimensions (such as those shown in Fig. 1.1). This technique has several advantages over other procedures, the most important of which is the avoidance of an invidious methodological defect present in one standard technique in which the experimenter supplies causes that he or she judges, a priori, to be internal or external, stable or unstable, and so on. As pointed out by several critics (e.g., Ross & Fletcher, 1985), such a procedure suffers from the problem that causal attributions tend to be ambiguous with respect to where they are located on particular causal dimensions. Consider, for example, the causal attribution "he hugged me because he loves me." This appears to be a stock internal, stable, and global attribution; but, in a given relationship, the attribution ("he loves me") may quite reasonably be judged by a particular subject as relatively transient and specific.

A more general problem with any technique that makes use of structured ratings (including both of those discussed previously) concerns the extent to which attributional questions instigate attributional processing that may be quite different to that which occurs spontaneously in real-life settings; even worse, attributions may seldom occur at all in real-life. To deal with this problem, several researchers have assessed unsolicited attributions by requiring subjects to recount their thoughts and feelings in response to descriptions of positive and negative relationship behaviors. Causal attributions that occur in such protocols can then be coded into *relationship-positive* attributions or *relationship-negative* attributions, depending on whether they conform to the prototypical happy or unhappy relationship pattern outlined in Fig. 1.1 (a technique devised originally by Holtzworth-Munroe & Jacobson, 1985). The results from studies using this technique demonstrate the same attributional differences between happy and unhappy couples in their unsolicited attributions, as are found in studies using structured ratings (Fletcher, Fitness, & Blampied, 1990; Grigg, Fletcher, & Fitness, 1989; Holtzworth-Munroe & Jacobson, 1985). Moreover, studies that have used both structured, experimenter-supplied ratings and a measure of unsolicited attributions have found good convergent validity correlations between the two attributional measures (Fletcher et al., 1990; Holtzworth-Munroe & Jacobson, 1985).

Overall, we think there is sufficient anecdotal and research evidence to conclude that attributions are alive and well in close relationships and do not occur simply in response to invasive attempts by psychologists to measure their occurrence. However, we acknowledge that explicit, conscious attributional activity is likely to be more intensive at certain times during relationship development, such as the initial stages, periods of conflict, or relationship dissolution (see Surra & Bohman, this volume). (For an analysis of the conceptual and methodological issues in studying spontaneous attributional activity, see Bradbury & Fincham, 1988a.)

Considerably more research attention has been directed at causal attributions than responsibility attributions. However, work dealing with responsibility attributions has confirmed the model shown in Fig. 1.1, producing a similar pattern of findings to that found with causal attributions; namely, people in happy relationships, compared to those in unhappy relationships, view positive behaviors as reflecting less positive intentions, motivated by less selfish concerns, and more worthy of praise; the opposite pattern applies to responsibility attributions for negative behaviors (for reviews, see Bradbury & Fincham, 1990; Fincham and Bradbury, in press).

To sum up, there is evidence of a robust correlation between attributions and relationship satisfaction. However, the fact that attributional patterns correlate with relationship satisfaction does not necessarily imply the existence of a causal relation between the two constructs, an issue we turn to next.

Is there a causal link between attributions and relationship Satisfaction?   We know of only one experiment that has attempted to assess the causal impact of attributions on relationship satisfaction. Seligman, Fazio, and Zanna (1980) manipulated the attributions that subjects in unmarried relationships gave for their relationships by encouraging partners to list reasons for continuing the relationship that had either an external focus (e.g., "I go out with my girlfriend because she has a car") or a focus internal to the relationship (e.g., "I go out with my girlfriend because we always have a good time together"). As predicted, subjects in the external focus condition expressed less love and a lower likelihood of marriage than subjects in the internal focus condition. One obvious problem with conducting experiments to address such questions is that it is manifestly unethical to do so, except in the case of marital therapy which attempts to increase relationship satisfaction. However, treatment outcome studies dealing with interventions designed to change attributions in marital therapy have yielded equivocal findings (see Fincham, Bradbury, & Beach, in press).

Fortunately, there are other methods, apart from experiments, that allow the causal status of the link between attributions and relationship satisfaction to be assessed. Longitudinal data, for example, allow one to tease out the probable direction of causation between two constructs. Fletcher et al. (1987) found that unmarried persons who attributed the maintenance of their relationships equally to themselves and their partners reported increased relationship satisfaction two months later (using multiple regression procedures that statistically controlled relevant time 1 variables). In a more ambitious study, Fincham and Bradbury (1987) reported that wives who produced more relationship-positive causal attributions and responsibility attributions increased their levels of relationship satisfaction 12 months later. Moreover, in both studies, relationship satisfaction at time 1 was unrelated to attributions at time 2 (using appropriate statistical controls at time 1), suggesting that attributions cause relationship satisfaction but not vice-versa.

Such findings add substance to the proposition that attributions and relationship satisfaction are causally related. But, as with all correlational data, longitudinal studies do not rule out the possibility that other unmeasured variables are responsible for the association between attributions and relationship satisfaction (the *missing variable* problem). Perhaps the two most plausible candidates as missing variables are depression and explanatory style. Most developing relationships go through periods of conflict or relative unhappiness. People who have negative explanatory styles may, in these circumstances, generate maladaptive attributions for their relationships that will, in turn, produce depression or relationship unhappiness. Alternatively, it may be that people who are depressed before entering their relationships will both be more likely to become dissatisfied in those relationships and tend to produce relationship-negative attributions (as a function of their depression). In short, depression and/or explanatory style may independently cause relationship satisfaction and attributions, which implies that there is no causal relation between relationship satisfaction and attributions.

Although such a causal scenario is consistent with the evidence showing that depression is negatively correlated with relationship satisfaction (Gotlib & Hooley, 1988), and that depression and attributions are also related (see Robins, 1988), three recent studies suggest that neither depression nor explanatory style is responsible for the correlation between relationship satisfaction and attributions. Fincham, Beach, and Bradbury (1990) found in their first study that the relations between responsibility attributions and relationship satisfaction were not mediated by depression in a community sample of married women. In a second study, they showed that the responsibility attributions of a group of clinically depressed and maritally distressed women did not differ from a group of nondepressed and maritally distressed women. Both groups, however, differed in the expected fashion from happily married women. Similarly, Fletcher et al. (1990) found that neither depression nor general explanatory style (assessed via questionnaire) mediated the relation between causal attributions and relationship satisfaction in a sample of subjects in long-term unmarried relationships (as expected, all three studies found more depressed subjects were more dissatisfied with their relationships).

In sum, the evidence supports the existence of a causal link between attributions (both causal and responsibility) and relationship satisfaction. Notwithstanding this conclusion, there remain some basic issues and problems with the model displayed in Fig. 1.1 and the research it has generated which we will now discuss.

Caveats and Cavils

The type of model illustrated in Fig. 1.1 has operated as an attributional workhorse in numerous areas of social psychology covering topics as diverse as sex differences in attributions (Deaux, 1984), learned helplessness models of depression (Abramson, Seligman, & Teasdale, 1978), and the group-serving bias in attributions (Fletcher & Ward, 1988). In all such models the pivotal underlying assumption is that once dispositional judgments are formed, there is an inherent tendency for such judgments to be maintained. Imagine how the social world would be experienced if this was not the case. Our partners would appear to change their characters with every action, while our relationship judgments would be on a continual roller coaster. Such variability would, to put it mildly, threaten the stability, predictability, and controllability of our social world (including our close relationships). Attributions can thus be viewed as one powerful means of maintaining the relative permanence of our beliefs, schemas, and judgments concerning our partners and relationships, in the face of apparently contrary and shifting evidence.

This continuity between the standard attributional model utilized in close relationship research and the attribution theories utilized in other domains of social behavior enhances the power and credibility of the model shown in Fig. 1.1. However, a less flattering way of interpreting this claim would be that these models are dressing up a relatively simple point concerning people's penchant for consistency in their affective and cognitive judgments. Gottman and Levenson (1984) hint at this when they state that "if a couple is unhappy, they will agree that almost any dimension of marriage that could be negative is in fact negative" (p. 70).

However, the evidence suggests that the relations between the causal dimensions and relationship satisfaction are not as simple as implied by either the model in Fig. 1.1 or Gottman and Levenson's comment. For example, Bradbury and Fincham's (1990) review of the literature revealed that the connection between the locus causal dimension and relationship satisfaction is less robust than that between the globality causal dimension and relationship satisfaction. In a similar vein, Fletcher et al.'s (1987) study found that the same attributional variable had subtly different relations with different components of relationship satisfaction: Although partners' judgments of relationship happiness, commitment, and love showed substantial intercorrelations (a typical result), subjects who attributed the bulk of the maintenance of the relationship to themselves, rather than their partners, reported high levels of love, moderate levels of commitment, and low levels of relationship happiness. An extreme version of this pattern fits the notion of unrequited love rather nicely; the unfortunate individual suffering from such a condition would attribute the maintenance of the relationship entirely to himself or herself, probably be moderately committed, and almost certainly by thoroughly miserable.

These findings suggest that one valuable direction for research is to examine the relation between attributions and relationship satisfaction using more subtle and complex models of both constructs. Componential theories of love, such as Sternberg's (1986) triangular theory of love which conceptualizes love or relationship satisfaction in terms of related but distinct components, may be a useful starting point for such research (see Sternberg & Beall, this volume).

A second lacuna in attribution research in close relationships concerns the paucity of work investigating attributions and constructs in addition to relationship satisfaction. There are many potentially important constructs including personality impressions, relationship beliefs, and so forth, that merit empirical and theoretical attention. To illustrate this point we consider the construct of depression—a topic we previously dealt with, but purely in terms of the possibility that depression might account for the correlation between attributions and relationship satisfaction. Recall that the research results do not support such a proposition. However, there are other causal models dealing with the links between depression, attributions, and relationship satisfaction that deserve attention. For example, the correlational and regression analyses reported in Fincham, Beach, and Bradbury (1990) and Fletcher et al. (1990) are consistent with the plausible possibility that depression influences relationship satisfaction which in turn affects relationship attributions. To put it another way, relationship satisfaction may mediate the relation between depression and attributions.

Another set of questions concerns the relation between depression and attributions within relationship settings. One important difference between attributional models of depression and close relationships is that research dealing with depression takes the *self* as the unit of analysis, whereas close relationship theories focus on the *relationship*. This distinction has the most clear-cut implications for (locus) attributions to one's partner; for example, an attribution to one's partner for positive behavior is clearly relationship-positive, whereas from the perspective of an attributional model of depression it would be viewed as negative for the self. Fletcher et al. (1990) found that increased depression was associated with a relationship-negative pattern of attributions rather than a prototypical self-negative attributional pattern. Of course, if we accept that self-esteem in close relationships is causally connected to the partners' behavior and also to the participants' relationship satisfaction, then it is hardly surprising that relationship-negative attributions (e.g., attributing negative events to one's partner) may have negative consequences for the self (such as increased depression). The upshot of this discussion is that examination of the role that variables, such as depression, may have with respect to attributions and relationship satisfaction can yield more powerful and accurate social-psychological models of close relationships.

The third, and perhaps most obvious direction for further research is the need to examine attributions in the context of *actual* interactive behavior. The few studies that have examined the relation between attributions and dyadic behavior are more or less consistent with the attribution model shown in Fig. 1.1. Fincham & Bradbury (1988a) found that more relationship-positive attributional patterns for relationship problems (both causal and responsibility) correlated positively with wives' positive behaviors and negatively with both husbands' and wives' negative behaviors in discussions of marital problems. Moreover, there was evidence that reciprocation of behaviors was related to the attributions for these marital problems. For example, wives were less likely to reciprocate positive behavior if they viewed the cause of the problem as global and if they saw their husbands' contribution as being intentional and selfishly motivated (Bradbury & Fincham, 1988b). In a similar vein, Bradbury (1990) found that married women who produced a relationship-positive pattern of causal and responsibility attributions for a particular marital problem tended to express more anger and contempt, but less interest and sadness, in a later discussion of the same problem. Finally, in an experimental study, Fincham & Bradbury (1988b) manipulated attributions for a negative partner behavior and found that spouses who were induced to locate the cause of the negative behavior in their partners, were more negative toward their partners in a subsequent discussion than were those who attributed the negative behavior to the circumstances (for a more detailed discussion of these studies dealing with the behavior-attribution link, see Fincham, Bradbury, & Scott, 1990).

In sum, there is some evidence that attributions are related to behavior. However, studies of on-line attributions as they actually occur during the interaction process have yet to be conducted. This is the methodologically demanding option, to be sure, but a critical step in the further investigation of attributions in close relationships (see Fletcher & Kininmonth, this volume, for a discussion of studying on-line cognition in dyadic interaction). However, the standard attribution model provides a limited theoretical base for examining attributions in the context of interactive behavior for reasons we will now discuss.

ATTRIBUTIONAL PROCESSING
OF INTERACTIONAL BEHAVIOR
WITHIN CLOSE RELATIONSHIPS:
BEYOND THE STANDARD ATTRIBUTION ACCOUNT

As indicated previously, the standard attribution account used in close relationship research is largely derived from ideas and assumptions in classic attribution theory. Although it has proved to be useful, we think it is time to develop a new, if not entirely different, theoretical base for attribution research: We therefore offer a model that goes beyond the standard attribution account in four important ways. First, attributional processes are located within a more general social cognitive context. This step is part of a general movement in recent attributional theorizing and will, hopefully, generate ideas and hypotheses concerning the relation between attributions and other cognitive processes and states. Second, we explicitly address the interactional context, and pay particular attention to the link between attributions and behavior. Third, we think there are some advantages to be gained from a model that adopts an information-processing approach in addition to the more structural schematic approach found in the classic attributional theories. Finally, we take into account important domain-specific features of close relationships, while retaining links with what we know about attributional processes in more general social settings.

At first blush, attempting to model the role of social cognitive processes in close relationships seems an impossibly complex business given the range and complexity of variables involved. However, a useful beginning point adopted by a number of authors is the distinction between *distal* and *proximal* variables (Bradbury & Fincham, this volume; Kelley et al., 1983). The distal context includes stable dispositional variables that predate the immediate proximal context, such as personality dispositions, cognitive style dispositions (e.g., explanatory style), chronic mood states, and relationship-relevant attitudes, beliefs, and expectations (e.g., level of relationship satisfaction, relationship beliefs). In contrast, the proximal context includes the immediate interactional and social context, and the related flow of cognition and affect that precedes a given cognition or behavior.

The overall model we will explicate, shown in Fig. 1.2, is an adapted version of the *contextual* model developed by Bradbury and Fincham (Bradbury & Fincham, 1989; this volume).[3] Figure 1.2 represents a snapshot of one small part of an interactional, conversational sequence of dyadic behaviors. The actor observes and encodes a behavior of his or her partner (let us assume a verbal behavior accompanied by the typical gamut of nonverbal behavior), further cognitively processes the behavior, then responds with a behavior directed toward the partner.

The following example will be used to illustrate the model. Mary is an optimistic and well-balanced individual with a positive, general attributional style. Mary is very satisfied with her marriage and strongly believes that her relationship is based on an equal partnership. One can see elements here of some of the categories listed in the *distal* context in Fig. 1.2 (e.g., relationship satisfaction, relationship account). One evening, after her first week of work outside the home, Mary is straightening up the living room and begins to think about the division of labor between herself and her husband (proximal context). Nathan (Mary's husband) notices Mary cleaning up, starts thinking about his own chores, and comments that he is getting fed-up doing the vacuuming (*partner behavior*). Initially, much of the processing associated with perceiving and encoding the verbal and nonverbal behaviors is fast and unconscious (*automatic processing*). Because of factors already described in the distal context and proximal context (e.g., commitment to equality, immediately prior thinking about sharing jobs), Mary is surprised and initially slightly upset. This motivates her to subject Nathan's behavior to in-depth, conscious processing (*controlled processing*) and to consider how to deal with Nathan's comment. Based on the subsequent relationship-positive attribution she produces ("Nathan is under heavy pressure at work"), and the fact that she does not want her mother (who happens

---

[3]The most important change to the Bradbury and Fincham model is the adoption of the *automatic* versus *controlled* distinction in place of the *primary* versus *secondary* distinction proffered by Bradbury and Fincham. The two distinctions are roughly parallel in meaning. However, we considered a labeling change was warranted given that the *controlled* versus *automatic* label is more commonly used in the cognitive and social cognitive literature, while the *primary* versus *secondary* distinction seems to be used to refer to greater variety of distinctions in the same literature (e.g., primary vs. secondary emotions).

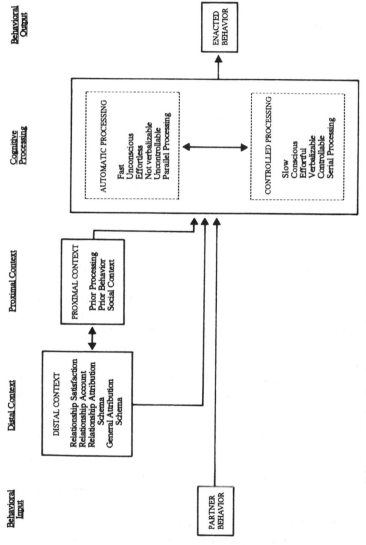

FIG. 1.2. Attributional processing of interactional behavior within close relationships: A social cognitive model.

19

to be in the next room) to be privy to a marital argument (*proximal context*), she decides not to confront the issue but responds with a reassuring comment to the effect that vacuuming is not really important.

Following this simple illustration of the model, we will next describe and discuss each component of the model in greater detail, concentrating on the role that attributions perform. We start with the heart of the model—the cognitive-processing component—where we will further discuss the distinction between *controlled* and *automatic* processing, and ask the questions: Are attributions automatic or controlled? What motivates controlled attributional processing in close relationships?

The Cognitive Processing Component: Controlled and Automatic Processing

Cognitive scientists are generally in accord that a good deal of cognitive processing takes place outside of conscious awareness and in parallel, rather than serially and consciously. Few situations illustrate the force of this proposition in as compelling a fashion as in a dyadic conversational context. A complex and intertwined flow of subtle, and not so subtle, stimuli need to be encoded, processed, and acted upon, including those related to the meaning of the verbal content, voice tone, and nonverbal behavior (including facial expression and posture). Moreover, each person needs to monitor and control his or her own verbal and nonverbal behavior so that it is, at least roughly, coordinated with his or her partner. It is difficult to see how such feats could be routinely performed without a large number of different processes being carried out simultaneously (i.e., in parallel).

In contrast to unconscious cognitive activity, conscious cognition involves some degree of phenomenological awareness, which is subject to verbal interpretation or description and which tends to be under the control of the individual. This contrast between two forms of cognition is commonplace in cognitive theory and has been given a variety of labels including *preattentive* versus *attentive* processing (Neisser, 1967), *primary* versus *secondary* processing (Bradbury & Fincham, 1989), and *unconscious* versus *conscious* processing (Branscombe, 1988), but perhaps the most popular characterization in cognitive psychology is that between *automatic* and *controlled* processing (Anderson, 1983; Posner & Snyder, 1975; Shiffrin & Schneider, 1977).

A key difference between the two processing modes is that controlled processing has attentional capacity constraints, unlike automatic processing, which has little or no capacity constraints. Automatic processing is thought to be fast, unconscious, effortless, not readily verbalizable, not controllable, and carried out in parallel. In contrast, controlled processing is relatively slow, conscious, effortful, verbalizable, controllable, and serially produced. This distinction is best represented as a dimension rather than in terms of discrete dichotomous categories, so that, for example, practice or learning will typically result in increasing automatization (Smith & Lerner, 1986). Finally, many processing tasks will involve both automatic and controlled processing acting either simultaneously or with rapid switching between modes (hence the double-headed arrow shown in Fig. 1.2).[4]

Attributions: Controlled or automatic?   This question has been hotly debated in the social cognitive literature, and is clearly a critical issue in evaluating the model in Fig. 1.2. We were earlier at pains to distinguish among three types of attribution: dispositional ascriptions, causal attributions, and responsibility attributions. Briefly put, we will argue that all three types of attributions may be present in both of the two processing modes, but that there are important qualitative differences between the kind of attributions that occur in the two modes, and associated differences in attributional processing. Because almost all the work related to these issues has been carried out in nonrelationship settings, research findings from the general social cognitive domain will be used to address these issues in close relationships.

The first question to consider is whether attributions (of any kind) exist at the automatic processing level. The most clear-cut evidence for the automatic processing of dispositional inferences has come from the program of research carried out by Uleman and his colleagues (for reviews see L. Newman & Uleman, 1989; Uleman, 1987). In a clever set of experiments, these researchers have found evidence that when subjects read sentences describing social events, they spontaneously infer dispositional ascriptions without either intending to or being conscious of doing so. Moreover, there is evidence that purely ascriptive dispositional processing tends to occur prior to explicit causal processing (e.g., Gilbert, Pelham, & Krull, 1988; Smith & Miller, 1983; Trope, Cohen, & Maoz, 1988). However, although simple, primitive attributional ascriptions may precede explicit and more complex causal attribution, this does not imply that causal attributions are *never* processed automatically or that dispositional ascriptions will *always* precede causal attributions. We present three arguments to support this proposition.

First, we take Read's (1987) point here that causal attributions are implicit in the act of encoding and comprehending a set of events. Indeed, we would argue that prototypical causal structures or events in the world are often directly and automatically perceived, requiring little or no higher order cognitive processing. To merely observe a particular behavior as an action involves some basic causal understanding that will appear as part of the observed behavior. For example, when I observe my wife pounding some wiener schnitzel flat with a mallet, the

---

[4]For an analysis of the *controlled* versus *automatic* distinction in relation to more general cognitive processes in marital relationships, see Fincham, Bradbury, and Scott (1990); for a comprehensive discussion of this distinction in relation to social cognition, see Uleman and Bargh (1989).

most basic causal aspects involved (the mallet's blows are causing the meat to become flatter, and my wife is causing the mallet to rise and fall) will appear as readily accessible features of the world, requiring little inferential work. Of course, if further attributional work is motivated, then more complex attributions will be involved that will require considerable inferential work (e.g., why is my wife making weiner schnitzel when she knows I hate it? Maybe she is doing it to annoy me—she never has forgiven me for accidentally killing the goldfish; perhaps her girlfriend is coming round to dinner, she loves red meat, etc.).

Second, the separation between causal attributions and dispositional ascriptions is not as straightforward as we have implied. The relation between the two concepts depends, in part, on what sort of dispositional theory is adopted (Fletcher 1984; L. Newman & Uleman, 1989). A behavioral theory of dispositions, such as Buss and Craik's (1983) "act frequency approach" interprets traits or dispositions simply as summary descriptions of observed behavior. By contrast, a causal theory of dispositions implies that there is some stable causal structure that produces or causes behavior under the appropriate conditions (see Zuroff, 1986).

According to Fletcher (1984), psychological theory implicit in everyday, commonsense psychology is probably more complex than either theory of dispositions, with different dispositions falling into both behavioral frequency and causal categories (also see L. Newman & Uleman, 1989). Consider, for example, describing one's partner as talkative or untidy—such attributions appear simply to constitute summary descriptions of regular behavior. On the other hand, attributions of beliefs, attitudes, or other mental attributes seem less obviously linked to behavior and more plausibly cited as internal causes of behavior. There are also many personality dispositions that straddle the mental and behavioral spheres and, hence, implicitly assume some causal dispositional structure that can produce the relevant behavior in the appropriate conditions (e.g., describing one's partner as insecure, warm, or insensitive). The upshot is that causal attributions may often be included, prepackaged and implicit, in the act of ascribing dispositions.

Third, in close relationships, causal attributions will often be produced as part of a well-practiced script and a set of stable personality and relationship impressions that require little, or relatively superficial, cognitive processing. Perhaps a wife's causal attribution that her husband's behavior is due to his insecurity was originally based on an agonizing and comprehensive causal analysis of his childish, attention-seeking behavior in public; once explained in this way, however, such an attribution may appear as part and parcel of his observable behavior and even his appearance. In short, cognitions that are originally part of the controlled processing stage may become an automatic and uncontrollable component of the encoding stage of information processing.

Many of the points made here concerning the links between causal attributions and dispositional ascriptions can be generalized to the links between responsibility attributions and causal attributions. In a similar vein to the proposition that dispositional ascriptions precede causal attributions, entailment models have been proposed in which blame attributions presuppose responsibility attributions, which, in turn, presuppose causal attributions (e.g., Fincham & Jaspars, 1980; Shultz, Schleifer, & Altman, 1981). That is, responsibility and blame attributions necessarily include some sort of causal attribution (even if it is of the primitive form X caused Y to occur), whereas causal attributions have little or no normative content of the sort found in responsibility and blame attributions.

However, we raise the same caveats as previously expressed concerning the order in which dispositional ascriptions and causal attributions are processed. First, it seems to us that on many occasions the responsibility and causal categories will be inextricably intertwined, particularly in close relationship contexts. For example, my partner's failure to remember my birthday may be attributed to her lack of love for me. This attribution could simultaneously be a dispositional ascription, a causal attribution, and a responsibility attribution with its attendant normative and blaming overtones. Second, as marital counselors know only too well, attributions, heavy with blame and invective, may become quite routine and automatic in distressed close relationships.

In sum, all three types of attributions may occur at both the automatic and controlled processing levels. This conclusion raises the important question of what factors motivate effortful, controlled, attributional processing, a question we turn to next.

When does controlled attributional processing occur?   This question is critical because it is related to the goals of the layperson and the associated functions of attributions. Weiner's (1985) review of the attribution research revealed two major triggers of explicit, conscious, attributional activity: negative events and unexpected outcomes.

The same factors, identified by Weiner (1985), have also been found to motivate conscious, explicit attributional activity in close relationships. Fletcher et al. (1987) reported that unsolicited causal attributions were more prevalent in unmarried partners' descriptions of their relationships when such relationships were unstable or when subjects were thinking about the possibility of separation. Holtzworth-Munroe and her colleagues (Camper, Jacobson, Holtzworth-Munroe, & Schmaling, 1988; Holtzworth-Munroe & Jacobson, 1985) have carried out several studies in which married subjects provided their thoughts and feelings in response to real or hypothetical behaviors. These studies have found that more attributions were produced for negative partner behavior than positive behavior. Fletcher and his colleagues (Fletcher et al., 1990; Grigg, Fletcher, & Fitness, 1989) have used the same technique, with subjects in unmarried relationships, and included self as well as partner initiated behaviors. The results showed that significantly more attributions were produced for negative behaviors (than positive behaviors), and that self-initiated behaviors evinced more attributions than partner-initiated behaviors.

A further point worth reiterating here is that attributions (dispositional ascriptions, causal attributions, and responsibility attributions) processed at the automatic level are likely to be either simple and data driven, or part of a well-rehearsed script. In addition, it seems likely that certain attributional dimensions will be especially influential at the automatic level. For example, we suspect that the locus (spatial location) of a cause may often be determined as part of automatic processing, simply because locus is likely to be a data-driven factor that is part and parcel of the encoded behavior. For example, if I see my partner baking a cake, I automatically assume that the cause resides in him. The causal dimensions of stability and globality are less obviously attached to the ongoing stimuli (i.e., data driven), and hence, may be less involved at the automatic processing stage.

It is also commonly believed that the judgment of intentionality is an important determinant of both causal and responsibility attributions (Fincham & Bradbury, in press; Heider, 1958; Jones & Davis, 1965). For example, Heider and others have suggested that personal dispositions are more readily inferred from intentional than unintentional behavior. In addition, Fincham (1985) and others (Shaver, 1985) have postulated that the assessment of intention is a critical factor in assessing responsibility and blame. How is intentionality assessed? According to Heider (1958) the layperson uses three criteria: *equifinality, local causality,* and *exertion.* Equifinality refers to the fact that intentional action is goal directed, implying that people will use a variety of strategies to attain a goal. Local causality is established when the actor is perceived as the originator of the behavior. Finally, Heider claimed that perceivers infer intention when exertion appears to be present. The critical point to note about this list is that these features are part of directly observable behavior, which means that intentionality judgments may often be data driven.

Recall the cake-baking example. We think it is apparent that the judgment that the cake-baking behavior is intentional rather than unintentional is data driven and perceived as a surface feature of the observed behavior.[5] The work of Smith and his colleagues (Smith, 1984; Smith & Miller, 1983) supports the point that judgments of intentionality may typically be data driven and automatically processed. If the above suggestions concerning the role of intentionality in the attribution process are correct, then this feature would facilitate the rapid and automatic attribution of both causal and responsibility attributions.

In contrast to the automatic level, controlled attributional processing can

---

[5]The term *intention* is used in different ways that are sometimes confused. Here, we are using the expression as a label that simply distinguishes *intentional* from *unintentional* behavior. However, the term is also sometimes used to refer to the motives or reasons that a person has for carrying out an action. According to this latter usage, intentions are actually causal or responsibility attributions. In the former usage they are not a class of attributions, although they may signal the appropriateness of certain kinds of attributions. For example, people are probably more likely to attribute motives or blame people for intentional behavior than unintentional behavior.

produce attributional accounts of astonishing complexity and sophistication in close relationship contexts judging by the verbal protocols produced by persons explaining important events in their own relationships, such as relationship dissolution (e.g., Fletcher, 1983a; 1983b). The stability and globality causal attribution dimensions are probably more theory driven than locus and intentionality judgments, and hence may become more important at this stage. Of course, it is also possible that in the controlled processing mode judgments of intentionality or causal locus may be processed anew and altered, leading to rather different attributions from the primitive, automatically generated attributions.

Another important factor that is likely to instigate controlled attributional processing is affective arousal. Indeed, it is a popular notion in emotion theories that autonomic nervous system arousal is part of a system especially evolved for alerting and directing the attention of the organism to some potentially dangerous or threatening state of affairs (e.g., Berscheid, 1983; Mandler, 1975). On this account, it is no accident that the key triggers of emotional arousal are the same as those that have been found to instigate explicit attributional processing (see Fitness & Strongman, this volume). However, the emotion labeling that occurs subsequent to the initial encoding of autonomic arousal may be influenced by later causal attributions. Weiner (1986) has argued that an initial attribution-independent emotion occurs that is subject to a primitive cognitive appraisal along a positive–negative dimension. Next, the individual makes a causal attribution along the three causal dimensions of locus, stability, and controllability. Subsequent labeling of emotions is held to depend on where these attributions are located on these dimensions. For example, pride will tend to be associated with the locus dimension, hopelessness with the stability dimension, and anger, pity, guilt, shame, and gratitude with the controllability dimension.

Weiner has made a valuable beginning in this area, and his theory has a plausible feel to it. However, his model may need some fine-tuning when applied to close relationships (see Fincham, in press). For example, it does not appear plausible that attributing the cause of a positive feeling to one's partner should reduce pride (as his theory predicts). In addition, Weiner's taxonomy of emotions may require revising in light of the wealth of emotion research dealing with emotion taxonomies (see Fitness & Strongman, this volume). Nonetheless, further examination of the links between attributions and emotions has the potential to provide a deeper understanding of attributional processes in close relationships.

Summary. To summarize this section, we have argued that attributions may occur at both the automatic and controlled processing levels, but that there are important differences between the kinds of attributions and attributional processing that occur in the two processing modes. Second, we concluded that controlled, in-depth attributional processing is motivated by unexpected events, negative events, and affective arousal. In the following two sections we discuss the remaining two components in our model—the proximal and distal contexts—with particular attention being paid to the influence these two factors have on attributions at both the automatic and controlled processing levels (see Fig. 1.2).

Proximal Context

The proximal context covers both the social context (with its associated norms) and the behavior and processing that have previously occurred in the immediate social interaction episode within which a particular behavior is located. This is a full-blown psychological model, so that the interactional and social contexts are taken into account only to the extent that they influence the cognitive processing of either partner.

As shown in Fig. 1.2, the proximal context can directly influence both the distal context and the cognitive processing component. The proximal context can influence attributional activity in a number of ways. For example, the social setting and the interaction episode will influence how behavior is perceived and interpreted, and hence indirectly determine the extent and nature of attributional processing. For example, a comment made to one's partner concerning his or her sexual peccadilloes may be interpreted as cruel by the partner in the context of a formal dinner party, but as open and honest in a private setting (with rather different attributions being instigated).

The other major impact of the proximal context is likely to involve the *priming* of attributional schemata or beliefs (in the distal context), which may in turn instigate or shape attributional processing. Alternately, factors in the proximal context may directly prime attributional processing (at the automatic or controlled levels). There is ample evidence from the social cognitive literature that such priming tends to occur without conscious awareness and beyond the control of the individual (Bargh, 1984; Higgins & Bargh, 1987). For example, viewing a play or thinking about a specific problem in one's relationship prior to some dyadic interaction may quite unconsciously prime a particular explanatory attribution for a partner's behavior (e.g., a deep-seated insecurity).

Finally, a potentially powerful way in which the proximal context may influence attributions or attributional processing is by creating affective states that may prime or color subsequent attributional activity. Simply being in a good or bad mood may predispose people toward relationship-positive or negative attributions (see Forgas, this volume; Scott, Fuhrman, & Wyer, this volume).

Distal Context

The distal context consists of relatively stable and permanent psychological characteristics. Hence, any information that is stored in long-term memory, or any personal disposition (traits, personality characteristics, or cognitive styles), is included in this component. However, although a potentially enormous range of material is *available* for retrieval, this material will vary in terms of its *accessibility*. Some constructs will only be retrieved on specific occasions, even within relationship settings, when they are primed by certain events or cues. Other constructs, sometimes termed *chronically accessible,* can permanently prime the generation of certain items, again potentially in an unconscious and unintentional fashion (e.g., Bargh & Tota, 1988). In a dyadic context, for example, we might expect that constructs such as relationship satisfaction, relationship beliefs, and so forth, will be chronically accessible and thus feature prominently in the generation of attributional processes.

In this section we discuss three different categories of attributional schemata that have received little attention in the close relationship literature: abstract social schemata, abstract schemata confined to the close relationships domain, and explanatory accounts that are specific to particular relationships.

The first, and most abstract category consists of general social attributional schemata that subsume relationship contexts. These would include such general individual difference variables as explanatory style (Peterson, et al., 1982) or the complexity of attributional schemata (Fletcher, Danilovics, Fernandez, Peterson, & Reeder, 1986). The extent to which such individual differences are related to attributional processes in close relationships has received little attention (for exceptions, see Bradbury & Fincham, 1988c; Fincham & Bradbury, 1989; Fletcher et al., 1990). These general causal attributional schemata will be built around the classic attributional dimensions already alluded to, such as stability, globality, and locus, although other causal dimensions such as the temporal dimension (where the cause is located in time) may also warrant inclusion (see Fletcher et al., 1986; Kelley, 1983). Responsibility attribution schemata will be built around the dimensions of blame, intentionality, and so forth.

The second type of attribution schemata, although still an abstract structure, is confined to close relationship contexts. Such schemata may differ in subtle respects from more general attributional schemata. For example, as we have previously argued, the interpersonal attribution target may become an important attribution category in such schemata. The relations between relationship-specific schemata and attribution schemata covering the entire social domain is, again, an open question; for example, an individual may have a positive attributional style for close relationships, but a negative attributional style for general social phenomena (although we might expect correlations between measures of individual differences from the two domains).

A third type of schemata is considerably more content specific and refers to a *particular* close relationship. Such an explanatory scheme will typically include a storylike account of the development of this relationship, an understanding of the major issues and problems in the relationship, and so forth. This rich knowledge base will include more than attributional material, and it will be related to the more abstract schemata noted above. However, presumably it will provide a highly accessible construct that will generate attributions at both the automatic and controlled levels. Harvey and his colleagues (Harvey, 1989; Harvey, Agostinelli, & Weber, in press) have made a valuable beginning in investigating the contents and the origins of such accounts.

Relationship-specific accounts will also be strongly related to interactional scripts or what Smith (in press) terms "if . . . then" production rules (derived from Anderson's, 1983, Act* model). The presence of such scripts probably accounts for the stereotyped fashion in which interactional patterns occur in long-term relationships—the associated cognitions (predictions, attributions, etc.) may be built into these behavioral scripts and hence become instantly available to conscious awareness if required.

Although attributions may often simply be read-off from the relationship account in the fashion indicated above, the more abstract schemata add considerable explanatory power to any general model of attributional processes. This is so for two reasons. First, it is difficult to explain how a given relationship account develops without postulating an a priori attributional framework. Second, unexpected or idiosyncratic behaviors occur often, even in the best regulated close relationships, requiring the individual to go beyond the content of the relationship account to generate the appropriate attributions. Indeed, as we have previously argued, it is in just such circumstances that controlled, explicit attributional activity is likely to occur. Unfortunately, there is little research that deals with the relation between these three types of schema, or how they influence one another over time during the development of the relationship. Clearly, this is rich territory for researchers.

Limitations of the Model

From a social psychological point of view, we think that the conversational situation covered in the proposed model represents a prototypical *social* activity that is central to the understanding of close relationship processes. However, complex as the model shown in Fig. 1.1 is, it of necessity involves over-simplifications and limitations. First, over the course of an interaction episode the cognitive processing stages will causally impinge on the proximal context, and over longer periods of time will also impact on the distal context, so that attribution processes may eventually influence the level of relationship satisfaction (as, indeed, some of the previously cited research suggests is the case). Hence, a more complete model would include complex feedback loops (that we have left out for the sake of simplicity). Second, this model does not deal with attributional processes that may take place outside behavioral interaction. Yet, clearly, such ruminative attributional analyses may occur frequently and exert enormous influences over subsequent behavioral interaction and the course of the relationship. Third, attributional processing may occur as a response to one's own behavior (which may strike one as surprising or unusually negative) rather than in response to one's partner's behavior.

Finally, we have confined our attention to private attributions rather than attributions that are part of publicly observable verbal behavior. There is evidence that couples talk openly about their explanations for each other's behavior (e.g., Holtzworth-Munroe & Jacobson, 1988), and that disagreements over the appropriate attributions are a common source of conflict in close relationships (Orvis, Kelley, & Butler, 1976). Such publicly expressed attributions may sometimes be a mirror image of privately expressed and rehearsed attributions. However, public and private attributions are different categories that may be subject to different causal contingencies and have different psychological consequences (see Bradbury & Fincham, 1988a).

THE LAYPERSON IN CLOSE RELATIONSHIPS: NAIVE SCIENTIST, COGNITIVE MISER, OR NAIVE LAWYER?

In the concluding section we return to a theme, referred to in the introduction, concerning the contrast between the naive scientist model in classic attribution theory and the less flattering picture of the layperson as cognitive miser popular in social cognition circles. Based on the frequency and importance of attributions of blame and culpability in close relationships (responsibility attributions), a third candidate is suggested as an appropriate metaphor for the layperson's cognition in close relationships—that of the naive lawyer (Fincham & Jaspars, 1980). For better or worse, such models have exerted considerable influence over social psychological research and theorizing and, to some extent, can be seen mirrored in the different chapters of this book. Hence, it is appropriate to consider which model best fits the layperson's cognition in close relationship contexts.

The cognitive miser model is based on a string of research findings in the 1970s and 1980s that the ordinary person's performance on social judgment tasks departed from normative inference or attribution models in consistent ways that suggested the presence of invidious social judgment biases—laypeople were purported to underestimate the causal role of situational determinants of behavior and overestimate the personal determinants (the so-called fundamental attribution error), to be poor statisticians, to be unduly influenced by prior theories while underutilizing data, and much more (Nisbett & Ross, 1980). More recent research and theorizing in social cognition have suggested an important caveat to this generalization, namely, that such social judgment biases are most apparent when social information is processed at the automatic level. In conditions that encourage such casual or automatic processing, laypeople typically rely on fallback heuristics (e.g., a simple rule attaching behavior to an underlying disposition) that produce characteristic biases or errors (such as the fundamental attribution error). However, under conditions that promote a more controlled and in-depth mode of cognition, these default heuristics tend to be corrected or discarded, hence reducing subsequent biases or errors (for extensive reviews substantiating this point, see Fletcher & Haig, in press; Klayman & Ha, 1987).

Applying this thesis to close relationships implies that attributions processed at the automatic level are likely to be less accurate and more prone to bias than those processed at the controlled level. On a more general note, we previously mentioned the sophisticated and complex nature of free-response explanations produced for important events, such as relationship dissolution. The fact that laypeople sometimes generate such sophisticated explanations for relationship events implies that they are concerned with such values as explanatory depth and the need to adequately integrate and account for disparate events in a coherent fashion—values that resemble our prototypical scientist rather than that of a lazy thinker or cognitive miser.

Our review of research suggests that negative or unexpected behavior and affective arousal in close relationships motivates controlled attributional processing. The naive scientist interpretation for such attributional activity is in terms of the need to understand, predict, or control the important events in our lives (all respectable scientific aims). However, alternative motivational interpretations for attributional activity are also plausible that are consistent with a less flattering view of human cognition as predominantly driven by the need to justify one's behavior, assess blame, or protect one's level of self-esteem—the naive lawyer model. Take, for example, the findings that self-initiated behaviors are particularly prone to attributional analyses. This is explicable either in terms of the naive scientist model or the less flattering naive lawyer image. For example, perhaps self-initiated behaviors produce more attributions because self schemata are more complex and variegated than schemata pertaining to our partners (at least in unmarried relationships). Alternately, it seems likely that self-initiated behaviors are particularly likely to instigate attributional thought in the form of justificatory maneuvers of various kinds.

Our analysis of this conundrum is essentially the same as that offered previously concerning the clash between the naive scientist and cognitive miser models: namely, that laypeople are both scientists and lawyers. As Fletcher and Haig (in press) note, attempting to rule out either motivational or cognitive/rational explanations or models is, in the end, a fruitless exercise because both views are surely correct: People are both rational and rationalizers—at times concerned with explanation, at times with justification, at other times with both, and at still other times with neither. Given the overwhelming centrality of close relationships in most people's lives, it should come as no surprise that either motivational or rational attributional processes may be dominant at different times or stages in those relationships.

To summarize, we have argued that laypeople's attributional analyses can be appropriately compared to all three models (naive scientist, cognitive miser, and lawyer). If this is accepted, then the proper question to ask becomes: *Under what conditions* in close relationships does lay explanatory activity fit the in-depth, detailed analyses of the naive scientist, the fast, casual processing of the cognitive miser, or the need to assess blame of the naive lawyer? We have proposed some tentative answers to this question. It remains for further research and theorizing to attempt more complete and detailed resolutions of these issues.

CONCLUDING COMMENT

In this chapter we have reviewed and discussed the extant research and theories dealing with attributional processes in close relationships and have presented a model of attributional processing within an interactional setting that attempts to locate attributional processes within a social, information-processing context. We have covered much ground and have not hesitated to be theoretically speculative. Notwithstanding the limitations of our attempt, we believe that continued work in this area holds the promise of increasing our understanding of both close relationships and of what we believe is a central component of social cognitive functioning: attributional structures and processes.

REFERENCES

Abramson, L. Y., Seligman, M. E. P., & Teasdale, J. (1978). Learned helplessness in humans: Critique and reformulation. *Journal of Abnormal Psychology, 87,* 49–74.

Anderson, J. R. (1983). *The architecture of cognition.* Cambridge, MA: Harvard University Press.

Bargh, J. A. (1984). Automatic and conscious processing of social information. In R. S. Wyer & T. K. Srull (Eds.), *Handbook of social cognition* (Vol. 3, pp. 1–43).

Bargh, J. A., & Tota, M. E. (1988). Context-dependent automatic processing in depression: Accessibility of negative constructs with regard to self but not to others. *Journal of Personality and Social Psychology, 54,* 925–939.

Berscheid, E. (1983). Emotion. In H. H. Kelley, E. Berscheid, A. Christensen, J. Harvey, T. Huston, G. Levinger, E. McClintock, A. Peplau, & D. Peterson (Eds.), *Close relationships* (pp. 110–168). San Francisco: Freeman.

Bradbury, T. N. (1990). *Cognition, emotion, and interaction in distressed and nondistressed couples: Towards an integrative model.* Unpublished manuscript, University of California at Los Angeles, Los Angeles.

Bradbury, T. N., & Fincham, F. D. (1988a). Assessing spontaneous attributions in marital interaction: Methodological and conceptual considerations. *Journal of Social and Clinical Psychology, 7,* 122–130.

Bradbury, T. N., & Fincham, F. D. (1988b). *The impact of attributions in marriage: Attributions and behavior exchange in marital interaction.* Paper presented at the 22nd Annual Convention of the Association for the Advancement of Behavior Therapy, New York.

Bradbury, T. N., & Fincham, F. D. (1988c). Individual difference variables in close relationships: A contextual model of marriage as an integrative framework. *Journal of Personality and Social Psychology, 54,* 713–721.

Bradbury, T. N., & Fincham, F. D. (1989). Behavior and satisfaction in marriage: Prospective mediating processes. *Review of Personality and Social Psychology, 10,* 119–143.

Bradbury, T. N., & Fincham, F. D. (1990). Attributions in marriage: Review and critique. *Psychological Bulletin, 3*, 3–33.

Branscombe, N. R. (1988). Conscious and unconscious processing of affective and cognitive information. In K. Fiedler & J. Forgas (Eds.), *Affect, cognition and social behavior.* Toronto: Hogrefe International.

Buss, D. M., & Craik, K. H. (1983). The act frequency approach to personality. *Psychological Review, 90*, 105–126.

Camper, P. M., Jacobson, N. S., Holtzworth-Munroe, A., & Schmaling, K. B. (1988). Causal attributions for interactional behaviors in married couples. *Cognitive Therapy and Research, 12*, 195–209.

Deaux, K. (1984). From individual differences to social categories: Analysis of a decade's research on gender. *American Psychologist, 39*, 105–116.

Fichten, C. S. (1984). See it from my point of view: Videotape and attributions in happy and distressed couples. *Journal of Social and Clinical Psychology, 2*, 125–142.

Fincham, F. D. (1985). Attribution in close relationships. In J. H. Harvey & G. Weary (Eds.), *Contemporary attribution theory and research* (pp. 203–234). New York: Academic Press.

Fincham, F. D. (in press). Understanding close relationships: An attributional perspective. In S. Zelen (Ed.), *Attribution: Extensions and applications.* New York: Springer Verlag.

Fincham, F. D., Beach, S. R., & Bradbury, T. N. (1990). Marital distress, depression, and attributions: Is the marital distress association an artifact of depression? *Journal of Consulting and Clinical Psychology, 57*, 769–771.

Fincham, F. D., & Bradbury, T. N. (1987). The impact of attributions in marriage: A longitudinal analysis. *Journal of Personality and Social Psychology, 52*, 739–748.

Fincham, F. D., & Bradbury, T. N. (1988a). The impact of attributions in marriage: Empirical and conceptual foundations. *British Journal of Clinical Psychology, 27*, 77–90.

Fincham, F. D., & Bradbury, T. N. (1988b). The impact of attributions in marriage: An experimental analysis. *Journal of Social and Clinical Psychology, 7*, 147–162.

Fincham, F. D., & Bradbury, T. N. (1989). The impact of attributions in marriage: An individual differences analysis. *Journal of Social and Personal Relationships, 6*, 69–86.

Fincham, F. D., & Bradbury, T. N. (in press). Cognition in marriage: A program of research on attributions. In D. Perlman & W. Jones (Eds.), *Advances in personal relations* (Vol. 2). Greenwich, CT: JAI Press.

Fincham, F. D., Bradbury, T. N., & Beach, S. R. H. (in press). Cognition in marriage and marital therapy. *Journal of Family Psychology.*

Fincham, F. D., Bradbury, T. N., & Scott, C. K. (1990). Cognition in marriage. In F. D. Fincham & T. N. Bradbury (Eds.), *The psychology of marriage* (pp. 118–149). New York: Guilford Press.

Fincham, F., & Jaspars, J. M. (1980). Attribution of responsibility: From man the scientist to man as lawyer. In L. Berkowitz (Ed.), *Advances in experimental social psychology* (Vol. 13, pp. 81–138). New York: Academic Press.

Fiske, S. T., & Taylor, S. E. (1984). *Social cognition.* Reading, MA: Addison-Wesley.

Fletcher, G. J. O. (1983a). The analysis of verbal explanations for marital separation: Implications for attribution theory. *Journal of Applied Social Psychology, 13*, 245–258.

Fletcher, G. J. O. (1983b). Sex differences in attributions for marital separation. *New Zealand Journal of Psychology, 13*, 245–258.

Fletcher, G. J. O. (1984). Psychology and common sense. *American Psychologist, 39*, 203–213.

Fletcher, G. J. O., Danilovics, P., Fernandez, G., Peterson, D., & Reeder, G. D. (1986). Attributional complexity: An individual differences measure. *Journal of Personality and Social Psychology, 51*, 875–884.

Fletcher, G. J. O., Fincham, F., Cramer, L., & Heron, N. (1987). The role of attributions in close relationships. *Journal of Personality and Social Psychology, 53*, 481–489.

Fletcher, G. J. O., Fitness, J., & Blampied, N. M. (1990). The link between attributions and happiness in close relationships: The roles of depression and explanatory style. *Journal of Social and Clinical Psychology, 9,* 243–255.

Fletcher, G. J. O., & Haig, B. (in press). The layperson as "naive scientist": An appropriate model for social psychology? In R. Hogan, R. Wolfe, & K. Craik (Eds.), *Perspectives in personality* (Vol. 4). Greenwich, CT: JAI Press.

Fletcher, G. J. O., & Ward, C. (1988). Attribution theory and processes: A cross-cultural perspective. In M. H. Bond (Ed.), *The cross-cultural challenge to social psychology* (pp. 230–244). California: Sage.

Gilbert, D. T., Pelham, B. W., & Krull, S. (1988). On cognitive busyness: When person perceivers meet persons perceived. *Journal of Personality and Social Psychology, 54,* 733–740.

Gotlib, I. H., & Hooley, J. M. (1988). Depression and marital distress: Current status and future directions. In S. Duck (Ed.), *Handbook of personal relationships* (pp. 543–580). New York: Wiley.

Gottman, J. M., & Levenson, R. W. (1984). Why marriages fail: Affective and physiological patterns in marital interaction. In J. C. Masters & K. Yarkin-Levin (Eds.), *Boundary areas in social and developmental psychology* (pp. 67–106). New York: Academic Press.

Grigg, F., Fletcher, G. J. O., & Fitness, J. (1989). Spontaneous attributions in happy and unhappy dating relationships. *Journal of Social and Personal Relationships, 6,* 61–68.

Harvey, J. H. (1987). Attributions in close relationships: Research and theoretical developments. *Journal of Social and Clinical Psychology, 5,* 420–434.

Harvey, J. H. (1989). People's naive understandings of their close relationships: Attributional and personal construct perspectives. *International Journal of Personal Construct Psychology, 2,* 37–49.

Harvey, J. H., Agostinelli, G., & Weber, A. L. (in press). Account-making and the formation of expectations about close relationships. *Review of Personality and Social Psychology.*

Heider, F. (1958). *The psychology of interpersonal relations.* New York: Wiley.

Hewstone, M. (1989). *Causal attribution: From cognitive processes to collective beliefs.* Oxford: Basil Blackwell.

Higgins, E. T., & Bargh, J. A. (1987). Social cognition and social perception. *Annual Review of Psychology, 38,* 369–425.

Holtzworth-Munroe, A., & Jacobson, N. S. (1985). Causal attributions of married couples: When do they search for causes? What do they conclude when they do? *Journal of Personality and Social Psychology, 48,* 1398–1412.

Holtzworth-Munroe, A., & Jacobson, N. S. (1988). Toward a methodology for coding spontaneous causal attributions: Preliminary results with married couples. *Journal of Social and Clinical Psychology, 7,* 101–112.

Howe, G. W. (1987). Attributions of complex cause and the perception of marital conflict. *Journal of Personality and Social Psychology, 53,* 1119–1128.

Jones, E. E., & Davis, K. E. (1965). From acts to dispositions: The attribution process in person perception. In L. Berkowitz (Ed.), *Advances in experimental social psychology* (Vol. 2, pp. 219–266). New York: Academic Press.

Kelley, H. H. (1967). Attribution theory in social psychology. In D. L. Vine (Ed.), *Nebraska symposium on motivation* (pp. 192–238). Lincoln: University of Nebraska Press.

Kelley, H. H. (1973). The processes of causal attribution. *American Psychologist, 28,* 107–128.

Kelley, H. H. (1983). Epilogue: Perceived causal structures. In J. Jaspers, F. Fincham, & M. Hewstone (Eds.), *Attribution theory and research: Conceptual developments and social dimensions* (pp. 343–369). London: Academic Press.

Kelley, H. H., Berscheid, E., Christensen, A., Harvey, J. H., Huston, T. L., Levinger, G., McClintock, E., Peplau, L. A., & Peterson, D. (Eds.). (1983). *Close relationships.* New York: Freeman.

Klayman, J., & Ha, Y. W. (1987). Confirmation, disconfirmation, and information in hypothesis testing. *Psychological Review, 94,* 211–228.

Kyle, S. O., & Falbo, T. (1985). Relationship between marital stress and attributional preferences for own and spouse behavior. *Journal of Social and Clinical Psychology, 3,* 335–351.

Mandler, G. (1975). *Mind and emotion.* New York: Wiley.

Neisser, U. (1967). *Cognitive psychology.* New York: Appleton-Century-Crofts.

Newman, H. (1981). Communication within ongoing intimate relationships: An attributional perspective. *Personality and Social Psychology Bulletin, 7,* 59–70.

Newman, L. S., & Uleman, J. S. (1989). Spontaneous trait inferences. In J. S. Uleman & J. A. Bargh (Eds.), *Unintended thought* (pp. 155–188). New York: Guilford Press.

Nisbett, R. E., & Ross, L. (1980). *Human inference: Strategies and shortcomings of social judgment.* Englewood Cliffs, NJ: Prentice-Hall.

Orvis, B. R., Kelley, H. H., & Butler, D. (1976). Attributional conflict in young couples. In J. H. Harvey, W. J. Ickes, & R. F. Kidd (Eds.), *New directions in attribution research* (Vol. 1, pp. 353–386). Hillsdale, NJ: Erlbaum.

Peterson, C., Semmel, A., von Baeyer, C., Abramson, L. Y., Metalsky, G. I., & Seligman, M. E. P. (1982). The Attributional Style Questionnaire. *Cognitive Therapy and Research, 6,* 287–299.

Posner, M. I., & Synder, C. R. (1975). Attention and cognitive control. In R. L. Solso (Ed.), *Information processing and cognition: The Loyola Symposium* (pp. 55–86). Hillsdale, NJ: Erlbaum.

Read, S. J. (1987). Constructing causal scenarios: A knowledge structure approach to causal reasoning. *Journal of Personality and Social Psychology, 52,* 288–302.

Robins, C. J. (1988). Attributions and depression: Why is the literature so inconsistent? *Journal of Personality and Social Psychology, 54,* 880–889.

Ross, M., & Fletcher, G. J. O. (1985). Attribution and social perception. In G. Lindzey & E. Aronson (Eds.), *The handbook of social psychology* (3rd. ed., pp. 73–122). New York: Random House.

Seligman, C., Fazio, R. H., & Zanna, M. P. (1980). Effects of salience of extrinsic rewards on liking and loving. *Journal of Personality and Social Psychology, 38,* 453–460.

Shaver, K. G. (1985). *The attribution of blame: Causality, responsibility, and blameworthingness.* New York: Springer-Verlag.

Shaver, K. G., & Drown, D. (1986). On causality, responsibility, and self-blame: A theoretical note. *Journal of Personality and Social Psychology, 50,* 697–702.

Shiffrin, R. M., & Schneider, W. (1977). Controlled and automatic human information processing: 2. Perceptual learning, automatic attending, and a general theory. *Psychological Review, 84,* 127–190.

Shultz, T. R., & Schleifer, M., & Altman, I. (1981). Judgments of causation, responsibility and punishment in cases of harm-doing. *Canadian Journal of Behavioral Sciences, 13,* 238–253.

Smith, E. R. (1984). Attributions and other inferences: Processing information about the self versus others. *Journal of Experimental Social Psychology, 20,* 97–115.

Smith, E. R. (in press). Content and process specificity in the effects of prior experiences. In T. K. Srull & R. S. Wyer (Eds.), *Advances in social cognition* (Vol. 4). Hillsdale, NJ: Erlbaum.

Smith, E. R., & Lerner, M. (1986). Development of automatism of social judgments. *Journal of Personality and Social Psychology, 50,* 246–259.

Smith, E. R., & Miller, F. D. (1983). Mediation among attributional inferences and comprehension processes: Initial findings and a general method. *Journal of Personality and Social Psychology, 44,* 492–505.

Sternberg, R. J. (1986). A triangular theory of love. *Psychological Review, 93,* 119–135.

Trope, Y., Cohen, O., & Maoz, Y. (1988). The perceptual and inferential effects of situational inducements on dispositional attribution. *Journal of Personality and Social Psychology, 55,* 165–177.

Uleman, J. S. (1987). Consciousness and control: The case of spontaneous trait inferences. *Personality and Social Psychology Bulletin, 13,* 337–354.

Uleman, J. S., & Bargh, J. A. (Eds.). (1989). *Unintended thought.* New York: Guilford Press.

Weiner, B. (1985). "Spontaneous causal thinking". *Psychological Bulletin, 97,* 74–84.

Weiner, B. (1986). *An attributional theory of motivation and emotion.* New York: Springer Verlag.

Weiner, B., Frieze, I., Kukla, A., Reed, L., Rest, S., & Rosenbaum, R. M. (1972). Perceiving the causes of success and failure. In E. E. Jones et al. (Eds.), *Attribution: Perceiving the causes of behavior.* Morristown, NJ: General Learning Press.

Zuroff, D. C. (1986). Was Gorden Allport a trait theorist? *Journal of Personality and Social Psychology, 51,* 993–1000.

2 Information Processing in Close Relationships[1]

Christy K.Scott
University of Illinois

Robert W. Fuhrman
University of Texas, San Antonio

Robert S. Wyer, Jr.
University of Illinois

Information processing is fundamental to interaction in close relationships. To understand the dynamics of such interaction, therefore, one must be able to specify the cognitive processes that mediate (a) partners' interpretations of each other's behavior, (b) their perceptions of the behavior's implications for themselves, their partner, and the relationship, and (c) the decisions they make about how to respond to this behavior. The importance of determining the cognitive mechanisms that govern the interactions that take place between relationship partners is widely recognized (Arias & Beach, 1987; Berley & Jacobson, 1984; Bradbury & Fincham, 1987; Fincham & Bradbury, 1987; Glick & Gross, 1975; Gurman & Knudson, 1978; Newman & Langer, 1983; Sillars, 1985). Nevertheless, these mechanisms have rarely been examined. Research has focused instead on the association between partners' relationship satisfaction and (a) their explanations of various types of relationship events (e.g., Fichten, 1984; Fincham, 1985; Fincham & Bradbury, 1987; Ross & Sicoly, 1979) or (b) beliefs about relationships (e.g., Eidelson & Epstein, 1982; Fincham & Bradbury, 1987; Weiss, 1984). The results of this research (for a summary, see Fincham, Bradbury, & Scott, 1990) are important. However, their theoretical interest is limited unless the factors that underlie them are understood.

The cognitive processes that mediate the transmission, receipt, and interpretation of information are the concern of research and theory in social cognition (for

[1]The writing of this paper and some of the research reported therein was supported by Grant MH 3–8585 from the National Institute of Mental Health. Appreciation is extended to the University of Illinois Social Cognition Group for stimulating many of the ideas expressed.

37

reviews, see Sorrentino & Higgins, 1986; Wyer & Srull, 1984, 1989). Unfortunately, most of this research has been conducted in laboratory settings within a limited set of research paradigms. Consequently, it does not capture the complexities of interpersonal communication in close relationships and the way that several different factors combine to influence this communication. Nevertheless, a conceptualization of information processing in close relationships in terms of theory and research in social cognition raises several important theoretical and empirical questions concerning the dynamics of these relationships. Our objective in this chapter is to call attention to these questions.

THE COMPONENTS OF INTERPERSONAL COMMUNICATION

Figure 2.1 describes a sequence of behaviors involving a man, A, and a woman, B. Person A performs a behavior or sequence of behaviors that he believes will attain a goal ($Goal_{A,1}$). These behaviors constitute a communication ($Comm_{A,1}$) that B receives and interprets. Her perception of the implications of this message ($Perc_{B,2}$) stimulates her to form a communication goal ($Goal_{B,2}$). She then generates a communication to A ($Comm_{B,2}$) that she believes will facilitate the attainment of this goal, and so on.

Communication is accomplished in a variety of ways (e.g., verbal, written, behavioral). However, many of the processes that underlie the transmission and interpretation of messages may be similar. In close relationships, behaviors that occur outside the context of verbal communication, and even in the absence of the partner, can be an important stimulant of later interactions. For instance, person A might stay out until 2 A.M. after promising to be home by 10. Person B's communication in response, mediated by her perception that A's behavior conveys hostility and rejection, might be to get up early and leave for work without speaking to B, thus conveying anger and resentment. The components of

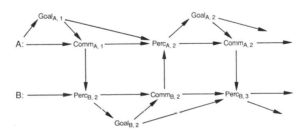

FIG. 2.1. Hypothetical segment of a communication sequence involving a man, A, and a woman, B. $Goal_{A,i}$, $Comm_{A,i}$ and $Perc_{A,i+1}$ denote A's communication goal at time 1, the communication he transmits, and his perception of B's response to this communication. Symbols pertaining to B are analogous.

Fig. 2.1 apply to these sorts of communications as well as those that occur during conversations.

Several factors can influence the relations among the components described in Fig. 2.1. For one thing, a person's perception of another's communication is determined not only by features of the communication itself, but also by the recipient's expectancies for the nature of this message. These expectancies, in turn, are influenced by concepts and knowledge that the participant has acquired before engaging in the interaction. As a result of these and other influences, there is often a discrepancy between a recipient's interpretation of a communication and the meaning that the communicator intends to convey. In addition, a recipient's perception of the implications of a communication will often lead him or her to experience positive or negative emotions. These emotions can affect the message that the recipient attempts to convey in return.

Figure 2.1 indicates the *possible* causal relations between the variables described. However, the actual relations may differ considerably in strength, and some of them may not exist at all. To the extent that a person's perception of another's message (and, therefore, the person's reactions to it) is determined by the person's own prior behavior and expectancies rather than by the actual content of this message, miscommunications can arise that have a substantial impact on the couple's interactions with each other. Our discussion in this chapter focuses on the factors that underlie these miscommunications and their consequences. We first conceptualize more precisely the components of communication denoted in Fig. 2.1. We will then turn to the cognitive processes that underlie the relations among those components and their implications for communication in close relationships.

The Communication

A *communication* is a configuration of verbal and nonverbal behaviors that intentionally or unintentionally convey information to another. These behaviors may or may not be intended to convey this information. We will typically focus on communications that occur in the course of a direct interaction (e.g., a conversation). However, many of the issues we raise are equally applicable to communications more broadly conceived.

Communications typically convey a specific fact, concept, thought, or emotional reaction. Some consist of only a single word, a facial expression, or a shift in body position or eye contact (Argyle & Dean, 1965; Noller, 1980). Others involve detailed accounts that extend over several minutes. For the purposes of this chapter, we define a communication in terms of the idea or thought being conveyed without regard to its length or the number of verbal and nonverbal acts that compose it.

Communications vary in meaning along dimensions that are either descriptive, affective, or both (Gaelick, Bodenhausen, & Wyer, 1985; see also

Watzlawick, Beavin, & Jackson, 1967). Moreover, this meaning can be conveyed either directly or indirectly (see Clark & Clark, 1977, for a discussion of indirect speech acts). For example, a husband's statement "It's cold in here" may simply provide descriptive information about the temperature. On the other hand, it can also convey the husband's wish that his spouse would turn up the heat or his anger at her pervasive tendency to set the thermostat too low.

The indirect meaning of communications is likely to vary with the amount of knowledge shared by partners. Married couples develop a private meaning system that allows them to convey both descriptive and affective information to which other listeners are not always privy (Gottman, 1979). To continue our example, the husband's statement that "It's cold in here" may be stimulated by a long history of heated discussions surrounding his wife's unwillingness to set the thermostat at the level he wants. If the statement is made in front of guests, however, the hostility it conveys might not be perceived by anyone other than his wife. (We discuss the factors that underlie partners' sensitivity to these indirect speech acts later in this chapter.) The emotional component of a message is often more important than the descriptive for understanding the effects of interpersonal communication on the quality of a close relationship (cf. Gaelick et al., 1985; Weiss, 1984; see also Bodenhausen, Gaelick, & Wyer, 1987). However, the two types of meaning cannot be considered in isolation, as our examples above indicate.

Communication Goals

Transmission goals.   A communication is usually generated with one or more specific objectives in mind. A common goal is to transmit descriptive, factual information. At the same time, one may wish to convey an opinion or attitude toward oneself or toward the recipient. Thus, the statement "I can fix your car for you" may be intended to convey not only factual information, but also that the speaker is competent, is superior to the other, or is concerned about the other's well-being. However, the goal of a communication is not always to convey information to its recipient. This is particularly true when the communication is nonverbal or consists of behavior that is performed in the recipient's absence. Thus, staying out until 2 A.M. after promising to come home early could be motivated by considerations other than the desire to convey hostility or rejection to one's spouse.

Reception goals.   The immediate goal of someone who receives a communication is presumably to understand it. Once the message has been received and understood, however, the recipient may be motivated to respond to it. If the message is conveyed in a conversation, for example, the recipient might wish to confirm or refute the validity of its implications, or to provide additional information about the topic being discussed. If the recipient experiences positive or negative emotional reactions to the communication, he or she might try to convey these reactions.

As these examples indicate, people's goals in a conversation are often influenced by their interpretation of each other's messages. Consequently, these goals are likely to change several times during the course of the interaction. Note also that to the extent that a communication is perceived to convey both descriptive and emotional meaning, each meaning component can activate a different communication goal, and these goals may combine to determine the content and form of the recipient's response.

Perceptions and Reactions of the Receiver

Three stages of perception should be distinguished. First, individual features of a verbal or nonverbal message are interpreted in terms of low-level semantic concepts that are necessary to understand its literal meaning (Wyer & Srull, 1989). The interpretation of communications at this stage occurs almost automatically.

At a second, higher level of encoding, both verbal and nonverbal features of a communication may be interpreted in terms of more general trait and evaluative concepts that pertain to the specific referent of the message. These concepts may also pertain to a more general category to which the referent belongs, or, in some instances, to the communicator. For example, the behavior of cheating on one's wife could be classified as deceitful or dishonest. Alternatively, the nonverbal behaviors that accompany a verbal message could be encoded as "warm," "hostile," or "unhappy."

At the third level, the *implications* of the encoded information are inferred. These implications, which can be evaluative, descriptive, or both, concern the specific referent of the communication. They can also concern the communicator, the recipient, or their relationship. The latter implications are often inferred on the basis of the recipient's prior knowledge of the speaker and their past interaction history. Thus, a husband's observation that "There were four cases of Lyme disease in Yosemite last week" might be perceived as an indication that the speaker is worried about contracting the disease. In the context of previous discussions with his spouse, however, it might also be interpreted as indicating that the speaker simply doesn't want to go to California and is inventing an excuse to cancel the trip. Such inferences often elicit affective or emotional reactions in the recipient that influence the recipient's response to the communicator's message.

A recipient's interpretation of a message and construal of its implications are obviously not always an accurate reflection of the meaning and implications that the communicator intends to transmit. One reason is that the recipient does not always attend to all of the features of a communication that are necessary to extract a communicator's intent. A woman's comment to a guest, "If my husband drives you home, be sure to wear your seat belt" might be intended as a good-natured ribbing, stimulated by a recent, atypical experience on the high-way. If the husband overhears the remark without noticing his wife's facial expression, however, he might interpret it as hostile or sarcastic. He might also misconstrue its affective implications if the prior knowledge he assumes to under-lie his wife's comment differs from the knowledge that actually stimulates it (e.g., if he believes that his wife is basing her remark on a general reaction she has had while riding with him, whereas she is actually only thinking about a recent, unavoidable near-accident). Many other factors that contribute to these misperceptions and miscommunications will be noted presently.

Summary

In discussing the components of Fig. 2.1, we have alluded to several more specific steps that intervene between the reception of a communication and the generation of a response. Suppose a man, A, transmits a message to his wife, B. The following steps may then occur:

1. *Initial encoding.* B interprets the communication in terms of concepts that are applicable for understanding its affective and descriptive meaning.
2. *Inference.* B determines the implications of the information for the refer-ent of the communication, for herself, or for her relationship with A.
3. *Affective reactions.* B experiences affective or emotional reactions based on her inference of the message's implications.
4. *Goal selection.* B decides the emotional and/or descriptive content of her message to A.
5. *Response generation.* B decides the language to use in conveying her message, and generates an overt response.

These component stages of processing are influenced not only by the content of A's communication, but also by a variety of situational and individual dif-ference factors that affect the subset of prior knowledge that B retrieves from memory and uses to perform the cognitive activities that occur at these stages. This knowledge can either be semantic or can consist of episodic information about A, about B, about their relationship to each other, or about other people and events. Figure 2.2 summarizes these cognitive stages and some of the factors that affect them. (This figure is essentially an elaboration of the processes that mediate the relation between $Perc_B$ and $Comm_B$ in Fig. 2.1.) In this chapter, we discuss the nature of these processes in some detail, focusing primarily on encoding and inference. First, however, some comments about the content and structure of social memory are in order.

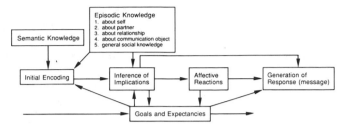

FIG. 2.2. Cognitive and affective factors mediating a recipient's perception of a relationship partner's communication and his or her response to this communication.

THE NATURE OF SOCIAL MEMORY

The interpretation of verbal or nonverbal communications and the perception of their implications are based on the knowledge one has acquired through social experience. This knowledge consists of general trait, behavior, and noun concepts that can be used to interpret verbal statements or observed actions, and general concepts of people and how they are likely to behave. It also includes memories of particular persons and of past experiences involving them. A considerable amount and diversity of stored knowledge can potentially be brought to bear on the interpretation of a given statement or behavior. In practice, however, only a small subset of this knowledge is applied. It is therefore important to understand the factors that determine which particular subset is likely to be retrieved and used.

Several theoretical models of social memory have been proposed (cf. Smith, 1984, 1990; Srull & Wyer, 1989; Wyer & Carlston, 1979; Wyer & Srull, 1986, 1989). Of these, the Wyer and Srull model is the most comprehensive. This conceptualization defines several different types of knowledge representations that are formed and stored in locations throughout the memory system, and postulates a set of rules that govern both their storage and retrieval. Several general features of this formulation provide a useful framework for our subsequent discussion. We first describe briefly the types of knowledge structures that the model assumes, and then consider the processes that underlie their identification and use.

The Content of Social Memory

The concepts and knowledge structures of greatest relevance to the concerns of this chapter pertain to traits, behaviors, people, and events.

Semantic concepts.   Semantic concepts exist in memory that refer to general categories of persons, attributes, and actions. Each concept consists of a verbal or nonverbal label (e.g., "man," "intelligent," "hits") and alternative sets of defining features. An attribute concept, for example, has a label ("honest," "friendly," etc.) and prototypic behaviors that exemplify it ("tells the truth," "smiles and says hello," etc.). A subset of attribute concepts refers to emotions ("happy," "angry," etc.). The features of these latter concepts can include not only overt behaviors but representations of internal physiological reactions that are either personally experienced or imputed to others. Action concepts, which refer to different types of social behavior, are analogous, although they differ from other concepts in form and complexity (cf. Wyer & Srull, 1989).

Person representations.   People often form mental representations of both specific individuals (one's spouse, etc.) and prototypic ones (lawyers, feminists, etc.). These representations can be of several types, including (a) a visual image, (b) a set of one or more general trait or behavior descriptions, and (c) situation-specific behaviors. Many such representations contain a number of interrelated features that can be either descriptive or affective. Thus, they may include emotional reactions that were experienced at the time the representation was formed. Both types of features may be activated when the representation is retrieved from memory. Person representations are formed in the course of pursuing a particular goal that requires their construction (e.g., forming an impression or predicting a future behavior). Several representations, therefore, are likely to be formed of the same person. These various representations constitute different units of knowledge about the person that are stored and retrieved independently.

Event representations.   An event representation typically consists of a temporally and/or causally related sequence of actions. These actions may pertain to a specific experience (e.g., last night's argument about visiting the in-laws) or to a more general category of experiences (e.g., discussions about money). Moreover, it may consist of events that occur in a particular situation or in different situations that extend over a period of time. Event representations, like person representations, are formed in the course of pursuing a goal. For this reason, they might not be a complete depiction of the sequence of actions to which they refer. For example, goal-irrelevant features of the original sequence might be omitted. This is particularly likely when the individual actions are encoded in terms of more abstract, goal-relevant concepts that do not capture all of their possible implications. Thus, the representation of a man's conversation with his wife could include either verbatim statements of what was said or a more general characterization of the events that occurred (e.g., "I said I didn't want to visit her parents and she got angry"). Such an encoding does not capture aspects of the woman's behavior that might, if considered, have other implications for her feelings and reactions. Each such event representation, like each person representation that is formed, functions as a separate unit of knowledge that is stored and retrieved as a whole, independently of other units.[2]

As our example implies, knowledge about an event can be contained in a person representation, and knowledge about a person can be contained in an event representation. A recognition of this fact is important in conceptualizing the basis for social judgments and decisions. One set of questions that arises from this conceptualization concerns the factors that determine when one representation rather than another is retrieved and later used as a source of knowledge about the people and events for which it has implications.

The Structure of Social Memory

Wyer and Srull (1986, 1989) conceptualized social memory as consisting of two main components. One, the *Work Space,* is a temporary depository of material that is or has recently been involved in the pursuit of a particular processing objective. This material may consist of stimulus input information, the concepts and knowledge that have been used to interpret it and construe its implications, and the results of this processing (e.g., abstract encodings of the information, inferences drawn from it). This material is only retained in the Work Space temporarily, however. A short time after the processing objectives to which it is relevant have been completed, the Work Space is cleared to make room for other goal-relevant information. Once this occurs, only the encoded representations that have been formed from the original input information (and have been transmitted to permanent memory) can be recalled and used as a basis for later judgments and decisions. In other words, features of the original information that are not contained in these representations are lost.

The second component, the *Permanent Storage Unit,* is analogous to long-term memory. This unit is conceptualized metaphorically as a set of storage bins. These bins have different functions. One, the *semantic* bin, serves as a mental dictionary. It contains attribute, action, noun, and emotion concepts that are used to interpret the denotative meaning of words, sentences, observed behaviors, and so on. Other, *referent* bins, which as a group constitute a cognitive encyclopedia, contain knowledge about general or specific persons, objects, or events. Each referent bin is denoted by a *header,* or set of features that define and circumscribe its contents. Thus, a person may have bins that refer to "my first date," "visiting my husband's parents," "Richard Nixon," and "last night's party at Mary's." Separate bins can refer to oneself (a "self" bin), one's spouse, and one's relationship (e.g., a "marriage" bin). These bins can pertain to either general refer-

---

[2]Event representations as we conceptualize them are very similar to *scripts* (Schank & Abelson, 1977). To avoid any confusion between our conceptualization of event representations and the characteristics and use of scripts as postulated by Schank and Abelson, however, we will adopt the more general terminology in this chapter.

ents, as in these examples, or more circumscribed ones (e.g., "fights with my wife"). General bins ("my wife") and circumscribed ones ("fights with my wife") can coexist, and the knowledge contained in them can differ.

Storage

Bins are used to retain information that is processed in pursuit of a particular goal that exists at the time the information is received. Therefore, although a piece of information often concerns more than one person or object, it is not necessarily stored in bins pertaining to all of these referents. Rather, it is stored in only the bin to which one's immediate processing goal is relevant. For example, a woman's conversation with her husband may have implications for the woman, for her spouse, for their relationship, and for some unrelated topic. Nevertheless, if the woman is thinking about the conversation with reference to her husband, a representation of it would theoretically be stored in her "husband" bin alone and not in other bins that refer to the relationship, to the woman herself, or to the topic of discussion. Moreover, if she is thinking about the conversation as a "bad time with my husband," she may store a representation of it in a "bad times with husband" bin rather than in the more general "husband" bin. Note that, as communication goals change in the course of a conversation, different aspects of the conversation are likely to be stored in different bins. The main point of this discussion is that knowledge about a particular person or object are often stored at several different locations. The importance of this point becomes apparent in the context of the model's assumptions concerning retrieval processes.

Retrieval

Bin selection.   When knowledge is required to attain a particular processing objective (i.e., to interpret new information, to make a judgment or decision, etc.), the Work Space is the first location searched. This means that goal-relevant knowledge that has been recently acquired and/or used is the most likely to be identified and used again. If no goal-relevant knowledge is found in the Work Space, however, a set of features (*probe cues*) are compiled that characterize the type of information being sought (e.g., "my wife"). A bin whose header contains these features is then identified.[3] The initial interpretation of individual

---

[3]Probe cues are determined primarily by processing objectives that stimulate the retrieval of information. That is, if a man is asked to make a comment about his wife, "wife" will presumably be a probe cue. However, Wyer and Srull (1986, 1989) postulated that other features that happen to be accessible in the work space at the time information is sought may sometimes be fortuitously included in the probe set. Thus, for example, if an emotion concept such as "hostile" happens to be activated at the time the man is searching for information about his wife, it may also be included, leading a "hostile wife" bin to be identified rather than the more general one. We discuss this possibility in more detail in the context of selective encoding.

pieces of new information typically requires the use of attribute, noun, or action concepts that are drawn from the semantic bin. If, however, the attainment of one's processing objective requires knowledge about a specific person, object, or event, this knowledge is typically drawn from a referent bin. In the latter case, the particular referent bin that is searched depends on the probe cues that are compiled. When information relevant to one's goal is contained in more than one bin, the information contained in bins other than the one that is identified by the probe cues will not be considered. In combination with the storage processes outlined earlier, this means that *information is likely to be retrieved only if one's objective at the time of retrieval concerns the same referent as one's objective at the time the information was acquired.*

A simple example helps to convey the implications of this restriction. A couple's argument over money may have implications not only for the financial issue being discussed but also for the quality of their relationship. Later, both partners are asked how happy they are with their relationship. To answer this question, the partners presumably search for information in their respective "relationship" bins. Whether aspects of their conversation about money are retrieved and used as bases for their responses depends on how each partner had thought about the conversation at the time it took place. Suppose the woman had thought about the conversation's implications for the quality of her relationship with her partner, whereas the husband's primary concern at the time was the financial issue being discussed. In this case, the woman would be more likely to use the conversation as a basis for judgment than the man.

Findings reported by Gaelick et al. (1985) are interesting to consider in the context of this example. Married couples described a conflict they were having in their relationship. Later, each person reviewed statements that were made during the discussion and rated them in terms of the love and hostility that the communicator intended to convey (as perceived by both the communicator and the recipient) and the affect that the recipient conveyed in response. Finally, partners reported their relationship satisfaction. Women's dissatisfaction with their relationship increased with the hostility that both they and their spouse perceived to characterize the conversation. In contrast, men's dissatisfaction was unrelated to either their own or their partner's perceptions of the hostility that was conveyed.

One possible interpretation of these findings is suggested by the considerations raised above. That is, women may be inclined to think about a conversation with their spouses in terms of its implications for their relationship at the time the conversation occurred, and, therefore, to store a representation of it in a "relationship" bin. In contrast, men may be more inclined to think about the conversation with reference to the issues being discussed. Consequently, women are more likely than men to retrieve and use their memory of the conversation and its affective quality when they are asked to evaluate their "relationship."

Our analysis is obviously oversimplified. It nevertheless helps to conceptualize conditions in which people describe their relationship as satisfying despite the fact that in other circumstances they refer to their spouse as belligerent and hard to get along with. It also allows one to understand why two partners might sometimes report quite different levels of relationship satisfaction, despite the fact that they experienced similar emotions during their interactions with one another.

Within-bin search for information. When several knowledge units are contained in a bin, three principles govern which unit is identified and used:

1. The search of a referent bin for goal-relevant information proceeds from the top down. Therefore, the information that is nearest the top of the bin (i.e., the most recently deposited information) is most likely to be identified.

2. When a knowledge unit of potential relevance to one's processing goal is available, a copy of it is retrieved. After it has been used, this copy is returned to the top of the bin from which it was drawn. Consequently, the likelihood of retrieving this same knowledge unit at a later time is increased.

3. No more knowledge is retrieved than is *sufficient* for attaining the goal at hand. Therefore, if two alternative units of information are equally applicable for attaining an objective, only the first unit that is encountered in the top-down search of the bin will be considered.

These postulates imply a strong recency effect of previously acquired (or used) knowledge on judgments and decisions. That is, when several different units of knowledge about a referent have implications for a judgment or decision, the one that was formed (or used) most recently (and, therefore, is nearest the top of the referent bin being searched) will most often be identified and applied, and other, equally relevant pieces of information will be ignored.

We are now in a position to turn to the various processes that we propose to underlie communication between partners in close relationships, beginning with encoding and interpretation.

ENCODING PROCESSES

The recipient of a communication must first understand what it means. This is achieved by encoding features of the message in terms of previously formed semantic concepts. The encoding occurs in two stages. First, the communication (e.g., a verbal description of an event, an observed behavior) is encoded in terms of noun and action concepts that are necessary to understand its denotative meaning. Then the information may be further interpreted in terms of semantic concepts at a higher level of abstractness. (For example, the behavior of swearing at Mary may be interpreted as "hostile.") Encodings at this second stage are not usually essential to understand the descriptive meaning of the information. Consequently, they only are performed if they are necessary to attain some goal or processing objective that requires them. Moreover, several alternative concepts can often be applied to the information at this level of abstractness, each of which has different implications. For example, swearing at Mary could be interpreted not only as "hostile," but also as "boisterous," "impolite," or "dominating."

Behaviors are more likely to be encoded in terms of specific trait or emotion concepts if they are inconsistent with expectations. Behaviors that are part of an established interaction pattern, for example, might simply be encoded as "typical" rather than in terms of a specific trait concept that they exemplify. Consequently, such behaviors might not be recalled when specific instances are sought that exemplify a particular trait. (Thus, if a man typically criticizes his wife, specific instances of this behavior will not be encoded into memory as "hostile," and so they will not be reported when the wife is subsequently asked why she believes her spouse to have this attribute.)

General Effects of Concept Accessibility on the Interpretation of Information

Research on the role of concept accessibility on the encoding of information (Bargh, 1984; Higgins & King, 1981; Wyer & Srull, 1989) converges on several conclusions concerning the factors that lead different trait concepts to be activated and used to interpret information. These conclusions take the form of postulates.

Postulate 1.   When people must interpret information in terms of an abstract concept, they are likely to encode this information in terms of the first applicable concept that comes to mind without considering other concepts that, although equally applicable, are less easily accessible (Higgins, Rholes, & Jones, 1977; Srull & Wyer, 1979, 1980).

Postulate 2.   The concepts that are likely to be most accessible at the time new information is received are ones that have been used most recently and/or most frequently in the past (Srull & Wyer, 1979; for discussions of the relative influence of recency and frequency, see Higgins et al., 1977; Wyer & Srull, 1989).

Postulate 3.   Information is only interpreted in terms of abstract concepts if this interpretation is necessary to attain one's immediate processing objectives.

Postulate 4.   Once information has been encoded into memory in terms of abstract concepts, the influence that these encodings have on judgments and decisions *increases over time* in relation to that of the original information.

Postulate 5.   Once information is interpreted in terms of concepts that are accessible at the time it is received, the information is unlikely to be *re*interpreted in terms of concepts that are activated subsequently, at the time a judgment or behavioral decision is requested (Carlston, 1980; Massad, Hubbard, & Newtson, 1979; Srull & Wyer, 1980).

These postulates have clear implications for communication in close relationships. Partners often make statements or perform behaviors that could be interpreted in terms of several different trait and emotion concepts. Suppose a woman comments to her husband that "I'm tired of spending time alone watching TV while you are at the football game." This statement could be interpreted as conveying hostility, sadness, or even love. Whether her husband applies any of these abstract emotion concepts may depend on whether his objectives at the time he receives the message require him to make such an encoding (see Postulate 3 above). That is, if the man is thinking about things that do not require an assessment of his wife's emotional state, he will not encode the comment in terms of any emotion concept at all. To the extent that such an encoding is relevant to the person's processing objective, the particular concept he accesses and uses is likely to be the first one that comes to mind (Postulate 1). The accessibility of this concept might be influenced by factors that have little to do with the conversation or the topic at hand (e.g., the content of a book the husband happens to be reading). Once this encoding is made, however, it can affect not only the man's immediate response to the woman's statement but the way in which the comment is stored in memory. Consequently the man may later remember his wife's statement as implying either "hostility' toward his work behavior or, alternatively, as implying that she is "sad" and "lonely." These encodings can, in turn, affect judgments, decisions, and later communications for which this knowledge has implications. Moreover, their effect could actually be greater after a period of time has elapsed than it is immediately after the woman's comment was made (Postulate 4).

Selective Encoding

The concepts that happen to be activated at the time information is received can influence not only how individual pieces of this information are interpreted, but also *which* aspects of the information are encoded and stored in memory. This is particularly true when a large amount of information is presented and it is difficult to pay equal attention to all of it. Under such circumstances, aspects of the information that can be interpreted in terms of easily accessible abstract concepts are more likely to be encoded into memory than other aspects that cannot be so easily interpreted (Srull & Wyer, 1989; Wyer & Srull, 1989). This selective encoding will influence the later recall of the information and judgments based on it. The concepts that lead to selective encoding, like those that affect the interpretation of individual pieces of information, can be activated by one's specific processing objectives at the time information is received (Wyer, Srull, Gordon, & Hartwick, 1982). However, they can also be activated by fortuitous experiences (e.g., one's mood) that have nothing to do with the people or objects to which the information refers (Bower, Gilligan, & Monteiro, 1981).

There is little direct evidence of these effects in research on the dynamics of close relationships. However, certain results of the study by Gaelick et al. (1985) are of heuristic interest. To reiterate, spouses discussed a marital conflict. Later, they viewed a videotape of the conversation and identified communications that they considered to be important. For each such communication, the communicator reported the feelings that he or she intended to convey, and the recipient indicated the feelings that he or she perceived in the communicator's message. It seems reasonable to suppose that concepts associated with negative emotions are more likely to be activated in the course of discussing a conflict than concepts associated with positive ones. Therefore, communications that convey negative emotions are more likely to be interpreted correctly. Consistent with this hypothesis, both men and women were more accurate in perceiving their partners' intentions to convey hostility than in perceiving their partners' intentions to convey love.[4]

Selective encoding effects are of methodological as well as theoretical importance. That is, differences in the recall of different types of information can reflect differences in the concepts that were used to encode the information at the time the information was received and, therefore, differences in the relative accessibility of these concepts. Some recent data collected by Scott, Bradbury, and Fincham (1989) are of interest in this regard. Marriage partners were given a list of behaviors pertaining to either themselves, ("I . . ." statements), their partners ("He . . ." or "She . . ." statements), or both ("We . . ." statements), and were asked to indicate whether each behavior had occurred during the past week. Later, they were asked to recall as many of these statements as they could, regardless of whether or not they had endorsed them. Recall differences were evaluated as a function of partners' marital satisfaction. Nondistressed partners generally recalled more "We . . ." statements ($M = 5.1$) than either "I . . ." statements ($M = 3.4$) or partner-specific statements ($M = 3.0$). In contrast, distressed partners recalled substaneously fewer "We . . ." statements ($M = 2.7$), than "I . . ." or partner-specific statements (3.8 and 4.3, respectively). This suggests that the concepts that were most easily accessible to persons who were satisfied with their relationship referred to themselves and their partner as a single unit, and so items that could be interpreted in terms of these concepts ("We . . ." statements) were more likely to be encoded into memory. In con-

---

[4]To confirm interpretation of the data, one would need to show that participants in discussions of positive experiences are more accurate in perceiving intentions to convey love than intentions to convey hostility. Nonetheless, the consistency of the results with a selective encoding hypothesis is worth noting.

trast, the concepts that were most accessible to distressed partners referred to themselves and their spouse as separate entities, and, therefore, the items that were interpretable in terms of these concepts were more likely to be encoded and stored.

Determinants of Concept Accessibility

In some instances, a person's objective when receiving a communication may be to understand it at a concrete, descriptive level. In this case, differences in the accessibility of higher order (e.g., trait) concepts will have little influence on its representation in memory (Postulate 3). Often, however, a recipient of a message will be motived to respond to it. This alone may be sufficient to induce the recipient to interpret the communication in more abstract terms. Under these circumstances, as well as when the recipient has a more specific purpose for acquiring the information, several factors can affect which particular concepts are applied.

Fortuitous experiences.   Experiences that are quite unrelated to a statement or observed behavior can activate concepts that are later used to interpret this communication (cf. Higgins & King, 1981; Wyer & Srull, 1989). Thus, for example, a man is more likely to interpret his wife's behavior as conveying hostility if he has just been watching a Clint Eastwood movie than if he has been watching a Jacques Cousteau documentary.

Situation-specific goals and intentions.   A person who wishes to convey a particular message, or to elicit certain reactions from the recipient, might activate concepts associated with these objectives. These concepts might influence the person's interpretation of the other's response. For example, an individual whose goal is to communicate love to someone is likely to interpret the other's response as conveying love, whereas a person who wishes to convey hostility is likely to interpret the other's reactions as hostile (Gaelick et al., 1985). These tendencies can lead people to perceive others as reciprocating the emotions they have personally tried to convey.

Expectations.   Partners inevitably acquire expectations for each other's comments and behavior. These expectations could be situation specific, or could be general ones that have developed over the course of the relationship. Some expectations are specific to certain types of information, topics, and situational contexts, whereas others are more pervasive. In either event, concepts activated by these expectations will often affect partners' interpretations of each other's actual behavior during a particular interaction.

The effects of couples' interaction history on their interpretation of one another's behavior may be self-perpetuating. Imagine a man who expects his partner to respond with hostility to his comments. He is apt to perceive her communication as confirming this expectation. Once this encoding is stored in memory, it may later be retrieved and used as a basis for his expectations in subsequent situations, affecting his interpretation of the spouse's messages in these situations as well. Therefore, the effects of expectations are self-reinforcing and may be very difficult to reverse.

Social learning. Bargh, Bond, Lombardi, and Tota (1986) identified differences in the chronic accessibility of trait concepts that combine additively with situationally induced differences in their accessibility to affect the interpretation of behavioral information. In another context, Markus (Markus, 1977; Markus & Smith, 1981) identified individual differences in the accessibility of trait concepts that are predictable from tendencies to apply the traits to oneself. In research on marital relationships, Markman (1979) found that marriage partners' dispositions to interpret each other's behavior positively (independently of its actual implications) predicted their satisfaction with their relationship several years later. This finding could indicate that general individual differences in the accessibility of concepts have pervasive effects on the interpretation of behavior in a relationship, leading to the establishment of general interaction patterns that are more or less satisfying to the parties involved.

Motivational factors. The effects of general goals and values on the interpretation of information was initially recognized by Bruner (1957). Klinger (1977) subsequently pointed out the role of "current concerns," often resulting from an unpleasant life situation (e.g., the loss of a job, a financial crisis, etc.), in the interpretation of information. A person who is experiencing financial difficulties, for example, may be disposed to encode everything in terms of its cost. Someone who is concerned about a tyrannical boss may interpret any person's behavior in terms of the anger or hostility it conveys. A man who is concerned about his poor grades in college may interpret a variety of experiences in terms of their implications for his competence or general self-worth.

As the above examples imply, concerns that have nothing to do with one's spouse can activate concepts that affect one's interpretation of the spouse's statements and behavior. Current concerns take on particular importance, however, when they *do* surround one's spouse or the quality of one's relationship. A woman who is suspicious of her husband's infidelity might activate concepts that lead her to interpret his passing remarks about female colleagues as having implications for past, present, and future sexual encounters with them. More generally, individuals who are currently concerned about the quality of their relationship are prone to interpret everything their partner says in terms of concepts that have implications for this relationship, and for their feelings about each other, regardless of whether these implications were intended by the communicator.

Personality differences. Several other individual differences in the concepts that are brought to bear on the interpretation of social experiences, which may have both motivational and learning components, may be related to various indices of personality. Differences in self-consciousness (e.g., Fenigstein, Scheier, & Buss, 1975) or self-monitoring (Snyder, 1974) might be associated with differences in the tendency to activate concepts or knowledge about either oneself or the other, respectively, for use in interpreting information. The effects of these factors have rarely been considered in empirical work on the determinants of concept accessibility. However, their implications for differences in the concepts that relationship partners typically bring to bear on the processing of one another's communications is well worth exploring.

The interpretation of a communication sometimes requires not only a consideration of the descriptive features of the message itself but also an assessment of the conditions that gave rise to it. Moreover, in deciding how to respond to the communication, the recipient might also infer its implications for the people and events to which it directly or indirectly pertains. For example, a wife whose husband says that she should take the children to visit her parents may infer that his comment is based on his knowledge that her elderly parents haven't seen their grandchildren in three years, and that this may be one of their last opportunities to do so. Alternatively, she may infer that her husband would like to spend some time away from her in order to carry on an affair with his secretary. Depending on which inference is made, the woman may interpret her husband's remark as either considerate or rejecting. Moreover, she may construe its implications for her husband's feelings toward her and for the prognosis of their relationship as either favorable or unfavorable. As this example suggests, a recipient's emotional and behavioral responses to a communicator's message depend largely on which of several possible inferences are made about the message's antecedents and consequences. The processes that determine which inference is made are discussed below.

The Accessibility of Event Representations

The antecedents and consequences of a communication are often determined on the basis of an event representation. This representation may be either specific to a particular experience and situational context or an abstraction of several different experiences. In either case, it can be conceptualized as a series of frames, each of which denotes a different action in a temporally and/or causally related sequence (cf. Abelson, 1976; Newtson, 1976; Wyer & Gordon, 1984; Wyer & Srull, 1989). When a verbal statement or observed behavior has features that compose one of the frames contained in such a representation, the representation is likely to be activated. Then the frames that occur earlier in the representation will be used to construe antecedents of the particular communication being considered, and frames that occur later will be used to infer its consequences. Often, features of a communication will match a frame of several different event representations. In such cases, inferences of its antecedents and consequences (and, therefore, the response that is ultimately made to the communication) depend on which alternative representation happens to be most accessible in memory.

The retrieval and use of an event representation are theoretically governed by processes similar to those we postulated to underlie the activation and use of semantic concepts to interpret individual pieces of information. However, whereas the semantic concepts are typically contained in the semantic bin, the event representations are usually retrieved from referent bins. This difference raises some additional considerations that are worth reviewing in the context of inference phenomena.

The Work Space is the first location searched for inference-relevant information. Therefore, if an applicable event representation has been activated very recently (e.g., earlier in the conversation), it is likely to be used. Otherwise, the representation that is used will be retrieved from a referent bin in Permanent Storage. In this case, the likelihood of retrieving a given representation depends on both (a) the position of the representation in the bin that contains it and (b) whether this bin is actually identified.

To the extent that the latter is the case, the retrieval of any given representation depends on whether the probe cues that govern the search compose the header of the bin in which the representation is located. For example, a woman's "husband" bin might contain a representation that concerns her husband's being frustrated at work, coming home and criticizing her. Her "relationship" bin might contain a representation that concerns her husband's resenting the time she spends with her friends and displacing this resentment by criticizing her. One frame in each representation portrays the husband as criticizing his spouse. Considered in context, however, these frames have different implications. Thus, imagine that in the course of dinner conversation, the woman interprets one of her husband's comments as a criticism. The representation she uses to infer the implications of this comment, and her reactions to it, depend on whether she happens to be thinking about the conversation with reference to her husband or with reference to the relationship and, therefore, whether "husband" or "relationship" is included among the probe cues that govern the search.

These considerations are particularly important when there are systematic differences in the type of representations that partners typically store in different bins. One might speculate, for example, that partners typically store sequences of events that have positive implications for the quality of their relationship in a "self" bin, but store sequences with undesirable implications for their relationship in a "spouse" or "relationship" bin. If this were so, the implications they are likely to perceive in their partners' messages would depend substantially on their goal when they receive these messages and, therefore, the referent that they happen to be thinking about.

The probe cues that lead a bin to be identified are not always directly relevant to one's processing objectives (see footnote 3). Irrelevant features that happen to be activated at the time information is sought may be fortuitously included. A study by Bower (1981) suggests this possibility. Specifically, subjects who were asked to recall their childhood experiences were more inclined to report experiences that were affectively congruent with their mood at the time (i.e., "happy" or "sad"). One interpretation of this is that, at the time subjects' childhood experiences occurred, they were stored in bins that were denoted in part by their affective quality ("happy" or "sad"). When subjects were later asked to recall their past experiences, affective features activated by their mood were fortuitously included among the probe cues that governed their search of memory, and so experiences were selectedly retrieved from bins whose headers contained these features.

By analogy, relationship partners may often organize their experiences in terms of affective as well as descriptive features. In other words, they may have separate bins that are restricted to "good relationship" experiences and "bad relationship" experiences as well as a more general "relationship" bin. Suppose a man happens to be in a bad mood at the time his spouse initiates a conversation. His mood could have been stimulated by factors that had nothing to do with either his relationship with his partner or the topic of his wife's comment. Nevertheless, concepts activated by his mood could lead him to draw a representation from a "bad relationship" bin to use when inferring the implications of his wife's statement rather than from the bin pertaining to his relationship in general. As a result, he might construe the implications of his wife's comments as undesirable, and this construal might influence his responses to them. Note that a representation of the wife's comment, along with its inferred implications, is stored in memory. This representation can later be recalled and used to interpret subsequent communications. This analysis implies that *unless misperceptions of a communication are corrected shortly after the message is received, these perceptions can have an enduring effect on memory for the communication and, therefore, on judgments and decisions that are based on it.*

It seems likely that event representations of the sort we have postulated, which are often idiosyncratic, will play a major role in construing the implications of communications that occur in the context of close relationships. However, responses to a communication are certainly not always mediated by inferences of the sort we have postulated. In addition, qualifications arise concerning the assumptions that (a) both the antecedents and consequences of a communication are typically considered when responding to a communication, and (b) only one representation is typically used as a basis for inferences. These matters are discussed below.

The Role of Communication Norms
in the Interpretation of Messages

When communications are conveyed in the course of a conversation, additional factors come into play that are not taken into account by the preceding analysis. For one thing, both the generation and interpretation of these messages may be governed in part by general normative rules of communication (Grice, 1975; Higgins, 1981). Three principles—informativeness, accuracy, and politeness— are particularly important. For reasons we will indicate, the application of these principles may have a substantial impact on a relationship partner's perceptions of the emotional content of a verbal message and affective reactions to it.

Informativeness.   Communications are usually expected to convey new information. Consequently, the recipient of a message typically assumes that the communicator has intended to be informative and attempts to interpret the message in a way that is consistent with this assumption. This phenomenon has particularly important implications when the literal meaning of the message is redundant with the receiver's prior knowledge and, therefore, would normally "go without saying." Under these conditions, the message may be assumed to be an indirect speech act and, therefore, to convey feelings and intentions that are not directly implied by it. Thus, to return to an earlier example, a husband's comment that "It's cold in here" would go without saying if his wife is in the same room. The nonredundant aspects of such a statement concern its *indirect* implications (i.e., the husband's irritation at his spouse for constantly setting the thermostat too low.) These implications might therefore be inferred by the wife, based on the assumption that the husband is trying to be informative. As this example suggests, the indirect implications of a message often pertain to its emotional meaning.

Communicators sometimes violate the informativeness principle unwittingly. This could occur either because they are unaware of what the recipient already knows, or because they simply fail to consider this factor. In either case, the receiver may impute meaning to the communication that the communicator did not intend. In our example, the husband may spontaneously have uttered "It's cold in here" upon feeling a chill, without first thinking about its information value. The wife, however, by applying the informativeness principle, may attribute motives and affect to her spouse that did not, in fact, exist.

A general conclusion is suggested by this example. That is, miscommunications occur whenever the communicator and the recipient have different perceptions of whether the direct implications of a communication are informative. Suppose a communicator assumes that the direct content of his message is already known by the recipient, and intends the message to be an indirect speech act that conveys feelings about the recipient or the topic being discussed. If the recipient actually does not have this knowledge, she may miss the indirect implications that the speaker intends to communicate. Alternatively, suppose a communicator attempts to convey information he incorrectly assumes is not already known by the recipient. In this case, if the recipient assumes that the speaker is aware of her knowledge, she may impute indirect (e.g., emotional) meaning to his message that he did not actually have.

Accuracy and politeness.   The information conveyed in communications should be accurate. At the same time, communications should not unnecessarily offend the receiver. These principles are often applied both in generating messages and in perceiving their implications. The application of the principles, however, often works one against the other. That is, communications may often need to be inaccurate in order to avoid hurting the recipient's feelings.

The most obvious example of a conflict between applications of the accuracy and politeness principles by partners in a close relationship occurs in the context of infidelity. However, many other situations arise of a much more trivial nature. For example, a man who believes that his wife would like the last piece of candy may profess that he personally does not. A common aspect of both examples is that a communicator's message often has more desirable implications for the recipient if it is interpreted as accurate than if it is not. Put another way, a communicator's application of the accuracy principle in generating a communication can often be detrimental to the quality of the interaction, at least in the short run. In contrast, a recipient's application of the principle can actually be beneficial.[5]

The politeness principle, of course, applies even when the descriptive content of a communication *is* intended to be accurate. People who wish to complain about another's behavior, or to point out a quality of the person that they find irritating, usually attempt to do so in a way that conveys this information without overly upsetting the person. Thus, they couch their criticism in terms that convey positive feelings toward the other, despite the behavior or attribute they find objectionable.

Correspondingly, recipients who apply the politeness principle will often attempt to interpret communications in a way that is not upsetting. Thus, even when a communication conveys anger, or a harsh criticism of the recipient's behavior, the recipient may try to interpret it in a way that minimizes its implications for the communicator's general feelings toward the recipient or their relationship, thereby lessening the negative affect that results from it. Thus, the man whose wife criticizes him for reading the newspaper while she is talking may tend to attribute this to a momentary flare-up, perhaps caused by a bad day at the office, rather than as an indication that she generally dislikes him and is dissatisfied with their relationship.

---

[5]Obvious exceptions to this conclusion arise when communicators engage in good-natured ribbing of the recipient that, if taken seriously, would be offensive. The conclusion may also not apply in the case of sarcasm. By and large, however, the conclusion seems likely to be correct.

It is interesting to speculate about the effects of applying the politeness principle to relationship satisfaction. Persons who attempt to interpret their partners' responses as consistent with the politeness principle should generally experience less negative affect toward their partners, and, therefore, should be more satisfied with their relationships than partners who typically interpret each other's messages as violating the principle. This should be true regardless of whether or not they apply the principle in their role as communicators.

Although politeness, accuracy, and informativeness are general normative principles in conversation, it is clear that they are not always applied. Individual differences may often exist in the tendency to invoke these principles across situations. On the other hand, it also seems likely that the tendency to apply the principles may vary with the particular situation in which the communication takes place or, more specifically, with features of the situation that lead different subsets of prior knowledge to be retrieved. To this extent, the application of the principles, and the perceptions of the implications of messages that result from their application, may be governed to a large extent by the processes we outlined earlier in this chapter.

Automaticity in Interpersonal Communication: The Role of Productions

There are undoubtedly many instances in which a recipient's response to a message is not mediated by any of the inference processes we have described. Smith (1984, 1990), expanding on Anderson's (1983) ACT* model, has postulated the existence of "If . . . then . . ." *production rules*. These rules, which are acquired through learning, determine responses to different configurations of stimulus conditions. These productions may often be applied automatically when the stimulus conditions that activate them occur. In the present context, suppose a communicator's message is encoded in terms that fulfill the "If . . ." conditions of a production. This production may then be activated and may generate the response specified in its "Then . . ." component without any of the cognitive processing we have postulated to guide inferences based on a previously formed event representation.

As a simplified example, suppose people have acquired a production of the form "If partner communicates emotion X to me, then communicate emotion X to partner." The use of this production would lead someone who has interpreted his or her partner's message as hostile to reciprocate this hostility without considering either the antecedents of the communicator's message or its implications. More generally, this means that, when the features of a communication and its situational context fulfill the conditions of a production, the accessibility of alternative event representations is not a factor underlying the recipient's response.

Productions undoubtedly govern communications in a wide range of situations in which interaction patterns have become routinized. For this reason, they are particularly likely to guide much of the communication that takes place in close relationships in which partners' modes of responding to each other have developed over a long period of time. The conditions in which communications are mediated by productions rather than a more deliberate construal of the implications of a communicator's message, and the implications of these different mediating processes, warrant further consideration.

The Role of Attributions in Communication Decisions

Even when communication decisions are mediated by the retrieval and use of an event representation of the sort we have postulated, these representations may not always be used in the way we have described. In particular, explanations of another's statement or behavior often may not be consciously taken into account in deciding how to respond to this behavior. Partners' tendencies to attribute each other's behavior to different factors, and the relation of these tendencies to marital satisfaction, have been the focus of much research and theorizing (see Bradbury & Fincham, 1990). According to the formulation we have proposed, however, the role of these attributions in deciding how to respond overtly to one another's behavior is unclear.

Specifically, suppose a recipient's construal of the implications of a communicator's message is based on an event representation of the sort we have postulated. This construal does not necessarily require a conscious attribution of the message to any particular factor. Once the frame of a representation that corresponds to the communicator's message has been identified, an explanation of the message would be generated by searching backward (through earlier frames of the representation), whereas its implications (consequences) are inferred by searching forward. One need not go backward before going forward. This means that the representation can be used to infer implications of a message, and may elicit emotional reactions, without any conscious consideration of the antecedent conditions that have led up to this message.

The above considerations imply that attributions per se may not be as important mediators of interpersonal behavior as one might intuitively expect. Because attributions are theoretically based on the same cognitive representations that guide recipients' inferences of the implications of a communicator's statement, data bearing on their nature may provide some insight into which types of representations are likely to be activated and used to construe these implications and, therefore, mediate the recipient's responses. However, these attributions are not themselves the cognitive mediators of these responses. Indeed, they may not even be thought about unless the recipient is asked, by an experimenter or another person, to generate them after the fact.

The Search for Alternative Explanations

In discussing the role of event representations in construing the antecedents and consequences of another's behavior, we have assumed that one and only one representation is considered. There are undoubtedly instances, however, in which an alternative explanation *is* sought. This is most likely when aspects of the first explanation considered are inconsistent with knowledge about the message and the conditions surrounding it. People are inclined to accept explanations of events that have positive implications for themselves, and to use these implications as bases for judgments, even when plausible alternative explanations are easily accessible (cf. Arkin, Gleason, & Johnston, 1976; Schwarz & Clore, 1983). However, they resist accepting explanations of events with negative implications for themselves unless no alternative explanation is immediately apparent. In the present context, this suggests that people are more likely to search for explanations of their spouse's comments if the first explanation they happen to consider has negative implications for themselves or their relationship than if it has positive implications.

AFFECTIVE REACTIONS, OVERT RESPONSES TO COMMUNICATIONS, AND RELATIONSHIP SATISFACTION

As indicated in Fig. 2.2, people's response to a communication is often mediated by their affective reactions to the message. This response may be a specific statement or behavior that is directed toward the communicator in the immediate situation. Or it may also be a subjective judgment or evaluation of the receiver, the communicator, or their relationship that is not publically expressed at the time. These latter responses may ultimately provide the basis for the receiver's satisfaction with the relationship as well as overt behavior performed in subsequent situations. We are unable to discuss in detail the role of affective reactions in communication processes in this chapter. However, a few general points are worth nothing.

The Influence of Affective Reactions on Behavior: Reciprocity in Emotional Communication

As we have emphasized throughout this chapter, the transmission of descriptive knowledge and the transmission of emotional content cannot be viewed in isolation. Emotional communications may nevertheless be governed by a somewhat different principle than descriptive communications, namely, *reciprocity*. Specifically, recipients of a communication may often attempt to convey feelings to the communicator that are similar to those that they perceive the communicator has conveyed to them.

Evidence of a reciprocity rule was obtained in the aforementioned study by Gaelick et al., (1985). That is, both male and female marriage partners who discussed a conflict they were having, reported attempting to reciprocate the emotions that they believed their partner had intended to convey to them. This was true regardless of whether the emotion involved was love or hostility. Note, however, that this does not mean that the emotion the communicator intended to convey was *actually* reciprocated. For actual reciprocation to occur, the recipient must of course perceive the communicator's intentions accurately. As we noted earlier, communications of hostility were perceived accurately in Gaelick et al.'s study, whereas communications of love were not. Consequently, only expressions of hostility were actually reciprocated; communicators' attempts to convey love did not systematically influence the love that their partners tried to convey in return. Note that, as a consequence of such an asymmetry, the frequency and intensity of the hostility conveyed in these interactions are likely to escalate over the course of the conversation, whereas the frequency and intensity of the love conveyed are not. (In evaluating this conclusion, however, it is important to bear in mind that the conversation investigated by Gaelick et al. concerned a conflict that partners were having. Whether the conclusion generalizes to other types of conversations is not clear.)

The tendency to reciprocate affectively positive or negative communications may vary over individuals. For example, distressed couples are more likely than nondistressed couples to reciprocate affectively negative communications (Gottman et al., 1976). This could indicate distressed and nondistressed couples differ in their tendency to apply the reciprocity principle. On the other hand, it is also possible that distressed and nondistressed partners apply the principle equally, but distressed partners perceive negative affect more accurately than do nondistressed. Note that nondistressed partners are more disposed than distressed partners to interpret behavior positively, independently of its actual content (Floyd & Markman, 1983). This finding is consistent with the second interpretation.

The Influence of Affect on Judgments of Relationship Satisfaction

The affective reactions that people experience may affect the processing of information at several different stages (Wyer & Srull, 1989). That is, concepts associated with these reactions may influence the way information is encoded and the knowledge that is retrieved and used to assess its implications. In addition, people use the affect and emotions they happen to be experiencing at the time they are called upon to report a judgment, as information about their reactions to the object being judged and, therefore, base their judgments on these reactions (cf. Schwarz & Clore, 1983; Strack, Martin, & Stepper, 1988). An important implication of this tendency results from the fact that people are often unable to distinguish clearly between the various sources of the affect they are experiencing. Consequently, their judgments are often influenced by their mood or by other factors that have had an impact on their emotional state for judgment-irrelevant reasons.

In the present context, this means that partners' reported satisfaction with their relationship can often be influenced by factors that have led them to experience positive or negative affect at the time of judgment for reasons that have nothing to do with the quality of their relationship per se. These factors, although transitory and situation specific, could have enduring effects. That is, once a judgment is made of one's partner or relationship, a cognitive representation of this judgment, or the reactions on which it is based, is presumably transferred to memory. Consequently, this representation might later be retrieved and used as a basis for future judgments and decisions independently of the conditions that initially gave rise to its construction.

This calls attention to the fact that the relationship satisfaction that partners report is governed by the particular subset of prior knowledge that they happen to retrieve and bring to bear on it. As noted earlier in this chapter, the retrieval and use of any particular subset of prior knowledge are likely to depend on the recency with which the knowledge was acquired. It may also depend on one's processing objectives at the time and, therefore, whether the information is located in the bin in which information is being sought.

This is not to say that judgments of relationship satisfaction are completely unstable. In many instances, affect may become associated with a general concept of "one's relationship" (or, in terms of the model we have proposed, it may become a feature in the header of one's "relationship" bin). To this extent, the affect may be elicited whenever the concept is activated and may be used as a basis for judgments without searching for specific experiences that bear on them. The formulation we offer helps to conceptualize the cognitive mechanisms that underlie differences in reported satisfaction. It may also help us to understand the relation between the satisfaction that partners report and the nature of the personal experiences they have had in interacting with each other. This relation may be much more complex than we sometimes think.

FINAL REMARKS

As Fig. 2.2 implies, and our discussion in this chapter testifies, a complete understanding of interpersonal communication in close relationships requires knowledge of not only the factors that influence each of several, different stages of information processing, but also how these stages are interfaced. The same variables may influence processing at different stages. Moreover, the results of processing at one point in a conversation can alter communication goals and expectancies, which can in turn, influence processing at later points. An empirical investigation of these matters may be difficult, given the constraints that are inherently imposed on research involving couples in close relationships. However, it is not impossible.

Our framework is useful in conceptualizing factors that influence the dynamics of interpersonal communication in close relationships and their potential impact on relationship satisfaction. Moreover, it raises specific questions and hypotheses that can be empirically investigated. Although any particular empirical finding may provide only one piece in a very complex puzzle, we are confident that the various pieces will ultimately be fit together to provide a useful conceptualization of the dynamics of close relationships.

REFERENCES

Abelson, R. P. (1976). Script processing in attitude formation and decision making. In J. S. Carroll & J. W. Payne (Eds.), *Cognition and social behavior*. Hillsdale, NJ: Lawrence Erlbaum Associates.

Anderson, J. R. (1983). *The architecture of cognition*. Cambridge, MA: Harvard University Press.

Argyle, M., & Dean, J. (1965). Eye-contact, distance and affiliation. *Sociometry, 28*, 289–304.

Arias, I., & Beach, S. R. H. (1987). The assessment of social cognition in the context of marriage. In K. D. O'Leary (Ed.), *Assessment of marital discord* (pp. 109–137). Hillsdale, NJ: Lawrence Erlbaum Associates.

Arkin, R. M., Gleason, J. M., & Johnston, S. (1976). Effect of perceived choice, expected outcome and observed outcome of an action on the causal attributions of actors. *Journal of Experimental Social Psychology, 12*, 151–158.

Bargh, J. A. (1984). Automatic and conscious processing of social information. In R. S. Wyer & T. K. Srull (Eds.), *Handbook of social cognition* (Vol. 3, pp. 1–43). Hillsdale, NJ: Lawrence Erlbaum Associates.

Bargh, J. A., Bond, R. N., Lombardi, W., & Tota, M. E. (1986). The additive nature of chronic and temporary sources of construct accessibility. *Journal of Personality and Social Psychology, 50*, 869–878.

Berley, R. A., & Jacobson, N. S. (1984). Causal attributions in intimate relationships: Toward a model of cognitive-behavioral marital therapy. In P. Kendall (Ed.), *Advances in cognitive-behavioral research and therapy* (Vol. 3, pp. 1–60). New York: Academic Press.

Bodenhausen, G. V., Gaelick, L., & Wyer, R. S. (1987). Affective and cognitive factors in intragroup and intergroup communication. In C. Hendrick (Ed.), *Review of personality and social psychology: Group processes and intergroup relations* (Vol. 9, pp. 137–166). Newbury Park, CA: Sage.

Bower, G. H. (1981). Mood and memory. *American Psychologist, 36*, 129–148.

Bower, G. H., Gilligan, S. G., & Monteiro, K. P. (1981). Selectivity of learning caused by affective states. *Journal of Experimental Psychology: General, 110*, 451–473.

Bradbury, T. N., & Fincham, F. D. (1987). Affect and cognition in close relationships: Toward an integrative model. *Cognition and Emotion, 1*, 58–87.

Bradbury, T. N., & Fincham, F. D. (1990). Attributions in marriage: Review and critique. *Psychological Bulletin, 3*, 3–33.

Bruner, J. S. (1957). On perceptual readiness. *Psychological Review, 64*, 123–152.

Carlston, D. E. (1980). Events, inferences and impression formation. In R. Hastie, T. Ostrom, E. Ebbesen, R. Wyer, D. Hamilton, & D. Carlston (Eds.), *Person memory: The cognitive basis of social perception* (pp. 89–119). Hillsdale, NJ: Lawrence Erlbaum Associates.

Clark, H., & Clark, E. (1977). *Psychology and language*. New York: Harcourt Brace Jovanovich.

Eidelson, R. J., & Epstein, N. (1982). Cognition and relationship maladjustment: Development of a measure of dysfunctional relationships beliefs. *Journal of Consulting and Clinical Psychology, 50*, 715–720.

Fenigstein, A., Scheier, M. F., & Buss, A. H. (1975). Public and private self consciousness: Assessment and theory. *Journal of Consulting and Clinical Psychology, 43*, 522–527.

Fichten, C. S. (1984). See it from my point of view: Videotape and attributions in happy and distressed couples. *Journal of Social and Clinical Psychology, 2*, 125–142.

Fincham, F. D. (1985). Attributions in close relationships. In J. H. Harvey & G. Weary (Eds.), *Contemporary attribution theory and research* (pp. 303–334). New York: Academic Press.

Fincham, F. D., & Bradbury, T. N. (1987). Cognitive processes and conflict in close relationships: An attribution-efficacy model. *Journal of Personality and Social Psychology, 53*, 1106–1118.

Fincham, F. D., Bradbury, T. N., & Scott, C. K. (1990). Cognition in marriage. In F. D. Fincham and T. N. Bradbury (Eds.), *The psychology of marriage.* (pp. 118–149). New York: Guilford Press.

Floyd, F. J., & Markman, H. H. (1983). Observational biases in spouse observation: Toward a cognitive-behavioral model of marriage. *Journal of Consulting and Clinical Psychology, 51*, 450–457.

Gaelick, L., Bodenhausen, G. V., & Wyer, R. S. (1985). Emotional communication in close relationships. *Journal of Personality and Social Psychology, 49*, 1246–1265.

Glick, B. R., & Gross, S. J. (1975). Marital interaction and marital conflict: A critical evaluation of current research strategies. *Journal of Marriage and the Family, 37*, 505–512.

Gottman, J. M. (1979). *Marital interaction: Experimental investigations*. New York: Academic Press.

Gottman, J. M., Notarius, C., Markman, M. H., Banks, S., Yoppi, B., & Rubin, M. E. (1976). Behavior exchange theory and marital decision making. *Journal of Personality and Social Psychology, 34*, 14–23.

Grice, H. (1975). Logic and conversation. In P. Cole & J. Morgan (Eds.), *Syntax and semantics: Vol. 3. Speech acts* (pp. 68–134). New York: Academic Press.

Gurman, A. S., & Knudson, R. M. (1978). Behavioral marriage therapy: I. A psychodynamic-systems analysis and critique. *Family Process, 17*, 121–138.

Higgins, E. T. (1981). The "communication game": Implications for social cognition and persuasion. In E. T. Higgins, C. P. Herman, & M. P. Zanna (Eds.), *Social cognition: The Ontario symposium* (Vol. 1, pp. 343–392). Hillsdale, NJ: Erlbaum.

Higgins, E. T., & King, G. (1981). Accessibility of social constructs: Information processing consequences of individual and contextual variability. In N. Canton & J. F. Kihlstrom (Eds.), *Personality, cognition, and social interaction* (pp. 69–121). Hillsdale, NJ: Lawrence Erlbaum Associates.

Higgins, E. T., Rholes, W. S., & Jones, C. R. (1977). Category accessibility and impression formation. *Journal of Experimental Social Psychology, 13*, 141–154.

Klinger, E. (1977). *Meaning and void: Inner experiencing and the incentives in people's lives*. Minneapolis: University of Minnesota Press.

Markman, H. (1979). Application of a behavioral model of marriage in prediction relationship satisfaction of couples planning marriage. *Journal of Consulting and Clinical Psychology, 47*, 743–749.

Markus, H. (1977). Self-schema and processing information about the self. *Journal of Personality and Social Psychology, 35*, 63–78.

Markus, H., & Smith, J. (1981). The influence of self-schemata on the perception of others. In N.

Cantor & J. F. Kihlstrom (Eds.), *Personality, cognition, and social interaction* (pp. 233–262). Hillsdale, NJ: Lawrence Erlbaum Associates.

Massad, C. M., Hubbard, M., & Newtson, D. (1979). Perceptual selectivity: Contributing process and possible cure for impression perseverance. *Journal of Experimental Psychology, 15,* 513–532.

Newman, H. M., & Langer, E. J. (1983). Investigating the development and courses of intimate relationships: A cognitive model. In L. Y. Abramson (Ed.), *Social-personal inference in clinical psychology* (pp. 120–137). New York: Guilford Press.

Newtson, D. A. (1976). Foundations of attribution: The perception of ongoing behavior. In J. Harvey, W. Ickes, & R. Kidd (Eds.), *New directions in attribution research* (Vol. 1, pp. 223–247). Hillsdale, NJ: Lawrence Erlbaum Associates.

Noller, P. (1980). Misunderstandings in marital communication: A study of couples' nonverbal communication. *Journal of Personality and Social Psychology, 39,* 1135–1148.

Ross, M., & Sicoly, F. (1979). Egocentric biases in availability and attribution. *Journal of Personality and Social Psychology, 37,* 322–336.

Schank, R. C., & Abelson, R. P. (1977). *Scripts, plans, goals and understanding.* Hillsdale, NJ: Lawrence Erlbaum Associates.

Schwarz, N., & Clore, G. L. (1983). Mood, misattribution, and judgments of well-being: Informative and directive functions of affective states. *Journal of Personality and Social Psychology, 45,* 513–523.

Scott, C. K., Bradbury, T. N., & Fincham, F. D. (1989). *Memory in close relationships.* Paper presented at Midwest Psychological Association Convention, Chicago.

Sillars, A. L. (1985). Interpersonal perception in relationships. In W. Ickes (Ed.), *Compatible and incompatible relationships* (pp. 277–305). New York: Springer-Verlag.

Smith, E. R. (1984). Models of social inference processes. *Psychological Review, 91,* 392–413.

Smith, E. R. (1990). Content and process specificity in the effects of prior experiences. In T. K. Srull & R. S. Wyer (Eds.), *Advances in social cognition* (Vol. 3, pp. 1–60). Hillsdale, NJ: Lawrence Erlbaum Associates.

Snyder, M. (1974). Self-monitoring of expressive behavior. *Journal of Personality and Social Psychology, 30,* 526–537.

Sorrentino, R. M., & Higgins, E. T. (Eds.). (1986). *Handbook of motivation and cognition.* New York: Guilford Press.

Srull, T. K., & Wyer, R. S. (1979). The role of category accessibility in the interpretation of information about persons: Some determinants and implications. *Journal of Personality and Social Psychology, 37,* 1660–1672.

Srull, T. K., & Wyer, R. S. (1980). Category accessibility and social perception: Some implications for the study of person memory and interpersonal judgment. *Journal of Personality and Social Psychology, 38,* 841–856.

Srull, T. K., & Wyer, R. S. (1989). Person memory and judgment. *Psychological Review, 96,* 58–83.

Strack, R., Martin, L. L., & Stepper, S. (1988). Inhibiting and facilitating conditions of the human smile: A non-obtrusive test of the facial-feedback hypothesis. *Journal of Personality and Social Psychology, 54,* 768–777.

Watzlawick, P., Beavin, J. H., & Jackson, D. D. (1967). *Pragmatics of human communication.* New York: Norton.

Weiss, R. L. (1984). Cognitive and behavioral measures of marital interaction. In K. Hahlweg & N. S. Jacobson (Eds.), *Marital interaction: Analysis and modification* (pp. 232–252). New York: Guilford Press.

Wyer, R. S., & Carlston, D. E. (1979). *Social cognition, inference and attribution.* Hillsdale, NJ: Lawrence Erlbaum Associates.

Wyer, R. S., & Gordon, S. E. (1984). The cognitive representation of social information. In R. S.

Wyer & T. K. Srull (Eds.), *Handbook of social cognition* (Vol. 2, pp. 73–150). Hillsdale, NJ: Lawrence Erlbaum Associates.

Wyer, R. S., & Srull, T. K. (Eds.). (1984). *Handbook of social cognition* (Vols. 1–3). Hillsdale, NJ: Lawrence Erlbaum Associates.

Wyer, R. S., & Srull, T. K. (1986). Human cognition in its social context. *Psychological Review, 93*, 322–359.

Wyer, R. S., & Srull, T. K. (1989). *Memory and cognition in its social context.* Hillsdale, NJ: Lawrence Erlbaum Associates.

Wyer, R. S., Srull, T. K., Gordon, S. E., & Hartwick, J. (1982). The effects of taking a perspective on the recall of prose material. *Journal of Personality and Social Psychology, 43*, 674–688.

3

On the Coherence of Mental Models of Persons and Relationships: A Knowledge Structure Approach

Lynn Carol Miller
Stephen J. Read
University of Southern California

> I saw John for the first time in a local bar, having a few drinks. He was a slim, attractive man, in his forties I'd say, tall with nice wavy black hair and a touch of gray. He wore a business suit, and his briefcase was sitting by the bar stool. I noticed he wasn't wearing a wedding band. He looked over at our table and seemed to nod in my direction. Wendy and I looked at each other and smiled. "He's all yours, Mary," she said. We told the bartender we'd like to offer that fellow his next drink. It didn't take long to get a response. "I'm John," he said, as he tipped his drink and asked if he could join us. John was attentive and charming. He told me I was attractive and that he'd had his eye on us since he came in. We both found ourselves listening and giving him the floor. He talked about his job, his recent failed marriage, and his college days at Princeton.

What do these actions mean? Why did Mary and Wendy invite John to their table? Why did he accept? What was he doing in the bar? Such kinds of questions are common in everyday life. As observers and interactants we want to understand events and so attempt to construct a coherent picture of sequences of actions, what individual are doing, and what they are like. Moreover, as relationships develop with time and further interaction, we construct more detailed models of our partner and the relationship. These models are critical for guiding behavior in interactions and in relationships. Yet we know surprisingly little about how people construct such models and how they cohere. The aim of this chapter is to outline a model of how people develop coherent models of others.

Coherence is a concept used by scholars in a variety of fields (e.g., linguistics, communications, cognitive science, philosophy, and psychology). Although definitions of coherence vary widely (see Kellerman & Sleight, 1989), a common theme concerns the extent to which elements (e.g., sentences in a text, propositions in a network, or speech acts in a conversation) go together to form a meaningful whole (Fisher, 1989). But what factors determine whether things go together or cohere? Although researchers have suggested a number of possibilities, we believe that the coherence central to social interaction is provided by theories, often causal and goal-based theories, concerned with how things are related to one another or go together (Murphy & Medin, 1985). These theories are often embedded in complex knowledge structures, such as those analyzed by Schank and Abelson (1977) (also see Galambos, Abelson, & Black, 1986; Schank, 1982).

Knowledge structures include goals, plans, scripts, roles, and themes. These structures enable us to make inferences from elements (e.g., behavior, speech acts, events) and to link these inferences and elements to help form coherent models of interactions, persons, situations, and relationships. We suggest that a variety of *principles of coherence* (Thagard, 1989) guide the development of these models and guide the choices we make among different competing mental models. Furthermore, we suggest that *seeking coherence* is an important and fundamental goal of understanding; it provides the underlying dynamic in the development of individuals' mental models of interactions, other persons, self, and relationships in the world. The more that people perceive that a model coheres internally and with other outside information, and judge it as more coherent than alternative models, the more that individuals are apt to feel that they understand events.

People construct models, and thus make *judgments of coherence,* at a variety of levels: at the level of specific short behavioral sequences; at the level of longer behavioral consequences and extended conversations; and at the level of elaborate models of persons, situations, and relationships over longer and longer time frames. People's models of the current interaction, as well as their more general models of their partners and relationships, play a major role in guiding their interactions. Thus, understanding how individuals develop coherent mental models is a fundamental issue in studying social interaction and developing relationships.

To further explicate what we mean by coherence and to investigate the process by which individuals develop coherent mental models, we first outline the knowledge structures that are apt to be used in developing coherent mental models (Miller & Read, 1987, in press; Read & Miller, 1989). Next we describe a model of how mental models of events, persons, and relationships are constructed and examine the principles of coherence (Thagard, 1989) that are applied in building mental models. In doing so we illustrate how the constructs that we often use in everyday parlance (e.g., traits, roles) can be economical labels for elaborate mental models and how attempts to develop and combine these models may shed light on (a) the goal-based structures that may underlie them and (b) what coherence principles are applied in their construction. Finally, we discuss the implications of this approach for interpersonal relationships.

KNOWLEDGE STRUCTURES USEFUL
FOR UNDERSTANDING PERSONS
AND RELATIONSHIPS

As the theory of Inter-personalism argues (Miller & Read, 1987, 1991; Read & Miller, 1989), goal-based structures (e.g., goals, plans, resources, and beliefs) provide a common language for thinking about the relations among persons and between persons and situations. Within this framework, stable individual differences are viewed as chronic configurations of the individual's goals, plans, resources, and beliefs. Similar structures can be used to conceptualize situations and relationships. Thus, the theory offers a common language of goal-based structures to analyze how individuals interact with situations and with each other. Earlier work (Miller & Read, 1987; Read & Miller, 1989) used these structures to outline a framework for thinking about cognition and behavior in relationships. Here we focus on the implications of this approach for understanding how people comprehend the behaviors of others and build coherent models of them. First, let us consider the building blocks of these structures in greater detail.

Building Blocks

Goals. A goal is something that the individual desires or wants to attain. Among the wide range of possible goals are basic biological needs, such as food, sleep, and sex; social goals, such as companionship, respect, love, security, and success; and more abstract goals, such as truth and justice. Goals that are particularly relevant to social relationships include, for example, making a positive impression, establishing an intimate relation or friendship, and avoiding rejection. In our earlier example, Mary may have desired a close relationship and possible marriage partner; she may have perceived that John had the same goals. John may actually have had the goals of wanting to impress and flatter her, and wanting physical intimacy. Individuals must infer partner goals from behavior; their inferences about partner goals may or may not overlap with actual partner goals.

Knowledge of relationships among goals is important for understanding behavior both alone and in interactions with others. Wilensky (1983) has analyzed extensively two major types of goal relations: intrapersonal goal relations, which are relations among the goals of a single individual, and interpersonal goal relations, which are relations among the goals of two or more individuals. Intrapersonal goals may be unrelated, they may overlap (in which case the same plan may achieve multiple goals), or they may conflict. Goal conflict may be due to one or more limitations (e.g., resource limitations such as insufficient time to carry out all of one's plans; state limitations, such as physically being unable to be in two locations at once; and limitations due to preservation goals, for instance, having an affair would endanger John's existing marriage). Interpersonal goals may compete (e.g., individuals' goals may be negatively related because only one person's goal can be pursued at a time or the attainment of one goal prevents the attainment of the other). For example, Mary may wish a marriage partner, whereas John may already be married, may not want a divorce, and may be just looking for an affair. There may also be goal concordance in which individuals' goals are positively related (e.g., because they both possess the same goal, or each individual's goals facilitate the other's). If both Mary and John just want a fling, then they could probably facilitate each other's goals. The implications of such goal configurations have been more extensively discussed elsewhere (Read & Miller, 1989).

Plans and strategies.   Plans are organized sequences of behavior aimed at the attainment of a goal. They are organized in a goal-subgoal hierarchy, composed of subsequences of behavior that are combined in an overall plan. Plans can vary tremendously in detail, from the quite sketchy to the highly detailed. Often, an individual possesses several alternative plans for a given goal. For example, if our goal is to establish a close relationship, we might choose between disclosing intimately and being particularly responsive to our partner's needs. The choice of a plan depends on factors such as the perception of the context, the availability of resources, and the judged likelihood that it would achieve one's goals. Mary and Wendy may perceive that John needs to talk, and perhaps the best way to allow him to achieve his goal is to listen; this may also achieve their goal of being perceived as likable and responsive, and may fit in with other person structures for Mary (e.g., to be perceived as feminine) or John (e.g., beliefs about what men and women are like and what one does to win a woman over). Although particular goals and plans are associated, a particular plan can often achieve several goals, and several different plans could be used to attempt to achieve the same goal.

Resources.   Plans have conditions that must be satisfied for them to be enacted. Satisfaction of some of these conditions depends on states of the world that are beyond the individual's control. However, satisfying these conditions often depends on the individual's possession and utilization of the necessary resources.

There are a number of different kinds of resources that are relevant to the successful enactment of social plans. Various taxonomies of these resources have been suggested (e.g., Foa & Foa, 1974; Wilensky, 1983). Here we focus on an abbreviated version of a taxonomy proposed by Read and Miller (1989). There are several general sources of resources: personal resources that the individual has access to individually, resources that are afforded by the situation, and resources that are available through our relationships with others.

Personal resources include (a) *cognitive resources,* which include mental skills, abilities, and strategies; (b) *knowledge* concerning the social and physical world as well as one's memories of past experiences and events; (c) *specialized talents and abilities,* such as musical and athletic skills; (d) *physical attributes,* including such things as physical attractiveness, body build, health, and energy level; (e) *social, expressive, and communicative skills;* (f) *position and status;* (g) *time;* and (h) *possessions,* such as money and physical objects that can play a role in plans. When we lack important resources we may fabricate having these resources to impress others and to encourage the belief that we are the type of person who fits their needs. Men and women are known to fabricate aspects of their appearance, and to exaggerate or fabricate other resources (e.g., social class, position, college backgrounds, intelligence). However, if we are attracted to another because of their resources (e.g., appearance, social and communication skills, money, inner spirituality, social status), and these are vital to the fulfillment of our goals, we are less likely to stay in the relationship if we discover we were mistaken in our initial judgment—or worse, deceived.

Situational resources are those afforded by a particular situation. For example, situations afford access to particular people and objects that may be important to our plans.

Finally, *relational resources* are afforded by our relationships with others. Among these are (a) *cognitive resources,* which include such things as transactional memories (Wegner, Giuliano, & Hertel, 1985) in which a couple's joint knowledge is greater than the sum of its parts; (b) *material resources,* such as a home, that a couple can only afford jointly; (c) *social and affective resources,* such as mutual love and social networks; and (d) *physical resources,* such as sex and resulting offspring.

Although our knowledge remains quite sketchy about the nature of different kinds of resources and their role in people's plans, it is quite apparent that there are important differences among resources. These differences have important implications for peoples' ability to carry out their plans and for the potential relations among plans (Read & Miller, 1989; Wilensky, 1983). Such resource differences may provide important clues as to when we should and should not expect consistency in behavior across situations. Furthermore, knowledge of the differences among resources may provide insight into how people can deal with various kinds of goal conflict. For example, John may perceive that he lacks the resources Mary needs to consider him for a sexual relationship. If he fabricates these, he may win her over; because he is not really interested in a long-term relationship, he will be long gone before she discovers the deception and he may have achieved his goal.

Beliefs.   Individuals possess an enormous number of beliefs about themselves, other people, and the world. These beliefs affect the choice and execution of goals and strategies. They also play a role in inferences about one's own and others' behavior. Beliefs may also influence the evaluation of the effectiveness and morality of plans. And beliefs may involve inferences about the characteristics and likely behavior of social objects, as well as inferences about the nature of our relationship with others.

Beliefs may be part of complex systems, in which some beliefs activate other beliefs in a given cluster. We may have schemas involving organized sets of beliefs about the self, others, relationships, or even about what we think others may think. Some of these schemas may be culturally shared (e.g., stereotypes, themes about roles, social norms and rules, scripts); some may be unique for the individual (e.g., mental models about what others generally are like, self-schemas) and how the individual views particular others or particular unique relationships (e.g., mental models of one's own marriage). For example, John may believe that others are basically not trustworthy, that you have to hurt others before they hurt you, that it is impossible to be close to others, and that you cannot depend upon others. In contrast, Mary may perceive that others are trustworthy and that she can depend upon them and feel close in relationships. It is noteworthy that beliefs and knowledge, viewed as a resource, involve some overlap. Beliefs, we would argue, could usefully be viewed as resources to the extent that they enable the utilization of plans to achieve goals.

Complex Structures

Using these basic building blocks a variety of more complex configurations can be constructed to represent persons, situations, and relationships.

Traits and other person structures.   We have argued (Miller & Read, 1987, 1991; Read & Miller, 1989) that stable individual differences can be conceptualized in terms of chronic configurations of four components: (a) an individual's chronic goals, (b) the plans and strategies for achieving those goals, (c) various resources that are required to successfully carry out the plans and strategies, and (d) beliefs about the world that affect such things as the likelihood of activation of goals and the execution of plans. Similar arguments about the importance of one or more of these components in the analysis of individual differences have frequently surfaced (Allport, 1937; Alston, 1970, 1975; Carbonell, 1979; Cattell, 1965; John, 1986; Mischel, 1973; Pervin, 1983). Although such configurations may be idiosyncratic to an individual, configurations that are shared across individuals in a culture will often be recognized by a trait label. Thus, we believe that traits can be analyzed in terms of the above four components.

John (1986) has recently presented an insightful conceptual analysis of traits that is similar to the above analysis and is in some ways more explicit. He has argued that the meaning of traits lies in underlying event scripts that are responsible for people's recognition of a behavior as an exemplar of a particular trait.

Such event scripts can be thought of as a general frame possessing a number of slots that can be filled by the appropriate concept. Among its slots are those for (a) a behavioral act, (b) the consequences of the act, (c) the roles and characteristics of the participants in the act, and (d) the goals and intentions of the participants. For example, consider John's analysis of the trait "charitable." To infer that someone is charitable, that individual must transfer a resource to someone and the recipient must be needy. In addition, the plan should use the appropriate resources; in this case the resource transferred should be something the recipient needs. Finally, actors should have the necessary goals: They must intend to benefit the recipient, and they must not expect to receive anything in return. Thus, the extent to which a behavior is a good exemplar of a trait should depend on how well the behavior matches the appropriate event script.

Interestingly, trait concepts often have embedded within them stories of the relationships between an actor and others. For example, when we use the trait "vindictive" we infer that there is a history between the actor and another, that the actor perceives that the other once harmed him, and that the actor is now in a position (e.g., has the resources) to reciprocate that harm and intends to harm (or has harmed) the other. Such examples suggest that the perceived goals of a behavior play an important role in trait inferences.

Consistent with the argument that goals are important components of traits, Read, Jones, and Miller (1990) have shown that ratings by one group of subjects of the extent to which a behavior achieved the goals associated with a trait strongly predict the confidence with which a separate group of subjects will make a trait inference from that behavior. Further, there is evidence that goals mediate the relations between various traits and the perception of obstacles to safer sex (Miller & Bettencourt, 1989).

The preceding components can be used to analyze the underlying structure of many traits and tell us much about the nature of the relations among traits that seem similar in some ways but quite different in others. For example, a lonely person and a sociable person may have very similar goals but differ in their plans, beliefs, and resources for goal achievement. Or individuals may have similar strategies, resources, and beliefs (e.g., self-monitors and sociable individuals) but differ in their goals. By considering these goal structures as components of traits, researchers should be better able to understand why expected behaviors do not consistently occur (e.g., a resource was unavailable) and why and when we might expect behavioral change (e.g., development of new skills or alternate strategies).

Also, the relationships among goals, as suggested in this model, may affect the choice of plan and the subsequent behavioral enactment. A person who desires intimacy and wants to avoid embarrassment may find intimate disclosures too risky and opt instead to engage in a behavior that, while not necessarily the most effective for either goal, is the most acceptable given the overall configuration of goals.

This approach to traits is exciting because it allows us to understand the dynamic significance of trait terms, concepts that can be incredibly rich. Further, it provides insight into how people can use traits to summarize and explain the complex models they construct of the goals, plans, resources, and beliefs of others.

Situation structures.   Argyle, Furnham, and Graham (1981) have presented an analysis of situations that parallels in many ways our analysis of person structures. First, they argued that a major component of a situation is the goals whose satisfaction the situation affords. Second, different situations have different roles associated with them; this makes some plans more salient, whereas others may be restricted. Third, in a given situation particular behavioral sequences can be enacted for achieving goals within that situation. Fourth, rules governing appropriate behavior are associated with different situations. Finally, many situations have associated with them particular resources that are important in carrying out plans. Therefore, in any given situation behavior should depend upon the type of match between the individual's structures and the parallel structures in the situation.

Relationship structures.   In addition to their use in analyzing individuals and situations, goal-based structures can be used to examine how individuals influence each other in a developing relationship over time. First, prior to or at the beginning of an interaction, an individual's goals, plans, resources, and beliefs may influence his or her choice of interaction partner for achieving various goals. For example, our views of how different partners may impact on our goals may considerably restrict who we date. Or our beliefs that married people should be faithful may keep us from achieving the goal of sexual intimacy with someone other than our spouse. Recent work on attachment styles suggests that perceptions of one's relationship with one or both parents and resultant models of self and others may influence dating (Collins & Read, 1990) and marital partner choices, and also patterns of vigilance, affect display, and satisfaction in interactions with current marital partners (Cooke & Miller, 1990). Furthermore, just as we may think of "possible selves" (Markus & Nurius, 1986), we may also think of "possible others" and "possible relationships" that we use to predict how our goal-based structures may interface with those of our partners (Miller & Jones, 1989). For example, in deciding whether to interact with someone we have been told is shy, we may take into account what some of the resource limitations of shy people might be (e.g., access to social networks, social skills deficits) and how these limitations might interface with our goal-based structures (e.g., we might have a working model that "a shy person would be OK with me because I'm so nonthreatening I'd really be able to bring him/her out of their shell").

In addition to these general relationship structures, as individuals come to know others they are more and more likely to develop a unique relationship in which individuals influence each other and a unique model of the relationship emerges. Like mental models of physical systems (Gentner & Stevens, 1983; Johnson-Laird, 1983), these mental models of particular relationships are causal models that represent the characteristics of the persons in the dyad, such as their goals, plans, resources, and beliefs, as well as representing the relations among these elements. These dynamic representations are constantly updated in response to new information. Furthermore, because they are causal models they can be run, so that we can use our model of a person to simulate how they might respond to some action of ours. Thus, such models could be used to guide our interactions with a particular partner and predict and explain behavior. Such representations are apt to take into account whether the other person's goals and plans mesh or conflict with one's own, whether present and possible future goal integration is possible (e.g., will it be possible to negotiate two careers?), whether one's personal resources will be depleted or enhanced by one's relationship with another, and how this relationship might change how we view others, ourselves, and our own future possibilities. Over time, individuals may develop fairly detailed models of their partners and how they are likely to respond to themselves. As a result, the mere presence of the partner may activate goal-based structures that are unique to a particular relationship.

Much of our information about others comes from observations of their behavior in social interaction. But how do we understand the meaning of behaviors in even a single social interaction? For example, let us consider a conversation. An interaction between a speaker and a listener is a dynamic interaction involving mutual influences in which the speaker and the listener are enacting behaviors based on prior inputs from and assumptions about this partner. To understand the meaning of a disclosure, for example, it is critical to understand why and how it is embedded as an utterance in a conversation. Clark (1985) noted:

> When a person talks, he can't just utter words aloud and expect to be understood. He must consider the people he is talking to, make an encyclopedia full of assumptions about them, and design his utterances accordingly. He must design what he says so that his specific addressees can figure out what he means, and they must interpret what he says assuming that he has selected it for them. (p. 227)

In addition, addressees, using a variety of linguistic and perceptual information as well as communitywide knowledge and beliefs, are also ascertaining the goals of the speaker and the speaker's intent, in developing a model of the speaker and of the interaction (Clark, 1985). How do individuals arrive at coherent models of the goals, plans, resources, and beliefs of those with whom they interact?

DEVELOPING MODELS OF THE INTERACTION, THE PARTNER, AND THE RELATIONSHIP

Several theorists (e.g., Abelson & Lalljee, 1988; Druian & Omessi, 1983; Lalljee & Abelson, 1983; Read, 1987) have argued that understanding a dyadic interaction is very similar to what happens when we read a short story or novel. As we progress we build a representation of the sequence of events. New information is integrated with the preexisting representation. We continually build and add to our model of the characters and the sequence of events (Read, 1987). Of course, unlike reading a novel, our ongoing interpretation of events affects how we respond to others and the situation, and how others respond to us. Thus, participants' interpretations of events are part of the changing flux of events as individuals mutually influence each other. We attempt to build coherent models of the interaction, of the people in it, and of ourselves, so we can coordinate, guide, and understand the meaning of our interactions with others. In order to have smooth interactions with others, these models of interactions, persons, and relationships should be at least compatible, if not shared (Miller, 1990). Precisely how do people construct their representations of interactions?

Connectionist Modeling and Parallel Distributed Cognitive Processing

To answer this question, we propose a model that is based on a connectionist model of comprehension (Kintsch, 1988; Mannes & Kintsch, 1989) and other work on parallel distributed cognitive processing (Rumelhart & McClelland, 1986; Thagard, 1989). The model includes two major steps. First, sets of concepts related to the input are activated; second, these activated concepts are organized into a coherent representation of the input. Although these steps can be understood on their own conceptual merits, certain aspects have been explicitly modeled in various computer simulations (Kintsch, 1988; Thagard, 1989).

Step 1: Activation of related concepts. Initially, input leads to the activation of a number of related concepts. Consider the earlier example of Wendy and Mary meeting John in a bar. An input like "bar" might activate related concepts such as "stool," "drink," or "pick up." Via taxonomic relations, categories such as "chair" might be activated by "stool"; "social meeting place" might be activated by "bar." Causal connections might activate other concepts. If we see a man spill a drink, it might activate the following thought, "Oh, no, he's going to get it all over her dress." A man's presence in a bar might activate goal-based concepts such as "he's trying to forget his troubles" or "he's trying to pick someone up." That is, a behavior may activate a particular goal (to forget one's troubles) that this behavior (drinking) is known to achieve. If we see this man approach a woman and inquire, "What's your sign?" we might via a part-whole relation activate the "pick up script" (Galambos, 1986). An action or object may also activate a role concept because it is an important part of the plans that are central to that role. For example, we may observe price quotes in a briefcase and wonder whether the owner is a salesperson.

Self-disclosures also provide a rich data source and allow one to make inferences beyond the present context about what partners are generally like or how they generally cope with situations and relationships. If John says, "I was just offered a promotion that I turned down because I didn't want to work so hard on weekends," such statements may activate other concepts (e.g., lazy, able, bon vivant). Additional behaviors may also activate related trait concepts. For example, if John interrupts Wendy a number of times, and only talks about his own feelings and experiences while bragging about his accomplishments, traits like "egocentric" and "self-centered" may be activated. Visual information about the individuals, including such things as the physical appearance of individuals (e.g., wavy hair, grey business suit, white, male, tall, middle aged) may activate stereotypes and concepts concerning race, age, gender, social class, roles, and so on.

Information about the context (e.g., a wall full of liquors and glasses, men initiating interactions with women) may activate additional concepts (e.g., bar or dating scene). Our own goals in the interaction, either as participant or observer, are also part of the context. For example, if we are interested in a long-term companion and this target is a middle-aged male, we may begin to assess whether or not this is a desirable candidate with whom to initiate an interaction. In doing so, we may wish to avoid meeting an alcoholic. Our goals may lead directly to the activation of concepts, or they may do so indirectly by affecting our attention to various aspects of the situation and our interaction partner. For example, we may wonder whether he is available. Does he look around, asking the bartender about someone who catches his attention? Does he attend to someone, offer another a drink, and so on? Do his behaviors suggest a plan (e.g., finding a date)? Concerns about whether he is an alcoholic may lead to the following type of information search: How many drinks does he order? How stiff are the drinks? How attentive is he to drinking? How quickly does he finish his drinks? Does he order a new drink before he finishes the last? Does he know the bartender? And so forth. In addition to the information available in the context we may also have knowledge about these individuals based on our past history with them and information that others have told us.

We can illustrate concretely the activation of concepts by returning to our example of Wendy and Mary in the bar. They observe John and later invite him to join them. Figure 3.1 shows a variety of pieces of information from the ongoing sequence (here E1 to E18) that may be activated for Wendy. This information may be active at the beginning of the interaction or it may be activated by events that occur later.

Wendy also makes inferences that allow her to summarize or explain the

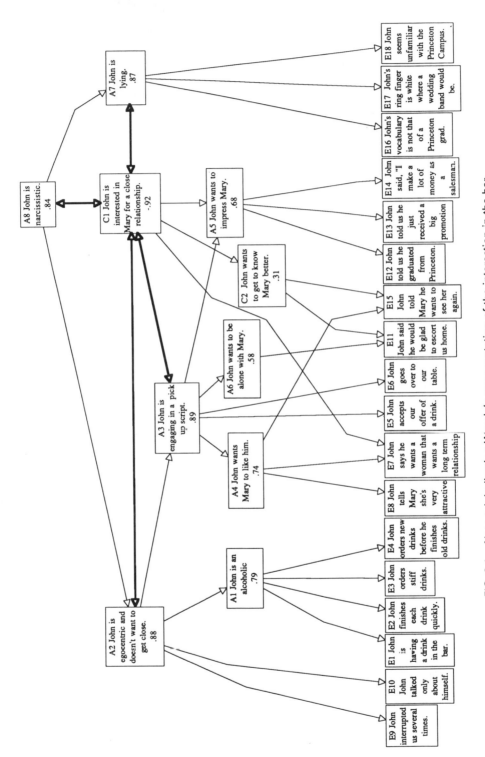

FIG. 3.1. Network indicating Wendy's representation of the interaction in the bar.

events that she observes. These inferences can vary from being relatively low level and specific, to being much more general and higher level. For example, as indicated in Fig. 3.1, Wendy may infer that a number of relatively lower level structures (e.g., John is egocentric, John is trying to pick up Mary) explain much of the data. These lower level structures may in turn be explained by a higher order structure, "John is narcissistic" and may cohere around it. Further aspects of this figure, such as the numbers associated with the boxes, are explained in the next section.

Kintsch (1988) suggested that concepts are initially activated somewhat promiscuously, with no real check on whether they are consistent with the context or with other activated concepts. Following this, the initial input and the activated concepts are linked into a network of concepts. Initially, this network includes a mix of information activated by the input that is relevant, irrelevant, or even inconsistent with the eventual representation of the event. At this point there is only a loose network of concepts that is not yet a coherent representation of the interaction.

We assume that there will be a strong preference for linking concepts that have causal and goal-based relations to each other (Galambos, et al., 1986). There are three general possibilities for how any two concepts may be linked. First, there may be a positive or excitatory link, where the activation of one concept will increase the activation of another. In Fig. 3.1 these are represented by the single-headed arrows. Concepts that are associatively related or have goal relations, causal relations, or part-whole relations (e.g., an action that is part of a script or plan) will be positively linked. Second, there may be a negative or inhibitory link, where the activation of one concept will decrease the activation of another. In Fig. 3.1, these are represented via the bold double-headed arrows. This occurs when concepts are inconsistent with one another. General examples are mutually exclusive roles, mutually exclusive category membership, mutually inconsistent event sequences, conflicting goals, mutually inconsistent explanations, and so forth. In Fig. 3.1, Wendy's inference that "John is egocentric and doesn't want to get close" seems inconsistent with the inference that "John is interested in Mary for a close relationship." Finally, there may be no relation between two concepts. The greater the number of positive (excitatory) links with other concepts and the smaller the number of negative (inhibitory) links with other concepts, the greater the degree of activation of a concept when activation is spread through the network.

Step 2: Spreading activation through the network. Once the initial loose network is built, a parallel constraint satisfaction process (e.g., Kintsch, 1988; Rumelhart & McClelland, 1986; Thagard, 1989) will be used to determine which of the activated concepts best characterizes the interaction and to arrive at a coherent, consistent representation of the interaction. In this process, activation is propagated through the links and concepts in parallel to arrive at the resulting level of activation for the concepts. The greater the number of excitatory links to a concept and the greater the strength of the links, the higher the activation of that concept. Conversely, the greater the number of inhibitory links and the greater their strength, the lower the activation of that concept. By this process, concepts that are not supported by other concepts in the network die out, and concepts that are supported are strengthened. Concepts that are highly activated are taken as the representation of the interaction up to that point.

This process runs in cycles, with each cycle corresponding to an action in the social interaction. For each cycle a new network is built consisting of new input, newly activated associated concepts, and information that is passed along from the previous cycle. Inferences, such as higher order knowledge structures, that receive high levels of activation will be among those that are passed on to the next cycle. In each cycle, we add new behaviors that are observed and any additional information to the representation. At this point, the new information, as well as the inferences from the previous cycle, will activate new concepts. These new concepts will then be connected into a network, and the parallel constraint satisfaction process will be applied. This cycle will continue throughout the interaction. As more data are received and more inferences are made, broader and more encompassing structures can be built. Further, inferences and representations at a number of different levels are created throughout this process.

In the preceding account we have talked about parallel constraint satisfaction processes in general terms. However, the details of how this is done (e.g., specified explicitly in different computer simulation programs) differ depending on the purpose and assumptions of a given model (e.g., Holyoak & Thagard, 1989; Kintsch, 1988; Rumelhart & McClelland, 1986; Thagard, 1989). One parallel constraint satisfaction process that is particularly useful for understanding how people form coherent models is Thagard's (1989) recent model of Explanatory Coherence. What makes Thagard's model and simulation particularly useful is that, unlike other connectionist models, this model and simulation are explicitly based on a set of assumptions about how higher order, causal, and goal-based theories are used to explain data and other inferences; consistent with Thagard's position, we would argue that explanatory links to causal and goal-based theories underly the coherence of mental models.

Thagard's Model of Explanatory Coherence

Thagard proposed several principles for evaluating the coherence of the network of data and hypothesized explanations. The operation of these principles is actualized by applying a parallel constraint satisfaction process to the network. Thus, these principles are implemented via a computer simulation, although the validity of these principles can be usefully considered quite apart from their connectionist implementation (see Read & Marcus-Newhall, 1990). First, the explanation that requires the fewest assumptions will be more coherent. This is the well-known principle of Parsimony or Simplicity. This follows from the structure of Thagard's (1989) model because the activation provided by a fact is divided among the hypotheses that are needed to explain it. More hypotheses mean less activation for each hypothesis. Second, an explanation that explains more facts, that has greater breadth, will be more coherent. Thus, an explanation that explains more facts than an alternative explanation is more coherent. Further, any given explanation becomes more coherent as more facts are introduced that support it. This is a natural outcome of the model because explanations that are connected to (explain) more facts receive more activation than do explanations connected to fewer facts. Third, explanations are more coherent if they are explained by higher order explanations. This follows because a higher order explanation contributes activation to the explanation it explains. Here we can see the importance of high-level knowledge structures in coherence. And fourth, explanations are more coherent if they are supported by an analogy to another system with the same causal structure. This follows because the analogous explanation provides activation to the explanatory hypotheses.

Because Thagard's (1989) simulation is a parallel process, connectionist model, it applies all the principles simultaneously to the entire set of explanatory propositions in judging the coherence of a set of propositions, rather than evaluating the principles and propositions one at a time. This is possible because these principles are actualized in terms of the ways in which data and explanatory propositions are connected in this model. Interestingly, it seems that the general notion of explanatory coherence and many of the principles that have been identified as the foundation of judgments of coherence naturally fall out of a model that depends on a parallel constraint satisfaction process.

Let us use our example of Wendy to make this process more concrete. Figure 3.1 is based on output from Thagard's (1989) Echo program. In that program, evidence or data (E1 to E18) are specified. In Wendy's hypothetical interaction, these inputs are generally observations of behaviors or statements made in a conversation. Higher order propositions that are inferences made about the data are also specified. In Fig. 3.1, propositions A1 to A8 involve negative inferences about John, and propositions C1 and C2 involve positive inferences regarding his intentions with respect to Mary.

Following this, it is necessary to specify what explains each data entry and which inferences explain other inferences. For example, C2 (John wants to get to know Mary better) explains E15 (John told Mary he wants to see her again). Analogies may be specified (although none are specified in this example) as well as contradictions. As indicated in Fig. 3.1, four contradictions are specified in Wendy's hypothetical model of John, all involving the inference "John is interested in Mary for a close relationship."

Data have excitatory links to hypotheses that explain them (e.g., E1:John is having a drink in the bar, is explained by A1:John is an alcoholic) and inhibitory links to hypotheses that are inconsistent with them (none present in this example). In addition, hypotheses that conflict have inhibitory links (A2:John is egocentric and doesn't want to get close, conflicts with C1:John is interested in Mary for a close relationship). Further, higher order explanations can explain (e.g., A3:John is engaging in a pick up script, explains A4:John wants Mary to like him) or contradict (e.g., A8:John is narcissistic, contradicts C1:John is interested in Mary for a close relationship) lower order explanatory hypotheses, which lead to excitatory and inhibitory links respectively. Finally, if a set of explanatory hypotheses are analogous to an already well established set of hypotheses, the established set of hypotheses will have an excitatory link to the proposed explanatory hypotheses (this is not illustrated here).

This set of data, and explanatory and contradictory propositions is then run. In each cycle (e.g., input in the conversation or behavior in a sequence), the activation level of every concept is computed. Activation levels at the point of last data entry in the behavioral interaction of Wendy and Mary are given in Fig. 3.1 for each higher order inference: for example, .31 for C2 (John wants to get to know Mary better); .84 for A8 (John is Narcissistic). These activations can be thought of as the relative strength of those inferences in Wendy's model of the interaction. At the end of the reported interaction in Fig. 3.1, we see that Wendy has two competing mental models of John—one more positive, involving higher order structures C1 and C2, and a more negative model involving higher order structures A1 to A8. Wendy's model of John coheres around the inference that "John is narcissistic" (A8). That construct is more coherent than "John is interested in Mary for a close relationship" (C1) because it has more breadth and because C1 receives negative activation from higher order structures that are well supported by the data.

Wendy's model that John is narcissistic, egocentric, lying, and engaging in a pickup script is fairly coherent (the actual coherence of the overall model could be calculated using a variation of a statistic called "Harmany"; Thagard, 1989, personal correspondence). Now compare Wendy's representation of John and this event against Mary's version of events (Fig. 3.2). First, Mary's representation involves a somewhat different, although overlapping set of data that are activated (or encoded). Second, Mary's inferences in general tend to be more positive, although the higher order inference, "John is a liar," does get activated. Still, that inference is deactivated by the contradictory alternative inference, "John is an impressive man," which receives considerably more activation from the data. Mary's inference that John is interested in a close relationship with her is thus, in contrast to Wendy, a leading hypothesis in her model of John. Still, Mary's model, although more positive, is far more fragmented and less coherent than Wendy's.

Advantages of this approach.   The type of model outlined here has several advantages over alternative, more serial models. First, in discussing models of

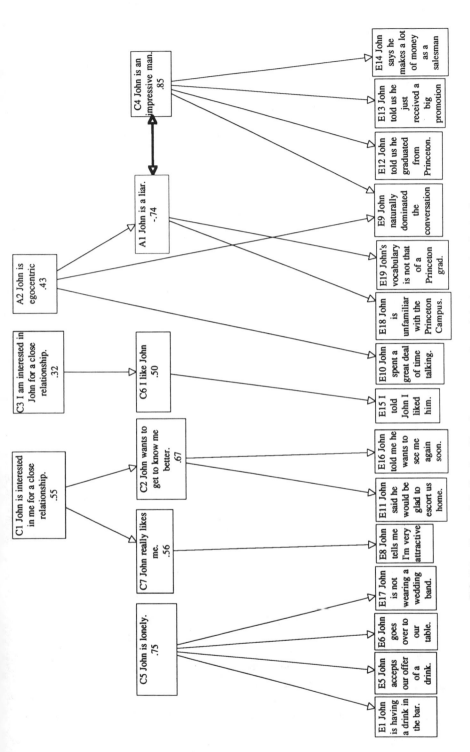

FIG. 3.2. Network indicating Mary's representation of the interaction in the bar.

discourse comprehension, Kintsch (1988) has pointed out that previous models need very smart inference rules that could figure out precisely what should be connected to what. A parallel constraint process does not need to be so smart, because it can start out with a somewhat incoherent network representation and settle on a representation that best fits, based on evidence from a number of sources. Second, it seems clear that the evaluation of the adequacy of the interpretation of a behavioral sequence often depends on the successful integration of multiple sources of information. A parallel constraint process makes it fairly easy to integrate information from a number of different sources simultaneously. Also, it seems intuitively obvious that in any social interaction there are far too many pieces of information available at the same time for people to integrate them sequentially. A parallel process allows them to be integrated at the same time, with each piece of information influencing each other piece of information.

In addition, this model helps us to understand how people choose among various characterizations of a sequence. Thagard's (1989) model provides an elegant approach to understanding how people might choose among alternative knowledge structures as characterizations of individuals' actions. Different scenarios could be constructed out of the same, or similar, set of facts, using different knowledge structures. Which knowledge structures are chosen and which scenario is constructed depends on which is more coherent. For example, as illustrated in Fig. 3.1, if two different structures, "John is interested in Mary for a pick up" versus "John is interested in Mary for a close relationship," were potentially applicable to an interaction, we should prefer the one that requires fewer assumptions (simplicity) and that is able to handle more of the sequence (breadth). In addition, we might prefer structures that are consistent with previous interpretations of similar events (analogy), for example, we just saw a soap opera about a guy like John. Further, the principle that a hypothesis will be more coherent if explained by other hypotheses suggests that a characterization of a sequence would be more coherent, and thus more likely to be selected, if it could be explained by other features of the people involved, such as personal characteristics, goals, or abilities. For example, "John is interested in Mary for a pickup" would be more coherent if it were explained by "John is narcissistic." Finally, Thagard's model suggests that we should be unsatisfied with the application of a structure to a sequence if it leaves many of the facts and events unaccounted for. Read and Marcus-Newhall (1990) have recently provided experimental evidence that such principles of explanatory coherence play an important role in people's evaluations of explanations for everyday social situations.

Thagard's (1989) model can be applied not only to the coherence of interactions, but also to the coherence of mental models of other people. Thagard argued that a system S will tend to have more global coherence than another if (a) S has more data in it, (b) S has more internal explanatory links between propositions that cohere because of explanations and analogies, and (c) S succeeds in separating coherent subsystems of propositions from conflicting subsystems. This analysis suggests ways in which individuals are apt to differ in the extent to which their models of others cohere. For example, more coherent models would be those in which an individual has more accessible other-relevant data (e.g., close friends who know one another well), in which there are more internal explanatory links between beliefs and behaviors, and those models in which coherent subsystems of beliefs and behaviors are effectively separated from conflicting subsystems.

Models of others are apt to differ both in the ways in which different behaviors and propositions are weighted, as well as the order in which inputs are encountered. As Thagard (1989) pointed out, the order of data entry can affect the likelihood that an individual will select a given hypothesis and retain it (even in the face of counterinformation and equally plausible alternative hypotheses). Analogies and preexisting knowledge structures (e.g., stereotypes) may also bias the process of perceiving persons and building models of them. For example, analogies from past relationships may bias how we construe propositions and behaviors of an individual in a current relationship. Thus, it is possible to examine how individuals differ idiographically in terms of the construction and coherence of their models. Figure 3.1 illustrates how Wendy may differ from Mary (Fig. 3.2) in her construction of events about John. At the same point in time (in the bar on their initial meeting), despite similar exposure to "stimulus input," Wendy's most coherent model of John, represented here in Fig. 3.1, is that he is narcissistic and just looking for a pickup; Mary's most coherent model of John, represented in Fig. 3.2, is that he is "interested in me for a close relationship."

Thagard's simulation provides an intriguing methodology to explore individual differences in the coherence of rich, idiographic models. In addition, because the output provides activation levels for higher order structures, it is possible to relate those levels of activation to other variables (e.g., positive or negative responses to partners, personality dimensions, the coherence of partner's models of the same interaction, understanding of the sequence and partner). It is also possible to plot changes in activations for new inputs over the course of an interaction or relationship to examine resultant changes in the mental models and activation of higher order structures.

In addition, by adding new evidence or inferences into a connectionist model, it is possible—at least hypothetically—to examine how such new information might affect a person's current representation. And, if part of the network was changed (i.e., for example, if one belief was altered), the model may be able to predict the likely higher order structures around which the resulting model would cohere. Such possibilities are exciting for therapists interested in forecasting how specific changes in a client's ways of construing events or others may influence the client's overall models.

Behavior and Its Fit with Existing Models

We previously discussed how individuals *develop* models of people and interactions. But how is new information integrated with already existing models? What determines a perception of fit or lack of fit? Because research in this area is, at best, sparse, we will offer some concepts and ways of thinking about this problem.

Latitude of fit. When we ask to what extent a sequence of actions fits with our current model, we use the model to guide our expectations. Much of this processing will be top down rather than bottom up. As a result, minor or perhaps even major deviations may be viewed as fitting the model until enough critical pieces are present that a "not fit" threshold is reached.

Because the meanings of behaviors often depend on context and their timing, relative to other actions and events, even the same behaviors may lead to very different inferences about the goals and other knowledge structures operative in a given interaction (Read, Druian, & Miller, 1989). Furthermore, initial hypotheses about the meaning of actions are likely to play a critical role in organizing subsequent information affecting what inferences are made. When we have pre-existing knowledge structures, such as traits, that have usefully been applied to a given person in the past, we may attempt to fit observed behaviors within these structures.

Some behaviors, for example, listening attentively, are more malleable with a wider latitude of fit than others. "Wide latitude" behaviors are those that would fit in easily with almost any preexisting interpretation of the other. These would include smiling and being nonverbally responsive. For example, if we see one partner smiling at another, that may fit with any number of traits attributed to this person by us in the past such as sociable, manipulative, warm, and superficial.

But not all actions may fit easily with existing structures. "Narrow latitude" behaviors, such as a slap or an insult, may fit with a much smaller number of potential structures. As a result, narrow latitude behaviors have a more limited range of possible meanings and are more restricted in their possible fit with existing structures. If an action departs from a prevailing model of the other, conscious processing is more apt to occur. The probability of such conscious processing should depend on the importance of the altered model for the relationship we are in, the extent to which discrepant information has accumulated in the past, and the ramifications for our own personal goals.

If we decide that a given model is no longer completely applicable to a person, there are several ways in which our conceptions might change. First, they may change in a quantitative way, as we decide that the individual is lower or higher on a particular dimension. We may have decided initially that Joe was highly sociable because when we first met him he was the life of the party, making jokes and being the center of attention. Then, we see him at a party where he does not know anyone and he spends the bulk of the evening listening to a few people but taking a back seat. One way we may alter our conception of him is to decide that he was not as sociable as we thought.

Alternatively, our model of Joe may change in a much more qualitative way. For example, we may develop a more complex model of Joe (e.g., Joe engages in really extroverted actions only when he is feeling comfortable and secure). Such a view suggests that we have a model of Joe as having a configuration of chronic structures (e.g., goals chronically salient to the person such as wanting to entertain but not wanting to be rejected) that given the appropriate situational factors (e.g., a relaxed, accepting setting) results in highly extroverted actions. Implicit in this view of Joe is the knowledge that Joe could engage in the behavior (he has the requisite abilities and skills), but the enactment of extroverted actions depends upon other factors. Our model may also change in other ways. We may discover that Joe only seems friendly and outgoing when he is trying to impress people in order to achieve his professional goals (e.g., status, wealth, power). We may, thus, alter our model of Joe from being sociable to being Machiavellian.

Previously we discussed how a new piece of information may fit within an existing structure. People also frequently combine multiple subsystems of information about individuals and attempt to develop coherent models of them. Next we discuss how structures such as traits and roles may be combined, and how such combinations may be viewed as miniature but complex mental models.

Conceptual Combinations and Coherence

Combining two trait concepts.   Asch and Zukier (1984) investigated how people formed an impression of an individual, when they were told that the individual was characterized by two apparently discordant trait terms such as cheerful–gloomy, generous–vindictive, or strict–kind. Subjects found it relatively easy to arrive at coherent interpretations of the individuals with these traits. However, the resolutions were clearly not simply the result of averaging the evaluations of the traits. Moreover, different resolution strategies were used for different trait pairs. Two important types of strategies that we would like to discuss are (a) inferring a higher order structure that explains the two apparently discordant traits and (b) one trait modifying the meaning of another.

When given the pair cheerful–gloomy, many subjects inferred a higher order knowledge structure that could explain both traits—for instance, that the individual was moody. This result can be explained straightforwardly in terms of our account of how people form models. According to this account, each trait activates a set of associated traits and concepts that are loosely linked. For example, the concept moody is likely to be activated because it is related to both gloomy and cheerful. Activation then spreads through the network, following Thagard's (1989) principles of explanatory coherence. The trait or concept that is most strongly activated, being the most explanatorily coherent, is moody.

The resolution for the generous–vindictive pair seems more complex. Many subjects suggested that the individual was only apparently generous, but was actually devious and scheming and used his or her apparent generosity in gaining revenge. Here, vindictive dominates the impression and strongly modifies our interpretation of the individual's generosity. Unlike the cheerful–gloomy pair, one member of the pair changes more than the other. This resolution process can be analyzed as follows. We have proposed that traits are composed of chronic configurations of four components: goals, plans, resources, and beliefs. Consistent with this position, John (1986) has argued that traits can be viewed as frames possessing roles or slots, where information is stored both about the defaults for those slots and the range of concepts or values that are acceptable for those slots.

Thus, generous and vindictive have, as part of their representation, slots for the goals associated with the trait and slots characterizing the behaviors that can achieve those goals. Further, there are constraints on the range of values that can fill those slots. For instance, the range of goals for vindictive seems fairly narrow. It is hard to think of vindictive individuals and their behaviors as having any goal other than to hurt someone. In contrast, there seems to be a greater range for the goals related to generous. Although the most likely goal is probably something like helping or benefiting someone, there are other reasons why someone is generous, including self-presentational and strategic reasons.

Thus, the model suggests the following account of how people construct a representation of an individual who is both vindictive and generous: When we encounter the trait vindictive it activates a narrow range of goals having to do with hurting others and gaining revenge. In contrast, "generous" probably activates a wider range of goals, among them the goal of helping others, as well as self-presentational goals. The activation of self-presentational goals may be particularly likely when vindictive and generous are encountered at the same time. Further, people may infer that the individual is being deliberately deceptive and trying to hide his or her true vengeful motives by acting helpful. These concepts are linked in a loose network, with the goal of helping others (implied by generous) connected by an inhibitory link with the self-presentational goals related to generous, the inference about deception, and the goals of hurting others and getting revenge (vindictive). At the same time, the self-presentational goals of generous will have a positive link with the goals of hurting others and getting revenge, because such self-presentational goals enable one to hurt others. In addition, the inference about deliberate deception will have a positive link with both the self-presentational goals and the goal of revenge. Then, when activation spreads through the network, the goal of helping others is strongly inhibited by the self-presentational goals related to "generous", by the goals of gaining revenge and hurting others, and by the inference about deliberate deception. On the other hand, the self-presentational goals related to generous, the inference about deliberate deception, and the goals associated with vindictive will mutually support one another because of their positive links.

One can carry out a similar analysis of the trait pair strict–kind, also investigated by Asch and Zukier (1984). Parallel to the above analysis, the range of acceptable goals seems greater for strict than for kind. There are multiple reasons why someone may be strict, including the goal of helping others, but it is hard to think of someone as being kind who does not have the goals of helping others. Thus, people can see strict behaviors enacted in order to be kind. For example, one may believe that children need discipline and will grow up to be psychologically healthier if they have that discipline.

It also seems quite plausible that for many people this conclusion is bolstered by, or even based entirely on, the retrieval of a stereotype or a particular memory of a strict teacher, coach, or parent who really did this because they wanted their charges to become moral and competent human beings. This would be an example of Thagard's (1989) principle that an explanatory relation is bolstered if it is supported by an analogy to another structure.

These examples are by no means exhaustive of the ways in which trait concepts, or indeed any social concepts, can interact. Asch and Zukier (1984) presented many other strategies that people use in combining discordant terms.

Combining social roles and traits.   In the present discussion we have focused on how trait concepts can be combined. However, it seems likely that this general kind of modification model could be applied to any situation in which concepts are combined. One example of this would be combinations involving social roles. Kraut and Higgins (1984) gave the example of the conceptual combination casual surgeon. The adjective *casual* by itself receives a positive evaluation as does *surgeon* alone, yet a casual surgeon receives a negative evaluation. But clearly the result of this combination does not depend just on the meaning of *casual,* because a casual professor receives a positive evaluation. Presumably what happens is that *casual* modifies the surgeon's performance of his job.

It is clearly the ways in which the concepts interact that are important. For example, consider combinations involving social roles, such as *feminist bankteller* and *Republican social worker,* where our model of such individuals clearly is not simply the addition of two concepts. Recent work by Hastie, Schroeder, and Weber (1990) and Kunda, Miller, and Claire (in press) demonstrate that our models of such individuals often include emergent attributes that are not due simply to the addition or averaging of the attributes of the two concepts. Or consider the combinations *aggressive man* and *aggressive woman.* Why might those combinations result in very different inferences? One exciting possibility is that stereotypes associated with men, such as assertive and instrumental, can be easily combined with aggressive, so that we may assume that this man falls in the typical range and that his being aggressive is in the service of being instrumental. On the other hand, stereotypes associated with women (e.g., warm, kind, caring, helpful) present a problem: One is unlikely to be aggressive in the service of being warm. One possibility is to focus on the dimensions (e.g., warm, kind, caring, helpful) associated with the concept "woman" and infer that this woman is not in the typical range. To combine this information, some observers might infer that this is an uncaring woman or a woman who is hurtful in contrast to the typical woman. Interestingly, if we knew that the same woman was both helpful and aggressive, a different conceptual combination might result; for example, she is aggressive in her sales job in trying to get leads but helpful at home. Or we might infer that she is aggressive (e.g., in her search for information) in trying to help others. It is an intriguing possibility to consider how this combination might be resolved differently for men. For example, this combination might be resolved as "men are helpful (e.g., with a client) in order to be more aggressive (e.g., competing against others in trying to secure the client's business)." Thus, what could differ for perceivers in evaluating factors such as gender are the presumed organization of goals stereotypically associated with men and women.

We do not believe that the combination of just two items at a time is completely representative of how people develop detailed impressions of others from the richer information typically available in social interaction. Rather, we view such conceptual combinations as model systems that allow us to study, in miniature, how concepts are combined to form more comprehensive concepts or models. It allows us to get a handle on what is an extremely complex process.

Interpersonal combinations. In addition to conceptual combinations of intrapersonal structures (e.g., traits, stereotypes, roles), individuals also combine information about one person with information about another in order to explain or make judgments about the dyadic relationship. For example, consider the tasks engaged in by matchmakers. They need to determine what it is about a woman and a man that will make a good combination. How do they do this? Do they take into account the goals of each person and the extent to which each person's resources enable these goals to be achieved? Do they consider how the individuals might go about achieving their goals and the related possible sources of conflict? Recently, Miller and Jones (1989) have explored the possible relationships that people create when given various different combinations of individual characteristics for men and women. When the same persons are matched with different partners, raters describe their relationships quite differently and make different prognoses about couples, depending upon the expected fit between partners. Interestingly, if the characteristics assigned to the male and female members of the pair were swapped, this altered the relationship prognoses. Thus, it would tentatively appear that gender stereotypes and sex roles, as well as trait inferences, may influence the development of mental models of possible relationships that individuals may have with each other.

Goals in the organization of impressions. Most of the examples we gave previously of conceptual combinations in impression formation involved traits. This was done largely for ease of exposition—traits are easy to talk about—

rather than because we believe that traits are primary in impression formation. Indeed, we would argue that the organization of person information around an individual's goals, plans, resources, and beliefs is at least as important, and maybe more important, than a trait-based organization. Moreover, there are a number of reasons for thinking that traits are only one among several possible organizational structures. For example, work by Hoffman, Mischel, and Baer (1984) demonstrates that people are more likely to organize information by traits when they think they will have to communicate an impression to someone else, rather than keep the impression private.

Further, from a functional perspective, in terms of building mental models that can be used to predict another's behavior and plan one's own, organizing information in terms of goals, plans, resources, and beliefs would result in a representation that is much easier to use for simulating another's behavior. First, in thinking about how an individual would interact with a given situation, it would seem much easier to think about how the goals, plans, resources, and beliefs of the individual would fit with the parallel structures in the situation, than purely in terms of traits. Similarly, in thinking about how two individuals would interact, it would seem much easier to think about whether the partners will mesh in terms of their goals, plans, resources, and beliefs, than it would be to think about them in terms of their traits. And even when traits are important in organizing impressions, we have argued that it is the underlying frame or event script that is critical in how people combine the trait with other concepts.

Further, although researchers have rarely focused on forms of organization other than traits, we already know that many other forms of organization are important. For example, we undoubtedly organize much of what we know about people in terms of their roles (Cohen, 1981; Cohen & Ebbesen, 1979). And Cantor, Mischel, and Schwartz (1982) have provided evidence that we organize information about others in terms of person-in-situation prototypes, where we explicitly represent the behavior of specific kinds of individuals in specific kinds of situations. Furthermore, Trzebinski (1989) has recently reviewed a large body of research demonstrating that goal-based structures of various types play a major role in the organization of social information (see also, Galambos et al., 1986).

IMPLICATIONS

Implications and Strengths of a Knowledge Structure Approach

As Abelson and Black (1986) argued, one hallmark of the knowledge structure approach is that it provides a unified cognitive architecture that can be applied to a variety of problems and tasks. There is both a common set of representations and a common set of processes that are available for use in a variety of problems and tasks, such as (a) planning one's own behavior, (b) predicting another's behavior, (c) explaining one's own behavior and the behavior of others, (d) autobiographical memory, (e) analogical reasoning, (f) learning, and so on. We see this as an important strength in an attempt to develop an understanding of coherent mental models within a comprehensive model of dyadic interaction.

Another advantage of the knowledge structure approach is that it provides a level of representation that captures higher order configural and emergent properties. For example, the concept of competition captures a particular kind of relation among the goals of two or more individuals in which only one individual can achieve his or her goals. Or if we think about a dating script, the notion of a date captures a whole configuration of information, much of which goes beyond the actual behaviors to such things as the goals and social norms involved in such a situation. In addition, the knowledge structure approach emphasizes the importance of goals and plans in providing the structure of many social categories, and the importance of action-oriented structures in the representation of social knowledge. Within such a framework it is possible to think about the coherence of dynamic and ever-changing mental models that are responsive to new input and that are apt to play an important role in directing behavior. These feats are difficult to imagine without higher order knowledge structures.

Implications for understanding persons.   In earlier work (Read, Jones, & Miller, 1990; Read & Miller, 1989) we have argued for the importance of a knowledge structure approach in understanding individual differences and traits, and the role of goals in mediating trait effects. Here, we have also argued that knowledge structures play an important role in the coherence of individuals' idiographic mental models. These mental models may be about the interaction, the other, relationships, or the self. In understanding events, individuals construct models based on a wide variety of input, inference, and higher order structures. Understanding how these factors are combined is critical for understanding why individuals differ in the ways they construe events, situations, and other persons, and respond differently to those factors.

Implications for relationships.   As a number of prominent interpersonal researchers (Kelley et al., 1983; Kenny, in press) have argued, central to the study of relationships is understanding how individuals mutually influence one another. To understand mutual influence, Kelley et al. (1983) argued that the "basic data of relationships must (1) identify the activities (e.g., the thoughts, feelings, acts) of each person that affect and are affected by the activities (thoughts, feelings, acts and so on) of the other, and (2) specify the nature of the effects of each person's activities on those of the other" (p. 12). We would concur but argue that, in addition, we need to know much more.

First, we need to know how activated thoughts, feelings, and perceptions of behaviors during an interaction are related to one another and to other knowledge structures regarding one's self, one's partner, and the relationship, and how such relations produce coherent models of the other and the interaction. To address this issue, we need a way to idiographically describe and explore these interconnections. Given the current framework we can (a) address simultaneously how the data fit together and are organized for the individual and embedded in higher order knowledge structures that provide for coherent models of interactions, others, self, and relationships; (b) examine changes in model coherence and the activation of structures on a moment-by-moment basis during a behavioral interaction; (c) predict how new inputs and their explanatory links are apt to affect the overall coherence of our mental models of the other; and (d) simulate how changes in an individual's model (e.g., as a result of therapy) might alter the important coherent models of the individual's partner.

Second, we need to understand how the individuals' models influence their subsequent behaviors, and how these models change during the interaction as new inputs are received. When Wendy develops a coherent model of John as narcissistic, that model is likely to result in negative, or sarcastic behaviors directed at John and attempts to persuade Mary that John is not the wonderful person Mary perceives him to be. On the other hand, Mary's model of John is apt to result in more positive behaviors from Mary toward John, such as smiling and disclosing intimately. Such behaviors are likely to be important inputs for John's inferences and subsequent responses. The resulting inferences must then be inserted into his existing models of the interaction, Mary, Wendy, himself, and actual and possible relationships with each of these women. For example, because Wendy is responding negatively to him he may see her as difficult and her relationship with Mary as an obstacle for achieving his goals. In contrast, he may perceive Mary's more positive behaviors as indicative of either a caring or a gullible person, depending upon his actual goals in the interaction. These new inputs influence not only the nature and coherence of John's models, but these updated models may, in turn, influence John's plans and subsequent behaviors (e.g., needing to get rid of Wendy, so taking her home first).

To further explicate the utility of the current model for relationship researchers, we now apply the current formulation to two areas of interpersonal research: work on marital attributions and work on attachments in relationships. Let us begin with marital attributions. In a recent review, Bradbury and Fincham (1990) argued that dissatisfied couples are more likely than satisfied couples to make negative attributions for partner behaviors; these attributions, in turn, may influence marital satisfaction (also see Fletcher & Fincham, this volume). Furthermore, attributions of partner intent may also affect subsequent actor behavior (Bradbury & Fincham, 1988). Thus, this line of research suggests one way in which couples mutually influence each other: One individual's behavior is influenced by his or her cognitions about the meaning of the other's behavior; this behavior in turn is apt to influence partner cognitions, perceptions of intentionality, and subsequent response. Research in this area is exciting because researchers are beginning to explore the links between attributions and subsequent behavior. Still, subjects' accounts in this research concerning the links between behaviors and intentions are limited and give us an incomplete account of the overall mental model that partners have of one another. By exploring how subjects explain the multiple behaviors of their partner over time, more detailed mental models could be explored and simulated, and serve to provide a basis for more detailed predictions concerning when partners' models of the other are likely to guide behavior, how these models overlap, and how partners may differently construe the same acts.

An important new area of research in interpersonal relationships is based on Bowlby's (1982/1969) attachment theory and is concerned with adult attachment styles (Collins & Read, 1990; Cooke & Miller, 1990; Hazan & Shaver, 1987), and how past relationships between children and parents may provide the basis for adults' mental models of relationships that may guide romantic relationships. Recent work with married couples (Cooke & Miller, 1990) also suggests that working models (Bowlby, 1982/1969) of past relationships with parents may be activated in a current interaction. Given the attachment framework, these activated models should then play a role in a coherent representation of one's current dating or marital partner. For example, if one's mother was clingy, we may be likely to construe a partner's behavior, such as "suggesting we both go shopping," as controlling and the person as intrusive.

How might such connections to past relationship models affect the behaviors in which individuals engage? The present work suggests ways of exploring the connections among behaviors and higher order knowledge structures, and the implications of these activations for models of one's partner; it also suggests ways of exploring the extent to which models of past relationships may be connected to structures relevant to our current relationship that contribute to coherent representations of the partner.

Theoretical models, such as the one presented here, may allow us to understand how people use a variety of units of information to develop models of *ongoing interactions*. They also simultaneously allow us to understand how detailed unique working models of the self and others continue to influence the behaviors of individuals within interactions *over extended periods of time*, and how past relationships and prior knowledge may influence our interpretation of events in our current ongoing relationships. The current theoretical account also has promise for helping us understand how individuals develop models not only of current relationships but also of possible or future interactions. Understanding such processes, and developing methods for their exploration, may be critical to advances in studying interpersonal processes. Understanding how we can think about, represent, and evaluate the coherence of mental models opens exciting doors for explaining how we develop models of our partners and relationships, and how such models play a central role in our close relationships.

REFERENCES

Abelson, R. P., & Black, J. B. (1986). Introduction. In J. A. Galambos, R. P. Abelson, & J. B. Black (Eds.), *Knowledge structures* (pp. 1–18). Hillsdale, NJ: Erlbaum.

Abelson, R. P., & Lalljee, M. (1988). Knowledge structures and causal explanation. In D. Hilton (Ed.), *Contemporary science and natural explanation: Commonsense conceptions of causality* (pp. 175–203). London: Harvester Press.

Allport, G. W. (1937). *Personality: A psychological interpretation.* New York: Henry Holt.

Alston, W. P. (1970). Toward a logical geography of personality: Traits and deeper lying personality characteristics. In H. D. Krefer & M. K. Munitz (Eds.), *Mind, science, and history* (pp. 59–92). Albany, NY: SUNY Press.

Alston, W. P. (1975). Traits, consistency and conceptual alternatives for personality theory. *Journal for the Theory of Social Behaviour, 5,* 17–48.

Argyle, M., Furnham, A., & Graham, J. A. (1981). *Social situations.* Cambridge, Eng.: Cambridge University Press.

Asch, S. E., & Zukier, H. (1984). Thinking about persons. *Journal of Personality and Social Psychology, 46,* 1230–1240.

Bowlby, J. (1982/1969). *Attachment and loss: Vol. 1. Attachment.* New York: Basic Books. (Original work published 1969).

Bradbury, T. N., & Fincham, F. D. (1988). *The impact of attributions in marriage: Attributions and behavior exchange in marital interaction.* Paper presented at the 22nd Annual Convention of the Association for the Advancement of Behavior Therapy, New York.

Bradbury, T. N., & Fincham, F. D. (1990). Attributions and marriage: Review and critique. *Psychological Bulletin, 107,* 3–33.

Cantor, N., Mischel, W., & Schwartz, J. (1982). A prototype analysis of psychological situations. *Cognitive Psychology, 14,* 45–77.

Carbonell, J. G. (1979). *Subjective understanding: Computer models of belief systems* (Computer Science Tech. Rep. No. 150). New Haven, CT: Yale University.

Cattell, R. B. (1965). *The scientific analysis of personality.* Chicago: Aldine.

Clark, H. H. (1985). Language use and language users. In G. Lindzey & E. Aronson (Eds.), *The handbook of social psychology.* 3rd edition (Vol. 2, pp. 179–231). New York: Random House.

Cohen, C. (1981). Person categories and social perception: Testing some boundaries of the processing effects of prior knowledge. *Journal of Personality and Social Psychology, 40,* 441–452.

Cohen, C., & Ebbesen, E. B. (1979). Observational goals and schema activation: A theoretical framework for behavior perception. *Journal of Experimental Social Psychology, 15,* 305–329.

Collins, N. L., & Read, S. J. (1990). Adult attachment, working models, and relationship quality in dating couples. *Journal of Personality and Social Psychology, 58,* 644–663.

Cooke, L., & Miller, L. C. (1990). *Attachment styles and marital interactions.* Unpublished manuscript, Department of Communication Arts and Sciences, University of Southern California, Los Angeles.

Druian, P. R., & Omessi, E. (1983). *A knowledge structure theory of attribution.* Unpublished manuscript, Grinnell College, Grinnell, IA.

Fisher, W. R. (1989). *Human communication as narration: Toward a philosophy of reason, value, and action.* Columbia: University of South Carolina Press.

Foa, E. B., & Foa, U. G. (1974). *Societal structures of the mind.* Springfield, IL: Thomas.

Galambos, J. A. (1986). Knowledge structures for common activities. In J. A. Galambos, R. P. Abelson, & J. B. Black (Eds.), *Knowledge structures* (pp. 21–47). Hillsdale, NJ: Erlbaum.

Galambos, J. A., Abelson, R. P., & Black, J. B. (Eds.). (1986). *Knowledge structures.* Hillsdale, NJ: Erlbaum.

Gentner, D. & Stevens, A. (1983). *Mental models.* Hillsdale, NJ: Erlbaum.

Hastie, R., Ostrom, T. M., Ebbesen, E. B., Wyer, R. S., Jr., Hamilton, D. L., & Carlston, D. E. (1980). *Person memory: The cognitive basis of social perception.* Hillsdale, NJ: Erlbaum.

Hastie, R., Schroeder, C., & Weber, R. (1990). Creating complex social conjunction categories from simple categories. *Bulletin of the Psychologic Society, 28,* 262–267.

Hazan, C., & Shaver, P. (1987). Romantic love conceptualized as an attachment process. *Journal of Personality and Social Psychology, 52,* 511–524.

Hoffman, C., Mischel, W., & Baer, J. S. (1984). Language and person cognition: Effects of communicative set on trait attribution. *Journal of Personality and Social Psychology, 46,* 1029–1043.

Holyoak, K. J., & Thagard, P. (1989). Analogical mapping by constraint satisfaction. *Cognitive Science, 13,* 295–355.

John, O. P. (1986). How shall a trait be called: A feature analysis of altruism. In A. Angleitner, A. Furnham, & G. Van Heck (Eds.), *Personality psychology in Europe: Current trends and controversies* (pp. 117–140). Berwyn, IL: Swets North America.

Johnson-Laird, P. N. (1983). *Mental models.* Cambridge, MA: Harvard University Press.

Kellerman, K., & Sleight, C. (1989). Coherence: A meaningful adhesive for discourse. In J. A. Anderson (Ed.), *Communication yearbook/12* (pp. 95–129). Newbury Park, CA: Sage.

Kelley, H. H., Berscheid, E., Christensen, A., Harvey, J. H., Huston, T. L., Levinger, G., McClintock, E., Peplau, L. A., & Peterson, D. R. (Eds.). (1983). *Close relationships.* New York: Freeman.

Kenny, D. A. (in press). Interpersonal perception: A social relations analysis. *Journal of Social and Personal Relationships.*

Kintsch, W. (1988). The role of knowledge in discourse comprehension: A construction-integration model. *Psychological Review, 95,* 163–182.

Kraut, R. E., & Higgins, E. T. (1984). Communication and social cognition. In R. S. Wyer, Jr., & T. K. Srull (Eds.), *Handbook of social cognition* (Vol. 3, pp. 87–127). Hillsdale, NJ: Erlbaum.

Kunda, Z., Miller, D. T., & Claire, T. (in press). Combining social concepts: The role of causal reasoning. *Cognitive Science.*

Lalljee, M., & Abelson, R. P. (1983). The organization of explanations. In M. Hewstone (Ed.), *Attribution theory: Social and functional extensions* (pp. 65–80). Oxford, Eng.: Blackwell.

Mannes, S. M., & Kintsch, W. (1989). *Planning routine computing tasks: Understanding what to do* (ICS Technical Report #89-9). Institute of Cognitive Science, University of Colorado, Boulder.

Markus, H., & Nurius, P. (1986). Possible selves. *American Psychologist, 41,* 954–969.

Miller, L. C. (1990). Intimacy and liking: Mutual influence and the role of unique relationships. *Journal of Personality and Social Psychology, 59,* 50–60.

Miller, L. C., & Bettencourt, B. A. (1989). *Interpersonal goals and intimate negotiations: Predicting 101 obstacles to safer sex.* Unpublished manuscript, Department of Communication Arts and Sciences, University of Southern California, Los Angeles.

Miller, L. C., & Jones, D. K. (1989). *I wonder if they would hit it off? Contemplating possible relationships.* Unpublished manuscript, Department of Communication Arts and Sciences, University of Southern California, Los Angeles.

Miller, L. C., & Read, S. J. (1987). Why am I telling you this? Self-disclosure in a goal-based model of personality. In V. J. Derlega & J. Berg (Eds.), *Self-disclosure: Theory, research and therapy* (pp. 35–58). New York: Plenum.

Miller, L. C., & Read, S. J. (1991). Inter-personalism: Understanding persons in relationships. In W. Jones & D. Perlman (Eds.), *Perspectives in interpersonal behavior and relationships* (Vol. 2, pp. 233–267). England: Kingsley.

Mischel, W. (1973). Toward a cognitive social learning reconceptualization of personality. *Psychological Review, 80,* 252–283.

Murphy, G. L., & Medin, D. L. (1985). The role of theories in conceptual coherence. *Psychological Review, 92,* 289–316.

Pervin, L. A. (1983). The stasis and flow of behavior: Toward a theory of goals. In M. M. Page (Ed.), *Nebraska Symposium on Motivation, 1982* (pp. 1–53). Lincoln: University of Nebraska Press.

Read, S. J. (1987). Constructing causal scenarios: A knowledge structure approach to causal reasoning. *Journal of Personality and Social Psychology, 52,* 288–302.

Read, S. J., Druian, P. R., & Miller, L. C. (1989). The role of causal sequence in the meaning of actions. *British Journal of Social Psychology, 28,* 341–351.

Read, S. J., Jones, D. K., & Miller, L. C. (1990). Traits as goal-based categories: The importance of goals in the coherence of dispositional categories. *Journal of Personality and Social Psychology, 58,* 1048–1061.

Read, S. J., & Marcus-Newhall, A. (1990). *Explanatory coherence in the construction of causal explanations.* Unpublished manuscript, University of Southern California, Los Angeles.

Read, S. J., & Miller, L. C. (1989). Inter-personalism: Toward a goal-based theory of persons in relationships. In L. Pervin (Ed.), *Goal concepts in personality and social psychology* (pp. 413–472). Hillsdale, NJ: Erlbaum.

Rumelhart, D. E., & McClelland, J. L. (1986). *Parallel distributed processing: Explorations in the microstructure of cognition. Vol. 1: Foundations.* Cambridge, MA: MIT Press.

Schank, R. C. (1982). *Dynamic memory: A theory of reminding and learning in computers and people.* New York: Cambridge University Press.

Schank, R. C., & Abelson, R. P. (1977). *Scripts, plans, goals and understanding.* Hillsdale, NJ: Erlbaum.

Thagard, P. (1989). Explanatory coherence. *Behavioral and Brain Sciences, 12,* 435–467.

Trzebinski, J. (1989). The role of goal categories in the representation of social knowledge. In L. Pervin (Ed.), *Goal concepts in personality and social psychology* (pp. 363–411). Hillsdale, NJ: Erlbaum.

Wegner, D. M., Giuliano, T., & Hertel, P. T. (1985). Cognitive interdependence in close relationships. In W. Ickes (Ed.), *Compatible and incompatible relationships* (pp. 253–276). New York: Springer-Verlag.

Wilensky, R. (1983). *Planning and understanding: A computational approach to human reasoning.* Reading, MA: Addison-Wesley.

4 Life Tasks, Personal Needs, and Close Relationships

Nancy Cantor
University of Michigan

Janet Malley
Middlebury College

In the study of cognition in close relationships, there has been considerable progress in explicating the attributions that partners make for each others' behaviors and the accounts given for the dissolution of relationships (Fincham, Bradbury, & Scott, 1990). This cognitive activity provides a critical basis for individuals to understand and to assess their relationships—to see where things went wrong and to potentially guide the relationship in more satisfying directions. Attributions of responsibility and assessments of who is doing the work to maintain a relationship are related to subsequent measures of relationship commitment and happiness (e.g., Fletcher, Fincham, Cramer, & Heron, 1987).

In extending this analysis of cognition in close relationships, we should begin to pay closer attention to the ways in which attributions, accounts, and relationship talk depend systematically on the goals and needs of the partners in a relationship. Individuals will, quite probably, make fewer attributions—positive or negative—about events that do not enhance or threaten their goals for the relationship. Whereas attention has been given in the literature to the detrimental influence of irrational beliefs or dysfunctional working models of relationships (e.g., Eidelson & Epstein, 1982; Hazan & Shaver, 1987), relatively little is known about individuals' goals in their relationships (cf. Miller & Read, this volume; Read & Miller, 1989).

Goals and needs influence how much thinking a person does about a relationship and what he or she thinks about while interacting with a partner. As Reis and Shaver (1988) have noted, close relationships depend on a process of creating intimacy. Individuals with a strong need for intimacy will think more about interpersonal processes as they pursue their daily life than those with a low need for intimacy (McAdams & Constantian, 1983). Goals for an interaction that orient the individual toward interdependence with a partner will encourage detailed, controlled information processing in the interaction (Erber & Fiske, 1984). These interdependent goals can come from the structure of the interaction situation (e.g., rewards dependent on cooperative behavior), or they can reflect dispositional orientations toward relationships (e.g., Clark, Muchant, Ouellette, Powell, & Milberg, 1987). Expectancies about what relationships involve and about how well one can perform a given task are reflected in individuals' strategic thoughts as they prepare for, take part in, and retrospect on their social interactions (e.g., Langston & Cantor, 1989).

Broadly stated, the influence of goals and needs on cognition in close relationships takes two forms. Goals and needs shape interactions directly through their selective, and frequently automatic, influence on attention, on the accessibility of content, and on the interpretation of events as they unfold. One function of cognition in close relationships is to make sense of events as they happen, and personal goals and needs provide an orienting framework in that discovery process (Kelly, 1955). Controlled or intentional processing of relationship events is also influenced by what an individual sees as the task for the interaction and by what he or she personally desires from that relationship. As individuals work on understanding relationships, in their attributions or accounts of what went right and what went wrong, they are guided by expectancies developed in the past. In turn, those understandings provide the basis for the initiation of new goals and new strategies for conducting future relationships (Cantor & Kihlstrom, 1987). In both automatic and controlled processing contexts, cognitive activity will be shaped in part by what the person is trying to do in the relationship (i.e., by his or her needs and goals).

In this chapter we consider how goals and needs take shape in close relationships, and the ways in which individuals bring to bear different expectancies as they pursue a relationship. We concentrate on explicating this cognitive-motivational framework for relationships with the objective of encouraging future work that links goals and needs to individual differences in attention, interpretation, and strategic planning in close relationships.

Goals and Needs in Close Relationships

Recently, there has been a revival of interest in self-articulated personal goals as units of individual differences that can be profitably analyzed as representations of personality (Cantor & Zirkel, 1990; Pervin, 1989). Individuals' personal goals can be considered in tandem with less directly accessible motive dispositions (e.g., Emmons, 1989; Little, 1989). Motive dispositions, such as the need for intimacy or power, are general and can be fulfilled in diverse ways by different people in different settings. An individual's self-goals, such as the personal project of increasing equity in a relationship, specify personal needs by providing a "recipe" for how that person will address that need in his or her current life. Analysis of self-articulated goals provides a way to measure the influence of personal needs as they guide attention, thought, and action in daily life (Klinger, Barta, & Maxeiner, 1980). Self-articulated goals can also add a dimension beyond personal needs because they often reflect the individual's plans for effecting change. People think deliberately about their experiences in important activities and relationships, and self-goals reflect their views of what is possible and feasible for the future (Markus & Nurius, 1986; Schlenker & Weigold, 1989).

One way to characterize the goals that individuals bring to their relationships is in terms of their current *life tasks* (Cantor & Kihlstrom, 1987). Individuals' construals of what relationships involve and of how they see themselves currently pursuing intimacy can be instructive in the analysis of cognition in close relationships. Life tasks reflect both personal needs and the demands and opportunities that the person perceives in the environment. Life tasks for interpersonal intimacy can vary in content and in salience, depending on personal needs and the avenues available for expression of those needs in relationships. A person's particular expression of a need for intimacy, for example, may depend on the opportunities available for the life tasks of care giving, conflict resolution, and open communication. Life tasks also constitute plans or guidelines in the service of creating more interpersonal communication in a relationship. In this way, life tasks both reflect the current status of personal needs as expressed in daily life, and set forth plans for change in interpersonal relations. As a reflection of personal needs, they direct attention and thought in need-fulfilling ways. As a framework for obtaining increased satisfaction, they can also direct intentional thought toward new forms of interpersonal closeness.

An important simplification in this discussion is the emphasis on one partner's tasks in the relationship, and on how that person's tasks might change over time. We agree fully with Clark and Reis' (1988) recent assessment that, with a few notable exceptions (e.g., Kelley et al., 1983), the study of interpersonal intimacy has been too much a study of individuals as separate actors, and too little about the interdependent *process* of creating intimacy in a close relationship. Nonetheless, as they also noted, it still helps to begin with some sense of what each partner brings to the relationship in terms of expectations, needs, tasks, and dispositional orientations, and that is where we begin the present analysis of individual motivation in close relationships.

Individuals bring many expectations and orientations to their relationships, but we focus only on the personal needs and life tasks that such individual attitudes may make salient in a close relationship. Styles of attachment and preferences for closeness in relationships should be reflected in the life tasks that individuals have for their relationships. A person with a preference for closeness in relationships probably has correspondingly many life tasks concerned with diverse aspects of interdependence, such as the sharing of household responsibilities, joint decision making, and time spent together (Berscheid, Snyder, & Omoto, 1989). Our discussion focuses primarily on such life tasks, although many more general orientations contribute to the impetus for individuals to set certain kinds of tasks, and to avoid others, in working on their close relationships.

With these qualifications in mind, we consider the role of life tasks and personal needs in close relationships. After briefly discussing the life task as a unit of analysis in personality, we identify two fundamental personal needs that provide a motivational foundation for individuals' different ways of framing life tasks. We then consider how individuals find avenues through their life tasks for pursuing intimacy with more or less vigor and success. In the fourth section we discuss how tasks, needs, and relationships might be expected to change and be reformulated at different points in a person's life. We argue that two central components of well-being, both for individuals and for their relationships, are the *fit* of personal needs with current life tasks in the relationship, and the *balance* of personal needs in a variety of life tasks, that complement rather than conflict, and that can be relatively easily integrated within the daily workings of the relationship. Finally, we discuss how tasks and needs might be related to cognition in close relationships.

LIFE TASKS AS MOTIVATIONAL
UNITS OF PERSONALITY

Life tasks are what individuals see themselves working on and devoting energy and thought to, in a particular period of life. These are the tasks, such as "finding a relationship" or "being a good parent," that both organize our daily life activities and at the same time give added meaning to those routines—life tasks represent both the here and now of our current activities and projects, and also the wishes that we have for the future. For example, we typically elicit life tasks by asking people to consider the tasks that they see themselves as working on in a particular life period, and then we ask for the specific life situations and activities that comprise the tasks for them (e.g., for college students the independence life task means doing their own laundry or making their own decisions). Another source for individuals' life task statements is in their reports of what they *wish* to be doing in the next few years, and framing the question in this way orients individuals toward future life tasks. Nonetheless, in both cases the core idea is that broad-based personal needs are transformed into tasks to be pursued in particular life contexts. Needs do not simply result in abstract images of the self as a certain kind of person but also in images of the self carrying out life tasks. When people talk about their life tasks, their statements reveal their activity choices, their efforts to change their routines, and the parts of their daily activities that currently bring satisfaction or stress and distress to them.

The task is a unit of analysis that is importantly centered in the life context of a person in a particular stage of life; as Erikson (1950) and Havighurst (1953) have noted, life tasks arise in large part from the age-related demands and opportunities set forth by a particular subculture that operate as a guide for what individuals should be working on at that time, in that culture, and in those life situations. For example, after graduation from college many students begin to voice commitment to finding an intimate relationship, and the timing and urgency of their concerns suggest that they are now feeling considerable social pressure. Similarly, the very content of the relationship task takes on a different cast for women than for men in this culture, with the former primarily pursuing communal efforts within the context of the close relationship and the latter often oriented toward agentic self-development within the security provided by the relationship partnership (Malley & Stewart, 1988; Rubin, 1983). Individuals work on and think about their tasks in a social context and in the shadows of age-related demands, and a life-task analysis is deliberately oriented toward uncovering the personal ways in which individuals internalize those interpersonal and age-related expectations. The life-task analysis is a way of understanding what the person is up to, vis à vis the tasks and expectations of his or her social group and life period.

Not only do individuals get their ideas for life tasks from the social groups and intimate partners with whom they interact, and from the broader sociocultural agendas within which they live and work, but also they evaluate progress on life tasks in a social comparison context. These interpersonal pressures on life tasks are particularly acute for social tasks; for example, spouses need to take into account each other's life tasks in the marriage and to evaluate the current state of the relationship in the light of these shared agendas (Little, 1989). Lack of awareness of a partner's tasks, and incompatibility of tasks between partners, can result in severe distress in a close relationship. Moreover, relationships need to leave room for growth, and one dimension of such flexibility is in the space that one partner gives the other for changing his or her life tasks. Frequently, one member of a relationship will feel pressured to enact an old task, whereas the individual may prefer to move on to new life tasks (e.g., the interdependence of a marriage built around shared parenting may feel overly confining after the children have grown). At one point in a marriage, for example, interpersonal intimacy may be built around shared communal tasks, whereas at other points that intimacy may look more like parallel play with each partner oriented toward more individualistic, agentic tasks. One way to document the dynamics of a relationship is to consider the changing nature of the life tasks that each partner pursues within the relationship over time; relationships in that sense can fulfill different task agendas in the life course of the partnership.

Individuals pursue many life tasks at once, and with different purposes in mind. For example, individuals may have some tasks that serve as confirmation of who they are now, verifying and even bolstering their sense of self ("I'm working on my relationship because I'm a very social person"). Other tasks may be explicitly growth promoting in that they present a new personal direction or a change in interests or behavior ("I'm trying to maintain my relationship because

I want to be less isolated socially"). In either case, however, tasks represent a relatively malleable part of personality, at least in theory, because they are enacted in, and given meaning by, specific sociocultural and age-related life contexts, and when those context change, so may the meanings of life tasks. Close relationships provide an arena for intimacy that may have very different meanings in different periods of life, or for different social groups, in terms of the life tasks to be enacted as part of the more general intimacy task. Whereas college students may actually be working on independence (from family) as part of their efforts at forging a serious relationship, and young married people may be looking to their relationship as a source of identity, first-time parents may construe working on intimacy as an effort at interdependence.

The changes in meaning of a life task across life contexts and periods come in several forms: A task may become especially *salient* and important in a particular context (e.g., interpersonal intimacy tasks may take on particular urgency after a divorce); a task may change in *content* in critical ways (e.g., intimacy may be more agentic in some life periods and more communal in others); and, in a related vein, a task may change as a function of *other tasks* that a person is simultaneously pursuing (e.g., early in a marriage the intimacy life tasks may be intertwined with working on personal identity, whereas later on working on intimacy may be more closely linked to issues associated with the task of shared parenting).

In our view, the life task is a unit of analysis with much promise for elucidating cognitive-motivational dynamics in close relationships. In particular, as noted above, life tasks place the needs of individuals concretely within their daily life activities and projects, as well as revealing the shared demands of their culture and social group. Life tasks also reveal much about the forward-looking or growth-promoting aspects of individuals' strivings. Analysis of life tasks can provide a window on the personal needs that are fulfilled in a close relationship, as well as the thought that is directed toward changing the relationship. Partners' tasks reflect at once on what they are doing in the relationship, what they are trying to do in it, and on what they are trying to change.

FUNDAMENTAL PERSONAL NEEDS

Although life tasks reflect many aspects of our selves and life situations, they also represent the practical and feasible manifestations of our underlying personal needs. Needs embody very generalized and broad-based wishes or wants (either conscious or unconscious), and specific life tasks allow the fulfillment of these needs. A generalized need for intimacy may be expressed through a variety of very different specific life tasks in a variety of life arenas, such as with family, among co-workers, and even in interactions with relative strangers. McAdams (1984) defines the need for intimacy, for example, as the "readiness for experiences of close, warm, and communicative exchange with others" (p. 45), which could well map onto a variety of life tasks associated with different life contexts and age-related demands. For the student, intimacy may come in the form of security derived from establishing a first truly close relationship; for the parent it may take a very different meaning in the desire to be close to a child, built upon the dependency of the infant and the care-giving routines of parenthood.

Theorists have suggested a variety of underlying needs that may be manifested in individuals' life tasks (e.g., Freud, 1961/1930; Murray, 1938). However, considerable theoretical consensus points to the importance of two fundamental needs representing a basic duality in life (Bakan, 1966; Freud, 1961/1930; McAdams, 1985; Parsons & Bales, 1955). Although these needs have been variously described, they may be best understood through Bakan's (1966) description of agency and communion.

According to Bakan (1966, esp. p. 15), agency is concerned with the individual self—self-protection, self-assertion, and self-expansion. The self, then, is focused on separating from others through individual expression and mastery, which can result in a sense of isolation, alienation, and aloneness. Communion, in contrast, is expressed through the individual's merging with the larger group and the sense of being at one with others. Thus, rather than encouraging separation, the urge is toward contact with others, union, and cooperation.

Considered this way, the personal needs for agency and communion may be viewed as a dialectic—each orientation, in turn, vying to become the predominant modal need. It may be that this dialectical process is an accurate characterization of agentic and communal needs over the life course, especially at earlier stages of psychological development when there may be less tolerance for a complex, and possibly conflicting, set of needs driving behavior. However, Bakan (1966) specifically argues that health and well-being rest on the ability to combine both orientations (see, Block, 1973). Although needs tend to be broad based and global, they are not static. As individuals encounter new life experiences, the expression of both agentic and communal needs through diverse life tasks may become more feasible and desired.

Agency and Communion in Close Relationships

What role might close relationships play in the expression and integration of communal and agentic needs over the life course? Conversely, how might relationships be changed by individuals' changing needs for agency and communion? Most straightforwardly, close relationships provide an arena of social life that encourages communion—individuals in close relationships work on tasks of interpersonal interdependence, such as sharing household duties in a fair and reasonable way, and of intimacy, such as learning to trust a partner and to disclose one's insecurities (Kelley et al., 1983). The relationship provides a context that enables and encourages an individual to work on communion.

Nevertheless, individuals can be more or less prepared to take on the communal aspects of a close relationship—they may not always want to invest in the interpersonal life tasks that create intimacy in a relationship. Instead, the relationship can take on meaning as an adjunct to the other more agentic tasks of the individuals' career, schooling, or participation in clubs. The pursuit of intimacy may take a secondary place, whereas agentic tasks in the relationship (e.g., balancing the family budget, building a beautiful home) receive more attention. The "close" relationship is not always a particularly intimate one (Clark & Reis, 1988).

In the process of trying to satisfy these needs through life tasks in the relationship, people sometimes come to change their motivational emphases altogether, as when a career-oriented individual finds a new arena for communication with his or her spouse and their newborn child. The relationship, which once was yet another arena for the pursuit of achievement or power, suddenly takes on a more communal cast via investment in the interpersonal life tasks of social support and caring for each other and for the child. The individual now develops a new communal orientation by working on new life tasks in the family context, and by working on his or her relationship in a different fashion. In other words, the analysis of life tasks provides a window on the current status of personal needs and on their evolution and integration over the life course. If we think of personal needs as the motivational underpinnings of close relationships (i.e., what each person brings to the relationship in terms of desires for finding certain kinds of meaning), and we think of daily life experiences of cooperation and conflict, of love, and anger, as the concrete outcomes of the relationship, then life tasks provide the link between *personal* needs and *interpersonal* outcomes. The satisfaction of personal needs through compatible life tasks in relationships, as well as in other areas, should enhance well-being.

ANALYZING LIFE TASKS IN CLOSE RELATIONSHIPS

Bakan's (1966) model of fundamental personal needs is very useful as a framework for the analysis of life tasks in close relationships. Relationships provide a context for both communal and agentic needs to be enacted in a variety of concrete life tasks. An intimate relationship provides a context for working on conflict resolution, on shared parenting, on personal dominance, and on enriched friendship circles—to name only a few of the relevant life tasks. Although we focus initially on individuals' feelings about, and pursuit of, interpersonal intimacy, other more agentic tasks are also pursued in close relationships (e.g., the up-and-coming young professional's conception of intimacy in marriage may have as much to do with personal achievement and power as with the pursuit of interpersonal closeness). It seems critical in the analysis of close relationships to consider the possible enactment of both communal and agentic needs in life tasks.

Individuals' interpersonal life tasks can serve as a starting point in the assessment of the centrality of need for communion. By examining the content of those tasks we can understand better exactly how, and to what extent, the person is pursuing communion in relationships. Appraisals of the importance and challenge of those tasks, and of the time spent thinking about them, are indicative of the individual's level of motivation for working to maintain and enhance the relationship. When interpersonal life tasks are very salient, they are likely to guide attention automatically to associated events that are relevant to relationships. Individuals who perceive their interpersonal life tasks as demanding but critical to master are likely to focus on those tasks, to think about them often, and even to plan deliberately for ways to pursue intimacy. Over time, as avenues for the pursuit of intimacy arise or become closed, changes in the expression of communal needs may occur (McAdams & Vaillant, 1982). The opportunity for new life tasks can precipitate a shift in the allocation of attention and thought, suggesting a new accessible framework for interpreting events.

The Salience of Intimacy Tasks

A life-task analysis always begins with the question of what an individual sees himself or herself as working on in a particular life period. For example, we might ask how much a particular person is working on and thinking about intimacy in his or her current life. The salience or centrality of intimacy life tasks can be assessed via a number of measures, some direct and others indirect. For example, in a recent study of life tasks among a group of 57 sorority women at the University of Michigan, Cantor et al. (1991 in press) asked the participants first to list their current life tasks and then to code these tasks into seven general task categories (e.g., "Making friends, getting along with others"; "Being involved with someone, finding intimacy—dating"; "Being on your own, away from family"). These women coded tasks of the following sort as representing intimacy: "Dealing with my long-term relationship"; "Dating, having someone to spend quiet time with"; "Maintaining a healthy and happy relationship with boyfriend, feeling loved, feeling good about yourself." They viewed the intimacy task category as covering both communal needs for sharing and interpersonal closeness, and agentic concerns about personal identity and the self-confidence achieved in a relationship.

The sorority women also provided appraisals of the meaning of these seven task categories in their current lives, by rating each task on 15 meaning dimensions, including initiative, importance, conflict, difficulty, and enjoyment. They appraised the intimacy tasks as moderately difficult and rewarding, in comparison to their "stressful" achievement tasks and their "easy" friendship tasks.

At a later phase in the semester-long study, 50 of these women participated in an experience-sampling study in which they provided reports of their activities and emotional states during five randomly selected times each day, for 15 days.

Each night during the experience-sampling study, they looked back over their beeper activity reports and rated the relevance of each event to each of the seven life-task categories. Not surprisingly, the intimacy task was not a frequent presence in their day-to-day thoughts, although it did capture attention regularly in social events, at meals, and even occasionally in the library while studying. When they were thinking about intimacy, these women reported heightened emotional involvement and positive affect, as compared to their reports of emotional experiences in events relevant to their other life tasks (e.g., while working on grades).

These life-task listings and experience-sampling reports provided a variety of measures of individual differences in the salience or centrality of intimacy life tasks in their daily lives (see Cantor et al., 1991 in press, for details of the methods and results). For example, whereas the intimacy tasks were perceived by the sorority group as a whole to be quite important, the tasks took on added significance and relevance in the lives of the 31 students who were currently involved in a serious relationship. They were more likely to spontaneously generate intimacy life tasks in their top five life tasks; they appraised the intimacy task as involving more personal initiative, more enjoyment and progress, and less stress than did their peers; they were more likely to see day-to-day events in the experience-sampling reports as relevant to their intimacy tasks, and also more likely to have felt emotionally involved and happy in those events than were their peers. Not surprisingly, they were more satisfied with their romantic life than were their peers who were not in a current relationship, and were more likely to attribute their performance in this domain to ability than were those peers. Hence, one facet of a serious relationship, at least in this social group in which intimacy is a highly valued task, is that it can enhance the salience of, and meaning invested in, daily life events that afford the pursuit of interpersonal closeness. For the women currently in serious relationships, the intimacy life task was an organizing force giving meaning to their daily lives (e.g., Klinger, 1977; McAdams & Constantian, 1983).

In considering the cognitive correlates of the heightened salience of intimacy life tasks, the notion of construct accessibility serves as a convenient organizing principle. Intimacy tasks were quick to come to mind for the women in relationships—they thought about intimacy often and took personal initiative in this domain. They were emotionally involved in events relevant to the intimacy tasks and used these tasks as a framework for interpreting and evaluating their daily life experience. Intimacy was on their minds and they were especially attuned to events that pertained to these central life tasks. They attended to feedback about their relationships, and their heightened sensitivity to interpersonal messages and events may even have encouraged interpersonal responsiveness on their partners' parts. Through automatic processes of selective attention, interpretation, and evaluation, such individuals can create an intensely *intimate* environment in their daily lives.

Conflict over Intimacy

One of the ways in which a life task can take on added meaning or presence for individuals is if it engenders *conflict,* by engaging their special involvement and/or draining energy from other task pursuits (Emmons & King, 1988; Little, 1983). In a sociocultural setting in which certain life tasks take on special meaning anyway, as the intimacy tasks apparently did in this sorority group, then thoughts and obsessions about the tasks (and the underlying need that they presumably reflect) can be quite riveting, and impact uniquely on the quality-of-life experience. For example, in the sorority sample, women who reported experiencing conflict about their intimacy tasks also reported thinking a great deal about them and taking much personal initiative in working on them, whether or not they were in a relationship. Their appraisals of how much working on this task engendered conflict in their lives were not related to ambivalence about the task but rather were indicative of a special commitment to this task, at the cost of other current tasks. (It should be noted here that intimacy task conflict was unrelated to whether or not they were involved with someone. Moreover, those women who were in conflict about intimacy were not more likely to be in conflict about their achievement life tasks.)

Life task conflict, when combined with commitment rather than ambivalence about pursuing the task, involves an interesting two-sided set of correlates as individuals navigate their tasks in their current life contexts. For example, in this sample, conflict about intimacy tasks not only involved obsessive thought and heightened stress, but also brought many benefits when an appropriate avenue for communal expression was attained in a serious relationship. For women in a serious relationship, *conflict* about intimacy tasks was actually associated with *more* perceived control over the intimacy tasks, whereas for women not in such a relationship it was associated with *less* control. Conflict implied a positive, rewarding involvement for those in relationships and a negative, discouraging involvement for those not in a current relationship. At the end of the semester, those who had initially described the intimacy tasks with conflict were *more* likely to be satisfied and *less* likely to want to change anything *if* they were in a relationship, and the reverse pattern was observed for the high- (versus low-) conflict subjects not in a relationship. Thus, in a life context in which a particular life task is highly valued, obsessive conflict can be rewarding if you feel that you are actively working on the task, but a debilitating influence if you cannot find an avenue for working on that central task.

These data suggest that whereas salience of a task elicits rather automatic attentional and interpretive cognitive activity, life task conflict (when it is not combined with ambivalence) adds a dimension of absorption that involves more controlled processes. This latter approach to intimacy tasks implies that individuals deliberately build intimacy in their lives. If a relationship exists, then this kind of deliberate thought can be constructive, although there is always the risk that one's partner will not commit equivalent energy to maintaining intimacy (Fletcher et al., 1987).

Intimacy and Other Life Tasks

Individuals pursue many life tasks at once, and therefore a central aspect of the meaning of a particular life task, like intimacy, is how that task pursuit relates to other current tasks (Little, 1989). These intertask relationships can take a number of forms. For instance, in some cases investment in one set of tasks, such as those involved with the pursuit of interpersonal intimacy and sharing, can result in a turning away from other task pursuits that seem to reflect a different set of concerns (e.g., achievement tasks). We have seen this kind of oppositional task relationship in a number of data sets, and both Emmons and King (1988) and Little (1983, 1989) have written extensively about such intertask conflict. In the sorority sample, for instance, the women with high intimacy task conflict and in a serious relationship were feeling less involved in their academic life tasks than were their peers (e.g., they reported spending less time thinking about academics and being less involved in academics; they were less emotionally involved in classroom situations in the experience sampling). Intimacy task conflict combined with the outlet of a serious relationship narrowed the focus of these women's thoughts and concerns. Whereas this narrowing of focus had not resulted in a debilitation of academic performance for these women (at least not yet), they were less involved and invested in this other major arena than were their peers. In contrast, the high-conflict subjects who were not in a serious relationship were actually quite involved in their achievement life tasks, and that involvement may even have precipitated or exacerbated some of their concerns about the state of their romantic life. Although task conflict can sometimes mean a positive sense of engagement and accomplishment, it also can create new issues of task balancing that require attention and adjustment.

We suggest that those sorority members who reported conflict about the intimacy tasks, but also spent more time thinking about intimate relationships, were driven by an underlying personal need for communion. For those women, having a serious relationship meant that their interpersonal tasks provided important outlets for their communal needs. This may be why these women perceived themselves as having greater control over the relationship; the intimacy tasks were fulfilling their needs—providing them with opportunities to experience communion and satisfying their underlying personal needs. In contrast, those sorority women who also devoted much thought to an intimate relationship, but did not have that avenue for expressing and satisfying their communal needs, were understandably feeling less in control of this critical life arena. When life situations allow for the pursuit of life tasks that meet personal needs, people fare better than when they cannot find a way to work on tasks that fit their needs (Malley, 1989).

The women in this study with intimacy life tasks available to meet an underlying personal need for communion were clearly invested in these satisfying tasks, and expended correspondingly less effort in alternative life tasks potentially available to them. For them, communion appeared to be a primary motivating force, and life experiences were principally focused on this need. In contrast, those experiencing unsatisfied needs for communion seemed relegated to directing energies to alternative, and, for them, less rewarding, life tasks. In some sense these women's life experiences were out of sync with their underlying personal needs. It is likely, however, that over time, either their tasks or their needs would change to provide for a better fit.

INTEGRATING NEEDS AND TASKS
IN RELATIONSHIPS

A longer term perspective is required to test people's capacity for achieving consistency between their personal needs and current life experience via satisfying life tasks, and to reveal the process of balancing multiple needs in diverse tasks. As a first step in this investigation we examined, in collaboration with Abigail Stewart and Elizabeth Vandewater, longitudinal data from a sample of highly educated adult women (for details of the study, see Murray Research Center of Radcliffe College, 1988, Data Resources Index; Stewart, 1986). We were interested in examining the relationship over time between personal need for communion and interpersonal life tasks for these adult women, and in whether they took opportunities to change their tasks with changing life circumstances. As part of that study, 55 women, graduates of a women's college in the Northeast, responded to a question about "what they wished to be doing in the next ten years" at each of three time periods: 10, 15, and 22 years after college. We coded their life-task listings from these statements of what they wished to be doing, using a five-category system: interpersonal tasks, career tasks, parenting tasks, life-style tasks, and self-development tasks. The women were also asked at each time period to look back over the past 10 years and to describe the high and low points of these years. We coded their statements for the prevalence of positive and negative concerns with interpersonal intimacy, and constructed a total score for each time period of need for communion from these open-ended life descriptions. The women had also provided detailed year-by-year accounts of their current life circumstances for the years between college and the first questionnaire, between the first and second questionnaires, and then between the second and the last questionnaires. From these year-by-year accounts, we tabulated any change in life circumstance, such as a new relationship, new child, and change in career, that occurred during the years covering the women's 20's, 30's, and 40's. These data allow us to make a preliminary assessment of the relationships over time between need for communion, interpersonal life tasks, and life circumstances.

Before turning to the full data, it is useful to consider some concrete examples of the course of these women's lives. The following two brief case descriptions serve to illustrate the patterning of needs, tasks, and life circumstances in the postcollege years.

1. Phyllis—working toward satisfying communion. Phyllis scored high in need for communion at all three data points, and although her life tasks seemed to reflect the desire for intimacy, she did not experience her interpersonal life with uniform satisfaction. Specifically, Phyllis had already married and had a young daughter by the time she completed her education. In this early period she continued to care for her daughter, and then a son, also spending her time cooking and sewing, while her husband pursued a rather separate life in law school. Early on Phyllis felt a lack of love and validation of her efforts from her husband and eventually divorced. Almost simultaneously, Phyllis took on a job she loved and entered graduate school, which she found intellectually satisfying although financially draining. Her tasks for the future during this early time period included advancing professionally in her career, writing books, having many friends and then finding the "perfect" mate. By her late 40's Phyllis had achieved at least some of these goals. In terms of her career, she had a teaching job and had published a book. Phyllis had also remarried by this time. Both of these activities constituted high points for Phyllis, although she also admitted to some disappointments in teaching and the low salary she received for that work. At this time Phyllis' tasks for the future, once again, concerned both her family and work lives, but the relative focus had shifted back to a primary interpersonal concern. She wanted to earn a lot of money in her job, provided it did not require more time commitment, because she also wanted to spend more time with her husband (preferably by having him work less).

2. Kathy—commitment to agency. In contrast to Phyllis, Kathy exhibited lower need for communion. Unlike Phyllis, Kathy tried work in several areas immediately after college, delaying marriage for a few years. After marriage, and while at home caring for young children, Kathy developed her artistic skills by both writing and sculpting. High points for this time period mostly reflect this work. Kathy enjoyed the fact that she could be known through her artistic expressions. Although she describes the love for her children as high points as well, she does not specifically mention her marriage as a high or low point. Her tasks for the future centered primarily on her development as a writer (e.g., publishing a book of her writings), and secondarily on her desire to watch her children grow and mature. By her late 30's Kathy was unhappy and bored with the motherhood role, and with life in an unstimulating bedroom community. Nevertheless, she felt it is her responsibility to be home for her children and, thus, was comfortable with her life-style because it provided her with the security and opportunity to develop her own artistic talents while the children were at school. Once again, Kathy's high points for this period revolved around her children and her art. By her late 40's Kathy made few changes in her life. Her family moved to a less stifling community and she continues to work on her art and writing. More recently she has taken on a part-time job because

she dislikes being financially dependent upon her husband. High points for this time period continue to center on her art. Kathy also expresses a sense of loneliness and feeling set apart from others. But, in discussing her marital relationship Kathy makes it clear that she does not expect companionship or intimacy from her husband. Instead, she sees her marriage as a means of obtaining security, which then allows her to pursue her artistic endeavors.

These two cases seem especially revealing of how personal needs in life tasks follow different temporal patterns for different individuals. Phyllis, scoring high on communal needs throughout these years, pursued tasks relating to intimacy in an uneven way—she began her postcollege years committed to marriage and family, spent many years postdivorce with career development as her central passion, and then with the passage of time and career successes returned to finding and spending time with the "perfect" mate, and to addressing more directly that need for communion. In contrast, Kathy, characterized predominantly as low on communal needs, developed and pursued fundamentally agentic life tasks. Throughout her 30's and 40's, her efforts were primarily devoted to developing and sustaining her art and writing. Even her marriage was viewed, not as an arena for companionship, but rather as providing the security necessary to sustain these agentic life tasks. It is noteworthy, however, that Kathy's most recent remarks, made in her 40's, reveal some unhappiness in her life; these principally revolve around the lack of communion in her life and a sense of loneliness and feeling apart from others. It may be that Kathy is beginning to feel some conflict about her almost singular agentic approach to her life tasks.

Changing Tasks and Needs over Time

In these two cases, as in many in the sample, the perhaps inevitable tensions between agentic and communal needs and tasks surfaced in one form or another, seeming to require some resolution over time. One potential resolution involves a sequential commitment, presumably across different periods of one's life, in which central task focus switches over time from agentic to communal tasks, or vice versa—this model is implicit in most theories of age-related tasks (e.g., Erikson, 1950; Levinson, 1978). We observed such a pattern of alternating task focus in the full sample from which the above cases were drawn. A pattern of shifting task focus emerged in response to the wishes question: Those women who foresaw relatively many career tasks when questioned in their 20's listed relatively many interpersonal tasks in the later period of their 40's. Women listing relatively many career tasks in the 40's questionnaire were also more likely to list many tasks concerned with *self* development, but not with interpersonal involvements. Hence, a task focus centered on career tasks seemed to facilitate an interpersonal orientation over time, although women with a career focus in their 40's were more likely to be self rather than interpersonally focused.

This shifting life task focus over time provides a window on the malleability of the motivational context for a close relationship. The perceived importance of a relationship may itself ebb and flow with these changing task foci—that is, when agentic tasks have risen to prominence, then the demands for a close, intense relationship may subside. Even as the individual continues to pursue a relationship (e.g., to be married and a parent), the other task focus may drain some of the intensity from that pursuit. Or this shift may take a slightly different form in which the meaning of the relationship changes to take on the flavor of these other, more central pursuits. For example, Phyllis wrote about parenting during her graduate school days as another job, a responsibility to accomplish, whereas earlier it meant everything to her sense of community, and later on she wrote about it in the context of a renewed focus on family closeness and shared intimacy.

The changing meaning of the close relationship may sometimes involve a withdrawal of task energy from the relationship. In other instances the relationship may be pursued with equal vigor, but as an outlet for a different set of perhaps more agentic task concerns. Kathy, for example, never expressed concerns with forging a sense of sharing and mutual trust with her spouse, concerns that always seemed to take a back seat to the pursuit of artistic accomplishment and self-expression. She maintained the relationship throughout those years, but seemingly more as an arena for self-development than as an expression of interpersonal communion. Nonetheless, hers was a successful relationship, presumably because it was based upon a mutual understanding of the marriage as providing instrumental support to each other rather than companionship.

Changing tasks in a relationship. We assume that there are many forces constraining individuals' pursuit of life tasks in a close relationship—gender, membership in a social group, and age all are related to intimacy and are reflected in people's construal of tasks. However, these social prescriptions also bring with them a certain freedom, that is, the opportunity for changing task focus and task meaning occasioned by major changes in life circumstances and in social reference groups, such as occur with divorce, shifting careers, and new parenting (Cantor & Langston, 1989; Levinson, 1978; Stewart, 1989). For example, in Stewart's longitudinal study of women's lives, changes in the structure of these women's lives, such as changing marital or relationship status, career shifts, or alterations in life-style (e.g., buying a house), were often reflected in the tasks they then set for themselves in the future. In particular, the more changes in any of those life areas (i.e., marriage, career, or life-style) in the age period from roughly their mid-30's to mid-40's, the more likely these women were to list relatively many interpersonal-relationship tasks in their wishes for the subsequent 10 years. In this sample, life-struture changes seemed to have their most consistent impact on the setting of interpersonal tasks, more so than in other task arenas, perhaps suggesting that this arena remained a central foundation for their life-task activity, even while they pursued other tasks. These women may have been intentionally making some of these life-structure changes as a means of allowing for achieving intimacy life tasks, or they may simply have used the opportunity provided by career and life-style changes to alter their relationships. In either case, this seemed to happen more as they got older (i.e., life-structure changes in their 20's were not reliably related to the setting of tasks in any particular domain, whereas the patterns were clear and strong in the data from their 30's and 40's).

Phyllis' story provides an example of this increasing focus on interpersonal tasks following life structure changes in both marital and life-style arenas, relatively late in her life. Her story suggests that it often takes a considerable amount of time and experience, and perhaps the accrued security in other life-task arenas (e.g., her professional security), to find alternative avenues for the expression of communal needs. For example, in her report provided in 1974 (10 years after college, during her graduate school days), she said, "Periodically now, I suffer acute attacks of confidence in my work and go to various people for confirmation that my work is good." Whereas by 1986, after several years and promotions in the ranks of her profession, and after a new marriage, she said, "Just recently, last one and a half years, I have a real sense of coming-into-my-own in my [work]. I am bursting with projects and feel able to do them." Similarly, a comparison of her wishes for the 10 years from the 1974 to 1986 questionnaires, reveals a shift in life-task priorities from the highest priority on career tasks (e.g., her first wishes in 1974 were to "Write books that are well-read and especially acclaimed. Advance rapidly through the ranks of [my profession].") to a complementary priority on interpersonal and life-style tasks (e.g., her first wishes in 1986 were to "Earn a lot of money. Move to a warm part of [the country], spend more time with my husband."). This shift in task focus does not involve a radical departure from investment in career tasks, but the emphasis has changed in ways that mirror her changing life environment.

Life tasks as avenues of growth. In searching for the precipitant of a shifting task focus over time, one hypothesis is that people find ways to set new life tasks to better reflect their underlying or pervasive personal needs. For example, those women in Stewart's (1989) study who had many career tasks in their 20's may have felt the need to work hard on intimacy by age 40. There is some suggestion of support for this rejuvenation hypothesis in these data. As noted earlier, we coded their statements about the high and low points in the past 10 years for evidence of positive and negative concern with intimacy (providing a total score of need for communion). In these data, the tendency to reflect *negatively* (but not positively) on one's experiences with intimacy over the past 10 years, was significantly associated with the setting of interpersonal life tasks for the future. Accordingly, one is tempted to claim that the focus on career and self tasks early on after college precipitated concerns about sacrifices in their interpersonal lives, and that the subsequent focus on interpersonal life tasks was in the service of achieving a better life-task balance.

Life tasks provide a relatively malleable means of working on agentic and communal personal needs, and when individuals feel unsatisfied in the expression of those needs, then changes in the structure of their life-task system may well follow if the conditions of life permit such a reallocation of energies. These shifting task systems rarely reflect the abandoning of either communal or agentic needs, but rather the reintegration of these needs in a different set of tasks that changes the balance of effort in one direction or the other. For example, when Phyllis turned her attention more vigorously to her second marriage and to the interpersonal tasks of relationship and family, her agentic concerns certainly did not vanish, but rather took a somewhat less central position—as she said, "Responsibility to my mate is now first, before career. This creates a tension. But I am more integrated into a social mainstream. Friends are married too—though not all." In this ever-changing task system, the meanings of agentic and communal needs come to change in light of the new tasks set by the individual. Phyllis' renewed commitment to her interpersonal life tasks was reflected, for example, not only in positive statements about her relationship, but also in some negative statements about her interactions in her career arena (e.g., she mentioned in her last questionnaire her troubles communicating with ill-prepared students, whereas most of her prior reports on her career were more strictly focused on her own work, and on her concerns about self-confidence). There is a close intertwining of tasks and needs, and the life structures (e.g., relationships, jobs) within which they are enacted; the entire system shifts to some degree when any one component changes.

The impetus for setting new life tasks often arises from the demands and the opportunities afforded by a current life context. This would seem to be especially true of the impact of the close relationship on the individual's motivational agenda. The interdependence entailed in a close relationship mandates a certain amount of attention to relationship life tasks (e.g., from negotiating the sharing of daily life chores to resolving conflicts over dominance), even though personal needs and orientations can make those relationship tasks seem more or less self-relevant (Clark et al., 1987; Swap & Rubin, 1983). This bottom-up chain of influence, in which participation in the relationship encourages certain interpersonal (communal) tasks to become salient, is also bolstered by the many sociocultural expectations associated with relationships. At the very least, women traditionally have assumed a variety of interpersonal tasks as a result of participation in close relationships (Malley & Stewart, 1988). Kathy, for example, expressed increasing reservations over time about the relative lack of intimacy in her life; she may well have been feeling the pressure of social expectations as well as simply becoming more interpersonally oriented through her parenting and marital tasks.

Another important facet of the dynamics of the motivational system is that working hard on particular tasks, such as "trying to understand my adolescent daughter" or "becoming close to my new husband's children," can result in the reformulation or refinement of one's fundamental personal needs, such as agency and communion. The day-to-day struggle with children can, for example, make one's need for communion more urgent or result in a sapping of energy for communion so that personal agentic strivings become more attractive. Because these rather abstract needs are given concrete meaning in light of the particular tasks encouraged by specific life contexts, the expression of these needs will be changed by a commitment to enacting them through certain tasks (e.g., whereas communion might mean sexual passion early in a relationship, it often changes meaning later on when the salient tasks are those of negotiating mutually satisfying styles of communication or of resolving conflicting values and life-style interests; see Holmes & Boon, 1990).

These dynamics place a special burden on the partners in a close relationship—the burden of keeping up with the current needs and most salient tasks of the spouse or partner. The shifting nature of task priorities and of the needs that they reflect was evident in the life patterns of many of the women in the Stewart (1989) sample. Although they often pursued relationships across the 20 years of the study, these relationships changed in meaning several times in this period, and the most apparently satisfying relationships were those in which such motivational flexibility was encouraged. Moreover, several respondents noted the importance of having partners who affirmed their tasks, and who allowed for shifting task priorities with the attendant shifts in the needs to be fulfilled in the relationship. In fact, this sharply tuned attention to the current tasks and needs of one's partner may be part of the empathy component of the "relational competence" that Hansson, Jones, and Carpenter (1984) associated with the maintenance of a healthy relationship (see also, Davis & Oathout, 1987). A key ingredient in the relationship recipe may well be individuals' recognition of opportunities to change tasks over time, to work on their relationships differently at different points in life, and to allow this flexibility for their partners as well as for themselves. A fair measure of self-validation may be derived from the responsiveness of a partner to one's new task agendas (Derlaga, 1984; Little, 1989). This negotiation process seems to implicate clearly the interdependence of a close relationship, and therefore to require an analysis of how partners react *together* to their needs and tasks.

Flexibility of Tasks and Needs in Close Relationships

As Reis and Shaver (1988) have pointed out, a critical component of intimacy is the feeling of mutual validation of each partner's central needs and interests by the other, and this reciprocal validation becomes a key task in a close relationship (Berg, 1984). Partners in a relationship can go a long way toward affirming (or invalidating) their partner's needs by defining the relationship so as to include (or exclude) the relevant tasks. If one spouse works hard to create a busy social life for the couple and the partner shrinks from engaging in that arena, then to the extent that the spouse depends on the relationship for intimacy tasks, he or she is likely to feel quite frustrated and invalidated in this relationship. The relationship has to provide an avenue for both partners to enact their central tasks, either in the course of their day-to-day interactions or by providing the partner with the time and freedom to work on his or her tasks in other places and with other people. This kind of mutual regard and support for each others' tasks can create a foundation of caring and responsiveness in a relationship that many have suggested to be more critical to intimacy than the exchange of tangible resources (see Holmes & Boon, 1990). In Harvey, Agostineli, and Weber's (1989) analyses of couple's retro-spective accounts of the failures in their relationships, the absence of shared interests and of compatible definitions of the relationship were central themes in couples' dissatisfactions. It is hard to feel close to someone when you do not like what he or she spends time on, or when what he or she is trying to accomplish makes little sense in terms of your definition of the relationship.

In building intimacy in a close relationship, thought needs to be given to understanding each other's working model of the relationship—the goals and tasks for self and other in the relationship. Acitelli (1988) has developed an interesting perspective on this process of intimacy building that emphasizes the constructive role of "relationship awareness." She suggested that, although men and women often differ in when and how much they like to talk about their relationships, both partners in a close relationship do benefit from heightened awareness of the habitual dynamics in their interactions. Similarly, the growing literature on attributional reasoning in close relationships focuses on the rela-tional attributions that partners provide as explanations for good and bad events in the relationship (Fincham, 1985; Howe, 1987; Newman, 1981). We would only add here that a constructive part of this metacommunication about the relationship would be some effort directed at arriving at an understanding of what each partner is doing, is trying to do, and is trying to change in the relationship, as well as some continued assessment of how supportive each partner is of the other's tasks (Little, 1989).

In many recent reviews of the literature on close relationships, theorists have argued that intimacy derives not so much from the specific exchange of rewards or the equity in duties in the relationship, but rather from the balancing of mutual regard and responsiveness over relatively long periods of time (Holmes & Boon, 1990). In our view, a central feature of this longer term equity is that the partners each have the opportunity to balance multiple needs, perhaps best viewed as agentic and communal in content, through the enactment of a variety of life tasks in the course of the relationship. A parent may newly invest in care giving as a grandparent, and a grandparent may find avenues for career tasks that were not available as a parent (Block, 1973). Whereas it may be hard to focus with equal vigor on different task arenas at once, over the years of a relationship individuals ought to feel that it is possible to work on new tasks both within and outside the bounds of the partnership.

LINKING TASKS AND NEEDS
TO COGNITION IN CLOSE RELATIONSHIPS

Our analysis of tasks and needs in close relationships has focused on the fit between an individual's personal needs and the life tasks that he or she can enact within a current relationship, and on the tendency to balance communal and agentic needs over time through life tasks in a relationship. At the core of this discussion is the assumption that close relationships are open to alternative construals (Kelly, 1955) as to the central needs to be satisfied and the tasks through which fulfillment is achieved. We assume that the set of feasible tasks in relationships is defined largely by the age-related and gender-differentiated demands of particular cultures. Individuals work within those social prescriptions, shaping an approach to relationships that serves their personal needs.

The process of shaping and enacting personally satisfying life tasks in close relationships is dynamic and interpersonal, but also involves a great deal of cognitive activity. People think about their relationships in a variety of ways (e.g., as security for achievement strivings, as the basis for communal satisfaction, as arenas for power). Life tasks represent the self-articulated bridge between personal needs and the structured elements of a relationship that provides the orienting framework for the individual. The individual's tasks for the relationship reflect his or her pressing personal needs, the interpretation that he or she has given to social prescriptions for intimacy, and the opportunities that he or she sees for pursuing intimacy, however defined, within current circumstances. The life task is an orienting framework that summarizes what the individual sees should be done in a relationship.

Individuals' life tasks in relationships frequently serve multiple purposes. On one hand, they complement or reflect consistent and pervasive personal needs (e.g., for the individual high in the need for intimacy, the task in a relationship is to preserve open channels of communication and reciprocal care giving). The life tasks specify those needs by showing how to enact them in current life contexts. Individuals high in need for intimacy will become experts in the task of giving and receiving social support; they will think automatically of the needs and desires of their partners, attending to subtle indications of hurt feelings or momentary flashes of anger. Life tasks are highly accessible recipes for relating to partners, that selectively and often automatically channel attention, interpretations, and evaluations in ways that fit personal needs.

Life tasks also represent the growth-promoting side of individuals' motivation and cognition in relationships. When we think about our relationships we focus not only on what we typically do in them (or on how they have gone in the past), but also on what we potentially could do in the future. Tasks represent dynamic beliefs that define plans for new ways of relating to others. In this sense, when people think and talk about their goals for relationships they intentionally deliberate on alternative tasks (e.g., "Should I put my effort into being more communicative, or should I just learn to accept her need for privacy?"). This more deliberate cognitive work on relationships is encouraged by unsatisfied needs and involves the construction of new life tasks to be enacted in a relationship. It is in this way that life tasks bring motivation and cognition most closely together as people mentally simulate their new tasks, mentally experiencing the satisfaction of personal needs in novel ways, and guiding their behavior perhaps one step closer to an ideal for the relationship.

The literature on cognition in close relationships tells us all too little about how much of people's thoughts and attention serves to automatically confirm prior needs, goals, and expectancies, and how much deliberate cognitive effort is expended to shape new alternatives for intimacy. The life-task construct can serve a heuristic function in encouraging analysis of both the self-confirming (need-fulfilling) and the self-changing (need-reformulating) cognitive efforts of individuals in close relationships. We look to future research to continue to build bridges across the motivation-cognition gap in the study of interpersonal processes.

ACKNOWLEDGMENTS

Preparation of this chapter was supported by a National Science foundation grant (BNS87-18467), and reflects collaborative research with Abigail Stewart and Elizabeth Vandewater, and with Carol Cook-Flannagan, William Fleeson, Christopher Langston, Julie Norem, and Sabrina Zirkel. We wish to thank Nancy Exelby for technical assistance in preparation of the paper and the editors Frank Fincham and Garth Fletcher for their comments on an earlier version.

REFERENCES

Acitelli, L. K. (1988). When spouses talk to each other about their relationship. *Journal of Social and Personal Relationships, 5,* 185–199.

Bakan, D. (1966). *The duality of human existence.* Boston: Beacon Press.

Berg, J. H. (1984). The development of friendship between roommates. *Journal of Personality and Social Psychology, 46,* 346–356.

Berscheid, E., Snyder, M., & Omoto, A. M. (1989). Issues in studying close relationships: Conceptualizing and measuring closeness. In C. Hendrick (Ed.), *Close relationships* (pp. 63–91). Newbury Park, CA: Sage.

Block, J. H. (1973). Conceptions of sex role: Some cross-cultural and longitudinal perspectives. *American Psychologist, 28,* 512–526.

Cantor, N., & Kihlstrom, J. F. (1987). *Personality and social intelligence.* Englewood Cliffs, NJ: Prentice Hall.

Cantor, N., & Langston, C. A. (1989). "Ups and downs" of life tasks in a life transition. In L. A. Pervin (Ed.), *Goal concepts in personality and social psychology* (pp. 127–168). Hillsdale, NJ: Erlbaum.

Cantor, N., Norem, J., Langston, C., Zirkel, S., Fleeson, W., & Cook-Flannagan, C. (1991). Life tasks and daily life experience. *Journal of Personality,* Special issue on daily events and personality.

Cantor, N., & Zirkel, S. (1990). Personality, cognition, and purposive behavior. In L. A. Pervin (Ed.), *Handbook of personality: Theory and research* (pp. 135–164). New York: Guilford Press.

Clark, M. S., Muchant, C. B., Ouellette, R., Powell, M., & Milberg, S. (1987). Relationship type, recipient mood, and helping. *Journal of Personality and Social Psychology, 53,* 94–103.

Clark, M. S., & Reis, H. T. (1988). Interpersonal processes in close relationships. *Annual Review of Psychology, 39,* 609–672.

Davis, M. H., & Oathout, H. A. (1987). Maintenance of satisfaction in romantic relationships: Empathy and relational competence. *Journal of Personality and Social Psychology, 53,* 397–410.

Derlega, V. J. (1984). Self-disclosure and intimate relationships. In V. J. Derlega (Ed.), *Communication, intimacy, and close relationships* (pp. 1–9). New York: Academic Press.

Eidelson, R. J., & Epstein, N. (1982). Cognition and relationship maladjustment: Development of a measure of dysfunctional relationship beliefs. *Journal of Consulting and Clinical Psychology, 50,* 715–720.

Emmons, R. A. (1989). Exploring the relationship between motives and traits: The case of narcissism. In D. M. Buss & N. Cantor (Eds.), *Personality psychology: Recent trends and emerging directions* (pp. 32–44). New York: Springer-Verlag.

Emmons, R. A., & King, L. A. (1988). Conflict among personal strivings: Immediate and long-term implications for psychological and physical well-being. *Journal of Personality and Social Psychology, 54,* 1040–1048.

Erber, R., & Fiske, S. T. (1984). Outcome dependency and attention to inconsistent information. *Journal of Personality and Social Psychology, 47,* 709–726.

Erikson, E. H. (1950). *Childhood and society.* New York: Norton.

Fincham, F. D. (1985). Attribution processes in distressed and nondistressed couples: 2. Responsibility for marital problems. *Journal of Abnormal Psychology, 94,* 183–190.

Fincham, F. D., Bradbury, T. N., & Scott, C. K. (1990). Cognition in marriage. In F. D. Fincham & T. N. Bradbury (Eds.), *The psychology of marriage* (pp. 118–149). New York: Guilford Press.

Fletcher, G. J. O., Fincham, F. D., Cramer, L., & Heron, N. (1987). The role of attributions in the development of dating relationships. *Journal of Personality and Social Psychology, 53,* 481–489.

Freud, S. (1961/1930). *Civilization and its discontent.* In Vol. 21 of the Standard Edition. London: Hogarth.

Hansson, R. O., Jones, W. H., & Carpenter, B. N. (1984). Relational competence and social support. In P. Shaver (Ed.), *Review of personality and social psychology, emotions, relationships, and health* (pp. 265–284). Beverly Hills, CA: Sage.

Harvey, J., Agostineli, G., & Weber, A. (1989). Account-making and the formation of expectations about close relationships. In C. Hendrich (Ed.), *Review of personality & social psychology* (Vol. 10, pp. 39–62). Newbury Park, CA: Sage.

Havighurst, R. J. (1953). *Human development and education.* New York: Longmans, Green.

Hazan, C., & Shaver, P. (1987). Romantic love conceptualized as an attachment process. *Journal of Personality and Social Psychology, 52,* 511–524.

Holmes, J. G., & Boon, S. D. (1990). Developments in the field of close relationships: Creating foundations for intervention strategies. *Personality and Social Psychology Bulletin, 16,* 23–41.

Howe, G. W. (1987). Attributions of complex cause and the perception of marital conflict. *Journal of Personality and Social Psychology, 53,* 1119–1128.

Kelley, H. H., Berscheid, E., Christensen, A., Harvey, J. H., Huston, T. L., Levinger, G., McClintock, E., Peplau, L. A., & Peterson, D. R. (1983). *Close relationships.* New York: Freeman.

Kelly, G. (1955). *The psychology of personal constructs.* New York: Norton.

Klinger, E. (1977). *Meaning and void: Inner experience and the incentives in people's lives.* Minneapolis: University of Minnesota Press.

Klinger, E., Barta, S. G., & Maxeiner, M. E. (1980). Motivational correlates of thought content frequency and commitment. *Journal of Personality and Social Psychology, 39,* 1222–1237.

Langston, C. A., & Cantor, N. (1989). Social anxiety and social constraint: When "making friends" is hard. *Journal of Personality and Social Psychology, 56,* 649–661.

Levinson, D. J. (1978). *The seasons of a man's life.* New York: Ballantine.

Little, B. (1983). Personal projects: A rationale and methods for investigation. *Environment and Behavior, 15,* 273–309.

Little, B. (1989). Personal projects analysis: Trivial pursuits, magnificent obsessions and the search for coherence. In D. M. Buss & N. Cantor (Eds.), *Personality psychology: Recent trends and emerging directions* (pp. 15–31). New York: Springer-Verlag.

Malley, J. E. (1989). *The balance of agency and communion: Adjustment and adaptation in single parents.* Unpublished doctoral dissertation, Boston University.

Malley, J. E., & Stewart, A. J. (1988). Women's work and family roles: Sources of stress and sources of strength. In S. Fisher & J. Reason (Eds.), *Handbook of life stress, cognition, and health* (pp. 175–192). London: Wiley.

Markus, H., & Nurius, P. (1986). Possible selves. *American Psychologist, 41*(9), 954–969.

McAdams, D. P. (1984). Human motives and personal relationships. In V. J. Derlega (Ed.), *Communication, intimacy, and close relationships* (pp. 41–70). New York: Academic Press.

McAdams, D. P. (1985). *Power, intimacy and the life story: Personological inquiries into identity.* Homewood, IL: Dorsey Press.

McAdams, D. P., & Constantian, C. A. (1983). Intimacy and affiliation motives in daily living: An experience sampling analysis. *Journal of Personality and Social Psychology, 45,* 851–861.

McAdams, D. P., & Vaillant, G. E. (1982). Intimacy motivation and psychosocial adjustment: A longitudinal study. *Journal of Personality Assessment, 46,* 586–593.

Murray, H. A. (1938). *Explorations in personality.* New York: Oxford University Press.

Murray Research Center of Radcliffe College. (1988). *Index to the data resources.* Cambridge, MA.

Newman, H. (1981). Communication within ongoing intimate relationships: An attributional perspective. *Personality and Social Psychology Bulletin, 7,* 59–70.

Parsons, T., & Bales, R. F. (1955). *Family, socialization and intervention process.* Glencoe, IL: Free Press.

Pervin, L. (Ed.). (1989). *Goal concepts in personality and social psychology.* Hillsdale, NJ: Erlbaum.

Read, S. J., & Miller, L. C. (1989). Interpersonalism: Towards a goal-based theory of persons and relationships. In L. Pervin (Ed.), *Goal concepts in personality and social psychology* (pp. 413–472). Hillsdale, NJ: Erlbaum.

Reis, H. T., & Shaver, P. (1988). Intimacy as an interpersonal process. In S. Duck (Ed.), *Handbook of personal relationships: Theory, relationships and interventions* (pp. 367–389). New York: Wiley.

Rubin, L. R. (1983). *Intimate strangers.* New York: Harper & Row.

Schlenker, B. R., & Weigold, M. F. (1989). Goals and the self-identification process: Constructing desired identities. In L. A. Pervin (Ed.), *Goal concepts in personality and social psychology* (pp. 243–290). Hillsdale, NJ: Erlbaum.

Stewart, A. J. (1986, November). *Social change and individual change in women's lives.* Paper presented at a conference on Women's Development at Mount Holyoke College, South Hadley, MA.

Stewart, A. J. (1989). Social intelligence and adaptation to life changes. In R. S. Wyer & T. K. Srull (Eds.), *Advances in social cognition* (Vol. 2, pp. 187–196). Hillsdale, NJ: Erlbaum.

Swap, W. C., & Rubin, J. Z. (1983). Measurement of interpersonal orientation. *Journal of Personality and Social Psychology, 44,* 208–219.

5
A Contextual Model for Advancing the Study of Marital Interaction

Thomas N. Bradbury
University of California, Los Angeles

Frank D. Fincham
University of Illinois

In their book, *Communication, Conflict, and Marriage,* Raush, Barry, Hertel, and Swain (1974) expressed strong discontent with the theoretical and methodological inadequacies that characterized prevailing research on marriage. Their study, noteworthy for its emphasis on observational rather than self-report assessments of interpersonal behavior, played a significant role in bringing about a new tradition of research on marriage in which the primary focus was on the overt behaviors exhibited by spouses in interaction. As a result of more than a decade of research conducted within this tradition, much is known about the behavioral correlates of marital dissatisfaction (see Christensen, 1987; Noller & Fitzpatrick, 1990; Weiss & Heyman, 1990) and about the impact that clinical modification of these behaviors can have on marital functioning (see Beach & Bauserman, 1990; Hahlweg & Markman, 1988).

Although the empirical aspect of the Raush et al. study stands as an enduring contribution, the theory underlying this work, which emphasized covert factors in marital interaction at least as much as overt factors, has received far less attention. An essential feature of this theory is the concept of *object relations schemata,* defined as

> organizing structures for experiential events. Schemata determine the meanings of events and the contingencies they have for thoughts, feelings, and actions. Object relations schemata develop from experiences with others; they organize images of oneself and others and the relations between oneself and others. . . . What is communicated between interaction partners depends on object relations schemata. (1974, p. 49)

The significance of highlighting the differential impact of the empirical and theoretical facets of the Raush et al. (1974) volume derives from recent developments in the study of marriage. Specifically, following demonstration of a robust association between overt behavior and marital satisfaction, there has been a growing realization that a complete account of marital interaction requires analysis of the affective and cognitive processes that accompany observable behaviors. Studies addressing these processes represent the beginning of a *mediational tradition* of research on marriage (Bradbury & Fincham, 1989; see also Glick & Gross, 1975; Gurman & Knudson, 1978; Margolin, 1983) in which greater emphasis is being placed on thoughts and feelings pertinent to marital interaction and marital quality. With this important development, it is clear that the study of marriage has arrived at a juncture long ago advocated by Raush and his colleagues. However, whereas Raush et al. provided little direct data with which to support or refute their theoretical position, the current situation appears to be marked by a wealth of provocative data that could benefit from greater conceptual guidance.

We offer in the present chapter a conceptual analysis to guide mediational research on marriage. In doing so, we elaborate upon the large body of research on overt behavior in marriage in order to begin working toward a more comprehensive view of the affective and cognitive underpinnings of marital interaction. The chapter is organized into three sections. In the first we discuss the rationale for a model that includes, but is not restricted to, overt behavioral aspects of marriage, and we then present a framework within which the behavioral data can be understood. Although it would be reasonable to propose that the theory posited by Raush et al. could be used in this regard, we maintain that their formulation requires further specification if it is to organize existing research and guide future data collection and, moreover, that it can be enriched with the advances made in the study of marriage over the past two decades. The second section is an attempt to apply our model to reinterpret existing research findings and to direct future research efforts for understanding marital interaction and dysfunction. The chapter concludes with a summary and overview, where we highlight major themes of the chapter and identify some of its limitations.

A CONTEXTUAL MODEL OF MARITAL INTERACTION

Rationale for an Expanded Conception of Marital Interaction

Introduction of any competing framework for understanding marital interaction requires examination of existing frameworks and a justification for any modifications that are made to them. Many factors make this a difficult task (e.g., much of the thinking about marital interaction has not been formalized into models), yet it is possible to extract some basic premises that have guided past research on marital interaction and to evaluate them in light of relevant data. Most salient among these is the view that distressed couples, compared to nondistressed couples, engage in interactions that are characterized by a higher rate of negative behaviors and a greater likelihood that negative behaviors will be reciprocated; opposite, albeit weaker, associations are sometimes posited for positive behaviors. These behavioral tendencies are also hypothesized to be a major *causal* agent in spouses' judgments of their marital quality.

Numerous cross-sectional studies present data consistent with the first of the above hypotheses, as distressed couples have been found to exhibit and reciprocate negative behavior at rates higher than those found for their nondistressed counterparts (for reviews, see Christensen, 1987; Schaap, 1984; Weiss & Heyman, 1990). In contrast, few studies have focused on the possible causal impact of behavior on marital quality, and their results are less compelling. Filsinger and Thoma (1988), for example, conducted observational coding of couples' interactions and examined the associations between the coded behaviors and spouses' later judgments of marital adjustment. Although higher rates of females' interruptions were consistent predictors of lower levels of males' marital adjustment up to 5 years later, the authors observed that "generally there were no significant relationships between behavioral predictors at Time 1 and dyadic adjustment at Times 2, 3, 4, and 5" (p. 792). Most notable in their absence were associations between base rates of negative behavior, reciprocity of negative behavior, and later marital adjustment.

A similar study by Gottman and Krokoff (1989) revealed the expected cross-sectional associations between coded behavior and marital satisfaction, but found that these associations were reversed when changes in marital satisfaction over a 3-year period were predicted. Thus, higher levels of negative behaviors were related concurrently to lower levels of marital quality and to *increases* in marital quality over time (although this latter effect failed to reach significance for wives' behavior), and higher levels of wives' positive verbal behaviors were related concurrently to higher levels of marital quality and to *decreases* in marital quality over time (see *Longitudinal Analyses of Interaction*, below).

In sum, a wealth of cross-sectional data support a model linking maladaptive overt behavior to lower levels of marital quality, yet recent longitudinal data make it difficult to sustain a model whereby maladaptive behavioral tendencies (e.g., more negative behavior, less positive behavior) are expected to exert a causal influence upon declines in marital quality. Although these longitudinal findings are not without limitations (e.g., they are based on small samples; no follow-up assessments of behavior were undertaken so as to determine the effect of satisfaction on later behavior), they do offer a clear rationale for proposing a model of marital interaction that extends beyond overt behavioral phenomena.

Specifically, it appears that any causal effect of behavior on marital quality is probably not straightforward and, even if it were, nevertheless would leave unanswered the question of how behavior exerts this effect.

We must emphasize that our calling for an extension of the behavioral perspective is by no means a novel proposal, as many writers in the clinical and empirical literatures have commented upon the limitations of such a narrow conception of marriage, especially in view of data indicating that (a) it is the nonverbal aspect of behavior rather than the content of speech that is most powerful in distinguishing distressed and nondistressed couples (e.g., Gottman, 1979), thus suggesting that the findings for overt behavior are masking potent affective variables, and that (b) spouses typically have quite different impressions of the events in their marriage (e.g., Jacobson & Moore, 1981), thus suggesting that cognitive variables are also highly influential in the course of marital interaction. Despite this common realization, however, the study of marital interaction is marked by "the absence of a dominant, coherent theoretical model" (Snyder, 1989, p. 3), and hence there is a pressing need to outline a framework that formalizes some of the recommendations that have been made for infusing the overt behavioral model with much greater attention to covert factors. Thus, while the field has moved well beyond an exclusively behavioral formulation of marriage, the directions it has taken are many and in need of organization.

Two points bear noting before we attempt to provide some of this needed organization. First, justification for expanding the behavioral formulation of marriage comes not only from behavioral data that appear at odds with that approach but also from findings that point to cognitive or other nonbehavioral variables which explain variance in marital quality, especially *changes* in marital quality. Nonbehavioral data of this sort, which supplement the argument advanced in this section, are described in later sections in order to address the issue of *how* a behavioral conception is best expanded. Second, the framework described here shares some features with the influential perspective on close relationships presented by Kelley et al. (1983, chap. 2), a necessary consequence of the broadly inclusive nature of the Kelley et al. model. The two approaches differ in significant ways, however, and we refer the reader to a discussion of these differences in Bradbury and Fincham (1989).

Overview of the Contextual Model

Among the most impressive features of marriage are, first, that almost every adult in the United States marries and, second, that the proportion of marriages ending in divorce is about 1 in 2 (Cherlin, 1981). It is these factors, together with the corollary observation that many nondivorcing spouses are discontented with their marriages, that justify careful conceptual and empirical examination of marital interaction and its relation to marital dysfunction. An equally impressive aspect of marriage is that it is exceedingly complex and thus requires consideration of many interrelated phenomena if it is to be understood. Rather than begin addressing this complexity by identifying a single class of related variables and determining their relation with marital quality (e.g., as was done typically in the behavioral tradition), we instead attempt to identify a small set of components that we believe capture, directly or indirectly, the essential features of marital interaction. Each component of the model itself represents a host of variables and processes, and taken together they may facilitate a more comprehensive portrayal of how marriages become better or worse. (For related presentations of the contextual model, see Bradbury & Fincham, 1987a, 1988b, 1989; and Fincham, Bradbury, & Grych, 1990).[1]

As shown in Fig. 5.1, five components for each of two spouses are proposed as necessary for understanding marital interaction. First, a spouse, who we will designate arbitrarily as the wife, engages in the *processing* of some stimulus, which is usually some event in the environment (processed via path a) or, perhaps more specifically, a *behavior* enacted by the husband (processed via path b). The processing stage involves a series of events (not shown in Fig. 5.1) that serve to impart meaning to the husband's behavior, beginning with an attentional/perceptual step that is followed by a step in which the wife extracts information from the incoming stimulus and forms some representation of it. We propose that this processing takes place along three dimensions, indicating the degree to which the behavior is positive versus negative, expected versus unexpected, and personally insignificant versus personally significant (see Bradbury & Fincham, 1987a). To the extent that evaluation of the stimulus yields a judgment indicating that it is positive or neutral, expected, and/or personally low in significance, the wife will consider some response alternatives and enact a behavior of her own (via path c) at that point. To the extent that evaluation of the stimulus yields a judgment indicating that it is negative, unexpected, and/or personally high in significance, the wife may have a globally negative affective response that may become specified further on the basis of the results of an attributional search. In this search the wife will identify a cause for the stimulus and seek possibly to assign responsibility for it; and on the basis of that interpretation, she will consider some response alternatives and enact one of them (again via path c). (See Fletcher & Fincham, this volume.) In either of these two cases (i.e., without and with additional processing), the resulting behavior will be accessible to the husband (via path b) and will serve in turn as a stimulus that the husband will process, which will lead in turn to his enacting a behavior (via path c), which the wife will process, and so on. This notion can be specified

---

[1]Although the contextual model is presented here in terms pertaining to marriage, we believe it is equally applicable to the many sorts of relationships in which dyadic interaction takes place. Our emphasis on the contextual model as it applies to the marital dyad stems from an ultimate interest in identifying factors that may give rise to marital dysfunction, so that it may be prevented or treated in clinical settings.

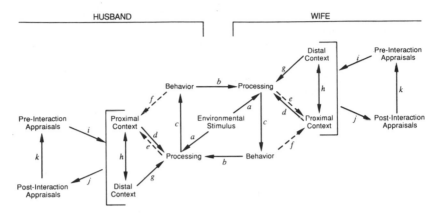

FIG. 5.1.   The Contextual Model of Marital Interaction. According to the model, a spouse processes an environmental stimulus (via path a) and/or a partner behavior (via path b), and that processing leads to the spouse's own behavior (via path c) which is then subject to processing by the partner. Processing is influenced by transient thoughts and feelings (via path d) that comprise the proximal context, which is updated frequently in the course of an interaction by feedback from the processing of partner behaviors (via path e) and by the spouse's reflections upon his or her behavior (via path f). Processing is influenced also by relatively stable psychological features of the spouse (via path g) that comprise the distal context, which is related bidirectionally to the proximal context (via path h). In addition, thoughts and feelings before an interaction, shown here as pre-interaction appraisals, will influence the course of the interaction (via path i), and events during the interaction will influence thoughts and feelings after an interaction (via path j), shown here as post-interaction appraisals. Finally, appraisals following one interaction will determine, in part, the nature of appraisals before a subsequent interaction (via path k). For clarity, depiction of the model has been simplified, especially in the processing stage; see text for further details.

further by noting that spouse behavior will have a public aspect (e.g., speech, facial movements, posture, gestures) and a corresponding private aspect (e.g., thoughts, feelings, physiology), and that it is the public aspect which will initiate most directly the partner's response.

The processing stage, which occurs very rapidly and typically without conscious awareness, is influenced by two other components or general classes of variables. One such component is the *proximal context,* which includes the transient, momentary thoughts and feelings that the wife experiences (usually as a result of prior events in the interaction); these thoughts and feelings provide an immediate frame within which each new partner behavior is processed (via path d). A spouse's proximal context is updated frequently in the course of an interaction, on the basis of his or her processing of partner behavior and environmental events (via path e) and the behaviors that he or she has enacted (via path f); for clarity, these two feedback paths are represented as dashed lines in Fig. 5.1.

A second component proposed to influence the processing stage (via path g) is the *distal context,* which, in contrast to the proximal context, includes relatively intransient, stable psychological characteristics of the spouse. Elements in the distal context, which are themselves interrelated, include personality and temperament; chronic mood states, expectations, goals, and rules for the relationship; beliefs about how relationships should function; and representations of the self, prior relationships, the partner, and the marriage. The distal context and the proximal context are themselves related bidirectionally (via path h), indicating that stable aspects of an individual are related to his or her thoughts and feelings within the interaction, and that stable aspects of an individual can change as a function of those thoughts and feelings.

This network of four components is embedded within a fifth and final component, which pertains to the *appraisals* that spouses make before and after their interactions. These appraisals influence (via path i), and are influenced by (via path j), the proximal and distal contexts, and thus affect indirectly the processing of behavior. Appraisals can be spontaneous thoughts or feelings or responses to environmental stimuli, and they can be either marital or nonmarital in focus. In addition, post-interaction appraisals from one interaction can influence pre-interaction appraisals before a subsequent interaction (via path k).

To summarize, because existing longitudinal data do not support the simple hypothesis that maladaptive behavior accounts for declines in marital quality, we argued for a model of marriage that includes but is not limited to behavior and marital satisfaction. We then described the basic components of a contextual model of marital interaction in which the partner's behavior in interaction is processed by the spouse, and that processing is qualified by responses to prior events in the interaction and by stable psychological features of the processing spouse (e.g., marital satisfaction). These events themselves influence, and are influenced by, the thoughts and feelings that spouses bring to an interaction and their reactions following interaction. An important next step of our presentation is to assess the degree to which such a formulation permits clarification of existing research and identification of new topics for study.

RESEARCH IMPLICATIONS OF THE CONTEXTUAL MODEL

The model outlined in the previous section is intended to facilitate an understanding of marital interaction and dysfunction. In this section we attempt to accomplish this task more directly by demonstrating how the model integrates existing findings and offers directions for new research. To simplify this task, several marital research domains are discussed, and in each case a review of findings is combined with suggestions for how those topics might be explored in the future. However, coverage of existing research will be selective rather than exhaustive, and where possible, attention will be given to studies that permit some degree of causal inference to be made.

Longitudinal Analyses of Interaction

Earlier we described a study by Gottman and Krokoff (1989) in which higher rates of negative behavior were related to lower levels of concurrent marital satisfaction but to increases in marital satisfaction over 3 years (although this only approached significance for wives). The cross-sectional findings mesh well with the large literature on marital interaction but leave unanswered the question of why behavior and satisfaction might be related. The contextual model (see Fig. 5.1) indicates that the processing stage is a critical intermediate step in this association, and research that begins to examine the processing stage is examined in the next section. In contrast, the longitudinal findings are unique in the marital literature and hence await replication, particularly in light of methodological uncertainties (e.g., small sample, low ratio of subjects to variables, uncertain clinical significance of changes in marital satisfaction, use of groups having extreme marital satisfaction scores; cf. Woody & Costanzo, 1990). If the validity of these results is granted, however, they raise the specific question of how negative behaviors lead to improvements in marriage as well as the general question of how events in marital interaction lead to changes in elements of the distal context, especially marital satisfaction. It is this general question with which we will be most concerned with here.

According to the contextual model, the behaviors that a spouse exhibits and the partner behaviors that she processes lead to changes in her transient thoughts and feelings, or proximal context (via paths e and f, respectively). Following an interaction the spouse will make appraisals of what has occurred (via path j) and, especially if the interaction was a negative one, those appraisals may yield unfavorable feelings and judgments about the marriage. Appraisals of this sort may in turn lead her (via path k) to approach a subsequent interaction with the expectation that her partner will be critical or unsupportive (via path i), such that her proximal (and possibly distal) context will predispose her to process partner behaviors in a negative fashion (via path d). This may lead to a confirmation of her earlier appraisal and, over time, to a stable belief that her marriage is unsatisfying (via path h) which will in turn influence later processing of partner behavior (via path g).

This series of events can be restated as follows: Spouses learn on the basis of their interactions and the appraisals that follow from them whether or not they are in a rewarding relationship, and this judgment influences later interactions. This learning is especially significant if it takes place in the context of *conflict,* which can be defined as perceived incompatibility of goals (see Fincham & Bradbury, 1991). Thus, if spouses engage in conflictual discussions and are left feeling threatened, unfairly criticized, hurt, and unsupported, they will approach subsequent interactions with the belief that they will be similarly destructive. They will eventually learn, or realize, that their marriage is not fulfilling their needs. On the other hand, if couples engage in conflicts and leave them feeling understood, appreciated, and respected (or at least *not* grossly misunderstood, unappreciated, and disrespected) and as though "the air has been cleared," then subsequent interactions will not begin in the face of biased proximal and distal contexts and spouses will gradually come to realize that the marriage can be a rewarding one. It follows that those couples who avoid conflict never have the opportunity to know whether theirs is a marriage that can "weather storms" and that those who engage in conflict routinely (and/or have more sources of conflict) will learn more quickly that their marriage is unhappy, barring the operation of strong processes to the contrary (e.g., a spouse's distal belief that conflict is a way the partner expresses his affection and that this is reasonable and satisfying for her).

Returning briefly to the results reported by Gottman and Krokoff (1989), we might infer from the foregoing argument that some spouses were able to exit their conflictual interactions with the belief that the conflict would not threaten the fabric of their marriage. Indeed, the realization that the marriage could withstand potentially damaging interactions may have contributed to the increases in satisfaction that were obtained. Although this would seem to be a surprising accomplishment in a sample comprised of a substantial proportion of distressed couples, the fact that couples had been married on average almost 24 years suggests that they had already learned quite well that they could withstand considerable conflict. Thus, replication of this study using a younger sample (i.e., couples who have not yet had as much experience with conflict) should yield a very different set of findings. Such a study should also include assessment of (a) interaction at several points in time to determine the extent to which behavior is a function of earlier satisfaction, and of (b) variables known to be highly correlated with satisfaction (e.g., depression) to determine whether they are contributing to longitudinal change.

In sum, we argue from the perspective afforded by the contextual model that spouses' judgments about their marital quality are a function of their accumulated experiences during and after interaction, especially interaction that involves perceived conflict in goals. Such a learning-based mechanism, which is undoubtedly influenced by many factors (e.g., environmental stressors, personality, experience in prior relationships) and which is not inconsistent with recent longitudinal findings, may aid in understanding how interactional events come to influence relationship judgments.

On-Line Judgments of Behavior

As noted in the previous section, the association between behavior and marital satisfaction leads naturally to the question of why these constructs are related, and the contextual model that we have outlined implicates the processing stage (and other components in the model to which it is linked) as a central factor in this association. To reiterate, the processing stage involves an attentional-perceptual step, followed by the formation of a representation of selected aspects of the partner's behavior, and an affective response. Then, depending upon the evaluation of that representation (i.e., along dimensions of positive versus negative, expected versus unexpected, and personally insignificant versus personally significant), behavior will follow directly or will follow an attributional judgment. It is possible that maritally distressed and nondistressed couples differ in any or all of these steps within the processing stage (or, of course, in none of them).

Recognizing the importance of the events interposed between spouses' behaviors, Gottman et al. (1976) devised a structured interaction task whereby every exchanged message was rated for its intended impact by the spouse who sent it and for its actual impact by the spouse who received it. All judgments were made on a 5-point scale ranging from very positive to very negative, and discrepancies between the intended impact of messages and their actual impact was examined among satisfied and dissatisfied couples. Results from this and subsequent "talk-table" studies typically show that spouses from both groups send messages with positive intended impact but that messages of distressed spouses are received with a negative actual impact (for a review, see Bradbury & Fincham, 1987b). Early studies suggested also that these judgments would be predictive of later satisfaction, although this possibility has now been called into question (see Markman, Duncan, Storaasli, & Howes, 1987).

In terms of the contextual model, this procedure requires spouses to attend to a partner behavior (path b), report on one of the steps within the processing stage (i.e., the globally positive versus negative quality of the partner's message), to behave presumably on the basis of that processing (via path c), and then to report on one aspect of their proximal context (i.e., the intended impact of their own message, path f). The assumption is that one element in the distal context, namely marital satisfaction, will influence one aspect of the processing stage (via path g).

Juxtaposing the talk-table procedure and the contextual model suggests a variety of directions for research. First, surprisingly little is known about the attentional and perceptual characteristics of spouses in interaction (see Fletcher & Kininmonth, this volume). The significance of this issue and how it might be studied have been treated at length elsewhere (Bradbury & Fincham, 1989) and we refer the reader to that discussion. Second, the contextual model makes salient the fact that nearly all research using the talk table addresses the relation between the intended impact of the behavior emitted by one spouse and the perceived intent of that behavior by the partner, an analytic approach that neglects the link between the processing stage and the processing spouse's own behavior (path c). This link is likely to be critically important because it is presumed that happily married spouses are somehow able to process, or edit, incoming negative behavior in a way that does not lead to its reciprocation, whereas distressed spouses possess this ability to a lesser degree and hence exhibit longer behavioral sequences marked by negative reciprocity.

Preliminary, albeit indirect, evidence of such *cognitive editing* was reported by Gottman (1979), who found that, whereas nearly all spouses were likely to reciprocate negative partner behavior, happily married wives proved to be the exception to this rule; they did not exhibit negative behavior after expressing a negative nonverbal reaction while listening to their husbands. Notarius, Benson, Sloane, Vanzetti, and Hornyak (1989) subsequently examined this process directly by conducting a standard talk-table study in which the link between spouses' perceived impact ratings and their own behavior (i.e., path c) was also examined. As anticipated, given that a negative partner behavior had been evaluated as negative by the receiving spouse, nondistressed wives were more likely to respond with a positive behavior than were distressed wives.

Apart from the observation that it appears to happen most among happily married wives, there are few clues as to why editing occurs. The contextual model suggests some possibilities in this regard. In terms of the processing stage, happily married wives may reciprocate negative behaviors less because they make attributions that are more benign (see next section) or because they are able to separate a negative evaluation of partner behavior from a judgment that it is self-relevant. In terms of the proximal context, happily married wives may be more sensitive to subtle changes in negativity, such that when a series of negative behaviors of decreasing intensity are exhibited by the husband she recognizes this shift and responds favorably. In terms of the distal context, happily married wives may recognize that the husbands' negative behaviors have not led to problems in the past (e.g., no post-interaction appraisals marked by strong negative affect) and thus they are able to discount them (e.g., in the processing stage), or they may have less experience with negative relationship events and hence have fewer negative associations with the behaviors, or they may possess the belief that "being argumentative never really solves anything."

In sum, studies using the talk-table procedure help to illuminate one aspect of the processing stage, which in turn has afforded a more thorough understanding of the association between negative reciprocity and marital dysfunction. There are few explanations for why happily married wives tend not to reciprocate negative behaviors, and we have attempted to show that the contextual model can serve as a source of hypotheses for this phenomenon. Nevertheless, we conclude with the important proviso that negative reciprocity has not been shown to be predictive of longitudinal declines in marital quality and hence there is no certainty as to whether the capacity for cognitive editing is ultimately beneficial or harmful in marriage. In fact, cognitive editing during interaction may lead some wives to the post-interaction appraisal that they are not permitted to express their true feelings in the marriage, which could lead to declines in marital quality over time.

Attributions for Marital Events

In the wake of clinical observation suggesting that explanatory or attributional variables were contributing to marital difficulties (e.g., Jacobson & Margolin, 1979), a large body of research emerged to address how happy and unhappy spouses differed in their explanations for events that occurred in their marriage (for reviews, see Bradbury & Fincham, 1990; Harvey, 1987). Results of this research indicate that, compared to nondistressed spouses, distressed spouses tend to make attributions that minimize the impact of positive relationship events ("He's being affectionate because things went well at work today") and that accentuate the impact of negative relationship events ("She's ignoring me in order to get back at me for coming home late last night"). There are also data to suggest that attributions of this sort are predictive of declines in marital quality over 12 months (Bradbury, 1990; Fincham & Bradbury, 1987), although this finding awaits replication in larger samples and across longer time periods.

When the contextual model is applied to the study of attributions, it becomes apparent that many aspects of attributional phenomena have yet to be studied in detail. Because the bulk of the extant research involves presenting spouses with relationship events (e.g., spouse behaviors, marital problems), asking them to rate those events along a series of attribution dimensions (e.g., locus, globality, blame), and correlating level of marital satisfaction with attribution judgments, it appears that our understanding of marital attributions pertains largely to their role as relatively stable elements within the distal context (cf. Baucom, Sayers, & Duhe, 1989; Holtzworth-Munroe & Jacobson, 1988). Although this is not insignificant, recognition of this limitation points to the possibility of asking different sorts of questions about attributions and investigating them as they are manifest in other components of the model.

One important question concerns whether attributions are related to behavior in interaction. Some studies show that attribution judgments made for a marital problem relate to behaviors (Bradbury & Fincham, 1991), sequences of behaviors (Bradbury & Fincham, 1988a), and specific affects (Bradbury, 1990) expressed in a discussion of that problem. However, it is not clear whether these findings result from actual attributions made in the processing stage (and possibly the transient proximal representation of attributions) or whether they result from a stable attributional style within the distal context (via paths g and c). One way to test these possibilities is to assess part of the processing stage by modifying the talk table described previously. This could be accomplished by requiring spouses to make an attributional judgment for each partner behavior (rather than a perceived impact judgment), and then examining the extent to which the on-line attribution judgments mediate the relation between the relatively stable attributions and the observed behavior.

A second question concerns whether the stable attribution judgments studied thus far, which appear to covary with stable affective judgments about the marriage, covary also with transient mood (via the proximal context and path h). (See

Forgas, this volume.) That is, are distressed spouses able to make benign attributions for partner behaviors when they are more optimistic about their marriage, or are such attributions simply not available in their cognitive repertoires? Likewise, do happily married spouses make less benign attributions as a result of their negative moods? In contrast to most research that has been done on attributions, addressing this question would require assessing attributions at times when spouses of varying levels of marital quality were experiencing positive and negative moods (either as they occur naturally or are manipulated experimentally). Determining that mood can influence attributions would lend support to path h in the model and would also raise questions about the circumstances that give rise to enhanced mood (e.g., paths e, f, and i). Establishing these links would be important, particularly in view of the possibility that transient affective reactions to the marriage may accumulate (through post-interaction appraisals, path j) and influence a spouse's pre-interaction appraisals (via path k), attributions about partner behavior (via path d), and subsequent judgments of marital satisfaction (via path h).

In sum, there is a substantial literature that documents the importance of attributions in marriage. In terms of the contextual model, however, it appears that only a limited range of attributional phenomena have been examined (specifically as distal judgments). We have attempted in this section to show how the model might be applied to reveal the nature of attributions in the processing stage and the proximal context, and to show how attributions in the distal context might change.

Psychophysiological Analyses of Interaction

Despite a long tradition of research on the physiological concomitants of social processes (e.g., Shapiro & Schwartz, 1970), it is only recently that investigators have begun to explore this topic in the domain of marital interaction. The impetus for such research derives from data suggesting that emotional responding during interaction accounts for behavioral differences between distressed and nondistressed couples (Gottman, 1979), and from the assumption that physiological indicators covary with emotional expression.

Following an initial study by Notarius and Johnson (1982) that offered some support for this approach, Levenson and Gottman (1983) reported that 60% of the variance in spouse's judgments of marital quality could be accounted for with a measure representing the degree to which a husband's and wife's autonomic physiology (i.e., heart rate, strength of heart contractility, sweating, and general somatic activity) covaried over the course of a problem-solving interaction. Specifically, higher levels of physiological linkage between interacting spouses were related to lower levels of marital quality, which was interpreted to mean that distressed spouses tend to get trapped in destructive cycles of behavior. Of greater relevance to the present discussion is a subsequent report on this project

(Levenson & Gottman, 1985; see also Levenson, 1989) that assessed the degree to which physiological variables would predict declines in marital satisfaction over a 3-year period. Surprisingly, significant prediction was afforded not by the measure of physiological linkage but by the mean levels of the physiological variables, and all findings tended to point toward a common conclusion: Higher levels of arousal at the initial assessment were predictive of greater declines in marital quality over 3 years. A further surprise to emerge from these data was that decreases in satisfaction were a function of levels of arousal measured in the 5-minute baseline period before the interaction began, as the spouses sat silently facing each other in anticipation of their conflict.

The explanations that Levenson and Gottman (1985) offered for their findings are significant because they underscore the importance of certain components of the contextual model. The most obvious of these are pre-interaction appraisals, which were assessed indirectly in the baseline period and which apparently had a strong association with marital satisfaction—an element in the distal context—a few years later. As the authors noted, "most crucially, [spouses] knew that they would soon be interacting with each other" (p. 91) and, on the basis of Fig. 5.1 we might infer that this period of anticipation typically influences the nature of the interaction (via path i), which in turn influences post interaction appraisals (via path j), subsequent pre-interaction appraisals (via path k) and, eventually, the distal context and marital quality (directly via path h and indirectly via paths e and f).

A second component of the model highlighted by this study is the distal context as noted by Levenson and Gottman (1985): "We believe that [the factor accounting for our findings] is the couple's past affective experience with interaction, compiled and summarized over the history of the relationship" (p. 91). This sets the stage for pre-interaction appraisals: "Over time, a couple develops a set of expectations about the prospect of interacting that is grounded in their past interactive experience" (p. 92), that in turn affect the interaction itself: "it is these pleasurable or unpleasurable expectations that account for the arousal differences we have observed. . . . These expectations are then carried over into the interactions themselves" (p. 92). We would refine this account by noting that individual spouses rather than couples develop sets of expectations, that the distal context is far more than a repository of memorable marital events (see next section), and that it is the *experience* of interaction (as represented in the proximal context and the post-interaction appraisals), probably more so than the interaction itself, that eventually produces change in marital quality.

Although the physiological data, if replicated, would point clearly to the value of incorporating events before (and, by implication, after) behavioral exchanges into a model of marital interaction, they would provide very little information about the utility of the contextual model for capturing specific events during the interaction itself. This is because variation in physiological data is related to the operation of many psychological processes—both affective and cognitive—so that inferences about any one of them become tenuous. One way to alleviate this problem would involve assessing in experimental paradigms the physiological responding of individual spouses to discrete audiotaped or videotaped stimuli, such as negative statements made by the partner. Although this would yield a less ecologically relevant study, such a loss would be compensated for by the increase in experimental rigor and the corresponding ability to make relatively specific inferences about the contextual model.

For example, groups could be established on the basis of significant elements in the distal context (e.g., maritally distressed vs. nondistressed; depressed vs. nondepressed; chronic vs. acute history of marital conflict; adaptive vs. maladaptive attributional style), appraisals and the proximal context could be systematically manipulated (e.g., induce positive vs. negative mood), different classes of stimuli could be presented (e.g., positive vs. negative; delivered by spouse vs. stranger), and the effects of these factors on physiological responding and self-reports of behavioral responding could be ascertained. This would allow examination of a variety of questions. For example, are distressed spouses with a maladaptive attributional style more physiologically aroused in response to negative partner behavior than distressed spouses with a benign attributional style? Does conflict history contribute to increases or decreases in physiological responding to negative stimuli? Is distressed spouses' physiological arousal to negative stimuli lessened if they are in a positive mood? The predictive value of such assessments on changes in marital quality over time could also be determined.

In sum, recent research on physiology in marital interaction highlights the role of pre-interaction appraisals and the distal context as essential factors in understanding changes in marital quality. We have observed that physiological applications to date permit few unambiguous inferences about other aspects of the contextual model, and have argued for complementary experimental research that allows for clearer investigation of the relation between maritally relevant stimuli and physiological responses to such stimuli, and of the many factors that moderate such responses.

Personality and Marriage

A distinctive feature of behavioral and social-learning approaches to marriage is that they are often silent on the role that individual difference variables play in marital dysfunction. In contrast to the common view, that interpersonal events give rise to marital problems (and hence are targets for clinical change), is the competing view that interpersonal events are a manifestation of individual differences and that intrapersonal factors thus warrant close investigation as contributors to variance in marital quality. This latter perspective served as the impetus for a 45-year longitudinal investigation of 278 marriages reported by Kelly and Conley (1987; cf. Bentler & Newcomb, 1978). In this study data were collected from spouses early in their relationships on several classes of variables, including spouses' personality (as rated by five acquaintances of each spouse), early social environment, and stressful life events, and couples were contacted intermittently thereafter to provide information on the status of their marriage.

For husbands who remained married, dissatisfaction was predicted by personality factors (e.g., higher levels of neuroticism, lower levels of impulse control, lower levels of agreeableness) and by higher levels of stressful events early in the marriage. Wives' later dissatisfaction was predicted by personality factors (e.g., high levels of neuroticism, lower levels of impulse control), by higher levels of stressful events early in the marriage, and by aspects of the early social environment (e.g., higher levels of instability and lower levels of emotional closeness in family of origin). Overall, a composite index of marital incompatibility was found to be a function of higher levels of husbands' and wives' neuroticism and of the husbands' lower level of impulse control. Kelly and Conley (1987) noted in their conclusion that

> most recent research on marital compatibility has taken more or less of an operant behaviorist standpoint in which intrinsic individual differences have been ignored. . . . The present findings are strongly at variance with this trend. . . . Personality characteristics must be taken into account in a comprehensive analysis of marital interaction. Many of the disrupted patterns of communication and behavior exchange that recent researchers have noted in disturbed couples may be seen as the outgrowths of the personality characteristics of the partners. (p. 36)

We believe that these findings offer strong support for expanding the behavioral model in the way we have outlined in this chapter, particularly insofar as a model of interaction must address stable psychological variables in addition to marital quality. Indeed, if we view Kelly and Conley's (1987) data in terms of Watson and Clark's (1984) reconceptualization of neuroticism as *negative affectivity,* or a cross-situational propensity for certain individuals to experience negative feelings and distress, then it would be surprising if this were unrelated to marital dysfunction. This follows from the view that such individuals "tend to focus differentially on the negative aspects of themselves, other people, and the world in general" (Watson & Clark, 1984, pp. 481–482). In terms of the contextual model, this implies that negative affectivity, as an element in the distal context, may exert a pervasive influence upon pre-interaction appraisals, the proximal context, the processing of partner behavior, behavior itself, and post-interaction appraisals. Nevertheless, much variance in later marital quality remains unexplained after personality factors are taken into account, and important questions remain about the relative contributions of intrapersonal and interpersonal aspects of marital interaction, and their interrelation, to marital functioning.

Kelly and Conley's (1987) findings are notable not only because they identify classes of variables that may alter the course of marriage, but also because, in conjunction with the contextual model, they suggest a range of mechanisms by which individual difference variables might operate. The most obvious process, that a spouse high in negative affectivity perceives partner behavior to be more negative than an individual low in negative affectivity, is conceptually quite similar to the notion of *sentiment override* that Weiss (1980) has introduced to the literature. By this term Weiss refers to how a spouse's global positive or negative feeling toward the partner leads to unconditional judgments about the partner that match the valence of that feeling. In terms of the contextual model, this implies that when a partner exhibits a behavior (via path b) the spouse will process that behavior largely as a function of feelings held toward the partner (via path g), independent of the nature of the partner behavior itself.

Although there are few data to our knowledge that document conclusively the operation and nature of sentiment override, we believe that sentiment override may prove to be an important aspect of marital interaction. However, we believe also that limiting any override process to only the affective evaluation that a spouse holds for the partner or marriage may be overly restrictive, because it seems quite likely that many other enduring psychological features of an individual will influence his or her reaction to marital events. Negative affectivity may be one such feature that predisposes a spouse to view partner behavior in an idiosyncratic fashion and, as the Kelly and Conley (1987) data suggest, such tendencies may accumulate to take their toll on marital quality. Depression may be another element in the distal context that affects the processing of partner behavior in the way suggested by Weiss' sentiment override. Kowalik and Gotlib (1987) have shown, for example, that depressed spouses are more likely than nondepressed spouses to rate their partner's behavior in interaction as less positive and more negative relative to ratings made by trained coders. This paradigm could be modified readily to determine whether other stable variables also impinge upon the processing of partner behavior and whether such an influence occurs above and beyond the effect of marital satisfaction.

In sum, whereas marital dysfunction has been understood commonly to be a result of maladaptive communication patterns, others have maintained that such patterns emerge from spouses' personalities, and they have provided data supporting this possibility. The contextual model suggests that neither perspective can provide a comprehensive treatment of marital dysfunction, particularly in view of likely reciprocal relations among interpersonal and intrapersonal variables. The notion that an individual difference factor might affect how partner behavior is processed was related to an expanded conception of sentiment override.

SUMMARY AND OVERVIEW

Psychological inquiry into marriage has burgeoned in the past two decades, yielding an impressive body of research that is beginning to reveal the vast and daunting complexity underlying marital interaction and marital dysfunction (see Fincham & Bradbury, 1990). A guiding premise of this chapter is that empirical growth in this domain has not been accompanied by explanatory theory, in part because models that capture the full range of marital phenomena have not been proposed and tested. As a preliminary step toward addressing this problem we outlined a model of marital interaction that transcends the well-documented association between overt behavior and marital quality by incorporating a variety of covert constructs that provide an affective and cognitive context within which the behavioral findings can be understood. The model specifies the arrangement of five broad classes of variables that appear essential for addressing how a given interaction between spouses unfolds and how it affects subsequent exchanges and judgments about the marriage. Specifically, a partner's *behavior* is subject to the spouse's *processing,* which in turn leads to that spouse's own behavioral response; the processing, which comprises a series of attentional, affective, and attributional steps, is influenced by both transient reactions to prior incidents in the interaction as represented in the *proximal context,* and by relatively stable psychological features of the processing spouse (e.g., marital satisfaction) as represented in the *distal context.* These four constructs are influenced by the thoughts and feelings, or *appraisals,* that spouses experience prior to an interaction and by the appraisals they make of their interactions after they are completed.

Description of the model was followed by its application to several recent developments in the study of marriage (i.e., longitudinal behavioral analyses of interaction, on-line judgments that spouses make of each other's behavior, attributions that spouses make for events in their relationship, psychophysiological analyses of interaction, and the role of personality in marriage), and for each of these developments examples demonstrated how the model could be used to identify new research directions. Our presentation was limited by its emphasis on breadth across marital domains rather than depth within any one domain, and the model itself awaits greater specification in a number of areas. These include the factors that determine when people begin and end their interactions, the important elements of the distal context and how they might be organized, the role of non-interactional events in marriage (e.g., work, leisure time), initial stages of marriages and mate selection, the nature of response selection following processing of a partner behavior, and how various components of the model are best assessed. Resolution of these and other issues is likely to emerge from a dialectic between requisite data (cf. Kurdek, 1991) and model refinement, and we particularly encourage investigators to address marriage longitudinally, so that the model may go beyond describing cross-sectional differences between distressed and nondistressed couples toward a stage of explaining how marriages falter and improve.

Independent of our particular analysis of marital interaction, we believe that now is an appropriate juncture in the psychological study of marriage for conceptual expansion, because so few of its facets are well understood and because so little is known about how a relationship that typically begins with so much promise can lead so frequently to despair and divorce. The behavioral findings that were instigated, in part, by the emphasis placed on interaction by Raush et al. (1974) have provided a strong foundation for such conceptual expansion, yet, whereas sophisticated observational research in the behavioral tradition could be undertaken with relatively straightforward hypotheses, the present mediational tradition is likely to prove much more challenging theoretically as greater attention is given to intrapersonal variables. We see this as a necessary task, however, because, as Watzlawick, Bavelas, and Jackson (1967, pp. 20–21) noted, "a phenomenon remains unexplainable as long as the range of observation is not wide enough to include the context in which the phenomenon occurs. Failure to realize the intricacies of the relationships between an event and the matrix in which it takes place, between an organism and its environment, either confronts the observer with something 'mysterious' or induces him [or her] to attribute to his [or her] object of study certain properties the object may not possess."

REFERENCES

Baucom, D. H., Sayers, S., & Duhe, A. (1989). Attributional style and attributional patterns among married couples. *Journal of Personality and Social Psychology, 56,* 596–607.

Beach, S. R. H., & Bauserman, S. K. (1990). Enhancing the effectiveness of marital therapy. In F. D. Fincham & T. N. Bradbury (Eds.), *The psychology of marriage* (pp. 349–374). New York: Guilford Press.

Bentler, P. M., & Newcomb, M. D. (1978). Longitudinal study of marital success and failure. *Journal of Consulting and Clinical Psychology, 46,* 1053–1070.

Bradbury, T. N. (1990). *Cognition, emotion, and interaction in distressed and nondistressed marriages.* Unpublished manuscript, University of Illinois, Urbana-Champaign.

Bradbury, T. N., & Fincham, F. D. (1987a). Affect and cognition in close relationships: Towards an integrative model. *Cognition and Emotion, 1,* 59–87.

Bradbury, T. N., & Fincham, F. D. (1987b). Assessment of affect in marriage. In K. D. O'Leary (Ed.), *Assessment of marital discord* (pp. 59–108). Hillsdale, NJ: Erlbaum.

Bradbury, T. N., & Fincham, F. D. (1988a). *The impact of attributions in marriage: Attributions and behavior exchange in marital interaction.* Paper presented at the annual meeting of the Association for Advancement of Behavior Therapy, New York.

Bradbury, T. N., & Fincham, F. D. (1988b). Individual difference variables in close relationships: A contextual model of marriage as an integrative framework. *Journal of Personality and Social Psychology, 54,* 713–721.

Bradbury, T. N., & Fincham, F. D. (1989). Behavior and satisfaction in marriage: Prospective mediating processes. *Review of Personality and Social Psychology, 10,* 119–143.

Bradbury, T. N., & Fincham, F. D. (1990). Attributions in marriage: Review and critique. *Psychological Bulletin, 107,* 3–33.

Bradbury, T. N., & Fincham, F. D. (1991). *Attributions and behavior in marital interaction.* Manuscript submitted for publication.

Cherlin, A. J. (1981). *Marriage, divorce, remarriage.* Cambridge, MA: Harvard University Press.

Christensen, A. (1987). Assessment of behavior. In K. D. O'Leary (Ed.), *Assessment of marital discord* (pp. 13–57). Hillsdale, NJ: Erlbaum.

Filsinger, E. E., & Thoma, S. J. (1988). Behavioral antecedents of relationship stability and adjustment: A five-year longitudinal study. *Journal of Marriage and the Family, 50*, 785–795.

Fincham, F. D., & Bradbury, T. N. (1987). The impact of attributions in marriage: A longitudinal analysis. *Journal of Personality and Social Psychology, 53*, 510–517.

Fincham, F. D., & Bradbury, T. N. (1990). *The psychology of marriage.* New York: Guilford Press.

Fincham, F. D., & Bradbury, T. N. (1991). Marital conflict: Towards a more complete integration of research and treatment. In J. P. Vincent (Ed.), *Advances in family intervention, assessment, and theory* (Vol. 5). London: Kingsley.

Fincham, F. D., Bradbury, T. N., & Grych, J. H. (1990). Conflict in close relationships: The role of intrapersonal phenomena. In S. Graham & V. S. Folkes (Eds.), *Attribution theory: Applications to achievement, mental health, and interpersonal conflict* (pp. 161–184). Hillsdale, NJ: Erlbaum.

Glick, B. R., & Gross, S. J. (1975). Marital interaction and marital conflict: A critical evaluation of current research strategies. *Journal of Marriage and the Family, 37*, 505–512.

Gottman, J. M. (1979). *Marital interaction: Experimental investigations.* New York: Academic Press.

Gottman, J. M., & Krokoff, L. J. (1989). Marital interaction and satisfaction: A longitudinal view. *Journal of Consulting and Clinical Psychology, 57*, 47–52.

Gottman, J. M., Notarius, C., Markman, H., Bank, S., Yoppi, B., & Rubin, M. E. (1976). Behavior exchange theory and marital decision making. *Journal of Personality and Social Psychology, 34*, 14–23.

Gurman, A. S., & Knudson, R. M. (1978). Behavior marriage therapy: I. A psychodynamic-systems analysis and critique. *Family Process, 17*, 121–138.

Hahlweg, K., & Markman, H. J. (1988). Effectiveness of behavioral marital therapy: Empirical status of behavioral techniques in preventing and alleviating marital distress. *Journal of Consulting and Clinical Psychology, 56*, 440–447.

Harvey, J. H. (1987). Attributions in close relationships: Research and theoretical developments. *Journal of Social and Clinical Psychology, 5*, 420–447.

Holtzworth-Munroe, A., & Jacobson, N. S. (1988). Toward a methodology for coding spontaneous causal attributions: Preliminary results with married couples. *Journal of Social and Clinical Psychology, 7*, 101–112.

Jacobson, N. S., & Margolin, G. (1979). *Marital therapy: Strategies based on social learning and behavior exchange principles.* New York: Brunner/Mazel.

Jacobson, N. S., & Moore, D. (1981). Spouses as observers of the events in their relationship. *Journal of Consulting and Clinical Psychology, 49*, 269–277.

Kelley, H. H., Berscheid, E., Christensen, A., Harvey, J. H., Huston, T. L., Levinger, G., McClintick, E., Peplau, L. A., & Peterson, D. R. (1983). *Close relationships.* New York: Freeman.

Kelly, E. L., & Conley, J. J. (1987). Personality and compatibility: A prospective analysis of marital stability and marital satisfaction. *Journal of Personality and Social Psychology, 52*, 27–40.

Kowalik, D. J., & Gotlib, I. H. (1987). Depression and marital interaction: Concordance between intent and perception of communication. *Journal of Abnormal Psychology, 96*, 127–134.

Kurdek, L. A. (1991). Marital stability and changes in marital quality in newlywed couples: A test of the contextual model. *Journal of Social and Personal Relationships 8*, 27–48.

Levenson, R. W. (1989). Psychophysiological research on marital interaction: Physiological and affective markers of marital satisfaction. *Psychophysiology* (Supplement), *26*, 10.

Levenson, R. W., & Gottman, J. M. (1983). Marital interaction: Physiological linkage and affective exchange. *Journal of Personality and Social Psychology, 45*, 587–597.

Levenson, R. W., & Gottman, J. M. (1985). Physiological and affective predictors of change in relationship satisfaction. *Journal of Personality and Social Psychology, 49*, 85–94.

Margolin, G. (1983). An interactional model for the behavioral assessment of marital relationships. *Behavioral Assessment, 5*, 103–127.

Markman, H. J., Duncan, S. W., Storaasli, R. D. & Howes, P. W. (1987). The prediction and prevention of marital distress: A longitudinal investigation. In K. Hahlweg & M. J. Goldstein (Eds.), *Understanding major mental disorder: The contribution of family interaction research* (pp. 266–289). New York: Family Process Press.

Noller, P., & Fitzpatrick, M. A. (1990). Marital communication in the eighties. *Journal of Marriage and the Family 52*, 832–843.

Notarius, C. I., Benson, P. R., Sloane, D., Vanzetti, N. A., & Hornyak, L. M. (1989). Exploring the interface between perception and behavior: An analysis of marital interaction in distressed and nondistressed couples. *Behavioral Assessment, 11*, 39–64.

Notarius, C. I., & Johnson, J. S. (1982). Emotional expression in husbands and wives. *Journal of Marriage and the Family, 44*, 483–489.

Raush, H. L., Barry, W. A., Hertel, R. K., & Swain, M. A. (1974). *Communication, conflict, and marriage*. San Francisco: Jossey-Bass.

Schaap, C. (1984). A comparison of the interaction of distressed and nondistressed married couples in a laboratory situation: Literature survey, methodological issues, and an empirical investigation. In K. Hahlweg & N. S. Jacobson (Eds.), *Marital interaction: Analysis and modification* (pp. 133–158). New York: Guilford Press.

Shapiro, D., & Schwartz, G. E. (1970). Psychophysiological contributions to social psychology. *Annual Review of Psychology, 21*, 87–112.

Snyder, D. K. (1989). Introduction to the special series. *Journal of Consulting and Clinical Psychology, 57*, 3–4.

Watson, D., & Clark, L. A. (1984). Negative Affectivity: The disposition to experience aversive emotional states. *Psychological Bulletin, 96*, 465–490.

Watzlawick, P., Bavelas, J. B., & Jackson, D. D. (1967). *Pragmatics of human communication*. New York: Norton.

Weiss, R. L. (1980). Strategic behavioral marital therapy: Toward a model for assessment and intervention. In J. P. Vincent (Ed.), *Advances in family intervention, assessment, and theory* (Vol. 1, pp. 229–271). Greenwich, CT: JAI Press.

Weiss, R. L., & Heyman, R. E. (1990). Observation of marital interaction. In F. D. Fincham and T. N. Bradbury (Eds.), *The psychology of marriage* (pp. 87–117). New York: Guilford Press.

Woody, E. Z., & Costanzo, P. R. (1990). Does marital agony precede marital ecstasy? A comment on Gottman and Krokoff's "Marital interaction and satisfaction: A longitudinal view." *Journal of Consulting and Clinical Psychology 59*, 499–501.

II COGNITION AND AFFECT

The chapters in the first section deal with broad, overarching theoretical frameworks. In this section, the chapters are less general in scope and are more concerned with the detail of research findings and methodologies that operate at the interface of cognition and close relationships. A major theme running through this section is the interplay between cognition and affect. Some chapters deal with the investigation of these phenomena as they occur on-line in the context of dyadic interaction. Other chapters more generally explore the role of affect or emotion in close relationships. Given that close relationships are perhaps the most central social context within which emotions are experienced and expressed, it is odd that so little prior attention has been given to the study of affect in close relationships. The contributions in this section make a valuable beginning in addressing this gap in our understanding.

Chapter 6 by Forgas, *Affect and Cognition in Close Relationships,* describes a research program dealing with the interdependence between cognition and affect in the context of interpersonal relationships. From the converging lines of evidence, he concludes that affect plays a central role in both the storage and representation of general relationship knowledge and specific relationship knowledge, and in terms of dynamic cognitive processes such as attention, memory, and social judgment.

In the next chapter, *Affect in Close Relationships,* Fitness and Strongman consider emotion theories, drawn from social psychology/social cognition and from clinical sources, that embody two competing views of the cognition-affect link: that emotion is simply a product of cognition, and that affect precedes cognition. They proceed to use one of the only prior theories of emotion in close relationships, developed by Berscheid, as a framework for relating cognitive appraisal theories of emotion to close relationship settings. These authors offer a unique, integrative analysis of the emotion literature and its application to close relationships.

The next two chapters deal with an important theme theoretically explicated in the first section, namely, the investigation of social cognition as it occurs on-line in the context of dyadic interaction. Chapter 8 by Noller and Ruzzene, *Communication in Marriage: The Influence of Affect and Cognition,* describes a program of research carried out by Noller and her colleagues that has explored the links between marital communication and a variety of affective and cognitive judgments. These studies have not only produced a fascinating set of findings, related to such variables as gender and marital satisfaction, but are also exemplars of how researchers can study close relationship processes in controlled but ecologically robust ways.

The following chapter by Fletcher and Kininmonth, *Interaction in Close Relationships and Social Cognition,* continues the theme of the previous chapter, and reviews the research that has examined cognition or affect as it occurs on-line in dyadic interaction. Two central claims in this chapter are that the interaction between on-going cognition and social behavior is eminently researchable with current techniques, and that this arena should occupy a central position if we wish to examine close relationships from a truly social psychological position.

The final chapter in this section by Sternberg and Beall, *How Can We Know What Love Is? An Epistemological Analysis,* is the most avowedly theoretical chapter in this section. However, it differs importantly from the chapters in the first section in that it examines a single, although clearly important, construct concerned with close relationships—love. Sternberg and Beall take the reader on a stimulating tour of the major theoretical approaches that have been advanced in the study of love. They discuss some important strengths and weaknesses of each theoretical approach (including cognitive and social psychological theories), and they conclude that these theories often address different concerns rather than present directly competing accounts. Accordingly, they favor what they term a *theory-knitting* approach in which the limitations of one theoretical or methodological approach are balanced by the strengths of another. Interestingly, this proposition is effectively illustrated by all the chapters in this section.

6 Affect and Cognition in Close Relationships

Joseph P. Forgas
University of New South Wales

Cognition, in the broadest sense of the term, is an essential ingredient of every close relationship. Any attempt to understand the psychology of interpersonal behavior and human social relationships must also by definition include the detailed study of the cognitive aspects of how people relate to each other. The recent history of psychology in general, and contributions to this volume in particular, bears witness to the growing importance of cognitive approaches and analyses in most fields of psychological enquiry.

Interpersonal events within a close relationship, such as a marriage, can only be properly understood through the careful analysis of covert, intrapersonal events such as the partners' thoughts and feelings (see Bradbury & Fincham, this volume). Within the context of this book, the present chapter seeks to make a complementary but no less important point: that affect and cognition cannot be adequately understood as separate, isolated domains, but must be studied as they interact with each other within the context of a close relationship (Forgas, 1983c). Indeed, perhaps in no other domain of psychology is this interdependence more important than in the study of close relationships.

In discussing the links between affect and cognition in close relationships, we begin with a brief overview of the historical background of this issue. The major part of the chapter is devoted to describing a number of converging research programs we have been involved in, dealing with the close interdependence of affect and cognition. This work may be readily subdivided into two complementary orientations: (a) Research looking at the role of affect in the way covert knowledge about relationships and interaction episodes is organized and cognitively represented; we may call this the static aspect of cognition. (b) Affect is also closely involved in the active, dynamic aspects of cognition, such as learn-

Support from the Australian Research Council and the German Research Foundation is gratefully acknowledged. Contact Joseph P. Forgas for reprints.

ing, attention, memory processes, associations, judgments, and decisions. Recent work in this domain is considered in the second half of the chapter.

The first section discusses empirical evidence demonstrating the critical role of affective characteristics in implicit cognitive representations of relationship scripts. Next, our research program on the cognitive representation of social interaction episodes is described, and the role of affect and feelings in such representations is reviewed. In the second half of the chapter, the role of affect in cognitive processes such as memory, attention, associations, and learning is considered. These processes play a central role in close relationships, particularly as they come to influence interpersonal perceptions, judgments, decisions, and attributions (Bradbury & Fincham, 1987; Fincham & Bradbury, 1989). Our recent research illustrating emotional biases and distortions in the perception and interpretation of ongoing interactive behaviors, and social perception and impression formation, is considered. Finally, our recently completed research illustrating the significant influences of transient emotional states on social attributions and interpersonal choices and decisions is summarized. The chapter concludes with an overview of the evidence for the role of affect in cognitive representations and processes in close relationships and an outline of some future directions for research in this important field.

AFFECT AND COGNITION:
THE HISTORICAL BACKGROUND

For most of the history of modern psychology in the 20th century, affect and cognition were regarded as separate, almost unrelated aspects of the human mind. Indeed, much cognitive psychology has traditionally operated on the basis of the implicit—and sometimes explicit—assumption that cognition is ideally "affect-less," with emotions being regarded as at best an interference, a potential source of distortions in cognitive processes. As Hilgard (1980) convincingly argued, this position is very much at variance with earlier, traditional conceptions of the human mind.

The artifical separation of human faculties into affect, cognition, and conation (i.e., feeling, thinking, and the will) first arose in the writing of Kant and Leibniz in the 18th century, when individualism, rationalism, and the study of consciousness first emerged as of critical importance. However, the tripartite division of the mind into feelings, knowledge, and desire did not initially mean that these faculties could be regarded as independent or even separate. Rather, philosophers and early psychologists thought of these domains as inseparable, different but complementary dimensions of one and the same psychological phenomenon. It was the emergence of modern empirical psychology, and the increasing fragmentation and compartmentalization of its subject matter in the 20th century, that ultimately led to the now-accepted consensus that somehow cognition, affect, and motivation can be profitably studied in isolation from one another.

It is only in the past several years that the close interdependence of affect and cognition has come to be once again recognized, with a growing number of theories and empirical papers in social, cognitive, clinical, developmental, and personality psychology explicitly dealing with this interrelationship (cf. Fitness & Strongman, this volume). The study of close relationships provides one of the most intriguing domains where the interaction of affect and cognition can be studied. After all, it is in our social relationships that affective experiences and reactions play a particularly important part (Argyle, 1991), and it could be argued that affect is the primary dimension of interpersonal behavior (Zajonc, 1980). In this chapter we concentrate on two complementary aspects of the affect/cognition link in close relationships: (a) the role of affect in the organization and representation of information that is relevant to a relationship (the static aspect) and (b) the role of affect in the processing of information in close relationships (the dynamic aspect).

THE ROLE OF AFFECT
IN THE COGNITIVE REPRESENTATIONS
OF RELATIONSHIP SCRIPTS

Human social relationships characteristically conform to culturally established patterns. Individuals from a given culture normally have a clear, implicit, cognitive representation of the range of relationship prototypes practiced in their milieu. One of the most fascinating domains where affect and cognition play an interactive role is the way people perceive and cognitively represent the alternative relationship scenarios, or scripts, practiced within their culture. Close relationships typically follow a well-established sequential path in their initiation, development, and eventual termination (Levinger, 1980; Surra & Bohman, this volume).

Relationship script is a term we may apply to the shared, consensual perceptions and representations that members of a given culture have about common and frequently enacted relationship scenarios. In most Western cultures, individuals share an understanding as to what relationship scripts typically entail, such as a one-night stand, a holiday affair, or an engagement to be married. One of the most critical tasks in the early stages of any relationship is for the partners to agree on a definition of a predictable, scripted pattern they expect the relationship to follow, a task of often prolonged and subtle negotiation.

The study of how such knowledge of behavioral scripts influences social understanding has been one of the most fruitful areas of social cognition research in recent years (Abelson, 1976, 1980; Miller & Read, this volume). In a sense, the knowledge of appropriate relationship scripts is an essential prerequisite of effective interpersonal behavior. The study of implicit representations of relationship scripts may give us important insights into how interpersonal knowledge is represented and organized, and in particular the role of emotion and affect in such cognitive representations.

Taxonomies of relationship scripts and their cognitive representation are still rare in the literature, a shortcoming noted by Huston & Levinger (1978). Of course, several descriptive or speculative a priori taxonomies of relationships have been proposed over the years, emphasizing features such as love, sex, or intellectual appraisal (e.g., Bolton, 1961; Reiss, 1960). Empirical studies, using factor-analytic or multidimensional scaling (MDS) methods, have indicated that descriptive features such as intimacy, visibility of behavior regulation (Marwell & Hage, 1970), or cooperativeness, intensity, equality, and socioemotional versus task orientation may be some of the characteristics that differentiate between various kinds of relationships (Wish, Deutsch, & Kaplan, 1976). One study has also reported intergenerational differences in relationship perception (Rands & Levinger, 1979). Interestingly, few of these taxonomies reflect the affective, emotional quality of relationship representations. Yet it seems reasonable to assume that the way a person feels about various relationship scripts may well play a more important role in his or her perceptions than the actual descriptive features of the relationship.

To explore the role of affect in cognitive representations of relationship scripts, it is important that we first define the domain of relationship scripts of interest and obtain a representative and ecologically valid sample of such scripts, a task often ignored in earlier research. In one of our studies, we chose to focus on romantic heterosexual relationships because of the extensive existing literature in this area, the obvious emotional character of most such relationships, and the particular relevance of intimate relationships to young people who were to be our subjects. We expected that implicit representations of relationship scripts would be largely based on affective, connotative characteristics rather than on denotative features.

In the first phase of this research we elicited a representative range of stimulus relationships in a free response study (see Fig. 6.1). A second sample of subjects from the same milieu—a much larger group of university students—was asked to make similarity judgments between the relationship scripts and to fill out a series of demographic, attitudinal, and personality questionnaires about themselves. The matrix of similarity judgments between each possible relationship script was used as input to an individual differences multidimensional scaling (MDS) analysis, which identified three underlying dimensions as defining the relationship space. (For more detail on the use of MDS procedures, see Forgas, 1982a,b).

Results showed that the three dimensions defining the relationship space could be empirically interpreted (through the fitting by multiple regression of separately rated bipolar labelling dimensions to the three axes of the relationship space) as reflecting the social desirability, love and commitment, and sexuality aspects of the relationships. Canonical correlation analyses of the coordinates of relationship clusters also showed that a priori categorical distinctions between relationships were significantly preserved in this relationship space, and that meaningful and readily interpretable differences in relationship cognition between judges could also be demonstrated. The three-dimensional relationship

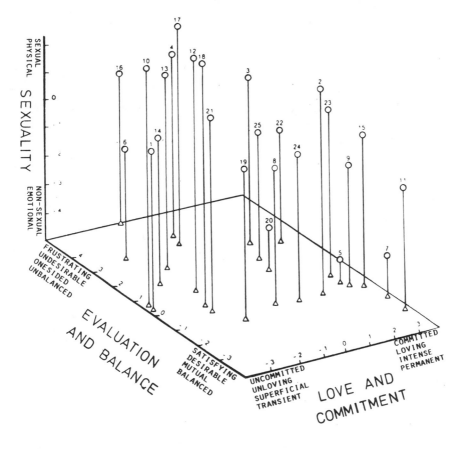

SEXUALITY

SEXUAL PHYSICAL

NON-SEXUAL EMOTIONAL

EVALUATION AND BALANCE

FRUSTRATING
UNDESIRABLE
ONE-SIDED
UNBALANCED

SATISFYING
DESIRABLE
MUTUAL
BALANCED

UNCOMMITTED
UNLOVING
SUPERFICIAL
TRANSIENT

COMMITTED
LOVING
INTENSE
PERMANENT

LOVE AND COMMITMENT

1. Verbal and physical flirting at a party, without follow-up.
2. A boy/girlfriend living together for a period after several months of dating.
3. A de facto relationship between two previously married people.
4. A young marriage after an unwanted pregnancy.
5. A permanent but nonsexual relationship between two young religious people.
6. A "going steady" relationship maintained to impress peers.
7. A long-lasting, close platonic relationship.
8. A steady relationship where each person goes out with other members of the opposite sex.
9. Widowers remarried in middle age, after several years of living alone.
10. A one-night sexual encounter.
11. A marriage of twenty-five years.
12. A mainly physical relationship with an older and more experienced person.
13. A school affair between teacher and pupil.
14. Brief, fluctuating relationships among members of a permanent social group.
15. A young marriage after a long, involved courtship.
16. A relationship in which only one of the partners is deeply involved.
17. Having an affair with a married person.
18. A short, mainly sexual affair between two young people.
19. An irregular, occasional dating relationship for mutual entertainment between two young people.
20. The continuation of a once personal relationship by letters and telephone calls from overseas.
21. A short, emotional holiday affair.
22. A long, involved "going steady" relationship at school.
23. "Love at first sight," followed by engagement, after a brief but intense relationship.
24. A short, mutual first love.
25. The recommencement of an old flame, that didn't work out before.

FIG. 6.1. A multidimensional scaling analysis of implicit cognitive representations of relationships, showing the relationship labels, and the best-fitting bipolar scales used to label the relationship dimensions (after Forgas & Dobosz, 1983).

space shown in Fig. 6.1 essentially shows how a hypothetical "average" member of this subject group perceived and cognitively represented differences between the relationship scripts.

The relationship characteristics underlying these representations are far more affective and evaluative in character than results from earlier studies seem to suggest, indicating the important role of feelings in perceptions and cognitive representations of relationships. Only the sexuality dimension appears to be descriptive rather than affective in character. Both social desirability and love and commitment are primarily evaluative features that reflect far more about how judges feel about this group of relationships, rather than the objective features of the relationships themselves.

In addition to constructing a relationship space for a particular milieu, this study also showed how individual members of a subculture differ in their cognitive representations of heterosexual relationships. There were substantial individual differences in the way romantic relationship prototypes were cognitively represented, leading to the conclusion that relationship cognition is not only affectively based, but is also closely related to a person's attitudes, personality, and previous heterosexual history (Forgas & Dobosz, 1980). For example, females tended to cognitively represent relationships more in terms of their social desirability rather than the sexual dimension, whereas subjects who scored high on extroversion relied on the sexuality dimension more heavily than on the desirability dimension. Love and commitment were also a more important feature to those who had a current romantic partner, and to those who had idealistic attitudes to love in general. This interdependence between personal characteristics and cognitive representations and processes is likely to receive far more attention in future research (Mayer & Salovey, 1988).

Affect may of course influence not only our cognitive representation of relationship scripts but ultimately our cognitive representations of a wide range of other phenomena, such as interpersonal episodes in relationships. Research demonstrating such influences is briefly considered next.

THE ROLE OF AFFECT
IN COGNITIVE REPRESENTATIONS
OF SOCIAL EPISODES IN RELATIONSHIPS

Social interaction between the partners is an essential characteristic of any relationship. It is through interaction that relationships are established, maintained, or terminated, and our past interactive experience and expectations play critical roles in guiding our interactive strategies (Forgas, 1985a). The implicit cognitive representation people develop about such interactions have been referred to as social episodes (Forgas, 1976, 1978, 1979, 1983a, 1983b). These representations of social situations are of course also strongly influenced by cultural, subcultural, and individual variables (e.g., Bond & Forgas, 1984; Forgas & Bond, 1985), and are to a greater or lesser extent shared among members of a particular social group.

The concept of social situation or social episode has a distinguished, if generally little appreciated background both in psychology and in sociology. Learning theorists, such as Kantor (1924) in his "interbehaviorism," have proposed that an individual should be studied as "he interacts with all the various types of situations which constitute his behavior circumstances" (p. 92). Despite the strong environmentalist position of learning theorists, this call was not seriously heeded until "situationism" became an important concept in contemporary social learning theory (Mischel, 1968). Social psychologists such as Lewin (1936) argued for a much more phenomenological conceptualisation of social situations: "the situation must be represented as it is 'real' for the individual in question, that is, as it affects him" (p. 25). The need to study and sample representative social situations recurs in the work of such influential psychologists as Blumer (1969), Brunswik (1956), Barker (1968), and many others. The social situation as an essential influence on meaningful social behavior is also central to the work of such eminent sociologists as Max Weber (1968), W. I. Thomas (1966/1928), Willard Waller (1961), and Goffman (1974). Social situations or episodes also constitute an essential part of social relationships, and affect seems to be a critical component of how such episodes are perceived and cognitively represented.

Recent work in cognitive social psychology confirms that affective states play an important role in the way we organize and store information about our past social episodes. Several experiments have found that people's recollections of particular episodes from the immediate past, or, indeed, even from their distant childhood, may be dominated by subjective feelings (cf. Bower, 1981). People who are experiencing an experimentally induced good mood are more likely to remember social episodes that are enjoyable and pleasant at the time, whereas people in a bad mood are more likely to recall spontaneously episodes that are unpleasant or depressing (cf. Bower, 1981). Research in clinical psychology also confirms this pattern: Emotion plays a critical role in how we remember and interpret social events, and depressed people are particularly prone to think about and recall unpleasant, negative episodes (Ottaviani & Beck, 1988; Roth & Rehm, 1980), particularly when it involves themselves. The interesting question arises: What role does affect play in our cognitive representations of social episodes?

As early as 1976, Pervin in a study of perceived situational dimensions noted: "what is striking is the extent to which situations are described in terms of affects (e.g., threatening, warm, interesting, dull, tense, calm, rejecting) and organized in terms of similarity of affects aroused by them" (p. 471). Similar conclusions have been reached in other studies, supporting Zajonc's (1980) claim that affective reactions play a critical and primary role in social perception and behavior.

In a series of empirical investigations over several years, we have looked at the way common, recurring social episodes are cognitively represented by individuals, groups, and subcultures. In these studies, the procedure typically involves collecting a representative range of commonly practiced interaction episodes from a group of subjects, selecting the most common and typical interactions from such a list, and then obtaining a reliable empirical measure of the perceived psychological similarity or relatedness between this group of episodes. This empirical information can be readily obtained in the form of direct similarity ratings, sorting procedures, or bipolar judgmental scales by a representative group of subjects familiar with the interaction routines studied (for a review, see Forgas, 1982a).

The overwhelming majority of such studies of social episodes are remarkable in that affective, connotative dimensions once again take precedence over other objective characteristics in people's cognitive representations. Commonly, characteristics such as pleasantness, feelings of self-confidence, anxiety or tension, or perceived intimacy and friendliness are the most important features that define a person's cognitive representation of his or her social episodes (Forgas, 1976, 1978, 1979, 1982a, 1983a, 1983b). It is also surprising to find that, in most of these studies, the number of common and recurring social episodes reported by people is far from unmanageable. In fact, most of our common and shared interactions seems to be variations on between 20 and 50 common themes. In well-established close relationships, the range of shared interaction types is probably even more limited. Examples of such shared episode scripts may include events such as having breakfast together, Saturday morning shopping, dinner party with friends, or going to see a movie together.

An example of a typical representation of an episode space is shown in Fig. 6.2. In this instance, subjects were members of a small academic group at a British university who were involved in an enduring pattern of close collegial relationships with each other, established over a period of several years. The group was composed of faculty members, research students, and other staff. Members of the group had regular social contact with one another, both inside and outside the department, in common social episodes such as participating in a seminar, having tea or coffee together, going to a dinner party, or going to the pub. The list of episodes included in this study was obtained from members of the group, who were able to list with a considerable degree of agreement their most common and recurring interactions. Once a list of representative social episodes was elicited, measures of perceived similarity between each pair of episodes were obtained and analyzed using an MDS program. The resulting episode space was defined by four largely affectively loaded dimensions: anxiety, feelings of involvement, evaluation, and social versus task characteristics; all but the last one of these turned out to be primarily affective in character.

If social episodes are perceived in terms of how people feel about them, there is good reason to believe that there may be significant individual differences in perceptions, depending on the individual characteristics of the judges. In the

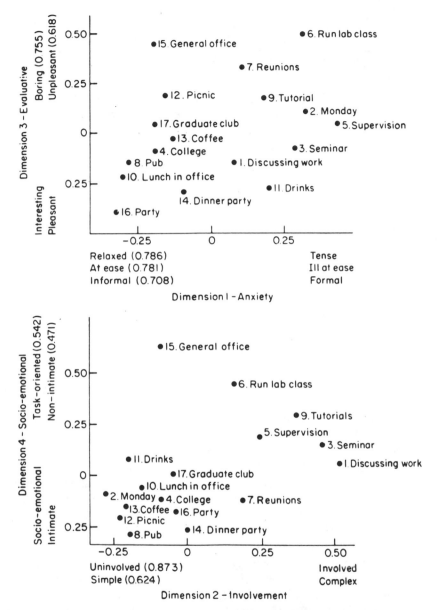

FIG. 6.2.   The perception of social interaction episodes by members of a close-knit academic group, showing the bipolar dimensions used to label the episode dimensions, and their associated regression coefficients (after Forgas, 1978).

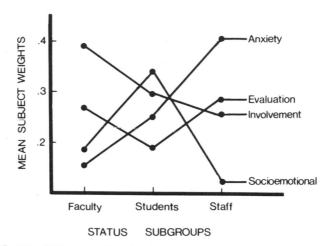

FIG. 6.3. Differences in episode perception between the three status subgroups: faculty, students and other staff with average subject weights on four episode dimensions for each group (after Forgas, 1978).

academic group we studied, status was perhaps the most salient feature differentiating group members. Would faculty members, research students, and other staff have significantly different representations of this group of social episodes? To evaluate this possibility, the mean dimension weights (indicating how much each subject relied on each episode dimension in his or her cognitive representation) between faculty, staff, and students were compared. Results showed the predicted differences. Evaluation was most important to faculty members, anxiety was the most salient episode dimension to other staff, and students saw episodes mainly in terms of their social or task orientation (Fig. 6.3).

What do this and other studies (for a review, see Forgas, 1982a) looking at the features determining cognitive representations of relationship scripts or social episodes tell us about the role of affect in personal relationships? Perhaps the most important conclusion is that cognition about interpersonal processes is hardly ever affectless. Even static, enduring cognitive representations of social stimuli are primarily emotional in character. This may have critical implications for our understanding of interpersonal relationships. The cognitions, expectations, and representations of individuals form a critical component of any human relationship. What these studies show is that perceptions and cognitive representations of both relationships and interpersonal events are strongly based on how a person feels about them. However, to the extent that affect seems to underlie much of our cognitive representation of information relevant to our relationships, we must also face the possibility that such perceptions may sometimes be biased or distorted, with potentially serious consequences for the success or otherwise of our relationships.

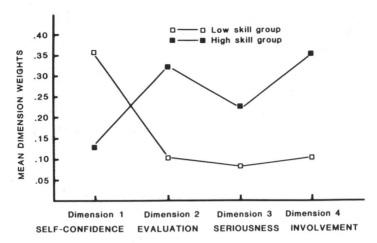

FIG. 6.4.   The role of social skills in cognitive representations of social episodes: average subject weights on four episode dimensions for socially skilled and unskilled subjects (after Forgas, 1983b).

These studies also have direct implications for clinical or counseling psychology as it relates to social relationships. Evidence is now available that social skills—surely one of the most important prerequisites for successful interpersonal relationships—are significantly related to a person's style of cognitively representing social episodes (Forgas, 1983b). In a study comparing the episode perception styles of subjects who scored high or low on measures of social skill, we found that socially unskilled subjects perceived interaction episodes primarily in terms of the anxiety and lack of self-confidence they elicited. In contrast, highly skilled subjects had a far more complex and differentiated perception of such interpersonal events. Figure 6.4 illustrates these differences in episode perceptions style (after Forgas, 1983b).

If affect plays such an important role in our static representation of social information about relationship scripts or common social events, it is likely that emotions also have a major influence on the dynamic aspects of cognition: the way we learn, remember, and judge social information. This issue is considered in the next section.

AFFECTIVE INFLUENCES ON PERCEPTIONS AND JUDGMENTS IN CLOSE RELATIONSHIPS

In addition to descriptive analyses of perceptions of social episodes and relationship scripts, in recent years researchers have also investigated the influence of affective and mood states on thinking about, remembering, and processing information about social stimuli, including other people (e.g., Bower, 1981,

1991; Forgas & Bower, 1987, 1988). There are at least two theoretical approaches that seek to explain how affect comes to play a role in social information processing, and both of these models have significant implications for the study of close relationships.

Within the social-psychological tradition, Schwarz and Clore (1988) proposed that affective states may function as sources of information about a social stimulus, thus influencing our perceptions and judgments. This view is consistent with much of the research on misattribution phenomena. The assumption is that judges, when confronted with a social stimulus (such as another person), in essence consult their temporary mood to infer their evaluative reactions; if they feel good, and if they have no readily available explanation for that feeling state, they use it as information and infer a positive reaction to the target. Experiments suggesting that only unattributed mood states are capable of influencing social judgments in this way found support for this model, and recently Clore and Parrott (1991) proposed that the "affect as information" notion may have broader implications than so far recognized.

The second, and one of the more influential models of how mood and cognition are related, comes from cognitive psychology and is based on a modification of the human associative memory (HAM) model put forward by Bower (1981, 1991).

Bower's (1981) semantic network model proposes that

> each distinctive emotion, such as joy, depression, or fear has a specific node or unit in memory that collects together many other aspects of the emotion that are connected to it by associative pointers . . . each emotion unit is also linked with propositions describing events from one's life during which that emotion was aroused. . . . Activation of an emotion node also spreads activation throughout the memory structures to which it is connected. (1981, p. 135)

Whenever an affective state is experienced, information associated with that state in the past becomes primed and is more likely to be recalled and used in information processing. Although this is essentially a memory model, dealing with the role of affect in information storage and retrieval, the predicted superior availability of affect-related information does have widespread implications for a variety of social domains, including close relationships.

The model predicts that emotional states should have an influence on (a) the selective recall of mood-consistent information, (b) the selective learning and attention to mood-consistent details in the environment, and (c) the mood-consistent interpretation of ambiguous social information. In conjunction, these cognitive processes imply that a variety of interpersonal processes, such as perceptions, judgments, decisions, and attributions, may be significantly distorted depending on the prevailing affective state of the individual. By influencing the availability of information, affective states facilitate the learning, retrieval, and interpretation of social stimuli in an affect-consistent manner.

These effects are particularly important in social perception and judgments. It seems to be an inherent feature of social perception that it is a highly selective and interpretive process (Heider, 1958; Kelly, 1955). The information for the social perceiver is rarely given but must be selected from an often exceedingly complex and ambiguous stimulus array, such as that represented by another person, and then must be further processed and interpreted. Affective states may influence not only what we see and pay attention to, but also what we remember, the associations we form, and the way we interpret the available information. Social perception is by definition a top-down process. We have known for some time that the enduring expectations, cognitive representations, and implicit theories of personality of a perceiver are often more important in social judgments than the actual characteristics of the target (Asch, 1952; Kelly, 1955). What the affect-priming model of Bower (1981) suggests is that much more transient, insubstantial variables, such as a perceiver's current mood state, may have equally important effects on social perception.

During the past several years, we have been engaged in a series of studies investigating the role of low-intensity, transient mood states in a variety of social perception and judgmental tasks. The affective states we studied are similar to the mild, nonspecific experiences of feeling good or feeling bad that are a common and fluctuating feature of everyday life, and are also an enduring feature of all close relationships.

In one of our studies (Forgas, Bower, & Krantz, 1984), we looked at the role of affective states in how people perceive and interpret their own social behaviors, and the behaviors of others. This is clearly one of the critical aspects of any social relationship, and affective biases in this process may have widespread consequences for the survival of a relationship. Subjects who were induced to feel happy or sad using a hypnotic mood induction technique were asked to look at a video recording of a social interaction they engaged in with another, previously unknown, person during the previous day. They were asked to identify and score positive skilled behaviors, and negative unskilled behaviors, both for themselves and for their partners as they observed them on the videotape.

We found (see Fig. 6.5) a strong and unexpected bias in how the behaviors recorded on the videotape were interpreted, according to the temporary mood state of the judge. Happy subjects tended to identify far more positive skilled behaviors than negative unskilled behaviors, both in themselves and in their partners, than did sad subjects. There was only one exception to this strong and consistent mood-induced bias in perceptions: Sad subjects tended to be more critical of themselves than their partners, probably because of the social norms constraining the negative evaluation of superficially known others.

Considering that the videotaped recording of a social interaction represents a far more objective and reliable medium for judging interactive social behaviors than is commonly available to social perceivers in everyday life, our experimental design presents a particularly challenging test of mood effects on judgments.

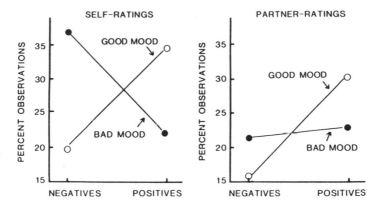

FIG. 6.5. The influence of affective states on the perception and interpretation of interactive behaviours for self, and for a partner, showing the average number of positive and negative acts seen by happy and sad subjects for themselves and their partners on a videotape (after Forgas, Bower & Krantz, 1984).

It seems reasonable to assume that everyday social judgments in close relationships that are not based on the objective evidence of a video recording may be even more likely to be influenced by a person's temporary mood than judgments of videotaped encounters. Of course, in close relationships, variables such as relationship satisfaction and a variety of other distal factors may also modify or even overwhelm the kind of automatic mood effects demonstrated here, a question that deserves more attention from researchers than it has received to date.

Following this surprising and rather counterintuitive demonstration of emotional distortions in social cognition and judgments, a series of follow-up studies helped us to specify the exact processes involved. In one of our experiments (Forgas & Bower, 1987), subjects participated in an impression formation task that involved reading about a variety of other persons on a computer screen and then making social judgments about these targets. The computer was programmed to accurately record how long each subject took to read each piece of information, and to make each impression formation judgment. Results showed that people tended to spend more time reading and learning about information that matched their mood state. This finding provides the first direct evidence that people do pay selective attention to, and learn better mood-consistent rather than inconsistent information, as predicted by the network model.

In our study happy subjects spent more time focusing on the positive characteristics of another person, whereas sad subjects preferred to look at negative details more; partners in a close relationship may well be similarly influenced in the way they appraise each other. Subsequent interpersonal judgments and attributions may then be distorted in an affect-consistent direction. Certainly the analysis of impression formation judgments in our study revealed the now-familiar mood-bias effect: Happy people made more positive, lenient judgments, whereas sad people were far more likely to be critical in their perception of the target character. Remarkably, the time taken to make each judgment was also influenced by mood: Mood-consistent judgments took less time to make than judgments that were inconsistent with the judges' prevailing mood. Once again, this is generally consistent with the predictions of the mood-priming model, which assumes that the superior activation and availability of mood-related constructs should be reflected in faster mood-consistent rather than inconsistent judgments.

The results of this experiment tended to support the predictions of priming models. By "spreading activation, a dominant emotion will enhance the availability of emotion-congruent interpretations and salience of congruent stimulus materials for learning" (Bower, 1981, p. 451). A richer associative base in turn may lead to the slower and more detailed processing of mood-consistent details in a learning task (Craik & Tulving, 1975), but the faster retrieval of mood-relevant details in a judgmental task. Mood-consistent details may also serve to enhance the intensity of existing moods, motivating judges to give such information greater attention. Mood-consistent details may also act to selectively remind subjects of congruent episodes from their past, again resulting in the slower and more detailed processing of such materials in learning tasks.

In other studies, we looked at the role of mood states in how young children learn, remember, and use information in their social judgments about others. Such mood-based distortions in interpersonal perceptions and evaluations may have important consequences for emerging patterns of friendship and social adjustment in childhood. Once again, significant mood-based differences in cognitive processing were found (Forgas, Burnham, & Trimboli, 1988), although the results were in some respects quite different from the adult data. For example, children demonstrated a significant negativity bias in their memory and judgments about others, something that could influence their emerging friendship patterns. Such negativity biases are rarely found with adults, who are presumably socialized to be particularly cautious in forming negative judgments about others, although a negativity bias may occur in close relationships. To the extent that children have a more restricted repertoire of emotional experiences, and may not have fully internalized adult norms of politeness, these differences were not entirely surprising.

Despite the overall support our studies provided for the associative network model, there are several problems that have also been identified. The effects of negative moods were found to be less consistent and enduring than positive mood effects. There are several possible alternative explanations for this. A critical part of socialization is to learn to control and deal with negative emotional states; it may be that the rules and norms pertaining to negative affect and its expression are superimposed on the kind of mood-priming processes predicted by the network model. If this were the case, we would expect that young children would be far more likely to give free expression to the kind of cognitive distortions associated with negative moods than adults do, and indeed, there is some evidence for such a difference from our research (Forgas et al., 1988). The relative volatility of negative mood effects on social perception and judgments may be contrasted to research on close relationships and indeed, on impression formation generally, where negative affect, events, or behaviors are generally found to have particularly significant effects (Forgas, 1985b). This apparent inconsistency may be reconciled, however, if we consider that it is precisely because people are aware of the greater salience and importance of negative information that they may consciously choose to control the influence of their negative moods when it comes to assessing others. A more detailed study of mood effects on social cognition and judgments in close relationships may help to clarify the nature of these processes.

A second suggestion is that positive and negative moods not only influence memory processes, but also selectively trigger different information-processing strategies. Negative moods in particular may be related to a slower, more detailed, and analytic kind of information-processing strategy, whereas positive moods lead to faster, more open, creative but also less analytic processing (Fiedler, 1991; Schwarz & Bless, 1991). Motivational as well as cognitive principles may be involved, as people are presumably motivated to control and escape from an aversive mood state, and this may lead them to consciously and selectively focus on potentially rewarding information. Some of these possibilities were examined in several of our recent experiments, where we looked at the effects of positive and negative moods on social decisions, choices, and attributions.

AFFECTIVE INFLUENCES
ON INTERPERSONAL ATTRIBUTIONS
AND DECISIONS

If mood states influence not only information storage and retrieval but also the way that information, once available, is used, this may have widespread implications for the way complex social judgments, attributions, and decisions are made. In several recently completed experiments, we looked at the role of short-term mood states in how people make attributions and inferences about each other, again one of the critical aspects of interpersonal relationships (Fletcher & Fincham, this volume). In a series of three experiments, the influence of mood on explanations of success and failure in self and others was investigated (Forgas, Bower, & Moylon, 1991). In the first study, subjects feeling happy or sad had to make attributions for the success or failure of a target person in a typical life dilemma, such as succeeding or failing in a job or winning or losing on an investment, a task previously successfully used in similar studies (Forgas, 1981). Generally, subjects in a good mood were likely to make positive, lenient attributions, preferentially identifying internal, stable causes for success, and external, unstable causes for failure. Although this study was successful in establishing that transient moods indeed predispose people toward more lenient or critical attributions, it suffered from several shortcomings. It only looked at attributions to others for hypothetical outcomes and was not designed to assess critically the role of cognitive as against motivational processes in the attribution outcome, one of the central issues in research on attributional biases.

In the next experiment, attributions were made for a real-life event, doing well or badly on an exam, and this time actor-observer differences were also investigated, by assessing attributions to the self as against others. The results again showed that positive mood resulted in more favorable attributions to both self and other. However, negative mood led to some surprising and paradoxical effects. Instead of displaying an increased self-serving bias, subjects in a bad mood were particularly critical of themselves, blaming stable and internal causes for their failure, and crediting unstable, external causes for their successes; yet this bias did not generalize to others, who continued to be given credit for succeeding, and little blame for failing (see Fig. 6.6).

These effects are difficult to reconcile with the affect-priming model, which predicts similar and balanced mood effects irrespective of the judgmental target, and both for positive and negative moods. However, our results are also inconsistent with motivational explanations of attributional biases, which predict that subjects should be most likely to engage in self-serving attributions when they need it most, that is, in a negative mood. The most likely account for this pattern of results is that affective states influence not only information storage and retrieval, as predicted by mood-priming models, but also preferred information-processing strategies. Affect may be seen as informing a person that "all is well in the world" (when in a good mood), or "watch out, there is trouble!" (when in a bad mood).

It makes adaptive sense, then, that people in a good mood engage in open, constructive, and relatively careless information processing, and as a result are strongly influenced by the superior availability of affect-consistent cognitions from their memory system. In close relationships, all things being equal, positive mood should correspond to an open, easy-going, and relatively uncritical cognitive style associated with lenient and generous interpersonal judgments and evaluations. Negative mood, in contrast, seems to lead to slow, detailed, and analytic processing of the available information, the imposition of controlled information-processing strategies, and particular focus on the self. This reaction may tend to result in conscious information-processing strategies that can counterbalance the effects of the greater availability of affect-consistent cognitions and may lead to particularly negative assessments of the self, without similar

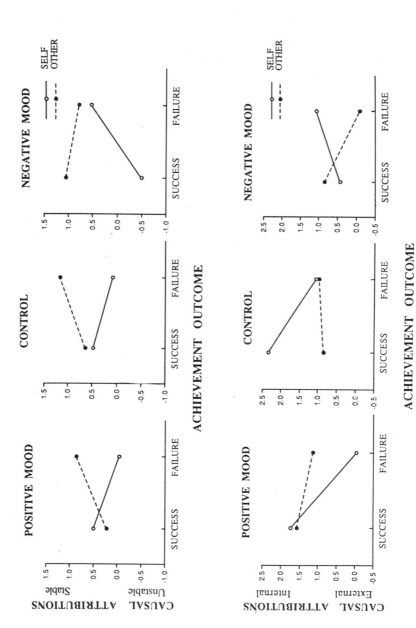

FIG. 6.6. The influence of affect on attribution judgments for success and failure outcomes for self and others for (a) attributions to internal vs. external, and (b) stable vs. unstable causes (after Forgas et al., 1990).

168

consequences for judgments of others. Of course, the picture may be far more complex in close relationships, where judgments of the self and judgments of the partner are not necessarily independent (Fletcher, Fitness, & Blampied, 1990).

There is also some support for the kind of self-partner differences we found from the clinical literature dealing with depressive affect and cognition. Clinically depressed patients exhibit a similar pattern to that found in several of our studies (Forgas & Bower, 1987, 1988; Forgas et al., 1984). Depressed people are often more critical of themselves than they are of others, tend to selectively blame themselves for negative outcomes, and are more likely to remember unpleasant or negative events than others do (Ottaviani & Beck, 1988; Roth & Rehm, 1980). The role of depression in marital attributions and satisfaction is also receiving increasing attention, and there is growing evidence that attributions exert a causal influence on judgments of relationship quality (Fincham & Bradbury, 1989).

As we come to see the role of affect in cognition as rather more complex and subtle than implied by the original mood-priming models, it may be possible to look at emotional influences on such complex and elusive cognitive tasks as interpersonal decisions and choices. There is some early evidence from the pioneering work of Schachter (1959) suggesting that a person's emotional state may have significant influences on interpersonal choices. It seems that people who are in a negative mood, as a result of being made anxious, not only prefer the company of others, but most prefer the company of those who are in a similar predicament, presumably because they assume that such partners may potentially be a source of comfort to them.

It is intriguing to consider whether negative moods may also trigger specific information-processing strategies targeted to achieve rewarding outcomes, a process that may underlie the kind of selective relationship preferences demonstrated by Schachter and others. In a related series of investigations, we looked at such interpersonal decisions by subjects who were experimentally made to experience a mild positive or negative affective state, as a result of succeeding or failing on a bogus test. Unlike Schachter's early studies, we were interested not only in the kind of interpersonal choices subjects made (the decision outcome), but also in the kind of information they selected and the decision-making strategies they adopted.

In this experiment (Forgas, 1989) subjects who were made to feel happy or sad had the task of selecting a partner for an anticipated cooperative task for themselves or another person from a number of potential candidates. Each of the candidates was described in a personal file in terms of a large number of relevant personal qualities, each recorded on a separate card. Some of the information related to the potential partners' ability to reward others, interpersonal skills and personality, and other details related to their intelligence and task competence. Subjects were asked to number every card (information unit) sequentially as they consulted it, and also rate their perception of the relevance of the information it

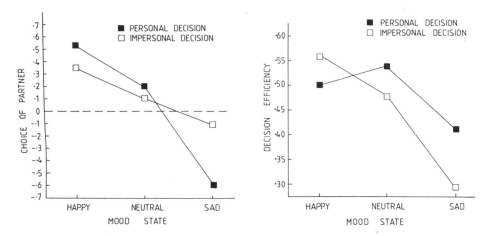

FIG. 6.7.   The effects of mood on interpersonal decisions for (a) partner choice, and (b) decision efficiency. Higher values indicate preference for more competent partners and more efficient decision strategies (after Forgas, 1989).

contained. In this way, we obtained a step-by-step record of the decision processes adopted by happy and sad subjects and their evaluation of the information
they dealt with.

Overall, we found that happy subjects reached a decision faster, were more
efficient in dealing with information and eliminating irrelevant details, focused
more on the task-related qualities of the potential partners, and ultimately made
choices that indicated preferences for competent rather then merely rewarding
partners. In other words, in a positive mood subjects adopted an efficient and
reasonably appropriate strategy by focusing on task-related features. In contrast,
sad subjects were slower, less efficient, and paid more attention to the personality
and social skills of potential partners. Ultimately, they preferred partners who
were socially rewarding rather than competent. As far as the actual decision-
making strategy was concerned, happy subjects were more likely to adopt a more
efficient, comparison-by-features type strategy in their decisions than were sad
subjects. A summary of the results is shown in Fig. 6.7.

SUMMARY AND CONCLUSIONS

The evidence outlined in this chapter has important and relatively clear-cut
implications for research on interpersonal relationships. Affect has a critical
influence on cognition in relationships (Bradbury & Fincham, 1987), yet the
precise nature of this influence is still far from clearly understood. The evidence
surveyed in this chapter illustrates both the static role of affect in the organization

and representation of social information that is relevant to relationships, such as knowledge structures about relationship scripts and interaction episodes, and the dynamic role of affective states in influencing information storage and retrieval, as well as the processing of relationship information. The results of our studies also suggest that the role of affect in cognitive representation of relationship scripts and interpersonal episodes in relationships is strongly influenced by personal and individual variables such as personality, social skills, and attitudes and values (Forgas, 1982a; Mayer & Salovey, 1988). Affect was also found to have a significant influence on social judgments and interpersonal decisions and attributions, according to the cumulative evidence of a growing number of investigations both by ourselves and others (Clore & Parrott, 1991; Fiedler, 1991; Forgas, 1989; Forgas & Bower, 1987, 1988; Schwarz & Clore, 1988). What are some of the implications of these findings for relationship research?

At the most general level, these results suggest that there is a general and pervasive tendency for people to perceive and interpret social events in terms of their feelings about them, and to organize their implicit knowledge of such information primarily in terms of connotative, affective dimensions. Close relationships are characterized by the richness and variability of the shared knowledge between the partners, and frequently, the same event or behavior is understood and interpreted by the partners very differently, despite their extensive share knowledge of each other and the context (Fincham & Bradbury, 1989). This is a phenomenon often observed in marriage counseling, and one of its underlying causes may well be the different feelings elicited by the same situation in two different people. In our research on social episodes, we were often surprised by how different the perceptions of identical episode domains may be for two individuals, due solely to their different affective reactions.

Given that close relationships are characterized by a particularly complex and elaborate shared context between the partners, and an extensive informational base partners possess about each other, mood-induced biases in information selection, retrieval, and interpretation of the kind demonstrated here may have particularly important consequences for decisions and judgments made within close relationships. There is some recent evidence suggesting that mood effects on cognition and judgments are most likely to be significant when the information base is complex and elaborate, selective and constructive processing is required, and the evidence is capable of supporting alternative interpretations (cf. Forgas, 1991). These conditions are by and large fulfilled in close relationships, suggesting that further research on affective influences on perceptions and attributions between partners in close relationships is amply justified. The methods described here are readily adaptable to empirically analyzing such covert, implicit perceptual differences between partners, and should be readily applicable to research on close relationships.

Apart from the major role of affect in static representations of social information, the studies outlined in the second part of the chapter indicated that affective states also have a potentially critical influence on information storage and retrieval, and a variety of social judgments, decisions, and attributions, both about ourselves and about others. This in turn suggests that critical decisions and judgments about a relationship or one's partner are more likely to be lenient and positive when a person is in a positive mood state, and more likely to be negative or critical when the judge is in a dysphoric mood. This conclusion must be tempered by a number of important qualifications, however. There is growing evidence suggesting that positive and negative moods are not equally effective in influencing information processing and judgments. Negative mood effects are typically less robust and more dependent on a variety of situational and contextual factors. Moreover, not all judgments are equally influenced by mood; we have seen that negative moods in particular are far more likely to influence self-relevant judgments and cognitions than judgments of others, at least when the targets are not intimately known. These exceptions suggest that in addition to the affect-priming principles proposed by Bower (1981), a variety of other factors— social, motivational, or personal in character—also influence how affective states influence cognition and ultimately, perceptions and judgments in interpersonal relationships.

We began this discussion by emphasising the important role that affect plays in cognition in close relationships. We may conclude by observing that, although much has been discovered about the information-processing and representational functions of affective states, not enough of this evidence has so far come from research directly concerned with close relationships. This is all the more regrettable because close relationships are particularly promising as an ecologically valid research domain concerning the links between affect and cognition. Given the growing sophistication of the theories and methods now applied in relationship research, to which this book bears clear testimony, studies of both the static and the dynamic aspects of the affect-cognition relationship will no doubt flourish in the future.

REFERENCES

Abelson, R. P. (1976). Script processing in attitude formation and decision making. In J. Carroll & J. Payne (Eds.), *Cognition and social behavior*. Hillsdale, NJ: Erlbaum.

Abelson, R. P. (1980). *The psychological status of the script concept* (Cognitive Science Technical Report No. 2). New Haven, CT: Yale University.

Argyle, M. (1991). A critique of cognitive approaches to social interaction and social judgments. In J. P. Forgas (Ed.), *Emotion and social judgments*. Oxford: Pergamon Press.

Asch, S. E. (1952). *Social psychology*. New York: Prentice-Hall.

Barker, R. G. (1968). *Ecological psychology*. Stanford, CA: Stanford University Press.

Blumer, R. (1969). *Symbolic interactionism*. Englewood Cliffs, NJ: Prentice-Hall.

Bolton, C. D. (1961). Mate selection as the development of a relationship. *Marriage and Family Living, 23*, 234–240.

Bond, M. H., & Forgas, J. P. (1984). Linking person perception to behavior intention across cultures: The role of cultural collectivism. *Journal of Cross-Cultural Psychology, 15*, 337–352.

Bower, G. H. (1981). Mood and memory. *American Psychologist, 36*, 129–148.

Bower, G. H. (1991). Mood congruity effects in social judgments. In J. P. Forgas (Ed.), *Emotion and social judgments*. Oxford: Pergamon Press.

Bradbury, T., & Fincham, F. (1987). Affect and cognition in close relationships: Towards an integrative model. *Cognition and Emotion, 1*, 59–87.

Brunswik, E. (1956). *Perception and the representative design of psychological experiments.* Berkeley: University of California Press.

Clore, G. L. & Parrott (1991). Moods and their vicissitudes: Thoughts and feelings as information. In J. P. Forgas (Ed.), *Emotion and social judgments*. Oxford: Pergamon Press.

Craik, F. I. M., & Tulving, E. (1975). Depth of processing and the retention of words in episodic memory. *Journal of Experimental Psychology: General, 104*, 268–294.

Fiedler, K. (1991). On the task, the measures and the mood: Research an affect and social cognition. In J. P. Forgas (Ed.), *Emotion and social judgments*. Oxford: Pergamon Press.

Fincham, F., & Bradbury, T. (1989). The impact of attributions in marriage: An individual difference analysis. *Journal of Social and Personal Relationships, 6*, 69–85.

Fletcher, G. J. O., Fitness, J., & Blampied, N. M. (1990). The link between attribution and happiness in close relationships: The roles of depression and explanatory style. *Journal of Social and Clinical Psychology, 9*, 243–255.

Forgas, J. P. (1976). The perception of social episodes: Categorical and dimensional representations in two social milieus. *Journal of Personality and Social Psychology, 33*, 199–209.

Forgas, J. P. (1978). Social episodes and social structure in an academic setting: The social environment of an intact group. *Journal of Experimental Social Psychology, 14*, 434–448.

Forgas, J. P. (1979). *Social episodes: The study of interaction routines*. New York: Academic Press.

Forgas, J. P. (1981). Responsibility attribution by groups and individuals: The effects of the interaction episode. *European Journal of Social Psychology, 11*, 423–431.

Forgas, J. P. (1982a). Episode cognition: Internal representations of interaction routines. In L. Berkowitz (Ed.), *Advances in Experimental Social Psychology* (pp. 59–101). New York: Academic Press.

Forgas, J. P. (1982b). Multidimensional scaling in social psychology. In A. P. M. Coxon & P. M. Davis (Eds.), *Key texts in multidimensional scaling* (pp. 144–162). London: Heinemann.

Forgas, J. P. (1983a). Episode cognition and personality: A multidimensional analysis. *Journal of Personality, 51*, 34–48.

Forgas, J. P. (1983b). Social skills and the perception of interaction episodes. *British Journal of Clinical Psychology, 22*, 195–207.

Forgas, J. P. (1983c). What is social about social cognition? *British Journal of Social Psychology, 22*, 129–144.

Forgas, J. P. (1985a). *Interpersonal behaviour: The psychology of social interaction*. Oxford & Sydney: Pergamon Press.

Forgas, J. P. (1985b). Person prototypes and cultural salience: The role of cognitive and cultural factors in impression formation. *British Journal of Social Psychology, 24*, 3–17.

Forgas, J. P. (1989). Mood effects on personal and impersonal decisions. *Australian Journal of Psychology, 40*, 125–145.

Forgas, J. P. (Ed.). (1991). *Emotion and social judgments*. Oxford: Pergamon Press.

Forgas, J. P., & Bond, M. (1985). Cultural influences on the perceptions of interaction episodes. *Personality and Social Psychology Bulletin, 11*, 75–88.

Forgas, J. P., & Bower, G. H. (1987). Mood effects on person perception judgments. *Journal of Personality and Social Psychology, 53*, 53–60.

Forgas, J. P., & Bower, G. H. (1988). Affect in social and personal judgments. In K. Fiedler & J. P. Forgas (Eds.), *Affect, cognition and social behaviour* (pp. 183–208). Toronto: Hogrefe.

Forgas, J. P., Bower, G. H., & Krantz, S. (1984). The influence of mood on perceptions of social interactions. *Journal of Experimental Social Psychology, 20*, 497–513.

Forgas, J. P., Bower, G. H., & Moylan, J. J. (1990). Praise or blame? Affective influences on attributions for achievement. Journal of Personality and Social Psychology, *59*, 809–819.

Forgas, J. P., Burnham, D., & Trimboli, C. (1988). Mood, memory and social judgments in children. *Journal of Personality and Social Psychology, 54*, 697–703.

Forgas, J. P., & Dobosz, B. (1980). Dimensions of romantic involovement: Towards a taxonomy of heterosexual relationships. *Social Psychology Quarterly, 43*, 290–300.

Goffman, E. (1974). *Frame analysis.* Harmondsworth, Eng.: Penguin.

Heider, F. (1958). *The psychology of interpersonal relations.* New York: Wiley.

Hilgard, E. R. (1980). Consciousness in contemporary psychology. *Annual Review of Psychology, 31*, 1–26.

Huston, T. L., & Levinger, G. (1978). Interpersonal attraction and relationships. *Annual Review of Psychology, 29*, 115–156.

Kantor, J. P. (1924). *Principles of psychology* (Vol. 1). Bloomington, IN: Principia Press.

Kelly, G. A. (1955). *The psychology of personal constructs.* New York: Norton.

Levinger, G. (1980). Toward the analysis of close relationships. *Journal of Experimental Social Psychology, 16*, 510–544.

Lewin, K. (1936). *Principles of topological psychology.* New York: McGraw-Hill.

Marwell, G., & Hage, J. (1970). The organization of role relationships: A systematic description. *American Sociological Review, 35*, 884–900.

Mayer, J. D., & Salovey, P. (1988). Personality moderates the interaction of mood and cognition (pp. 87–99). In K. Fiedler & J. P. Forgas (Eds.), *Affect, cognition and social behaviour.* Toronto: Hogrefe.

Mischel, W. (1968). *Personality and assessment.* New York: Wiley.

Ottaviani, R., & Beck, A. T. (1988). Recent trends in cognitive theories of depression. In K. Fiedler & J. P. Forgas (Eds.), *Affect, cognition and social behaviour* (pp. 209–218). Toronto: Hogrefe.

Pervin, L. A. (1976). A free response description approach to the study of person situation interaction. *Journal of Personality and Social Psychology, 34*, 465–474.

Rands, M., & Levinger, G. (1979). Implicit theories of relationship: An intergenerational study. *Journal of Personality and Social Psychology, 37*, 645–661.

Reiss, I. (1960). Towards a sociology of the heterosexual love relationship. *Marriage and Family Living, 22*, 139–145.

Roth, D., & Rehm, L. P. (1980). Relationship between self-monitoring processes, memory and depression. *Cognitive Therapy and Research, 4*, 149–157.

Schachter, S. (1959). *The psychology of affiliation.* Stanford, CA: Stanford University Press.

Schwarz, N., & Bless, G. (1991). Happy and mindless, but sad and smart? The impact of affective states on analytic reasoning. In J. P. Forgas (Ed.), *Emotion and social judgments.* Oxford: Pergamon Press.

Schwarz, N., & Clore, G. L. (1988). How do I feel about it? The informative functions of affective states. In K. Fiedler & J. P. Forgas (Eds.), *Affect, cognition and social behaviour* (pp. 44–62). Toronto: Hogrefe.

Thomas, W. I. (1966/1928). Situational analysis: The behavior pattern and the situation. Reprinted in M. Janowitz (Ed.), *W. I. Thomas on social organization and social personality* (pp. 154–167). Chicago: Chicago University Press.

Waller, W. (1961). *The sociology of teaching.* New York: Wiley.

Weber, M. (1968). *Economy and society.* New York: Bedminster.

Wish, M., Deutsch, M., & Kaplan, S. (1976). Perceived dimensions of interpersonal relations. *Journal of Personality and Social Psychology, 33*, 409–420.

Zajonc, R. (1980). Feeling and thinking: Preferences need no inferences. *American Psychologist, 35*, 151–175.

7

Affect in Close Relationships

Julie Fitness
Ken Strongman
University of Canterbury

The study of affect in close relationships is simultaneously a fascinating, yet exasperating experience. On the one hand, because most human beings describe their close relationships in terms of their feelings and emotions (love, hate, fear, anger, contempt, gratitude, and so on), one has a sense that, of all possible theoretical and empirical approaches to close relationships, the affective is possibly the most basic and the most meaningful.

On the other hand, the affective approach is also, without doubt, one of the most difficult areas in psychology to conceptualize, analyze, and theorize about in a meaningful way. Primarily, this is a function of the problematic nature of affect, or emotion, as a readily definable, observable, measurable entity. The term *affect* is a theoretical construct, typically used as a catch-all generic to include all manner of phenomena that could loosely be described as emotional. Consequently, until recently, psychologists working within the area of close relationships (and elsewhere) have usually opted to study more easily operationalized variables, such as observable behavior, than to tackle the seemingly nebulous, subjective world of emotions and moods. This is not so true of the clinical arena, where therapists have been struggling since the advent of psychoanalysis to understand and deal more effectively with emotional phenomena; indeed, a sizable part of our folk wisdom about emotions is a legacy of Freudian analysis. On the whole, however, research and theory building have proceeded in a parallel rather than interactive fashion within the separate topic areas of emotion and close relationships, and the amount of academically based research into affective phenomena that has been specifically conducted within an interpersonal context is both minimal and fragmentary.

Happily, we believe a stage has now been reached where a significant point of convergence between these two topic areas (emotion and close relationships) is in sight. This point of convergence can be loosely defined in terms of *cognition,* a concept that subsumes a wide range of conscious and unconscious phenomena (such as perception, memory, language, appraisal, evaluation, beliefs, attitudes, expectations, and problem solving). Within the field of emotion, the most recent empirical and theoretical work has underscored the extreme difficulty of accounting for emotion without considering the central and necessary role of cognition (Strongman, 1987). Similarly, within the field of close relationships, the importance of understanding cognitive processes and their role in relationship satisfaction is reflected in the burgeoning research and theorizing in this area. Cognition, then, forms a pivotal point at which the two fields of inquiry merge and overlap.

Consequently, the focus of this chapter is on cognition and its role in emotion within the wider context of close relationships. The first goal is to describe some of the behavioral and physiological approaches that have been taken to the study of affect in relationships (with particular focus on Gottman's studies of interactive, emotional behavior in the laboratory). We suggest ways in which such approaches might be most profitably integrated and enriched with a consideration of cognitive phenomena. The second goal is to sketch the current state of knowledge concerning the cognition–emotion relationship within the interpersonal context. As the first step toward this goal, we discuss cognitive aspects of emotion in close relationships from the perspective of those who hold that emotion is simply a product of cognition (Ellis, 1962). Then, we approach the cognition-affect relationship from the other direction and describe Clarke's (1987) work on affective sequences in marriage from an affect-first perspective. In addition, we cover in some detail Leventhal's (1979, 1982) integrative perceptual motor theory of emotion and evaluate its application in a marital therapy setting (Johnson & Greenberg, 1985). Our reasons for focusing on the clinical literature are twofold. First, we consider that therapies such as Ellis' (1962) rational emotive therapy and Johnson and Greenberg's (1985) emotionally focused therapy represent clear exemplars of the theoretical positions noted above. Second, we believe it is appropriate to consider such literature, given the amount of work that has been generated from a clinical perspective concerning the emotion–close relationship interface.

The final goal is to identify the most obvious gaps in our understanding, and to make some theoretical and methodological suggestions for further exploration in this area. Using Berscheid's (1983) analysis of emotion in close relationships as a framework, we relate her theory to current understandings about cognition and emotion, with particular reference to cognitive appraisal theories and prototype analyses of specific, interpersonal emotions. In particular, we argue that multifaceted research programs that incorporate self-reports of subjective and cognitive variables, reliable observations of emotional behavior, and a consideration of physiological variables will permit a more sophisticated analysis of emotional phenomena in close relationships than has hitherto been attempted.

BEHAVIORAL INDICES OF AFFECT

Behaviorally oriented theorists and researchers account for emotion in terms of observable emotional behaviors rather than internal states. Their approach has been particularly influential in the field of marital therapy, where therapists strive to deal with couples' so-called emotional problems and behaviors on a daily basis. Behavioral therapists do not usually regard emotion as being directly relevant to a couple's problems; rather, they typically seek to avoid the distraction of emotional displays (Coyne, 1986), and attempt to deal with troubled couples' emotions, such as anger, disappointment, hurt, and hatred, by relegating them to the role of symptoms of relationship distress. Once these troubling emotions have been safely categorized and accounted for in this way, they can be viewed as superfluous to the real problems causing the distress—for example, low rates of mutually reinforcing behaviors and communication skill deficits.

Where behaviorally oriented researchers have dealt with affect, they have tended to define it in terms of behavioral displays. For example, in his early pioneering work dealing with marital interaction, Gottman (1979) defined affect as "nonverbal behaviors of the speaker during message transmission," rather than as an "inner, emotional state" (p. 79). He videotaped married couples' interactions in the laboratory and had observers code the affective component of each message as positive, negative, or neutral, using the Couples Interaction Scoring System (CISS). In this system, affect is rated via three channels: facial expression, tone of voice, and body position or movements.

Results consistently indicated that distressed couples evince higher rates of negative affect than nondistressed couples; also, that distressed couples are more likely to reciprocate each other's negative affect than nondistressed couples. These findings have been confirmed by several researchers (e.g., Margolin & Wampold, 1981; Revenstorf, 1984; Schaap, 1982), leading Notarius and Herrick (1989) to confidently claim that negative affect reciprocity is the most critical feature of distressed marital interaction.

In addition to its role in indicating current distress, however, negative affect reciprocity can also be predictive of changes in marital satisfaction. In the first of a series of combined behavioral observation, affective self-report and physiologically monitored interaction studies, Levenson and Gottman (1983) videotaped 30 couples in three situations: first, as they were waiting together quietly, second, as they discussed the day's events for 15 minutes, and third, as they attempted to solve a marital problem for 15 minutes. Three years later, 19 of the 30 couples were located and their marital satisfaction assessed (Levenson & Gottman, 1985). Results indicated that negative affect reciprocity at Time 1 was strongly predictive of change in marital satisfaction at Time 2. Specifically, declines in satisfaction were associated with greater reciprocity of the husband's negative affect by the wife, and less reciprocity of the wife's negative affect by the husband. Thus, according to Levenson and Gottman, a vicious affective cycle tends to become set up in distressed couples' interactions, with the wife expressing increasing amounts of negative emotion while the husband withdraws emotionally. She reacts with increasingly intense negative affect, and the husband either distances himself still further or becomes devastatingly expressive as he loses emotional control (Notarius & Johnson, 1982).

Coding Couples Specific Emotions: SPAFF

Measuring and classifying affective behavior in a global fashion as either positive or negative are straightforward procedures and have the distinct advantage of parsimony. Moreover, this hedonic dimension is often claimed to be central in classifying emotions. For example, from the results of his studies on the dimensions of emotion, Russell (1978) claimed that pleasure–displeasure is the major dimension within the semantic domain of emotion terms. Similarly, based on their prototype studies of emotion, Shaver, Schwartz, Kirson, and O'Connor (1987) argued that the positive versus negative dimension is the only meaningful distinction between emotion categories. However, over the past 10 years it has become increasingly obvious that people in close relationships actually experience an enormous number of emotions. Although each of these can be subsumed within an overall pleasurable or displeasurable category, we consider the amount of useful information that can be gleaned from this approach is limited. For example, when researchers speak of "negative affect reciprocity" between distressed marital partners, it is never clear from the global affect codes whether or not the same affect is being reciprocated—does anger evoke anger, or contempt or sadness?

In recognition of this problem, Gottman and his colleagues (Gottman & Levenson, 1986) recently developed a coding scheme to separate some of the components of negative affect into sadness, anger, disgust or contempt, fear and whining, and positive affect into affection, humor, interest, anticipation, excitement, or joy (SPAFF: Specific Affect Coding System). Coders classify speech units according to SPAFF in a rather intuitive way by considering a gestalt of nonverbal cues, including voice tone, verbal content, facial expression, and body movement. Several studies using this system have underscored the utility of refining global affect categories into more discriminable components. In one conflict discussion, for example, Gottman and Levenson (1986) found that 77.7% of the husband's negative affect consisted of anger and contempt, whereas these emotions accounted for only 6.7% of the wife's negative affect. However, 93.2% of her negative affect consisted of whining, sadness, and fear.

Similarly, in a longitudinal study Gottman and Krokoff (1989) found a wife's expression of contempt and anger correlated negatively with her current marital satisfaction, but positively with a change in her satisfaction. A wife's fear predicted a decline in her satisfaction, whereas a husband's whining predicted a decline in his; her sadness predicted a deterioration in satisfaction for both partners. Gottman and Krokoff (1989) argued that the wife has a complex role as emotional manager of marital disputes. On the one hand, she must encourage her husband to confront disagreements, but not to whine, whereas on the other hand, she should express her own anger openly, without being fearful or sad and without provoking her husband to turn off and withdraw emotionally. The entire procedure sounds like a good deal of hard emotional labor.

Gottman's attempts to go beyond global affect measures and differentiate the kinds of emotions partners express are laudable. However, we believe the SPAFF coding scheme presents some problems. For example, although observers coded specific affects displayed in the videotaped interactions, the couples themselves indicated their affect on a rating dial, from very negative through neutral to very positive (on a nine-point scale). Thus, in order to assess the validity of the observers' coding, the SPAFF categories had to be collapsed into global positive and negative ones, so providing a very limited test of the scheme's utility. A second problem relates to the SPAFF emotion coding categories, which could only be described as arbitrary. On the one hand, some of them appear to be derived from easily classifiable emotional behaviors (such as whining) rather than from theoretical accounts of discrete emotion categories (e.g., Izard, 1977), although on the other hand, given that coders are trained to classify emotions on the basis of an overall expressive display, some of the codes would appear to be barely discriminable on the basis of observable behavior (e.g., "humor" and "joy," "anticipation" and "interest"). Thus, while Gottman (1979) claimed to eschew premature theorizing, in this case he does appear to have developed a coding scheme according to a rough a priori theory about the most commonly experienced (or at least expressed) emotions in interactive contexts. This theory may be suspect. For example, using SPAFF, coders would presumably be unable to classify "surprise," "relief," "embarrassment," "guilt," and "frustration," or discriminate between "fear," "worry," and "anxiety"—emotions that may be highly relevant in interpersonal interactions. Indeed, a recent study on dating partners' most typical emotional reactions to self- and partner-initiated relationship behaviors found that "disgust" and "contempt" (SPAFF categories) were very infrequently reported, whereas "frustration," "embarrassment," and "worry" (not included in SPAFF) were relatively frequently reported. Subjects also discriminated between "sadness" and feeling "hurt" in their self reports (Fitness & Fletcher, in press).

Finally, it should be noted that Polivy (1981) and others have commented at some length on the emotion blending that typically occurs in laboratory based, mood-induction studies. Here, as in the real world (no doubt), emotions can occur in rapid sequence and people often experience mixed emotions. Thus, while SPAFF represents a move in the right direction away from gross measures of positive or negative affect states, it is clear that more research is called for in developing an emotion classificatory system adequate for capturing a full range of interpersonal affective behaviors.

PHYSIOLOGICAL INDICES OF AFFECT

There is no doubt that physiological arousal is a very important aspect of emotional experience, although theorists and researchers have not (as yet) been very successful in identifying different emotional states on the basis of differential physiological response patterns. The rationale behind the physiological approach to emotion is that autonomic nervous system arousal is a necessary, though not sufficient, condition for the experience of emotion (Mandler, 1975). Thus, evidence of physiological arousal during a dyadic interaction is a reasonably good indication that an individual is experiencing emotion of some kind (unless the interaction involves vigorous physical activity such as exercising or playing sport together).

Along with coding observable affective behavior, Gottman and others have also measured various physiological indices of affect and have identified some reliable physiological effects that distinguish distressed from nondistressed couples. For example, Levenson and Gottman (1983) found that, during a 15-minute discussion of a marital problem, the level of interrelatedness between spouses' physiological reactions (heart rate, skin conductance, vasculature, and muscular activity) was much higher in distressed couples than nondistressed couples. Indeed, 60% of the variance in marital satisfaction could be accounted for in terms of this linkage. They speculated that a couple's previous experience with problem-solving discussions (perhaps better defined as arguments), along with their expectations about the likely course of the current discussion, leads to increased physiological arousal levels in both partners.

In their follow-up study, Levenson and Gottman (1985) found that high physiological arousal (on all measures) at Time 1 was strongly predictive of declines in marital satisfaction 3 years later. For example, the correlation between the husband's heart rate during the problem discussion and his decline in marital satisfaction was .92, while the correlation between the wife's skin conductance level during the discussion and her decline in satisfaction was $-.76$. In sum, these studies show that high levels of physiological upset in both partners, along with high levels of self-reported and objectively observed negative affect (and negative affect reciprocity), are both concomitants and predictors of marital distress.

Escape Conditioning Model

Given that arguments between unhappy couples tend to escalate in long spirals of increasing negativity, the physiological arousal accompanying conflict discussions may be long lasting and subjectively very unpleasant. Consequently, behavioral sequences that permit escape from the interaction, and that reduce physiological arousal levels, should be reinforcing for both partners in a conflict discussion. Gottman and Levenson (1986) examined marital interactions for such

180

escape moments, or points in the interaction, when both partners experienced a reduction in physiological arousal from a high level (upset) to a relatively low level (calm), and the reinforcing behavioral sequences accompanying such moments. In general, they found such sequences to be typically detrimental to long-term marital accord. For example, one woman who was hardly ever angry or contemptuous in nonescape moments tended to express anger and contempt in 53% of escape or tension-reducing moments. This corresponds with Levenson and Gottman's (1985) observation that distressed wives' typical emotion expressions tend to comprise mainly fear and sadness. With sufficient conditioning trials, this wife's display of anger is likely to become associated with reduced physiological arousal for both spouses, and, over time, relationship disputes will probably be settled with an expression of the wife's temper, when she has finally had enough. Alternately, Bradbury and Fincham (1987) suggested that many couples' escape moments may comprise laughter (by both spouses) at the wife's incompetence, as she takes the blame for the preceding argument.

Gottman and Levenson (1986) argued that this escape-conditioning model explains a great deal of the observed predictability and rigid behavioral sequences characteristic of distressed couples' interactions. In addition, they speculated that the same model might account for the more harmonious exchanges between happy couples. If such couples typically escape from negative interaction sequences and associated autonomic nervous system arousal by making warm, loving responses, then after a number of conditioning trials this may become a habitual, positive means of relieving tension and restoring calm in the relationship.

Gender Differences in Arousal

Gottman and Levenson (1986, 1988) also speculated that there are differences between men and women in their ability to deal effectively with autonomic nervous system (ANS) arousal. They proposed that males show greater autonomic nervous system responses to stress and recover more slowly than females; therefore, the arousal associated with negative affect is subjectively more intense, unpleasant, and persistent for males than females. They argued that males might tend to withdraw emotionally when arguments become too heated because they are simply trying to regulate their levels of negative arousal. However, and somewhat ironically, if males typically deal with stressful arguments by means of extreme negative affect control, or stonewalling (deliberately suppressing emotional expression and verbal responses in the course of an argument), they may actually be intensifying their ANS arousal rather than reducing it (Gottman and Levenson, 1988). This emotional intensification is particularly likely to happen if the arousal is accompanied by specific kinds of negative cognitions and attributions concerning the irresponsibility and general hatefulness of the spouse and her behavior (Epstein, 1984). Similarly, Revenstorf (1984) made the point that suppressing emotional responses may be associated with psychosomatic complaints, citing Sifneos (1973), who suggested that many patients with psychosomatic disorders are also alexithymic, that is, unable to decode and express emotions.

One difficulty with the concept of characteristically greater male arousal arises from the literature on affect intensity (Larsen & Diener, 1987). Affect intensity is an individual difference characteristic that relates to temperament, or an individual's regular experience of strong emotions, regardless of specific content or hedonic tone. That is, individuals with high affect intensity scores experience both positive and negative emotions more intensely (but not necessarily more frequently) than those with low scores. In contrast to Gottman's hypothesis concerning greater male ANS arousal, research in this area consistently shows that women in general have higher affect intensity scores than men (e.g., Larsen & Diener, 1987). Perhaps this means that, although women become just as aroused (if not more so) than men, they are able to deal with their arousal more efficiently. Then again, perhaps it is part of men's stonewalling techniques to perceive their arousal as being less intense than it really is. Clearly, there is room for more research in this area.

Of course, potential physiological gender differences notwithstanding, an individual's learning history and the cultural milieu in which he or she is raised are bound to be pivotal factors in influencing emotional expressivity. Indeed, social constructivist theorists of emotion (e.g., Hochschild, 1983) would claim that it is a society's implicit and explicit emotion rules that largely determine each partner's understanding of his or her negative (and positive) arousal and subsequent behavior (appropriate or otherwise). For example, along with stonewalling, another common male response to marital stress involves the use of physical violence. Dutton, Fehr, and McEwen (1982) hypothesized that many males have learned to interpret the arousal associated with a change in intimacy levels between themselves and their partners as anger, when in fact they may be experiencing anxiety because the partner has acted independently, or conversely is making demands on them they cannot meet. Dutton (1984) reported the results of a study that compared self-report affective responses of wife assaulters and control males to videotaped portrayals of husband–wife conflicts. It was found that physically assaultive males (compared to control males) reported high levels of anger when the woman was presented as dominant and leaving the relationship. Similarly, in a study of inequity and emotions in close relationships, Sprecher (1986) found anger to be the most usual negative emotion associated with a man's perception that he had been unfairly treated in a relationship. Although women also tended to experience anger in the same situation, they were more likely than men to experience sadness and depression. Sprecher explained this in terms of women's tendency to internalize blame for negative events, as opposed to men's tendency to externalize it. Given that many women remain attached to abusive males despite their violent behavior, an interesting issue for future research would be to investigate the wife's interpretation both of her husband's violent behavior, and also of her own emotional responses to it.

Future Directions for Physiological Research

The physiological approach to the investigation of emotion in close relationships has several problems; for example, measurement and recording techniques are intrusive. Also, as Harvey, Hendrick, and Tucker (1988) pointed out, instrumentation is expensive and requires a high degree of expertise to operate efficiently, and of course couples must be willing to have electrodes hooked to them as they discuss their relationship. Consideration must also be given to theoretical issues pertaining to the interpretation of physiological data and emotion differentiation. Mainstream emotion researchers have encountered enormous difficulties in discriminating among emotions on the basis of discrete physiological patterns of activity (Strongman, 1987). Thus, measures of physiological arousal are, at best, only gross indicators of affect (or rather, affective arousal).

One promising technique for differentiating between emotions is the use of facial electromyographic (EMG) measurements to detect micromomentary facial muscle movements. This technique has had some success in discriminating between depressed and nondepressed subjects (Greden, Genero, Price, Feinberg, & Levine, 1986), and such a procedure is potentially very useful as an ongoing indicator of affect (both global and discrete). Again, however, the procedure is intrusive and, as yet, discriminates only the most basic affective states. For most researchers a more practical route may be to employ videotaping procedures and score facial expressions by means of an accurate coding system, for example, the Facial Action Coding System, or FACS (Ekman & Friesen, 1978), a procedure Gottman and his colleagues (e.g., Gottman & Levenson, 1986) have frequently used in their interaction studies. On this note, we should also point out that Smith (1989) has made an excellent beginning in linking certain cognitive appraisal dimensions (such as anticipated effort, agency, and perceived obstacle) with facial and physiological indices of affect, such as changes in heart rate and eyebrow tension. Although he does not claim that his research is likely to produce a battery of physiological indices to serve as substitutes for verbal measures of emotion, we believe this kind of integrative research provides a potentially powerful technique for laboratory-based analyses of interpersonal affective behavior.

COGNITION AND AFFECT

Over the past 10 years, a number of emotion theorists have been absorbed in the intriguing task of attempting to define and describe the relationship between cognition and emotion. Although some theorists have claimed that emotion and cognition are independent systems, with emotion preceding cognition (e.g., Zajonc, 1984), others have asserted that some form of cognitive appraisal (no matter how fleeting) must precede all emotional states (e.g., Lazarus, 1984). Although these two positions have been commonly understood to be mutually exclusive, a good many theorists hold a more moderate, interactive, and integrative view of the relationship between cognition and emotion (e.g., Leventhal, 1979). Naturally, the implications of this theoretical debate have filtered down into various aspects of close relationship research and therapy. Consequently, although some relationship theorists and researchers work predominantly from within the cognition-before-affect perspective (e.g., Ellis, 1962), others work from within the opposite framework (e.g., Clarke, 1987). Recently, however, some researchers and clinicians have oriented themselves toward a more integrative theoretical structure (e.g., Johnson & Greenberg, 1985).

In the next section, we describe and discuss these different perspectives with respect to close relationships. Our aim is to shed some light on the more general theoretical issues involved, and also to illustrate the necessity of considering cognition and cognitive phenomena if we wish to make sense of emotions in interpersonal contexts.

The Cognition-Before-Affect Perspective: RET

Ellis (1962) was one of the earliest researchers to concentrate specifically on clients' cognitions and ideas (particularly the irrational ones) rather than their behaviors. Ellis believes that emotion is always a product of cognition (or as Shakespeare succinctly put it, "There is nothing either good or bad but thinking makes it so"). Consequently, the aim of Ellis' therapy (Rational Emotive Therapy: RET) is to challenge and modify clients' irrational beliefs in order to alleviate intense levels of negative affect and distress. Ellis and Harper (1961) identified five irrational ideas, or beliefs, that typically lead to marital disturbance and distress, including "My partner must love me constantly" and "My partner must fulfill all my needs." Clearly, these are impossible demands, yet such implicit beliefs are the product of a Western culture that emphasizes romantic ideals and happiness ever after if you can only find the right person. However, Ellis and Harper claimed the most pertinent irrational idea that leads to marital distress is the belief that emotion is uncontrollable. If your partner does something reprehensible, then he or she has caused your anger, or unhappiness—consequently, only your partner can relieve your distress, and you are a helpless victim (emotionally) of his or her actions toward you. In fact, as Ellis and Harper pointed out, your anger or unhappiness is a result of your appraisal of what your partner has done: Change your appraisal ("It's not so bad, really") and your emotion should change accordingly. For example, in a fascinating (if rather spine-chilling) chapter about rational and irrational jealousy, Ellis (1977) described how he managed to completely "talk himself out" of this highly unpleasant emotion by refusing to "catastrophize" the fact that his partner was interested in another. He went so far as to claim that partners who love each other can eradicate jealousy altogether if they would only talk to themselves rationally when confronted with threatening situations.

RET certainly has the potential to help uncover the kinds of dysfunctional explicit cognitions and implicit assumptions that elicit (or accompany) and reinforce negative emotions, and our theoretical knowledge would benefit from a thorough, methodical research program in the area. However, although RET might be a valuable therapeutic tool for couples whose irrational beliefs are setting impossible goals for either partner, there is still a behavioral flavor to the implicit message it communicates—one of emotions as disturbances, annoying end-products of faulty reasoning processes to be kept firmly in line, in order that we can all lead rational, affectively controlled lives, or, as Solomon (1981) so neatly put it, "It's ok to have an emotion, but don't get emotional about it" (p. 179). To Ellis and other theorists of his persuasion (e.g., Beck, 1967), negative emotions are perceived as arising entirely from inappropriate cognitions, and the message is that we can think or talk ourselves out of experiencing acute anger, hurt, and jealousy. However, Taylor and Brown (1988) have documented a great deal of research in social, personal, clinical, and developmental psychology that indicates that normal people possess unrealistically positive views of themselves and their ability to control their environment and the future. Conversely, depressed people tend to assess themselves and their situations without the benefit of such rosy illusions. This may be a case where irrational thinking serves to protect against negative emotion, rather than elicit it (Holt & Lee, 1989).

With respect to RET in close relationships, it is important to consider what happens to a relationship within which the emotions of one or the other partner have been sufficiently watered down or thought out so as not to be disturbing. With all the clinical evidence suggesting that women want men to stop withdrawing emotionally, to stop being so rational, and to express their emotions more openly (Eichenbaum & Orbach, 1983), it is possible that therapies such as RET are simply perpetuating and reinforcing a method of emotion control already used by a great number of men in Western society. It is interesting to speculate that for every woman who has known the frustration of having a man explain to her why her emotion is neither appropriate nor rational, there is probably a man who has been instructed from his earliest years that he ought not experience any emotions at all (other than anger, lust, and bonhomie, perhaps).

The Affect-Before-Cognition Perspective: Clarke's Affective Sequences in Marriage

Ellis' position on the absolute primacy of cognition is extreme and not universally shared. Other researchers, for example, Rachman (1981), have pointed out that modifying cognitions does not necessarily lead to changes in emotional experience. Indeed, there are times when no amount of conscious cognitive work can alleviate or alter an intense emotional experience. For example, a spouse may know that he or she is loved and cherished, yet still experience periods of chronic anxiety and insecurity. Moving to the other extreme of the cognition-affect relationship, Clarke (1987) has recently carried out research into negative emotions in close relationships from an affect-first perspective. Clarke believes that psychological processing is carried out by a three-level, hierarchical system, within which the affective processing system is superordinate to the cognitive system. Indeed, Clarke believes that if we study people's life accounts and examine their motivations for making particular choices along the way, the relative unimportance of cognitive—by which he clearly means conscious and rational—factors becomes clearly evident. Clarke speaks of the core of a close, interpersonal relationship as constituting a dialogue of the emotions, and he conceives affect to be an extremely powerful influence on a couple's perceptions and experience of each other.

In a study designed to delineate some of the most frequently experienced emotional patterns and sequences in married couples, Clarke (1987) had married subjects think of the most typical kinds of emotional sequences and progressions that occurred in marriage (e.g., from romantic love to happiness, and then to boredom or contempt, etc.), drawing on their own knowledge or their knowledge of other people's marriages. Subjects had to think of the sequences in terms of months and years, rather than minutes or hours, and to report emotion reciprocity patterns in strict partner alternation sequences. Each subject then built up five different representations of emotion sequences from nine sets of prearranged emotion clusters (derived from an earlier study on the prevalence of 72 emotions in seven different types of interpersonal relationship; Clarke, Allen, and Dickson, 1985).

The most interesting results of this exercise centred on three negative emotion groups, or clusters. The first group comprised emotions of boredom, insecurity, tension, loneliness, fear, bitterness, rejection, depression, indifference, suspicion, disloyalty, dislike, coldness, hate, guilt, regret, despair, confusion, and feeling unsympathetic and unfulfilled. The second group comprised emotions of anger, restlessness, rivalry, jealousy, envy, and feeling selfish, quarrelsome, and indebted. The third group comprised emotions of anxiety and feeling passive and tied down. Together, these three groups made up what Clarke referred to as an emotional subsystem; that is, a spouse's experience of an emotion from one cluster would typically elicit an emotion in the partner from the second or third cluster, whereupon the first partner would reciprocate with an emotion from within the same subsystem. According to the sequential maps that Clarke was able to draw from his results, these emotion groups appeared to be so richly interconnected that, once within the negative subsystem, a couple would have some difficulty extricating themselves from it. In fact, couples could only escape the subsystem through ashamed types of emotions (which also, unfortunately, led *into* the subsystem). Otherwise, entry was through a cluster of emotions comprising feelings of independence, commitment, generosity, finding the other entertaining, and feeling appreciated, content, and confident.

Given that subjects were instructed to follow a strict partner reciprocity rule, one can imagine a number of intriguing situations in which, for example, one partner's confidence and independence lead to the other's insecurity and loneliness. This in turn makes the first partner feel angry and quarrelsome, which triggers anxiety in the second partner. The first partner might then feel guilty or cold or regretful—but the only way to break the cycle is to feel ashamed, whereupon (presumably) he or she stops doing whatever it was that made the other partner feel miserable, and all is well. Conversely, the depressed partner may feel ashamed of his or her selfishness and break the cycle that way. However, because ashamed emotions can also lead back into the subsystem, the whole cycle may be set to repeat itself indefinitely. Given the rather large number of possible emotional states within the different clusters, one can construct a number of equally plausible scenarios that could conceivably make emotional sense.

At the macro level, the results of this study are interesting in that they identify (albeit very loosely) some of the kinds of emotional progressions and patterns in which the typical couple might expect to be engaged at different times over the course of their relationship. However, at a more micro level, the analysis is less useful and, indeed, difficult to interpret with any confidence. One problem relates to the fact that many of Clarke's (1987) emotion groups consisted of a number of emotions that many theorists would consider discrete and unrelated, for example, anger, fear, contempt, and sadness (Izard, 1977). Similarly, neither Harrison's (1986) factor study of emotion terms nor Shaver et al.'s (1987) prototype study of emotions grouped depression emotions (despairing, lonely, rejected) with fear, (afraid, confused, tense, insecure) guilt, and hatred emotions (unsympathetic, cold, bitter, dislike). However, all these emotion terms comprise one cluster in Clarke's study.

Given that theorists are only now beginning to map out the interconnections and discontinuities between the different kinds of discrete emotions within a number of his subsystems, Clarke's account of emotional progressions between subsystems is too vague and imprecise to be of any predictive value. However, these kinds of data might prove more useful when they have been integrated with a thoroughly detailed analysis of the behaviors and cognitions that accompany not only the shifts between emotional subsystems (accurately and usefully defined), but also the shifts from one discrete kind of emotion to another within each subsystem.

An Integrated Approach to Emotion and Cognition

From the preceding discussions of Ellis' cognition-first and Clarke's affect-first perspectives, it is clear that the suggestion that affect is, at least partly, independent of cognition (Zajonc, 1984) leads us into theoretically troubled waters if we choose to define cognition and affect as mutually exclusive phenomena. For example, Zajonc (1984) claimed affective experience can become conscious before cognition does—people tend to feel first; however, as Parrott and Sabini (1989) pointed out, this is only a problem if one equates cognition with consciousness. Indeed, affect and cognition share a good many properties—both can be affected by drugs, both can be difficult to verbalize, both can become automatic (see Shiffrin & Schneider, 1977, for a review of automatic cognitive processing), and the cognitive work that precedes either phenomenon can become truncated (Parrott & Sabini, 1989). Thus, rather than debating which comes first, cognition or affect, we believe a more sensible strategy is to conceptualize the relationship between the two phenomena as a fluid, interactive one. In any number of contexts, emotion may influence cognition (see Forgas, this volume), whereas cognition (even the briefest appraisal) must always accompany emotion. The challenge then lies in explicating the shifting relations between the two.

In this respect, Leventhal's (1979) perceptual motor theory of emotion represents an excellent attempt to account for many facets of emotion and emotional experience, and provides a sound framework for a good deal of research and theory building into affective phenomena (particularly within the close relationship context). Leventhal proposed that emotion processing occurs at three levels: the expressive motor level, the schematic or perceptual level, and the conceptual or abstract level. The expressive motor level is an innate, prewired emotion system that does not require prior learning for its elicitation. It generates the discrete feeling states (such as fear) and expressive reactions that comprise the "primary affective palette" (Leventhal, 1982, p. 128).

The schematic level consists of a record in memory of emotional episodes. This record stores in a schematic fashion both the autonomic and expressive motor acts that accompanied the emotional episode, along with its contextual details. When a similar situation is encountered, the schema is reactivated without deliberate or conscious thought. Thus, these schemata shape our perception and experience of the world without our effort or awareness, a phenomenon sometimes referred to as first-order knowledge (Levy, 1984). Emotional schemata operate independently of conscious, deliberative cognition. They act as filters to focus attention on particular stimulus features and so help to form (implicit) expectations, generalizations, and prototypes. Leventhal speculated that, once developed, such schemata are the major source of ongoing emotional experience, as we increasingly react in terms of our own expectations about the world rather than to actual external stimuli.

Finally, the conceptual or abstract level includes at least two kinds of processing: verbal and performance. The verbal component stores our memories about feelings, along with their antecedents and consequences. Information at this level can be verbalized—but Leventhal (1982) stressed that this verbalization is by no means a verbal paraphrase of schematic memory. Indeed, one's ability to conceptualize and talk about one's emotional experience is frequently limited to the most salient aspects that can be recalled after the event, and the actual feeling component can be almost impossible to recapture in words. The performance component of the conceptual level is developed as we practice expressing, recognizing, and controlling our emotions. Unlike the expressive motor display, the performance component is more voluntarily controlled (as we learn, for example, to turn the tears on or off). Leventhal claimed that all three mechanisms operate simultaneously and only the product, or synthesis, of their interaction can be observed.

Therapeutic Application of Leventhal's Theory of Emotion

Drawing on Leventhal's theory, Johnson and Greenberg (1985) worked from the opposite end of the therapeutic spectrum to Ellis and the cognitive behavioral marital therapists. Their focus has been almost exclusively on the affective, as opposed to the cognitive, aspect of couples' problems (emotionally focused therapy, or EFT). They have claimed that emotion is the primary source of information people have about the world and ongoing events, and have viewed clients as active perceivers who construct interpretations and meanings of events and stimuli on the basis of their current emotional states. Emotion itself is defined as "a construction arising from a complex synthesis of concepts, schemas, and expressive motor responses which then form the basis for the perception of new experience and the creation of meaning" (Greenberg & Johnson, 1986, p. 3). Thus, the focus of therapy is current emotional experience, through which the spouse is currently perceived and appraised.

Johnson and Greenberg (1985) identified three types of emotional experience: primary or authentic, secondary or reactive (e.g., when a person's expression of anger is really a defense against an underlying fear of losing their partner), and instrumental, such as crying for attention. The therapist's task is to evoke and affirm the authentic emotion, challenge the reactive emotion, intuitively probe for the underlying real affect, and ignore the instrumental displays. The rationale behind these procedures is that by experiencing authentic emotion and its associated "hot" cognitions (e.g., a belief that one is unlovable, which leads to a fear of being abandoned) an individual can begin to deal more effectively with the real issue that might be underlying his or her constant irritability or defensiveness. Another hope is that if spouses can witness each other's authentic emotions (and consequently, vulnerabilities), they will be moved to compassion and understanding.

In a study to assess the therapeutic effectiveness of EFT in comparison with cognitive behavioral marital therapy (BMT), Johnson and Greenberg (1985) randomly assigned 45 couples seeking therapy either to EFT, cognitive BMT, or a no treatment group for eight sessions. Their conclusions were that, although both treatments afforded significant improvements in goal attainment and target complaint reduction, EFT was the superior treatment for improving marital adjustment and increasing intimacy levels. However, their approach is not without its detractors, both at a methodological and theoretical level. For example, as Coyne (1986) noted, EFT is a reaction to the excesses and deficiencies of the overly cognitive (or indeed behavioral) approach. However, it also constitutes an exclusive orientation toward what should only be regarded as the third angle of the therapeutic triangle (R. M. Schwartz, 1982). Coyne also pointed out the philosophical difficulties inherent in the concept of "real" emotions underlying reactive emotions, and noted (perhaps cynically) that it is rather naive to expect that the expression of authentic emotion will always elicit compassion and good will from the spouse.

In response to some of these criticisms, Greenberg and Johnson (1986) claimed they do not regard emotion as a *ding an sich,* awaiting release within an individual, but as a functional connection between people and their environment. Evoked emotion is newly synthesized from current experience and is not present prior to synthesis. However, there appears to be a conceptual confusion here (probably an inevitable result of an attempt to integrate Leventhal's theoretical account with a predominantly psychodynamic orientation). On the one hand, Greenberg and Johnson (1986) claimed that they were evoking newly synthesized emotions from current experience, but on the other hand they stated that EFT accesses underlying vulnerability and "unexpressed anger" (p. 21), and that they strove to "empathetically evoke underlying feelings by facilitation, not force" (p. 22). To resolve this inconsistency, we believe Greenberg and Johnson should refer to the evocation of implicit scripts and cognitive-emotional schemata, rather than underlying emotions per se. As Israelstam (1989) pointed out, partners perceive each other and their interactions through the tinted lenses of their individual belief systems, for example, beliefs about one's lovableness (or lack of it) or beliefs about the dangers of dependency and getting too close. Such implicit beliefs, when explicitly expressed, are likely to be accompanied by strong negative emotions (which Greenberg & Johnson would no doubt classify as primary, or authentic), for example, fear and distress. From this point of view, Johnson and Greenberg's methodology is similar to the trouble-shooting perspective taken by many cognitive behavioral therapists (Jacobson & Gurman, 1986). In this procedure, couples are encouraged to get into a dispute in the therapist's presence. At various points, the therapist interrupts the negative interaction and elicits from each spouse, in turn, his or her thoughts and feelings, paying particular attention to underlying meanings and affect. Finally, a retrospective analysis identifies behavioral options on the basis of the thoughts and feelings expressed.

However, such therapies are typically conducted without any explicit, affective theoretical structure. By contrast, Johnson and Greenberg's approach gains strength from Leventhal's conceptual framework. In view of this, they might resolve confusion by lessening their insistence that their therapy is so heavily emotion focused. In fact, EFT appears to be an integrated approach that pays a good deal of specific attention to affective *and* cognitive phenomena within interactional settings, and that is no doubt effective in promoting more constructive behaviors between spouses inside and outside of therapy.

Our conclusion is that, for therapy to have more than a cosmetic effect on relationship adjustment, therapists must be aware of the subtle and complex interplay between affect, cognition, and behavior. As R. M. Schwartz (1982) has pointed out, each is fair game for intervention, depending on the individual, the type of event, and the context. On a more theoretical note, Baucom, Epstein, Sayers, and Goldman Sher (1989) have pointed out the lack of research into the different kinds of cognitive phenomena (e.g., assumptions, standards, and expectations) characteristic of distressed (and nondistressed) couples. Clearly, there is enormous scope for both clinicians and academic researchers to explore and elucidate the role of emotional schemata and to specify the affective and behavioral concomitants of different kinds of attributions, beliefs, and assumptions in distressed and nondistressed couples.

EMOTION IN CLOSE RELATIONSHIPS: BERSCHEID'S ACCOUNT

We now move on to describe some of the specific theorizing about emotions in close relationships that has been slowly building up over the past few years, beginning with the seminal theoretical work elegantly articulated by Berscheid (1983). Her analysis was structured within the framework of a broad-based, evolutionary theory of emotion developed by Mandler (1975), who proposed that autonomic nervous system arousal is a necessary condition for emotion (although not sufficient), and that such arousal is typically triggered by a change, or interruption, in an organism's ongoing activities. In effect, arousal alerts the organism to a potentially dangerous state of affairs, and directs attention to the source of the arousal. Then, within the limits imposed by its cognitive-interpretive system, the organism analyzes the meaning and relevance of the stimulus to its ongoing welfare, activities, and plans. If the interrupting stimulus can be removed or dealt with quickly, or if a substitute response is available that permits the activity sequence or plan to be completed, then emotion may not be experienced. However, if the route to completion is perceived to be quite blocked, then negative emotion is typically elicited.

Mandler (1975) pointed out that much of an organism's day-to-day activity is routinized and automatic, and runs in organized action sequences (e.g., getting up and dressed in the morning, finding one's way to and from work, preparing meals, getting ready for bed). In turn, many of these organized action sequences constitute hierarchical structures of higher order plans, or goals, such as buying a house, becoming a brain surgeon, or marrying well. All these organized action sequences and higher order plans are potentially subject to a great deal of interference, or interruption, from the small—such as discovering as you are driving to work that your partner has neglected to put gas in the car—to the large, such as learning that your partner no longer shares your dream of a successful marriage and wants a divorce. According to Mandler's theory, these interruptions, if accompanied by physiological arousal, should lead to the experience of "hot," negative emotion, the intensity of which depends on such factors as the unpredictability, novelty, complexity, importance, and negativity of the interruption. (The link with cognition becomes clear when we note that unpredictable, novel, negative, and important behaviors are also those most likely to elicit attributionalizing; Fletcher & Fincham, this volume).

Berscheid (1983) took as her starting point Kelley et al.'s (1983) definition of a close relationship as one in which a couple's interdependence patterns are characterized by high frequency and strength, covering a diverse range of activities, for a relatively long duration of time. Berscheid postulated that the greater the number of interconnections to each other's activities and plans a couple have, the greater the potential for interruption—that is, when one partner does something unexpected or out of sequence, or fails to do something expected. If these interruptions are accompanied by physiological arousal, then, in accord with Mandler's theory, negative emotion should also be elicited. Berscheid referred to such interdependence patterns as the amount of emotional investment (or interruptibility potential) a couple have in their relationship.

Clearly, then, as long as a couple's interdependence patterns and sequences are smoothly meshed, there may be very little intense emotion experienced in the relationship. Indeed, in relationships that are extremely well meshed and harmonious, partners may be quite unaware of their emotional investment until the relationship is terminated, and all the hidden connections with each other are abruptly severed. As Berscheid, Gangestad, and Kulakowski (1984) commented, "the nature of the emotional apparatus is such that awareness and appreciation of emotional ties may be lost over time. But, aware or not, an emotional price will be paid upon dissolution of a relationship" (p. 462).

Still working from within the interruption perspective, Berscheid (1983) also proposed an explanation for the elicitation of very intense, or "hot" positive emotions in close relationships. Her hypothesis was that stimulus events that suddenly and unexpectedly remove obstacles or previously interruptive stimuli, or that complete an activity or plan earlier than expected, are likely to elicit strong, positive emotion. Consequently, within a close relationship, if each partner has the resources to remove obstacles for the other, and/or to unexpectedly complete each other's organized action sequences or higher order plans, then both are likely to experience strong, positive emotion towards each other. Indeed, Berscheid described the conditions for the experience of intense romantic love as the "sudden unexpected realization that another is able and willing to help one fulfill one's most cherished plans and hopes" (p. 155).

From a developmental perspective, it is clear that in the early stages of a relationship, provided one or both of the partners have uncompleted plans and hopes (e.g., to get married, or have a family) or are in a continuing, negative state of interruption (e.g., feeling lonely), then the potential exists for a good deal of strong positive emotion as one individual is perceived to be in a good position to fulfill the dreams and alleviate the loneliness of the other. No doubt one of the conditions for the continuing experience of such intense emotions is for couples to make plans together that require each other's participation to fulfill. Similarly, with respect to less intense positive emotions, many contented couples engineer pleasant surprises for each other and help each other out in various ways, consequently eliciting warm and loving emotions toward each other on a day-to-day basis.

Berscheid's analysis is finely argued and intuitively plausible, and some of her predictions have also been empirically supported. For example, in a study on emotion frequency and labeling in dating relationships, Fitness and Fletcher (in press) found that partner-initiated, relationship-relevant behaviors (both positive and negative) elicited twice the number of self-reported emotions in an individual than did self-initiated, relationship-relevant behaviors. Clearly, we are most likely to experience emotion in a relationship when our partner does something to surprise or interrupt us (whether pleasantly or not). Similarly, in his longitudinal study of 234 dating subjects, Simpson (1987) found the factors that best predicted emotional distress on relationship termination were those that indicated high levels of emotional investment (i.e., partners' degree of closeness or interdependence with each other, duration of the relationship, and ease of finding alternative partners with whom activities could be meshed) as opposed to such factors as sexual involvement, relationship satisfaction, or personality variables such as self-monitoring. This study makes salient the important observation that relationship satisfaction and degree of interdependence or closeness cannot be treated as the same variable. Indeed, it is a commonplace observation that highly interdependent couples may be acutely unhappy and dissatisfied with their relationships, whereas satisfying relationships may be maintained with any number of people without substantial interdependence or emotional investment.

Although Berscheid's analysis provides a fine theoretical basis for work on emotions in close relationships, in itself it has not, as yet, engendered very much research activity, probably because it deals with emotions in a somewhat global fashion. For example, although it is useful to know that a partner-caused interruption to another's activities, hopes, wishes, or plans is likely to elicit arousal and emotion, to make a start at a fine-grained analysis of specific emotions within a specific context, such as marriage, we must acquire a detailed knowledge of the interruptee's cognitive appraisal (or evaluation) of the situation. Also necessary is information about proximal, priming variables, such as current mood, and distal variables, such as the interruptee's expectations, assumptions, and theories about the self, the partner, the relationship, and which emotions are appropriate to express (or even appropriate to acknowledge feeling) within an intimate relationship. In the next part of the chapter we discuss the concepts of cognitive appraisal, prototypical emotion knowledge, and the social construction of emotion with particular reference to the interpersonal context. Our aim is to sketch the kind of work that is being done in these areas and to suggest some useful directions for future research. We conclude with a brief summary of the main issues covered in the chapter.

THE ROLE OF COGNITIVE APPRAISAL IN EMOTION

Research into cognitive appraisals and emotion draws on the work of Arnold (1960) and Lazarus (1966). The goal is to describe the kinds of personal meaning analyses, or appraisal dimensions, that elicit particular emotions. In general, the accumulated results of these studies can be divided into two major areas: first, the constitutive appraisal dimensions of particular emotions (e.g., Roseman, 1984; Smith & Ellsworth, 1985, 1987), and second, the typical course of these emotions—their antecedents, physiological, and behavioral components, their regulation and consequences (e.g., Scherer, 1986). In general, appraisal theorists would agree that differing perceptions of the goal relevance, pleasantness, agency, and control of an event or stimulus are important features in the elicitation of different emotions. Of these features, however, the most critical is what Roseman (1984) called motivational consistency, or the relevance/importance of an event to one's needs, plans, desire, hopes, and wishes. Lazarus and Smith (1988) claimed this appraisal is of primary importance for our survival and well-being, and its constituents are *motivational relevance* (does it matter to me?) and *congruence* (is it good for me?)

To illustrate the links between such appraisals and emotions, we briefly describe Roseman's (1984) theory, which proposes that every emotion is the result of a match or mismatch between what people want (motivational consistency) and what they perceive they are getting. Thus, if I get what I want, my reaction is joy; if I don't get what I want, my reaction is sadness. Conversely, if I get what I don't want, my reaction is distress, or anger, whereas if I don't get what I don't want, I feel relief. Other dimensions are also involved, such as causal locus (self, other, or circumstances) and amount of perceived control over an event or stimulus. Although the precise number and nature of these cognitive dimensions are still to be determined, the real strength of the appraisal approach lies in its capacity to account for emotions, not simply as products of interruption, but as meaningful responses to goal/need/wish attainment or frustration. For example, if a couple is planning to go to a concert together and the husband arrives home from work so late that they cannot go, the wife may react with anger if she blames him for his thoughtlessness, or with depression if she interprets the event as a reflection of his lack of love for her. Alternately, the wife may react with relief when he finally arrives home, grateful that he has not had an accident, or even with contempt at his inability to be on time for anything. As Roseman (1984) pointed out, individuals will come to desire certain outcomes and wish to avoid others on the basis of their learning history. Some individuals may learn to appraise situations primarily in terms of negative events that might occur (such as being abandoned) and so feel chronically insecure or anxious, whereas others may consistently experience praise as the absence of criticism, and so feel relief rather than joy when they have done well. Clearly, there is no discrepancy here between such learned appraisals and Leventhal's concept of emotional schemata, through which, he proposed, we experience the world (and each other).

Analysis of Specific Emotions

We believe that a thorough-going analysis of cognitive appraisal profiles for specific emotions within specific contexts should become one cornerstone of emotion research. Because the emphasis remains predominantly global and abstract, no one is yet much the wiser when it comes down to the issues that most concern the layperson in a close relationship—that is, the whys, hows, and wherefores of powerful, interpersonal feelings such as love, hate, and jealousy. It has only been comparatively recently, for example, that the emotion of love was considered a fitting topic for research at all, and although psychologists have written possibly millions of words about aggression, the word *hate* is rarely mentioned in psychology textbooks, despite its status par excellence as a motivator of aggressive behavior. Similarly, jealousy has been cited as one of the leading causes of homicide in the Western world (Daly, Wilson, & Weghorst, 1982), yet it is not a common topic of either research or theory in social psychology (Buunk & Bringle, 1987). Admittedly, the situation has changed somewhat with respect to love (see Sternberg & Beall, this volume), yet the majority of empirical research focuses on love as an entirely abstract phenomenon, a relationship quality, or static entity that two people possess in relation to each other.

Possibly the most affectively oriented and lively research into the emotion of passionate love has been carried out by Hatfield and her colleagues (for a review, see Hatfield & Rapson, 1987). One result of this research program has been the development of the Passionate Love Scale (Hatfield & Sprecher, 1986), which measures cognitive, emotional, and behavioral indicants of the experience of passionate love. However, as Hatfield and Rapson (1987) commented, the next step is to explore what factors elicit (or release) love, as opposed to those that cause it to subside. Indeed, this is the case for the majority of powerful, interpersonally relevant emotions, such as hate, jealousy, frustration, hurt, and worry. Despite the amount of research conducted so far, we still have only the vaguest notions about what precipitates these emotions, how they feel, what kinds of cognitions typically accompany them, how they are typically expressed and controlled, and why, and what their consequences are, within a close relationship.

Prototype Analysis

Along with cognitive appraisal research, another way of exploring these features of emotion is through prototype analysis. Prototype research has been profitably conducted for many years within mainstream cognitive psychology (e.g., Rosch, 1978); Fehr and Russell (1984), Shaver et al. (1987), and Schwartz and Shaver (1987) have illustrated its utility for analyzing people's emotion knowledge, including the antecedent and consequent conditions (cognitive, physiological, and behavioral) characteristic of different emotions. Clearly, this kind of research within a close relationship context would be an invaluable adjunct to physiological and behavioral assessments of actual emotional experience (e.g., Gottman's interactional analyses).

A good example of this approach in action is provided by Fehr's (1988) meticulous prototype analysis of the concepts of love and commitment. She was able to tease apart and identify clusters of behaviors, physiological symptoms, and cognitive variables relevant to the experience of love (as opposed to commitment); for example, feelings of butterflies in the stomach and increasing heart rate, along with behaviors such as laughing, mutual gaze, and helping each other, and constant thinking about each other. However, this analysis was still conducted context free and, as such, may not have tapped into the truly distinctive features of the emotion of love (feeling loved, feeling loving) within, for example, a marital setting.

Along with gathering data about people's actual experience of different emotions toward each other in close relationships, we also need to analyze people's emotion knowledge, their implicit beliefs about emotion, and the way a particular culture encourages or discourages the experience and expression of specific, discrete emotions. The kind of prototype analysis that takes both the individual and cultural features of emotion into account is perhaps best exemplified in some of the work carried out by social constructivist theorists of emotion (e.g., Averill, 1982; Hochschild, 1983; Solomon, 1981). The social constructivist approach regards emotions as complex syndromes, constructed from within each individual's social world, and comprising physiological, behavioral, cognitive, and social components (no one of which is necessary or sufficient to define a particular emotion). Thus, in order to obtain a complete picture of an emotion, such as anger or love, one needs to research its natural history; to discover its prototypical features (e.g., cognitive, physiological, and behavioral accompaniments), within specific contexts (such as the intimate one). Some particularly good examples of this kind of detailed emotion analysis are included in Harré's (1986) collection of essays on the social construction of various emotions (e.g., Sabini & Silver's, 1986, analysis of envy, Armon-Jones', 1986, description of the social functions of emotions, and Averill's, 1986, account of the acquisition of emotions during adulthood). Clearly, there is a need for such comprehensive analyses of specific emotions within specific, close relationship contexts, in which the rules for emotional experience and express are, no doubt, both idiosyncratic and influenced by a diverse number of cultural understandings. The advantages of taking a prototype perspective to close relationship research have also been noted by Ginsburg (1987), who believes researchers must discover culturally prescribed relationship rules, including emotion rules and affective prototypes, if they are to obtain real insights into human personal relationships. After all, people constantly make use of their implicit emotion knowledge to understand and manage their interpersonal interactions. Consequently, relationship and emotion prototype data provide a fund of hypotheses about emotional elicitation, expression, control, and consequences in relationships.

Methodologically speaking, with respect to both prototype and cognitive appraisal research, we believe there are a number of possible options. For example, subjects can be required to imagine themselves participating in emotional stories or vignettes of relationship interactions and report their ongoing thoughts and feelings. G. E. Schwartz and Weinberger (1980) have noted that subjects tend to respond physiologically to an imagined situation in much the same way as they respond to an actual situation, suggesting that information gathered in this way is of reasonable validity. Alternately, researchers can ask subjects to recall a specific, highly emotional relationship incident and report details of their thoughts and feelings. Such reports can be audiotaped or recorded by means of a comprehensive questionnaire that combines open-ended and specific questions about the incident with a number of appraisal scale measures (Scherer, 1986). Such retrospective self-reports constitute a rich source of data on emotions and appraisals. Individuals and couples could also be intensively interviewed about recent emotional incidents in their relationships, making it possible for researchers to compare partners' accounts. Alternately, couples might be persuaded to keep daily emotion diaries for subsequent analysis.

Ideally, researchers should use as many methodological techniques as they can when conducting research in any area. However, this is particularly important for the study of emotion in close relationships, where the number of theoretical, empirical, and therapeutic approaches are so diverse. We believe the most productive strategy is to supplement, as far as possible, the kinds of self-report methods described above with behavioral and physiological observations (a strategy Clark & Reis, 1988, call triangulation). Such a strategy not only lends greater validity to research findings, but also enhances the breadth and richness of the data.

SUMMARY AND CONCLUSIONS

Throughout this chapter, our major theme has been the role of cognition in emotion within the context of close relationships. We began with an examination of specific emotional behaviors and physiological symptoms in the laboratory, and described the ways in which such behaviors and symptoms are related to marital distress. Clearly, thorough documentation of the physiological and behavioral expressions of emotion in distressed and nondistressed couples such as that carried out by Gottman and his colleagues is of great value. However, this work leaves a large gap in our understanding of the origins of such affective phenomena, both at the proximal (e.g., cognitive) and distal (e.g., societal) levels.

The next section of the chapter was concerned with the relation between cognition and emotion. We looked at theory, research, and therapy from the perspectives of both cognitive and affective primacy, and argued the case for adopting a more integrative model of cognition-emotion interaction. The role of cognitive appraisal in the elicitation of emotion, along with emotion prototype research, was described and discussed with particular reference to Berscheid's (1983) theory of emotion in close relationships. Her analysis was shown to comprise a valuable framework from within which the influence of proximal and distal variables (e.g., cognitive appraisals and emotional concomitants of relationship events) can be demonstrated and explored.

Finally, some methodological strategies for further research in the cognitive appraisal and emotion prototype area were suggested. We concluded that the best strategy for research is the multimethod one, involving an alliance between experimental, quasi-experimental, survey, self-report, and behavioral observational methods, both laboratory and field based. It is difficult to conduct nonintrusive, nonreactive, ethical research in the study of affect in close relationships. Nonetheless, there is clearly a need to supplement laboratory and clinically based observations of emotional behavior with more ecologically valid measurements. There is ample scope here for the imaginative and sensitive researcher to devise ways of obtaining reliable data with the least disturbance to a couple's relationship. The use of such methodological strategies, supplemented with laboratory and clinical observations and integrated with sophisticated emotion theory, holds promise for real advances in our understanding of this important area.

REFERENCES

Armon-Jones, C. (1986). The social functions of emotion. In R. Harré (Ed.), *The social construction of emotions* (pp. 57–82). Oxford: Basil Blackwell.

Arnold, M. B. (1960). *Emotion and personality: Vol. 1. Psychological aspects*. New York: Columbia University Press.

Averill, J. R. (1982). *Anger and aggression: An essay on emotion*. New York: Springer-Verlag.

Averill, J. R. (1986). The acquisition of emotions during adulthood. In R. Harré (Ed.), *The social construction of emotions* (pp. 98–118). Oxford: Basil Blackwell.

Baucom, D. H., Epstein, N., Sayers, S., & Goldman Sher, T. (1989). The role of cognitions in marital relationships: Definitional, methodological and conceptual issues. *Journal of Consulting & Clinical Psychology, 57*, 31–38.

Beck, A. (1967). *Cognitive therapy and the emotional disorders*. New York: International Universities Press.

Berscheid, E. (1983). Emotion. In H. H. Kelley, E. Berscheid, A. Christensen, J. Harvey, T. Huston, G. Levinger, E. McClintock, A. Peplau, & D. Peterson (Eds.), *Close relationships* (pp. 110–168). San Francisco: Freeman.

Berscheid, E., Gangestad, S., & Kulakowski, D. (1984). Emotion in close relationships: Implications for relationship counseling. In S. D. Brown & R. W. Lent (Eds.), *Handbook of counseling psychology* (pp. 435–476). New York: Wiley.

Bradbury, T., & Fincham, F. (1987). Assessment of affect in marriage. In K. Daniel O'Leary (Ed.), *Assessment of marital discord* (pp. 59–108). Hillsdale, NJ: Lawrence Erlbaum Associates.

Buunk, B., & Bringle, R. (1987). Jealousy in love relationships. In D. Perlman & S. Duck (Eds.), *Intimate relationships: Development, dynamics and deterioration* (pp. 123–147). Beverly Hills: Sage.

Clark, M. S., & Reis, H. T. (1988). Interpersonal processes in close relationships. *Annual Review of Psychology, 39,* 609–672.

Clarke, D. (1987). Emotion, decision, and the long-term course of relationships. In R. Burnett, P. McGhee, & D. Clarke (Eds.), *Accounting for relationships* (pp. 3–21). London: Methuen.

Clarke, D., Allen, C., & Dickson, S. (1985). The characteristic affective tone of seven classes of interpersonal relationship. *Journal of Social and Personal Relationships, 2,* 117–120.

Coyne, J. C. (1986). Evoked emotion in marital therapy: Necessary or even useful? *Journal of Marital and Family Therapy, 12,* 11–13.

Daly, M., Wilson, M., & Weghorst, S. (1982). Male sexual jealousy. *Ethology and Sociobiology, 3,* 11–27.

Dutton, D. G. (1984). Interventions into the problem of wife assault: Therapeutic, policy and research implications. *Canadian Journal of Behavioral Science, 16,* 281–297.

Dutton, D. G., Fehr, B., & McEwen, H. (1982). Severe wife battering as deindividuated violence. *Victimology: An International Journal, 7,* 13–23.

Eichenbaum, L., & Orbach, S. (1983). *What do women want?* Great Britain: Michael Joseph.

Ekman, P., & Friesen, W. V. (1978). *Facial action coding system*. Palo Alto, CA: Consulting Psychologist Press.

Ellis, A. (1962). *Reason and emotion in psychotherapy*. New York: Lyle Stuart Press.

Ellis, A. (1977). Rational and irrational jealousy. In G. Clanton & L. Smith, (Eds.), *Jealousy* (pp. 170–179). Englewood Cliffs, NJ: Prentice-Hall.

Ellis, A., & Harper, R. (1961). *Creative marriage*. New York: Lyle Stuart.

Epstein, S. (1984). Controversial issues in emotion theory. In P. Shaver (Ed.), *Review of personality and social psychology* (Vol. 5, pp. 64–88). Beverly Hills, CA: Sage.

Fehr, B. (1988). Prototype analysis of the concepts of love and commitment. *Journal of Personality and Social Psychology, 55,* 557–579.

Fehr, B., & Russell, J. A. (1984). Concept of emotion viewed from a prototype perspective. *Journal of Experimental Psychology: General, 113,* 464–486.

Fitness, J., & Fletcher, G. J. O. (in press). Emotion labeling in close relationships. *New Zealand Journal of Psychology.*

Ginsburg, G. P. (1987). Rules, scripts and prototypes in personal relationships. In S. Duck (Ed.), *Handbook of personal relationships* (pp. 23–41). Chichester, Eng.: Wiley.

Gottman, J. M. (1979). *Marital interaction: Experimental investigations*. New York: Academic Press.

Gottman, J. M., & Krokoff, L. J. (1989). Marital interaction and satisfaction: A longitudinal view. *Journal of Consulting and Clinical Psychology, 57,* 47–52.

Gottman, J. M., & Levenson, R. (1986). Assessing the role of emotion in marriage. *Behavioral Assessment, 8,* 31–48.

Gottman, J. M., & Levenson, R. (1988). The social psychophysiology of marriage. In P. Noller &

M. A. Fitzpatrick (Eds.), *Perspectives on marital interaction* (pp. 182–199). Clevedon, England: Multilingual Matters.

Greden, J., Genero, N., Price, L., Feinberg, M., & Levine, S. (1986). Facial electromyography in depression. *Archives of General Psychiatry, 43,* 269–274.

Greenberg, L. S., & Johnson, S. (1986). When to evoke emotion and why: Process diagnosis in couples therapy. *Journal of Marital and Family Therapy, 12,* 19–23.

Harré, R. (Ed.). (1986). *The social construction of emotions.* Oxford: Basil Blackwell.

Harrison, L. (1986). The grouping of affect terms according to the situations that elicit them: A test of a cognitive theory of emotion. *Journal of Research in Personality, 20,* 252–266.

Harvey, J., Hendrick, S., & Tucker, K. (1988). Self report methods in studying personal relationships. In S. Duck (Ed.), *Handbook of personal relationships.* Chichester, Eng.: Wiley.

Hatfield, E., & Rapson, R. (1987). Passionate love: New directions in research. In W. Jones & D. Perlman (Eds.), *Advances in personal relationships* (Vol. 1, pp. 109–139). Greenwich, CT: JAI Press.

Hatfield, E., & Sprecher, S. (1986). Measuring passionate love in intimate relationships. *Journal of Adolescence, 9,* 383–410.

Hochschild, A. (1983). *The managed heart.* Berkeley: University of California Press.

Holt, C., & Lee, C. (1989). Cognitive behavior therapy re-examined: Problems and implications. *Australian Psychologist, 24,* 157–169.

Israelstam, K. V. (1989). Interacting individual belief systems in marital relationships. *Journal of Marital and Family Therapy, 15,* 53–63.

Izard, C. (1977). *Human emotions.* New York: Plenum Press.

Jacobson, N. S., & Gurman, A. S. (Eds.). (1986). *Clinical handbook of marital therapy.* New York: Guilford Press.

Johnson, S., & Greenberg, L. (1985). Emotionally focused couples therapy: An outcome study. *Journal of Marital and Family Therapy, 11,* 313–317.

Kelley, H. H., Berscheid, E., Christensen, A., Harvey, J., Huston, T., Levinger, G., McClintock, E., Peplau, L., & Peterson, D. (Eds.). (1983). *Close relationships.* San Francisco: Freeman.

Larsen, R., & Diener, E. (1987). Affect intensity as an individual difference characteristic: A review. *Journal of Research in Personality, 21,* 1–39.

Lazarus, R. (1966). *Psychological stress and the coping process.* New York: McGraw-Hill.

Lazarus, R. (1984). On the primacy of cognition. *American Psychologist, 39,* 124–129.

Lazarus, R., & Smith, C. (1988). Knowledge and appraisal in the cognition-emotion relationship. *Cognition and Emotion, 2,* 281–300.

Levenson, R. W., & Gottman, J. M. (1983). Marital interaction: Physiological linkage and affective exchange. *Journal of Personality and Social Psychology, 45,* 587–597.

Levenson, R. W., & Gottman, J. M. (1985). Physiological and affective predictors of change in relationship satisfaction. *Journal of Personality and Social Psychology, 49,* 85–94.

Leventhal, H. (1979). A perceptual motor processing model of emotion. In P. Pliner, K. R. Blankstein, & I. M. Spiegel (Eds.), *Advances in the study of communication and affect: Vol. 5. Perception of emotions in self and others* (pp. 1–46). New York: Plenum.

Leventhal, H. (1982). The integration of emotion and cognition: A view from the perceptual–motor theory of emotion. In M. Clark & S. Fiske (Eds.), *Affect and cognition: The seventeenth annual Carnegie symposium on cognition* (pp. 121–156). Hillsdale, NJ: Erlbaum.

Levy, R. (1984) The emotions in comparative perspective. In K. Scherer & P. Ekman (Eds.), *Approaches to emotion* (pp. 397–412). Hillsdale, NJ: Erlbaum.

Mandler, G. (1975). *Mind and emotion.* New York: Wiley.

Margolin, G., & Wampold, B. (1981). Sequential analysis of conflict and accord in distressed and nondistressed marital partners. *Journal of Consulting and Clinical Psychology, 49,* 554–567.

Notarius, C., & Herrick, L. (1989). The psychophysiology of dyadic interaction. In H. Wagner & A. Manstead (Eds.), *Handbook of social psychophysiology* (pp. 393–419). Chichester, Eng.: Wiley.

Notarius, C., & Johnson, J. (1982). Emotional expression in husbands and wives. *Journal of Marriage and the Family, 44,* 483–489.

Parrott, W. G., & Sabini, J. (1989). On the "emotional" qualities of certain types of cognition: A reply to arguments for the independence of cognition and affect. *Cognitive Therapy and Research, 13,* 49–65.

Polivy, J. (1981). On the induction of emotion in the laboratory: Discrete moods or multiple affect states? *Journal of Personality and Social Psychology, 41,* 803–817.

Rachman, S. (1981). The primacy of affect: Some theoretical implications. *Behavioral Research and Therapy, 19,* 279–290.

Revenstorf, D. (1984). The role of attribution of marital distress in therapy. In K. Hahlweg & N. S. Jacobson (Eds.), *Marital interaction: Analysis and modification* (pp. 325–336). New York: Guilford Press.

Rosch, E. (1978). Principles of categorization. In E. Rosch & B. B. Lloyd (Eds.), *Cognition and categorization* (pp. 27–48). Hillsdale, NJ: Erlbaum.

Roseman, I. (1984). Cognitive determinants of emotion: A structural theory. In P. Shaver (Ed.), *Review of personality and social psychology: Emotions, relationships and health* (Vol. 5, pp. 11–36). Beverly Hills, CA: Sage.

Russell, J. (1978). Evidence of convergent validity on the dimensions of affect. *Journal of Personality and Social Psychology, 36,* 1152–1168.

Sabini, J., & Silver, M. (1986). Envy. In R. Harré (Ed.), *The social construction of emotions* (pp. 167–183). Oxford: Basil Blackwell.

Schaap, C. (1982). *Communication and adjustment in marriage.* Amsterdam: Swets and Zeitlinger B. U.

Scherer, K. R. (1986). Studying emotion empirically: Issues and a paradigm for research. In K. Scherer, H. Wallbott, & A. Summerfield (Eds.), *Experiencing emotion: A cross cultural study* (pp. 3–27). London: Plenum Press.

Schwartz, G. E., & Weinberger, D. A. (1980). Patterns of emotional responses to affective situations: Relations among happiness, sadness, anger, fear, depression and anxiety. *Motivation and Emotion, 4,* 175–191.

Schwartz, J., & Shaver, P. (1987). Emotion and emotion knowledge in interpersonal relations. In W. Jones & D. Perlman (Eds.), *Advances in personal relationships* (pp. 197–241). Greenwich, CT: JAI Press.

Schwartz, R. M. (1982). Cognitive behavior modification: A conceptual review. *Clinical Psychology Review, 2,* 267–293.

Shaver, P., Schwartz, J., Kirson, D., & O'Connor, C. (1987). Emotion knowledge: Further exploration of a prototype approach. *Journal of Personality and Social Psychology, 52,* 1061–1086.

Shiffrin, R. M., & Schneider, W. (1977). Controlled and automatic human information processing: II. Perceptual learning, automatic attending and a general theory. *Psychological Review, 84,* 127–190.

Sifneos, P. (1973). The prevalence of alexithymic characteristics in psychosomatic patients. *Psychotherapy & Psychosomatics, 22,* 255–262.

Simpson, J. (1987). The dissolution of romantic relationships: Factors involved in relationship stability and emotional distress. *Journal of Personality and Social Psychology, 53,* 683–692.

Smith, C. (1989). Dimensions of appraisal and physiological response in emotion. *Journal of Personality and Social Psychology, 56,* 339–353.

Smith, C., & Ellsworth, P. (1985). Patterns of cognitive appraisal in emotion. *Journal of Personality and Social Psychology, 48,* 813–838.

Smith, C., & Ellsworth, P. (1987). Patterns of appraisal and emotion related to taking an exam. *Journal of Personality and Social Psychology, 52,* 475–488.

Solomon, R. C. (1981). *Love: Emotion, myth and metaphor.* New York: Anchor Press/Doubleday.

Sprecher, S. (1986). The relation between inequity and emotion in close relationships. *Social Psychology Quarterly, 49,* 309–321.

Strongman, K. (1987). *The psychology of emotion* (3rd ed.). Chichester, Eng.: Wiley.
Taylor, S., & Brown, J. D. (1988). Illusion and well-being: A social psychological perspective on mental health. *Psychological Bulletin, 103,* 193–210.
Zajonc, R. (1984). On the primacy of affect. In K. Scherer & P. Ekman (Eds.), *Approaches to emotion* (pp. 259–270). Hillsdale, NJ: Erlbaum.

8

Communication in Marriage: The Influence of Affect and Cognition

Patricia Noller
Melodie Ruzzene
University of Queensland

The main goal of this chapter is to explore the link between cognition and affect, and the relationship of both to communicative processes in marriage. The primary focus is on processes involved in marital communication at three different levels: judgments of affect, judgments of intention, and attributions of blame and causality.

We assume that marital communication is a complex undertaking that is shaped by the cognitive and affective processes of both the message-sender and message-receiver. As Guthrie and Noller (1988) noted, knowing how spouses perceive and interpret each other's behavior is at least as important for understanding marital interaction as is their actual behavior.

The complexity inherent in marital communication is evident in Bradbury and Fincham's (1987) model of the communication process in marriage. In this model, cognitive and affective processes are involved in the processing of communicative events by both spouses, as well as the proximal (situational) and distal (historical) contexts in which they are operating. Bradbury and Fincham (1989) defined the proximal context as residual thoughts and feelings from prior events in the interaction, whereas the distal context includes thoughts and feelings arising from previous interactions as well as the psychological characteristics of each of the partners and of the relationship. As these researchers (1987) noted, "spouses are active participants in the observational task and see their partner's behavior through perceptual biases and filters that have been established over the course of their married life" (p. 50).

Close relationships are characterized by interdependence and a high degree of emotional involvement arising from the personal salience of relationship events for each partner, and the considerable extent to which the behavior of the partner is interpreted as personally relevant. For this reason, we assume that affective and cognitive processes assert their influence on communicative events in marriage in a unique fashion, as compared to less intimate contexts. The high levels of arousal generated in close relationships are likely to amplify the impact of both positive and negative cognitions and affect.

Bradbury and Fincham (1987) have underlined the close connection between cognition and feeling in marriage, and point to the difficulty of examining these as independent processes. Cognitions engender feelings, and feelings elicit thought processes. We agree with that position in the sense that any focus on cognition must recognize, explicitly or tacitly, the role of the cognitive processes under study as part of an ongoing chain of rapidly occurring, reciprocal, thought-feeling interactions. Similarly, any focus on affect would also need to acknowledge the role of cognition in contributing to, and being affected by, the emotional state.

We do not entirely agree, however, as Bradbury and Fincham assert, that separate and independent study of these two processes can only hamper their further clarification. For the present, at least, there would seem to be value in attempting to examine cognition and affect separately in order to relate each to particular behavioral outcomes. Studying each construct separately may also help us to better understand the degree to which one spouse's emotional state affects both the partner's emotional state and/or that spouse's perceptions of his or her partner's emotional state. Moreover, it is important to include both affective and cognitive variables in studies of marital communication, so that we can understand more clearly how they relate to each other.

The impact of affect and cognition on marital communication will be examined here in terms of communication quality. Communication quality may be defined in terms of (a) the degree of understanding that is evident between spouses as they interact with each other and (b) the way in which spouses explain their partners' behavior, especially behavior which relates to problem issues.

It is taken for granted that marital harmony is strongly related to effective communication between spouses, and that effective communication, to some optimal degree, involves spouses' understanding of each others' thoughts and feelings, personal experience of life in general, and the marital relationship in particular. To this extent, we focus on the accuracy of interpersonal judgments of the intended meaning and affective components of behavior as a way of understanding the conditions under which empathic accuracy may or may not arise. For example, we assume that distressed spouses are operating in a very different affective climate from nondistressed spouses, and that this climate influences interpersonal judgments and their associated communication outcomes.

Communicative events can be examined in terms of both accuracy and bias, where accuracy refers to whether the perception or judgment is correct or incorrect, and bias refers to a systematic tendency to make errors of perception or judgment in a particular direction. A study by Noller (1980) provides a concrete example of this kind of bias and its operationalization. Errors made by spouses in decoding the nonverbal messages of their partners were scored in terms of the direction of the error. Spouses who interpreted positive messages as neutral or negative, or neutral messages as negative, were considered to have made errors in a negative direction, whereas those who interpreted negative messages as neutral or positive, or neutral messages as positive, were considered to have made errors in a positive direction. Errors were scored in such a way that the mean scores would indicate any bias to make errors in a particular direction, as well as the strength of that tendency.

In addition to examining the accuracy or bias with which spouses judge each other's behavior, in this chapter, we also attempt to examine how the occurrence of behavior itself is explained by spouses. In this manner, as with accuracy, we hope to understand the relationship between different types of attributions and the conditions under which these attributions may arise. We know that cognitions that assign responsibility and/or blame have a major effect on the way one spouse responds to offending or pleasing behavior from the other (Bradbury & Fincham, 1990; Madden & Janoff-Bulman, 1981). It is therefore important to consider attributions when examining the effects of cognition and affect on communication in marriage.

In this chapter, we highlight three sets of data coming from our own work. These data examine accuracy and bias in (a) the decoding of nonverbal messages between spouses, (b) judgments about partner affect and intentions in an emotional situation, and (c) attributions for relationship events. In each data set, the variables under study are examined in relation to spouses' beliefs about the quality of their marital relationship.

Initially, we describe data involving the decoding of nonverbal messages between spouses and examine the effects of sex and marital adjustment level on the accuracy with which such messages are interpreted. This section focuses on studies carried out by Noller (Noller, 1980, 1981, 1984; Noller & Venardos, 1986) involving the decoding of standard content messages. We then examine data involving spouses' judgments of each other's intentions during emotional situations involving anger, depression, and affection (Guthrie & Noller, 1988). Again, we detail the effects of sex and marital adjustment level on the accuracy with which spouses judge their partners' intentions, as well as the positivity of those intentions, in a range of affective situations.

The third data set to be described involves judgments of both intentions and affect elicited in the same study. The judgments were made in relation to partner behavior emitted while spouses were discussing a long-standing conflict issue. In addition, spouses in this study were asked to make attributions about the causes of the problem issue under discussion, and about their own and their partners' problem-related behavior.

Our intention is to use the findings from these three sets of data to explore the relationships between accuracy at judging partner affect and more cognitive variables such as judgments of partner intention and attributions for partner behavior. Following Bradbury and Fincham (1987), our basic thesis is that these cognitive variables affect marital communication through their effects on the proximal and distal contexts in which marital communication takes place. We argue that the attributions of distressed spouses create a negative distal context for marital communication, which then increases the probability that the spouses will misunderstand each other's messages. Of course, these misunderstandings are also likely to have their own effect on the context, particularly the proximal context, and will lead to further cognitions that will intensify the negativity of both the distal and proximal contexts. In the following sections we present the findings that impinge on these issues, and then consider the implications of these findings for Bradbury and Fincham's model.

THE DECODING OF NONVERBAL MESSAGES
BETWEEN SPOUSES

Noller's (1980) methodology involved husbands and wives sending each other ambiguous verbal messages that could be interpreted as positive, neutral, or negative, depending on the accompanying nonverbal cues. (See Table 8.1 for an example of a message and its possible meanings.) Each spouse acted as both an encoder (the person conveying a message) and a decoder (the person interpreting the message sent by the encoder). The decoder's task was to decide which of the three types of message (positive, neutral, or negative) his or her spouse was sending.

To control for the quality of the encoding in this study, the messages that the spouses sent to each other were videotaped and shown to groups of judges who performed the same decoding task as the spouses, but from the videotape. Messages correctly decoded by two-thirds of judges were categorized as good communications, whereas those decoded less accurately were categorized as bad communications. On the basis of these categories, errors could be labeled as encoding errors (neither the spouse nor the judges were able to decode the message accurately) or decoding errors (the judges were able to decode the message accurately, but the spouse was not). Husbands low in marital adjustment made more encoding errors and more decoding errors than those high in marital adjustment. These findings were replicated in a later study (Noller & Venardos, 1986). An analysis that looked at the direction of errors showed that husbands were more likely to make errors in a negative direction (e.g., decode a positive message as neutral or negative), whereas wives were more likely to make decoding errors in a positive direction.

Several aspects of these findings need to be highlighted. First, those in less happy marriages tend to misunderstand each other more frequently than other couples. Just how these misunderstandings occur is not clear, although it seems

TABLE 8.1
Example of Cards Used by the Encoder and the Decoder for the Standard Content Task

Card Type	Section	Content
Encoding card	situation	You and your husband are sitting alone on a winter evening. You feel cold.
	Intention	a. You wonder it it's only you who are cold or if he is cold, too.
	Statement	I'M COLD, AREN'T YOU?
Decoding card	situation	You and your husband are sitting alone on a winter evening. You feel cold.
	alternatives	a. You wonder if it's only you who are cold or if he is cold, too.
		b. You want him to warm you with physical affection.
		c. You think he is being inconsiderate in not having turned up the heat by now and you want him to turn it up straight away.

likely that they are related to both how the messages are sent and how the messages are received. Both encoding and decoding are presumably affected by the cognitive and affective context created by the quality of the couple's relationship. Second, there is a clear tendency for the husband's communication accuracy to be the critical discriminator between couples high and low in marital adjustment. Gottman and Porterfield (1981) also found evidence that husbands have a deficit in decoding nonverbal cues.

Third, husbands and wives seem to differ in the direction of their errors. Wives are more likely to assume positivity where none was intended, whereas husbands are more likely to assume negativity where none was intended. Gaelick, Bodenhausen, and Wyer (1985) found similar effects, using a different methodology. On the other hand, Gottman et al. (1976) found that marital adjustment had the strongest effect on the decoding process, with both husbands and wives in unhappy marriages interpreting their partners' messages more negatively than they were intended. Although this latter finding fits the conventional wisdom, there are several methodological points that should be noted. The stimuli in this "talk-table" methodology adopted by Gottman involved both verbal and nonverbal messages (whereas those used by Gottman and Porterfield, 1981, and Noller, 1980, involved only the nonverbal channel, because the verbal channel was controlled), and there was no attempt to validate the ratings of intent that were given by the sender. Spouses low in marital satisfaction may be unaware of the negativity inherent in their messages. Alternatively, the impact of a message on a distressed spouse may be more strongly related to that spouse's general expectations and assumptions than to the actual message that was sent. This distinction between perceived intent and impact is discussed in detail by Bradbury and Fincham (1989).

A further study (Noller, 1981) was carried out to examine the relations between accuracy at decoding the spouse and accuracy at decoding strangers. All the married couples taking part in the earlier study decoded a standardized video of five married couples sending each other the same messages used previously. Although spouses low in marital adjustment were no less accurate at decoding strangers than those high in marital adjustment, both husbands and wives low in marital adjustment decoded their spouses less accurately than they decoded strangers. These findings suggest a decoding deficit that is specific to the relationship between the spouses. What seemed to be a communication skills deficit in the husbands is, in fact, a performance deficit specific to their relationships with their spouses. It is likely that this decoding deficit is related to the affective and cognitive context in which the decoding takes place. This context seems to make it difficult for spouses to decode their spouses' messages with the same level of skill they exercise in decoding the messages of strangers. For this reason it is important to analyze understandings and misunderstandings in marriage, at the message level, in relation to judgments of affect and intention, and attributions of blame.

This study involving the decoding of strangers also underlines some important findings about sex differences in decoding nonverbal cues. Although Noller (1980) found that males and females were equally accurate at decoding their spouses, Noller (1981) found that the females were more accurate than males at decoding strangers. Thus, there seem to be clear sex differences in the decoding of strangers, but no differences between the sexes when spouses are being decoded. These findings replicate the pattern of findings in other research (Hall, 1978, 1979; Zuckerman, Lipets, Koivumaki, & Rosenthal, 1975).

Noller (1986) has suggested that females may do better at decoding strangers because they are more aware of the general social rules for decoding nonverbal messages. On the other hand, when the decoding depends more on knowledge of an individual's typical nonverbal behaviors, then males decode as well as females. We will return to some of these findings and interpretations when we attempt to integrate the various findings in this area.

In the next section we report a study involving spouses' judgments of their partners' intentions during an interaction in which the emotion of anger, depression, or affection was involved. Once again, we are interested in accuracy, but on this occasion we focus on the accuracy with which spouses attribute intentions to each other, as well as any systematic tendency to attribute particular types of intentions. We expected distressed spouses to be less accurate and more negative in their attributions of intention than nondistressed spouses.

JUDGMENTS ABOUT PARTNER INTENTION IN AN EMOTIONAL SITUATION

In a very different type of study from those discussed in the previous section, Guthrie and Noller (1988) had spouses interact in situations involving different emotions and then make a global assessment of their spouses' intentions using open-ended responses. Their methodology involved the improvization technique used by Raush and his colleagues (Raush, Barry, Hertel, & Swain, 1974), with the coaching modification used by Rubin (1977) and described by Gottman (1979). The aim of this procedure was to make sure that the situations were as salient as possible for individual couples and also involved the particular emotion we were interested in studying.

The researchers first interviewed the spouses separately and asked for details about situations in which they would typically be angry with their partner or feel depressed about their marital relationship. Spouses were then instructed to act out these scenarios, which were videotaped. Each couple was required to enact a total of six situations—anger, depression, and affection situations for both the wife and the husband. A standard situation was used for affection, with spouses being asked to imagine that they had been watching television with their partners and were feeling very affectionate toward them.

Immediately following each interaction, subjects answered a number of questions about their perceptions of the interaction. These questions concerned their perceptions of the affect they and their partner were experiencing, their own intentions during the interaction, their judgments about their spouses' intentions, and their ratings of the positivity of their own and their spouses' behavior. Statements about their own and their partners' affect and intentions were given in the form of open-ended written responses.

Because spouses reported their own intentions, as well as their judgments about the intentions of their partners, the two versions of the intentions relating to each person in each situation could be rated for similarity. Groups of students rated the pairs of intentions (e.g., the wife's report of her intention in the anger situation and the husband's judgment of her intention in that same situation) on a six-point rating scale, where 1 = not at all similar and 6 = exactly the same. Irrespective of whether they were the expressor (the one who had suggested the situation because it was one in which they typically felt angry or depressed) or the receiver, low marital adjustment spouses were less accurate in judging the intentions of their partners. There were no differences between husbands and wives, and only one difference related to the particular emotion being expressed: Depressed spouses were better able to judge their spouses' intentions than were affectionate spouses.

The intentions were also rated individually in terms of their positivity, again by groups of students. The intentions of spouses low in marital adjustment were rated more negatively than those of spouses high in marital adjustment for situations involving both depression and affection. On the other hand, marital adjustment did not seem to affect the positivity of intentions ascribed in the anger situations, and all subjects attributed more positive intentions (when they were angry) to themselves than to their partners.

These findings indicate a clear tendency for unhappy spouses to misunderstand each other's intentions in situations involving high levels of affect. On the other hand, there seems to be little difference between distressed and non-distressed couples in how positively they rate their partners' intentions in anger situations—intentions were seen as equally negative, irrespective of the level of marital adjustment. It seems that situations involving anger are seen as negative, whatever one's level of marital adjustment.

The self-serving judgment that one's own intentions in anger situations are more positive than those of one's partner is interesting. The implication seems to be that spouses see themselves as controlling their anger better and expressing it more positively than their partners. This issue is discussed at a later point when we report data concerning attributions of responsibility and blame.

Of the two research programs reported so far, one involved perceptions of affect only, whereas the other involved judgments of intention only. If we are to argue, however, that judgments of intention have an impact on perceptions of affect (or vice-versa), then it is important to be able to directly relate the two types of data. In the next section, we describe a study in which judgments of affect and intention can be directly compared.

JUDGMENTS ABOUT PARTNER AFFECT
AND INTENTION IN
AN EMOTIONAL SITUATION

Ruzzene (in preparation) examined, within the same study, both the cognitive and affective components of marital interaction when spouses were involved in trying to resolve conflict. Fifty couples (15 classified as nondistressed, 22 as moderately distressed, and 13 as distressed) were videotaped while discussing a long-standing problem issue that was specifically relevant to their relationships and salient to both partners in terms of its ongoing effects on marital happiness. Following the discussion, spouses provided information about the way they had experienced the interaction themselves, the way they thought their partners had experienced the interaction, and about their causal explanations for the problems being discussed.

Specifically, these data involved judgments of self and partner affect and cognition during interactions that focused on conflict, together with related attributional decisions concerning the conflict issue. Thus, the accuracy of spouses' judgments of each other's communication could be related to their causal attributions in a way not possible when these two types of data are examined in separate studies. The data relating to accuracy in communication is discussed first, whereas data reflecting attributional processes is outlined at a later point.

Following the discussion of their problem issue, spouses were asked to describe their own intentions and their own predominant affective state for the interaction as a whole, as well as their perceptions of the intentions and predominant affective state of their partners. In addition, six significant events, comprising three behaviors emitted by the wife and three behaviors emitted by the husband, were selected by husbands and wives, respectively, during a review of the videotaped interaction. Spouses were asked to select those partner behaviors that had the most impact on their own feelings during the interaction. Having selected these significant events, spouses described, in their own words, the intentions they believed motivated each partner behavior, and rated the positivity of the accompanying affect. Meanwhile, their partners indicated their actual intentions for the same behavior under examination, and the actual affective state they were experiencing at the time.

Finally, spouses indicated the impact that their partners' behaviors had exerted on their own affective state, as well as the impact they thought their own behaviors had produced on their partners' affective state. Affect ratings for the significant events were made on a scale ranging from -7 = extremely negative to $+7$ = extremely positive. All spouses provided the required information concerning each significant event selected by either themselves or their partner, immediately after observing it on videotape. Table 8.2 shows examples of significant events chosen by distressed and nondistressed spouses, together with partner-attributed and self-attributed intentions and affect ratings. Thus, global intentions and affect for the interaction as a whole were obtained through open-ended responses by spouses, as were intentions for the six significant events. On the other hand, affect associated with the significant events was measured in terms of positivity ratings.[1] The information so obtained made it possible to assess the accuracy and similarity of partners' judgments of intentions and affect.

---

[1]Perceived and self-reported affect for the six significant events was also measured using a 64-item checklist based on Leary's (1957) Circumplex Model. In this way, information about the nature of the affect accompanying each event was obtained. These data will not be reported here.

TABLE 8.2
Examples of Significant Events and Associated Affect Ratings

		Affect Ratings	
Distressed Couple			
H's statement	"I'm a difficult person to live with."		
H's intention	To make a rhetorical statement knowing it was not really true	s.a. int + 2	p.a. imp + 3
W's judgment of H's intention	To be annoying. Patronizing!	p.a. int -1	s.a. imp - 4
Nondistressed Couple			
W's statement	"No. You haven't forgotten about it."		
W's intention	(He) doesn't want to discuss the issue	s.a. int + 1	p.a. imp - 2
H's judgment of W's intention	She wants to keep the issue going.	p.a. int + 2	s.a. imp - 1

Note. H = husband; W = wife
s.a. int = self-attributed intentional affect; p.a. int= partner-attributed intentional affect
s.a. imp = affective impact of partner on self; p.a. imp = perceived affective impact of self on partner.

Global Intention and Affect

Transcripts of the spouses' statements describing their intentions and affect were presented to groups of no fewer than 10 introductory psychology students. The students rated the degree of similarity between pairs of statements describing partner-attributed and self-attributed intentions (i.e., the content of the intentions), and partner-attributed and self-attributed affect (i.e., the type of affect), for the same event and the same individual. As in the Guthrie and Noller (1988) study, the average similarity rating for each pair of statements was taken as an index of spouses' accuracy or understanding of their partners' intentions in the interaction. For example, the average similarity rating for the statements "to make a rhetorical statement knowing it was not really true" (the husband's stated intention) and "To be annoying. Patronizing!" (the wife's judgment of his intention) was 3.4 on a scale of 1 = not at all similar to 6 = very similar.

With regard to the interaction as a whole, spouses in all three marital adjustment groups exhibited a similar degree of accuracy in inferring what their partners actually wanted to achieve during the discussion. In contrast to these judgments of intention, the degree of accuracy associated with spouses' perceptions of their partners' affective states differed according to marital adjustment level, $F(2,94) = 5.20$, $p < .01$. Distressed husbands and wives were markedly less accurate than happier spouses. That is, although exhibiting similar levels of understanding about their partners' intentions, distressed couples were much less sensitive to their partners' feeling states than other couples. Being aware of partner affect as well as partner intentions has important implications for spouses' responses to their partners' behavior, and for the interactional outcomes that may arise from these responses. For instance, knowing the intentions of one's partner will not necessarily lead to an appropriately congruent response if one imagines that the partner is feeling assertive and confident, when he or she is actually feeling apprehensive and frustrated. Transcripts of spouses' self-attributed and partner-attributed affect reveal examples of such discrepant evaluations—even when their judgments of intentions are rated as relatively accurate. For instance, one wife judged her husband's predominant affect during the discussion to be "comfortable—because he likes discussions" and "contented—because he really believes he is totally correct." Her husband, meanwhile, reported feeling "frustrated—because she [wife] cannot admit the problem." The possibility that general intentions may be accurately perceived, whereas emotions are not, underlines the complexity of marital communication and confirms the need to study these processes at different levels.

Although this finding differs from those observed by Guthrie and Noller (1988), the result needs to be understood in terms of the research context. First, the issues being discussed in the present study were long-standing and presumably involved often expressed differences between each spouse's particular aims and goals. It is therefore not surprising that spouses generally had a similar degree of understanding about their partners' intentions in the discussion. Second, in terms of the immediate methodology, spouses in the present study collaborated to choose the topic and may have conveyed something of their goals and intentions during that discussion. Nevertheless, despite spouses' shared history and experience of their partners' intentions, empathic understanding of each other's affect was less evident in distressed couples than other couples.

Judgments of Intentions, Affect, and Impact for Significant Events

Judgments of intention. As previously, the degree of agreement between the content of the self-attributed and partner-attributed intentions associated with significant events was determined using objective similarity ratings provided by raters. These varied according to the sex of the observer spouse and the marital adjustment of the couple, $F(2,94) = 3.32, p < .05$. Distressed and moderately distressed wives were least accurate in judging their partners' intentions for specific interaction events, whereas nondistressed wives were most accurate at this task. Thus, although more global attributions of partner intention were similarly accurate across the three levels of marital adjustment, when relating to specific events within an interaction, less understanding was displayed by distressed wives as compared to nondistressed wives and husbands (see Table 8.3).

Affect ratings. Our first aim was to examine differences in the affective climate of these problem-related discussions. Comparisons were made among the marital adjustment groups for the positivity of self-attributed and partner-

TABLE 8.3
Mean Accuracy Ratings of the Content of Partner-Attributed Intentions for Significant Interaction Events

	Nondistressed	Moderate	Distressed
Husbands	3.45	3.55	3.35
Wives	3.57	2.79	2.77

Note. Accuracy ratings on a scale from 1 = not at all similar to 6 = very similar.

attributed affect, both for intentions and impact, for each of the six significant events. As previously indicated, positivity of affect was measured on a scale of -7 = extremely negative to $+7$ = extremely positive, these ratings being provided by the subjects themselves.

With regard to affect associated with intentions, significant differences were observed between marital adjustment groups and between sexes. Distressed spouses' self-attributions of intention were more negative than those of nondistressed spouses, $F(2,276) = 3.16, p < .05$, and husbands' self-attributions of intention were more negative than those of wives, $F(1,276) = 4.38, p < .05$. In addition, distressed spouses' partner attributions of intention were more negative than those of nondistressed spouses, $F(2,276) = 14.35, p < .001$, and husbands' partner attributions of intention were more negative than those of wives, $F(1,276) = 3.80, p = .05$. Thus, when making judgments about their own and their partners' intentions for significant events in the interaction, distressed spouses and husbands attributed more negative intentions, both to themselves and to their partners, than did nondistressed spouses and wives, respectively (see Table 8.4).

The affect associated with impact for the significant events also varied according to marital distress and sex (see also Table 8.4). Partner attributions were

TABLE 8.4
Positivity of Self-Attributed and Partner-Attributed Affect for Intentions and Impact for Significant Events

	Nondistressed		Moderates		Distressed	
	H	W	H	W	H	W
p.a. int	-0.6	1.1	-0.3	-0.2	-2.4	-2.0
s.a. int	0.4	0.5	-1.0	0.2	-0.7	-0.1
p.a. imp	-0.1	-0.3	-1.0	-0.5	-2.4	-1.9
s.a. imp	-0.8	0.2	-0.5	-2.2	-1.8	-2.6

Note. H = husband; W = wife
Scale from +7 = very positive to -7 = very negative. Means are based on averages across both positive and negative significant events.
s.a. int = self-attributed intentional affect; p.a. int = partner-attributed intentional affect; s.a. imp = affective impact of partner on self; p.a. imp = perceived affective impact on self on partner.

TABLE 8.5
Correlations Between Self-Attributed and Partner-Attributed Affect for Significant Interaction
Events

	Nondistressed	Moderate	Distressed
Accuracy Across Couples			
Accuracy of speaker judgments of affective impact on listener	.39[c]	.22[b]	.24[a]
Accuracy of listener judgments of intentional affect of speaker	.28[a]	.31[c]	.15
Consistency Within Subjects			
Consistency between listener's affective impact and partner-attributed intentional affect	.60[c]	.44[c]	.12
Consistency between speaker's intentional affect and perceived affective impact on partner	.37[c]	.52[c]	.21

Note. Ns for these correlations are derived from the number of significant events for each group as a whole;
for nondistressed, $N = 89$; for moderates; $N = 121$; for distressed, $N = 72$.

[a] $p < .05$.

[b] $p < .01$.

[c] $p < .000$.

significantly more negative for distressed spouses of both sexes than they were for nondistressed spouses, $F(2,276) = 11.32, p < .001$. Moderate and distressed wives' self-attributions, meanwhile, were more negative than those of all other spouses, $F(2,276) = 5.70, p < .01$). These findings support recurring observations concerning the relative level of negativity among maritally distressed groups for both self and partner-attributed affect, and is consistent with such concepts as negative affect reciprocity and escalation of negativity in distressed couples (e.g., Gottman, 1979).

A further aim of this study was to look at the accuracy and consistency with which spouses judged each other's affective experience. Spouses' ratings for both their own and their partners' affect were compared in terms of correlations across couples between self-attributed and partner-attributed affect, for both intention and impact across the significant events. Recall that these ratings were provided by the subjects themselves (see Table 8.2 for examples). Because each event being rated was initiated by one spouse, correlations were split into those for the speaker and those for the listener. Thus, comparisons between ratings yielded four indices of couples' affective communication—two from the speaker perspective and two from the listener perspective. Specifically, correlations computed across subjects represent accuracy of speaker and listener judgments, and those within subjects represent perceived consistency between judgments, or level of perceived affective rapport, for both speaker and listener.

Overall, correlations in Table 8.5 reveal a higher degree of association between nondistressed spouses' self-attributed and partner-attributed affect than is

TABLE 8.6
Accuracy Correlations for Intentional Affect and Impact for Significant Interaction Events

	Affect for Intentions		Affect for Impact	
	H	W	H	W
Nondistressed	0.32[a]	0.17	0.41[b]	0.41[b]
Moderate	0.45[c]	0.18	0.20	0.35[b]
Distressed	-0.10	0.32	0.40[c]	0.69[c]

Note. Ns for these correlations involve the number of significant events for husbands and wives in each group; N = 44 for nondistressed husbands; N = 45 for nondistressed wives; N = 61 for moderate husbands; N = 60 for moderate wives; N = 36 for distressed husbands; N = 36 for distressed wives.
[a] $p < .05$.
[b] $p < .01$.
[c] $p < .001$.

true for distressed couples. Specifically, nondistressed spouses (as listeners) were more accurate than distressed spouses in judging the affect associated with their partners' intentions (partner-attributed intentional affect vs. self-attributed intentional affect), and in judging the impact of their own behavior (as speakers) upon their partner (partner-attributed impact vs. self-attributed impact). Moreover, judgments of own intentional affect and impact of self on partner (for the speaker) and judgments of partner intentional affect and impact of partner on self (for the listener) were more consistent for spouses from the higher marital adjustment groups than they were for spouses from the low marital adjustment group. Thus, although high marital adjustment couples were more accurate in their understanding of each other's affective communication than low marital adjustment couples, both nondistressed and distressed couples appear to have been aware, at least to some extent, of the respective levels of high and low rapport in their interactions.

When sex differences in the patterning of these correlations were examined within each marital adjustment group, husbands and wives exhibited different levels of accuracy depending on whether the focus was affect associated with intentions, or affect associated with impact. The pattern of correlations between self-attributed and partner-attributed affect for both intentions and impact (see Table 8.6) suggests that spouses, particularly wives, were more accurate at assessing their partners' affect when they were communicating to the partner rather than when the partner was communicating to them. On the other hand, although nondistressed husbands' judgments of their wives' affect were similarly accurate, irrespective of who was communicating to whom, distressed husbands displayed less accuracy when their wives were communicating to them than when they were communicating to their wives.

If wives are inclined to be demanding when discussing marital problems (Gottman & Levenson, 1988), it makes sense that assessing the impact of their own communications upon their husbands would be a highly salient task (for predicting their husbands' most likely response). This interpretation fits with Noller's (1984) findings with regard to gaze behavior, where distressed spouses monitored their partners' behavior much more closely when they themselves were the speakers than when they were the listeners. On the other hand, husbands' relatively low levels of accuracy when judging their partners' intentions may indicate an unwillingness to acknowledge their partners' intentions, and could be linked to their tendency to withdraw and avoid discussions of problem issues (Christensen, 1988; Noller, 1988).

Accuracy at judging both intentions and affect.   Because the same subjects made judgments of their partners' intentions and their partners' affect, we were able to directly relate accuracy at judging intentions to accuracy at perceiving affect. We did this by calculating the correlations between ratings of the *similarity* of self-attributed and partner-attributed intentions and the *discrepancy* between ratings of self-attributed and partner-attributed affect associated with those intentions. These correlations represent the degree of likelihood that accurate assessment of intentions is associated with accurate judgments of accompanying affect. If couples are similarly accurate in their judgments of intention and accompanying affect, we would expect negative correlations between these two measures, because similarity ratings increase while discrepancy scores decrease with greater accuracy.

This issue is central to models of interactional processes (e.g., the contextual model of Bradbury & Fincham, 1987), which involve implicit assumptions about the relationship between thoughts and feelings in the communicative process, for example, that accurate judgments of intention imply accurate understanding at the affect and message levels. It seems reasonable to assume that the affective reactions and subsequent behavioral responses of the observer spouse would be dependent, not only on correct interpretation of his or her partner's intentions (e.g., to express a desire for change in the status quo), but also on the nature of the affect that he or she sees accompanying such intentions (e.g., dominant, frustrated, neutral). The importance of ascertaining whether or not accurate judgments of intentions are a sufficient condition for accurate judgments of affect is apparent.

In fact, there were no significant correlations between accuracy for intentions and accuracy for affect for any of the marital adjustment groups or either sex. This finding with regard to specific events occurring during the interaction is consistent with those obtained in relation to the interaction as a whole. It seems that there is no reason to assume that accurate judgments of partner intention and affect go hand in hand. As noted, the present data for judgments of affect are in the form of ratings of positivity rather than judgments of the nature of the affect being experienced. Work is presently in progress to obtain further clarification of this issue with data representing spouses' qualitative descriptions of their part-

TABLE 8.7
Correlations Between Negativity of Intentions and Accuracy of Affect

All spouses	-0.18[a]
Nondistressed	0.02
Moderates	-0.19
Distressed	-0.09
Males	-0.31[b]
Females	-0.02

[a] $p < .05$
[b] $p < .08$

ners' affect (e.g., loving, frustrated, angry), along with their judgments of cognitions.

Given that distressed spouses are both less accurate and more negative in the intentions they ascribe to their partners (e.g., Guthrie & Noller, 1988), it is possible that negativity, rather than accuracy of judgments of intention, is related to inaccuracy in judgments of affect. In other words, the negativity of spouses' judgments of their partners' intentions may predict the degree of accuracy in judgments of partner affect. Because we had obtained only spouses' ratings of the affect they thought accompanied their partners' intentions, and not their assessment of the negativity of the thoughts embodied in those intentions, we could not test this hypothesis directly. However, we were able to compare outsider ratings of the negativity of spouses' judgments of those partner intentions with the level of accuracy exhibited in spouses' judgments of partner affect. The more negatively outsiders rated the spouses' judgments of partner intentions, the less accurate were the spouses' affect judgments (see Table 8.7). Specifically, husbands were less accurate in their judgments of affect when the intentions they attributed to their partners were rated as negative by outsiders. These findings indicate that, for husbands, attributing negative intentions decreases accuracy in judgments of associated affect. These correlations also provide further support for the possibility that husbands' decoding of affect (more than wives') influenced their attributions of intention.

Bias in Judgments of Affect

In this section, as in the studies mentioned earlier, we define bias as the systematic tendency to make errors in a particular direction. This bias is measured in terms of the size and direction of the discrepancy between spouses' ratings of the affect accompanying their own stated intentions, and their partners' ratings of that same affect. As noted earlier, these ratings were obtained on a scale of $+7 =$ very positive and $-7 =$ very negative.

Comparisons among marital adjustment groups indicated, as would be expected, that discrepancies for distressed spouses were larger and more negative than those for nondistressed spouses, $F(2,47) = 7.32$, $p < .01$. Whereas high marital adjustment couples' tended to make smaller errors in a positive direction, low adjustment couples made larger errors in a negative direction.

The findings arising from this study generally support previous research indicating superior levels of empathic accuracy and lower levels of negativity for the more adjusted couples. However, some observations suggest that long-standing conflict issues, presumably often discussed, provide a special context for understanding the quality of couples' communication. For judgments of intention (cognition), the accuracy of spouses' judgments did not vary with marital adjustment for the interaction as a whole, but did vary in the expected direction, at least for wives, when significant events in the interaction were considered. The accuracy of judgments of affect, meanwhile, varied according to marital adjustment for the interaction as a whole, and according to sex and marital adjustment for significant events in the interaction.

Overall, nondistressed spouses were more empathically aware of each other's affective states than were distressed spouses, whereas husbands and wives exhibited different levels of accuracy when judging affect associated with intentions, and affect associated with impact. Most notably, wives were more accurate at attributing partner affect for impact than for intentions, and distressed husbands were more accurate at attributing partner affect for intentions than for impact. In addition, there was evidence that the accuracy with which spouses assessed their partners' intentions did not necessarily predict the accuracy of their assessments of the accompanying affect. The possibility that accuracy on one judgmental task does not ensure accuracy on the other is an important consideration for models of marital communication.

Finally, evidence of biases in spouses' evaluations of each other's affect associated with intentions was presented. In brief, this evidence underlined the self-perpetuating nature of couples' interactional processes whereby the affective and cognitive processing of distressed spouses are likely to maintain, or even augment, the level of negativity in their communications with each other, whereas the processing of nondistressed spouses is likely to maintain or augment the positivity of their communications.

Attributions

Attributions are judgments or conclusions about the causes of events in a social environment and are assumed to be important determinants of behavior (Fiske & Taylor, 1984; Jones et al., 1972), particularly in the context of close relationships (Bradbury & Fincham, 1989; Fletcher & Fincham, this volume; Harvey, Wells, & Alvarez, 1978; Revenstorf, 1984; Thompson & Kelley, 1981). Traditionally, the most important distinction between possible causes for events is that of the person versus the situation, that is, between imputing an individual's dispositional characteristics as the major cause of a given event versus the environmental circumstances in which the event occurs. More recently, these two categories have been expanded and modified. Newman (1981a, 1981b) has proposed a third interpersonal category of attributions, whereas a number of researchers' (see Bradbury & Fincham's, 1990, review of the literature) have distinguished between causal attributions and attributions of responsibility and blame, suggesting that each of these categories has different implications for the attributor's affective response to the stimulus event (Fincham, Bradbury, & Grych, in press).

The findings reported here reflect attributions associated with marital problems that are relatively long-standing (i.e., a source of intermittent conflict in an ongoing sense) and recognized as such by both partners. This context may be contrasted to those studies that present one or more isolated incidents or behaviors—naturally occurring or hypothetical—as the stimulus for eliciting spouses' attributions. Results arising in the present context, therefore, provide further insight into spouses' attributional behavior as it relates to mutually acknowledged, ongoing sources of marital disharmony.

As previously described, couples selected the problem issue they wished to focus on in the study and were subsequently asked to indicate how they viewed this problem on a number of attributional dimensions. The attributions involved judgments about major causes of the problem and about their own and their partners' problem-related behavior. In addition, couples were asked how seriously they regarded the problem issue, how much control they thought they had over its recurrence, how permanent they perceived its causes to be, and how resolvable they thought the problem ultimately was. The responses to all of these questions, examined in terms of marital adjustment and spouse gender, are presented in the following sections.

Locus of causal attributions.   To ascertain how spouses explained the occurrence of the problem discussed in the videotaped interaction, we asked them to rate six possible causes on a scale from 1 = very unlikely cause to 6 = very likely cause. The description of each cause began with the phrase "Something to do with . . ." followed by (a) your personality, (b) your behavior, (c) your partner's personality, (d) your partner's behavior, (e) your relationship with each other, and (f) outside circumstances.

The six causal loci were drawn from literature that differentiates between personality and behavior attributions (Janoff-Bulman, 1979), and that proposes an interpersonal category of attributions over and above the more traditional person-situation classifications (Newman, 1981, 1981b). Presenting a range of possible causes enabled us to examine the separate causal loci relative to one another, that is, as a pattern of responses reflecting the *relative* importance of each possible cause, rather than assuming that endorsement of one cause implies rejection of another.

Preferences for different loci of attributions.   The six causal loci were rated differently by all subjects, with the most strongly endorsed causal locus being the

TABLE 8.8
Locus of Attributions for All Spouses

Own personality	4.8_a
Own behavior	4.3_b
Partner personality	4.2_b
Partner behavior	4.0_b
Relationship	3.2_c
Outside circumstances	3.1_c

Note. Means with different subscripts differ from each other at $p < 01$.
Scale from 1 = very unlikely cause to 6 = very likely cause.

respondent spouse's own personality (see Table 8.8). Own behavior, partner personality, and partner behavior were the next most strongly rated causes, whereas the relationship and outside circumstances were rated as the least important of the six possible causes. These results emphasise the importance of personality and behavior, relative to the relationship and outside circumstances, in spouses' judgments of causality for long-standing problems.

Two points need to be noted regarding these results. First, few attribution studies involve videotaped interactions prior to sampling the subjects' attributional responses. It may well be that the procedure of being videotaped while discussing a problem issue promoted unusual levels of self-focused attention. Such a focus may encourage and enhance considerations of personal responsibility for spouses, both individually and as a couple, resulting in stronger ratings for person-based attributions.

A second important aspect of these results is that, although spouses in general did not discriminate between their partners' personality and behavior as causal factors, they did differentiate between their *own* personality and behavior. This differentiation by spouses suggests that it is appropriate to consider these two dimensions of person attributions separately. Janoff-Bulman (1979) has presented evidence of individual differences in perceptions of control over personality and behavior, with personality being seen as less amenable to change than is behavior. Such differences in perceptions of the controllability of causal factors could have important implications for understanding the proximal and distal contexts in which problem-related interactions occur. Evidence presented below supports this proposition.

Differences among groups on each locus of causality.   There were no differences between marital adjustment groups in the extent to which own behavior, partner personality, or outside circumstances were seen as causes of the problem. Marital adjustment groups did differ, however, in the extent to which spouses invoked their own personality (distressed and nondistressed more than moderates, $F(2,44) = 3.31$, $p < .05$), partner behavior (wives more than husbands, $F(1,44) = 9$, $p < .005$), and the relationship itself (distressed more than moderates and nondistressed, $F(2,43) = 5.42$, $p < .01$). There was also a trend for

TABLE 8.9
Locus of Attributions According to Sex and Marital Adjustment Level

	Nondistressed		Moderates		Distressed	
	Husbands	Wives	Husbands	Wives	Husbands	Wives
Own personality	5.4	4.7	4.1	4.6	5.1	5.5
Own behavior	4.3	4.1	4.1	4.1	4.2	5.0
Partner personality	3.7	4.1	3.8	4.8	4.3	4.8
Partner behavior	3.1	3.9	3.6	4.2	3.9	5.5
Relationship	2.8	1.7	3.2	3.0	4.1	4.7
Outside circumstances	2.8	3.2	3.4	3.5	2.8	2.9

wives to invoke partner personality as causal to a greater extent than husbands, $F(1,46) = 3.14$, $p = .08$. (A summary of ratings is presented in Table 8.9.)

The fact that subjects seemed to place special emphasis on the contribution of their own personality to the problem is made especially interesting by the presence of a curvilinear relationship between marital adjustment and the extent to which this cause was invoked. If both distressed and nondistressed spouses similarly emphasize their own personality in causal explanations, it would be reasonable to assume that the implications of such an attributional decision for marital adjustment must be different in each case. To understand this finding, we can refer to the overall pattern of results. Whereas nondistressed spouses—and, indeed, distressed husbands—generally attribute greater causality to themselves than to their partners, distressed wives seem to consider their own and their partners' levels of causality to be roughly equivalent. In addition, whereas the pattern for all other spouses is to invoke partner personality over partner behavior as a causal factor, distressed wives place greater causal importance on their partners' behavior than on their partner's personality. Given that partner-related causes are seen as less controllable than one's own, and that behavioral causes are seen as more controllable than characterological ones (Janoff-Bulman, 1979), this pattern suggests that distressed wives are likely to perceive themselves as having relatively less control over problem resolution, and to place a greater onus for change onto their husbands—without necessarily expecting this change to occur. Thus, although distressed and nondistressed spouses are similar in the extent to which they see their own personalities as the cause of the problem, they may differ substantially, at least where wives are concerned, in terms of how this particular causal explanation meshes with perceptions of other causes.

The implications for further interaction are that wives may be more likely than husbands to demand that their partner change their behavior, leading to the cycle of demand and withdraw described by Noller and Fitzpatrick (1988). The finding that wives more than husbands focus on partner behavior as a causal factor is also consistent with stereotypic images of wives as demanding/approaching and husbands as pacifying/withdrawing. In addition, the tendency to account for problems in terms of causes over which one has little control is consistent with the idea of low efficacy expectations for problem resolution, which is associated with lower levels of marital adjustment (Fincham et al., in press). This interpretation is supported by other findings reported below.

Immediately after rating the possible causes of their problem, spouses were asked to rate their own and their partners' problem-related behavior on a number of dimensions. To the extent that husbands and wives do hold each other's behavior as causal, it seems important to ascertain whether or not there are any differences in judgments of own versus partner behavior on a number of dimensions that have been described in terms of their implications for relationship quality (Bradbury & Fincham, 1990; Fincham et al., in press; Holtzworth-Munroe & Jacobson, 1985; Madden & Janoff-Bulman, 1981). Specifically, spouses were asked to rate their own as well as their partner's problem-related behavior on the dimensions of globality, stability, temporary mood state, responsibility, and blame. A summary of the ratings is presented in Table 8.10.

Before presenting the results arising from these data, it is important to note that spouses' ratings of the seriousness of their problem was related to both

TABLE 8.10
Mean Attribution Ratings on All Dimensions by Sex and Marital Adjustment

	Nondistressed		Moderates		Distressed	
	H	W	H	W	H	W
Global						
Self	2.13	2.13	3.00	3.05	3.67	4.25
Partner	2.13	2.53	2.84	2.90	3.58	4.33
Stable						
Self	2.73	4.00	3.71	3.86	4.08	3.92
Partner	3.86	3.87	3.95	4.42	4.08	5.00
Mood						
Self	2.73	3.20	2.90	2.40	2.41	2.25
Partner	2.80	2.73	2.20	2.10	2.00	1.83
Voluntary						
Self	4.64	4.74	4.00	3.79	3.58	3.83
Partner	3.07	3.71	3.42	3.68	3.66	3.83
Intentional						
Self	1.87	2.93	2.89	3.39	2.83	3.50
Partner	2.60	2.07	3.67	2.55	3.16	3.08
Selfish						
Self	2.20	2.27	3.28	3.14	3.00	3.66
Partner	1.27	2.07	1.76	2.62	1.92	3.75
Blameworthy						
Self	2.60	2.07	3.19	3.05	2.33	3.42
Partner	1.87	2.00	1.71	2.81	1.42	2.67
Praiseworthy						
Self	2.57	2.21	2.71	2.76	3.17	2.25
Partner	4.14	2.85	3.81	2.52	4.17	3.00

Note. H = husband; W = wife
Self = own behavior
Partner = partner behavior
Scale from 1 = not at all to 6 = very much

marital adjustment level and a number of the dimensions outlined above. Therefore, all data reported below were analyzed using seriousness ratings as a covariate, with marital adjustment as a between-subjects variable, and sex of spouse as a within-subjects variable.

Globality and Stability Attributions

Distressed spouses more than moderate and nondistressed spouses perceived problem-related behavior to be present in many other areas of the marriage, $F(2,42) = 6.95$, $p < .005$. The relative pervasiveness of distress-maintaining behaviors, as much as the nature of the behaviors themselves, is confirmed as an important factor in predicting marital satisfaction (Fincham, 1985; Fincham, Beach, & Baucom, 1987; Fincham, Beach, & Nelson, 1987; Fincham & O'Leary, 1983; Holtzworth-Munroe & Jacobson, 1985). However, spouses in this study did not distinguish between their own problem-related behavior and that of their partners in terms of globality.

On the dimension of stability, ratings differed according to sex and marital adjustment. Wives rated problem-related behavior as being more stable than did husbands, $F(1,45) = 4.93$, $p < .05$, and partner behavior was regarded as more stable than own behavior, $F(1,45) = 9.01$, $p < .005$. A three-way interaction between marital adjustment, sex, and own versus partner behavior, $F(2,45) = 9.01$, $p = .05$, indicated that distressed wives were most likely and nondistressed husbands least likely to expect problem behavior to continue to occur in the future.

Temporary Mood State Attributions

Distressed and nondistressed spouses of both sexes were equally likely to attribute problem behavior to a temporary mood state. In addition, all spouses saw their own behavior as being more likely due to a temporary mood state than was their partners' behavior. Thus, as noted earlier, although spouses generally regarded their own personality as an important cause of the problem issue, they seem to imply, in a self-serving way, that their own problem-related *behavior* is more related to temporary factors than is their partners' problem-related behavior.

Responsibility and Blame Attributions

Research in the past decade has questioned the idea that attributions of causality necessarily lead to judgments of responsibility and blame. In a marital context, this means that a spouse may judge his or her partner as the cause of a given problem, but the extent to which the partner is held responsible or blamed will be determined by other factors. In theory, these factors would include the manner in which the partner is able to account for his or her actions, and the extent to which that accountability is deemed to invite censure or negative evaluation by the spouse. In terms of its implications for marital harmony, it is the assignation of responsibility and blame, rather than causality, that may have the greater significance, being most closely linked with such negative affective reactions as anger, guilt, or shame (Fincham et al., in press). In addition to measuring attributions of blame directly, the present study examined a number of dimensions upon which responsibility and blame are thought to rest (Bradbury & Fincham, 1990).

Voluntariness. Ratings on this dimension showed that spouses regarded their partner's problem-related behavior as less voluntary than their own, $F(1,42) = 8.62$, $p < .01$. However, further analyses revealed that this differentiation between partners' and own behavior was only exhibited by nondistressed spouses, $F(2,42) = 4.47$, $p < .02$. Nondistressed spouses, unlike other spouses, seemed to believe that their own behavior could have been avoided, and tended to make allowances for their partners' behavior in a way that other spouses did not.

This finding is in contrast to results reported above concerning locus of causality, in which distressed spouses seemed more inclined to explain behavior in terms of external factors. Nondistressed spouses, unlike distressed spouses, seemed ready to acknowledge internal factors that may contribute to the occurrence of problem-related behavior, suggesting a greater willingness on their part to take some responsibility for the recurrence of that behavior in the future.

Intentionality/foreknowledge of consequences. An interaction between sex of spouse and own versus partner behavior, $F(1,42) = 6.57$, $p < .02$, showed that wives believed that their own behavior was more intentional in its impact than was their husbands' behavior. Husbands, in conrast, believed that the impact of their own behavior was less intentional than that of their wives.

It is reasonable to assume that self-serving biases on the part of both spouses are involved in this finding. Wives may have believed that, although they themselves were more likely to know the impact their own behavior would have on their husbands, their husbands were less aware of the effects of their behavior on the wives. Wives seemed to have more confidence in their understanding of their husbands while having less confidence in their husbands' understanding of them. It is also possible that wives viewed their own behavior during conflict as more intentional *and* more constructive than that of their partner.

Husbands, on the other hand, may have judged their wives as being more responsible for the impact of problem-related behavior than they themselves were. That is, husbands may have believed that their actions were more often misunderstood by their wives, while at the same time implying that their wives were more likely to be aware of how they would react to the wives' actions. Thus, wives' proximal context could involve a statement like "He (an insensitive male) doesn't realize how his behavior is affecting me, whereas I (a warm and caring female) know how my behavior affects him"; husbands' proximal context could involve the complementary statement "She knows how her behavior affects me, whereas I (a logical rational male) can't be expected to understand how she (an emotional female) is going to react to my behavior." Findings relating to judgments of intentions and affect reported earlier would suggest that these contextual attitudes are reasonably well founded.

Selfish motives.   Distressed spouses were more likely to attribute selfish motives to problem behavior than other spouses, $F(2,44) = 6.13, p < .005$, and wives generally were more likely to attribute selfish motives to problem behavior than were husbands, $F(2,44) = 9.68, p < .005$. However, husbands and wives differed in their perceptions of selfishness for their own and for partner behavior, $F(1,45) = 6.09, p < .02$. Wives regarded both their own and their partners' problem behavior as equally selfishly motivated, whereas husbands saw their partners' behavior as less selfishly motivated than their own behavior, and less selfishly motivated than was true for wives.

Blame.   Overall, wives attributed blame to a greater extent than husbands for problem issues. Distressed wives particularly attributed more blame to problem behavior than did nondistressed wives and all husbands, and all spouses blamed their partners' behavior more than their own.

Praise.   Wives attributed less praise for problem-related behavior than did husbands, and spouses as a whole saw partner behavior as more praiseworthy than their own behavior. This latter finding, however, was largely due to husbands, $F(1,44) = 3.88, p = .06$, and could reflect the tendency for husbands to be the reconcilers in situations of low conflict (Gottman, 1979).

In summary, problem-related behavior was seen as more global and stable by distressed spouses than by nondistressed spouses. In addition, unlike nondistressed spouses, distressed spouses did not make allowances for the controllability of their partners' problem-related behavior in comparison to their own behavior. Husbands and wives, meanwhile, exhibited similar viewpoints concerning the intentionality of each other's behavior, with both spouses assuming that wives have a greater awareness of the likely impact of behavior than do husbands. It is possible, however, that the views held by each spouse, although similar in content, would differ in their self-serving implications.

Taken together with the finding concerning preferred locus of causality for problems, these results suggest that, for distressed spouses, causal attributions that involve problem-related behavior are likely to be associated with low efficacy expectations for problem resolution. The overall results also suggest that distressed spouses are less likely to assume some responsibility for change. In terms of the proximal and distal contexts in which interaction occurs, such a position is likely to mitigate against problem resolution and lead to more entrenched and polarized behavior patterns between unhappy spouses.

As well as indicating a number of self-enhancing biases, these findings point to the relatively higher degree of negativity likely to be associated with wives' judgments, particularly in the low marital adjustment group. Wives were generally more negative in their attributions of blame, more likely to attribute selfish motives, and less likely to praise than was true for husbands. In all, wives' judgments concerning selfishness and blame, as observed in this study, would tend to be associated with relatively high levels of affect. That is, in terms of Fincham et al.'s (in press) model of likely affective outcomes associated with attributional activity, wives in conflict would seem to be relatively more prone to both anger (other directed) and guilt (self directed). These findings are reminiscent of the stereotype of the demanding emotional wife and the pacifying rational husband, which we return to in a later section.

Attributions and Judgments of the Problem

Locus of causality and judgments of the problem.   Across all marital adjustment groups, correlations were calculated between ratings of importance of each of the causal loci and judgments of the seriousness, controllability, permanence, and resolvability of the problem. These correlations indicate the extent to which a given causal explanation is related to evaluations that have implications for spouses' efficacy expectations for the resolution of the problem. Such expectations have important implications for the manner and extent to which spouses attempt to cope with their difficulties.

The more seriously the problem was regarded, the more likely were spouses to invoke partner personality and the relationship itself as causes. Also, the more the spouses attributed the causes to partner personality and/or behavior, the more the problem was seen as permanent and beyond their control. Attributions to partner personality, then, carry implications that the problem is serious and arises from a permanent cause over which there is little control. These attributions are highly likely to be distress maintaining because spouses may resort to forcing their partners to change as the only solution. Under this kind of pressure, partners may become even more resistant to changing aspects of themselves, and react by increasing their own demands for change. Such a process is consistent with clinicians' reports that couples generally come into therapy entrenched in their habitual patterns of blaming the problems in the relationship on each other.

Globality, stability, and judgments of the problem.   Correlations were again calculated between ratings of the globality and stability of the problem's causes, and ratings of the seriousness, controllability, permanence, and resolvability of the problem. The more the problem-related behavior was seen as global and stable, the more likely the problem was to be considered serious, beyond the respondents' control, associated with permanent causes, and unresolvable. The perceived globality and stability of the partner's behavior were particularly likely to be associated with these distress-maintaining evaluations of the problem, suggesting the high salience of partner behavior compared with own behavior where problems are concerned.

Although the finding that distressed couples are more inclined to consider problem-related behavior as having stable and global causes is not new (Fincham & O'Leary, 1983; Holtzworth-Munroe & Jacobson, 1985), showing the link between these attributions and spouses' evaluations of the problem confirms the assumptions underlying the interpretation of much of this research. As noted earlier, spouses who perceive their serious problems as uncontrollable, unresolvable, and due to permanent causes are likely to be communicating in contexts that are characterized by low expectations for positive change. Once again, there is evidence of a pattern of judgments and beliefs that would provide a distal context almost certain to mitigate against the likelihood of constructive initiatives for change.

Responsibility, blame attributions, and judgments of the problem. Blame-worthy *partner* behavior was associated with judgments that the problem was serious, due to permanent causes, unresolvable, and beyond the respondent's control. Selfishness of partner motives was also associated with perceived permanence of problem causes and unresolvability. These findings highlight the fact that partners are more likely to be blamed for deeply entrenched problems that are seen as unresolvable and that seem to arouse considerable affect. It should also be noted that, where spouses regarded their own behavior as blameworthy and selfish, they were also more likely to see the problem as serious and due to permanent causes, although not necessarily unresolvable or beyond their control.

CONCLUSIONS

Although the evidence is by no means complete, data involving spouses' understanding of interaction events and their related attributional processes provide empirical evidence of a number of connections between elements in the proximal and distal context and the quality of marital communication. Distressed spouses, especially wives, approach problem discussions within a framework where problem-related behavior is seen as pervasive and unlikely to change, and where partner behavior, deemed selfish and blameworthy, is highlighted as a primary cause of the problem. Distressed spouses' evaluations of their problems seem to mitigate against any sense of self-efficacy or control, being associated with few perceived alternatives for achieving desired outcomes. In addition, solutions to the problem tend to be seen as requiring the unlikely eventuality of partner cooperation and change. (He needs to change and he probably won't, so there is nothing I can do!) The fact that spouses place so much emphasis on personality (both their own and their partners') as a causal factor is also likely to decrease expectations for change.

Judgments of communication events arising in the distal context just described seem to reflect the negative climate in which distressed couples are operating, and to contribute to that climate. Across the data sets it is quite clear that distressed spouses, who perceive and experience more negative affect, have problems in accurately identifying both the affect experienced by their partners during conflict episodes, as well as their partners' goals and intentions. This lack of rapport with their partners presumably affects the proximal context in which they are interacting (the updating process referred to by Bradbury & Fincham, 1989) and the distal context in which future interactions will take place. Subsequent judgments are also likely to be affected, exacerbating still further the tendency for error.

Intentions ascribed to partners were generally more negative than those that these same partners were prepared to acknowledge. However, distressed spouses seem to put the worst possible interpretations on their partners' motives. Again, this negativity is likely to contribute to the proximal context and affect communication through inaccurate decoding at the message level. Given that husbands tend to make message-level errors in a negative direction, and that distressed husbands make more errors than their nondistressed counterparts, it seems that the communication of these husbands is most likely to be affected by their tendency to see their spouse in a more negative light. If distressed husbands are particularly unskilled at discerning their wives' affective state, the stage is set for distressed couples to display optimal misunderstanding and polarity in their interactions.

On the other hand, distressed wives made more errors than other spouses in making judgments about intentions for specific events. Yet we do not see these misunderstandings reflected in decoding problems at the message level. Perhaps wives, even distressed ones, are more able to separate their message-level decoding from their beliefs about what their partner is trying to achieve. As Noller (1986) has suggested, the decoding of wives may reflect a cognitive activity based primarily on the nonverbal cues in the particular situation and their understanding of the social rules that govern these nonverbal behaviors.

Even when spouses were able to identify their partners' overall intentions, however, they were not necessarily able to identify their affect. Thus, identifying the partner's intentions appropriately does not ensure understanding at the affective level. So, while misunderstanding at the cognitive level may lead to misunderstanding at the affective level, understanding at the cognitive level does not automatically lead to understanding at the affective level.

How are these misunderstandings about intention likely to affect other problem communication behaviors? Negative affect reciprocity (Gottman, 1979) and related behaviors like cross-complaining, summarizing self, insults, and putdowns are likely to be motivated by beliefs about the partners' negative intentions. For example, assuming that the partner is being competitive might lead to the belief that it is necessary to win at all costs, even if the effects on the relationship are negative.

It was suggested earlier that distressed wives would be particularly likely to want to coerce their partners into changing their behavior while at the same time having low expectations of this ever actually occurring. It was also suggested that the wives' tendency to attribute selfish motivation and blame to their partners' problem-related behavior and their own personality would lead to such negative affective outcomes as anger and guilt. Taken together, these findings relating to cognitive and affective processes in conflict situations suggest that wives' interpretations of their husbands communications are especially likely to be influenced by the proximal context in which the interaction is taking place. It is, therefore, of some interest to note that distressed wives seem especially concerned with their partners' reactions, as indicated by the accuracy they exhibited at judging reactions as against intentions and their greater accuracy, relative to other spouses, at judging reactions. It is possible that distressed wives have a high personal investment in their partners' responses in terms of their own motives for changing partner behavior, their pessimism about this change, and the level of anger and guilt arising from attributions that blame their partners, and to some extent themselves, for the fact that their needs are not being met. For distressed wives, the comparison between perceived and desired partner reactions would be especially salient.

Although wives regarded their own and their partner's behavior as equally selfishly motivated, husbands saw their partner's behavior as less selfishly motivated than their own behavior. Husbands also believed that their partner's behavior was less worthy of blame and more worthy of praise than their own behavior. That is, husbands seem to be somewhat more benign in their judgments of wives.' behavior as compared to their own. Perhaps this tendency is due to stereotypes of women as being more nurturing and more positively disposed to work on relationship issues than are males.

Wives' attributions, on the other hand, generally seem to provide a more negative distal context for marital communication than is true for husbands. Moreover, as we have already noted, the proximal context in which wives communicate is likely to contain some elements of pressure or demand toward their partners. Perhaps husbands' unwillingness to engage in problem discussion with their wives is a result of their recognition of this negativity and demand emanating from their wives (Gottman & Levenson, 1988). On the other hand, this very unwillingness is likely to increase their wives' sense of frustration and helplessness and lead to more negative behavior on their wives' part in a vain attempt to get their husbands involved.

Levenson and Gottman (1983) examined the physiological arousal of husbands and wives as they discussed a marital problem. These researchers provided evidence of strong physiological linkage between distressed spouses—they are both likely to be highly negatively aroused and their arousal levels are likely to be similar. In a later study (Levenson & Gottman, 1985) they were also able to show that declines in couple satisfaction over the next 3 years could be predicted from the couples' level of arousal measured as they waited to discuss their issue during a baseline measurement period. Such findings suggest that the mere expectation of engaging in conflict is very stressful for these couples.

Gottman and Levenson (1988) discussed the tendency for distressed husbands to retain their high level of physiological arousal during the discussion, with the level only falling when the discussion is terminated. They suggested that this high level of arousal may be the reason that husbands tend to avoid discussions of marital problems and try to withdraw from them (see Christensen, 1988; Noller, 1988). But what is the source of this high level of arousal? Although the more physiologically reactive male "may not be as well equipped by nature and by nurture to adapt to life's more chronic stresses" (Gottman & Levenson, 1988, p. 199), there is a possibility that their relatively high arousal levels are, in part, due to differences in the dynamics of conflict interactions for husbands and wives. Perhaps this arousal is a response to the way distressed wives deal with problem discussions, and the expectations that these husbands build up of being blamed for the conflict and being expected to take responsibility for what changes need to be made. Levenson and Gottman (1985) themselves explained husbands' high arousal in terms of negative expectations based on their past experience of conflict situations. (Guthrie & Noller, 1988, discussed cognitions that may explain the heightened levels of arousal in conflict situations for husbands.) As Bradbury and Fincham (1989) interpreted these cognitions as aspects of the distal context in which communication about conflict takes place, we may say that husbands' distal context would predispose them to curtail the interaction as quickly as possible, or at least to restrict their level of involvement.

In viewing the pattern of cognitive and affective processes that make up the distal context of distressed and nondistressed spouses' interactions and the differential nature of their communication, previously stated notions about the downward spiral of negativity that characterizes distressed couples' interactions, and the self-maintaining positivity of nondistressed couples' interactions have been well supported in this research. The difficulty of interrupting the negative cycle in distressed communications is self-evident. Although there is still much to be understood about the relationship between cognition and affect in marital communication, the degree of support for the importance of proximal and distal contexts as influences on the effectiveness of spouses' communication points toward a need to investigate the origins of these contexts in the initial phases of marriage or even the premarital context. A detailed understanding of the factors that contribute to the development of the cognitive and affective climate in which spouses relate to each other would appear to have much to offer for both researchers and therapists.

REFERENCES

Bradbury, T. N., & Fincham, F. D. (1987). Affect and cognition in close relationships: Towards an integrative model. *Cognition and Emotion, 1,* 59–87.

Bradbury, T. N., & Fincham, F. D. (1989). Behavior and satisfaction in marriage: Prospective mediating processes. In C. Hendrick (Ed.), *Review of personality and social psychology* (Vol. 10, pp. 119–143). London: Sage.

Bradbury, T. N., & Fincham, F. D. (1990). Attributions in marriage: Review and critique. *Psychological Bulletin, 107*, 3–33.

Christensen, A. (1988). Dysfunctional interaction patterns in couples. In P. Noller & M. A. Fitzpatrick (Eds.), *Perspectives on marital interaction* (pp. 31–52). Cleveland & Philadelphia: Multilingual Matters.

Fincham, F. D. (1985). Attribution processes in distressed and nondistressed couples: 2. Responsibility for marital problems. *Journal of Abnormal Psychology, 94*, 183–190.

Fincham, F. D., Beach, S. R., & Baucom, D. H. (1987). Attribution processes in distressed and nondistressed couples: 4. Self-partner attribution differences. *Journal of Personality and Social Psychology, 52*, 739–748.

Fincham, F. D., Beach, S. R., & Nelson, G. (1987). Attribution processes in distressed and nondistressed couples: 3. Causal and responsibility attributions for spouse behavior. *Cognitive Therapy and Research, 11*, 71–86.

Fincham, F. D., Bradbury, T. N., & Grych, J. H. (in press). Conflict in close relationships: The role of intrapersonal phenomena. In S. Graham & V. Folkes (Eds.), *Attribution theory: Applications to achievement, mental health, and interpersonal conflict*. Hillsdale, NJ: Erlbaum.

Fincham, F. D., & O'Leary, K. D. (1983). Causal inferences for spouse behavior in maritally distressed and nondistressed couples. *Journal of Social and Clinical Psychology, 1*, 42–57.

Fiske, S. T., & Taylor, S. E. (1984). *Social cognition*. New York: Random House.

Gaelick, L., Bodenhausen, G. V., & Wyer, R. S. (1985). Emotional communication in close relationships. *Journal of Personality and Social Psychology, 49*, 1246–1265.

Gottman, J. M. (1979). *Marital interaction: Experimental investigations*. New York: Academic Press.

Gottman, J. M., & Levenson, R. W. (1988). The social psychophysiology of marriage. In P. Noller & M. A. Fitzpatrick (Eds.), *Perspectives on marital interaction* (pp. 182–202). Cleveland & Philadelphia: Multilingual Matters.

Gottman, J. M., Notarius, C., Markman, H., Banks, S., Yoppi, B., & Rubin, M. E. (1976). Behavior exchange theory and marital decision making. *Journal of Personality and Social Psychology, 34*, 14–23.

Gottman, J. M., & Porterfield, A. L. (1981). Communicative competence in the nonverbal behavior of married couples. *Journal of Marriage and the Family, 43*, 817–824.

Guthrie, D. M., & Noller, P. (1988). Married couples' perceptions of one another in emotional situations. In P. Noller & M. A. Fitzpatrick (Eds.), *Perspectives on marital interaction* (pp. 153–181). Cleveland & Philadelphia: Multilingual Matters.

Hall, J. A. (1978). Gender effects in decoding nonverbal cues. *Psychological Bulletin, 85*, 845–857.

Hall, J. A. (1979). Gender, gender roles, and nonverbal communication skills. In R. Rosenthal (Ed.), *Skill in nonverbal communication: Individual differences* (pp. 32–67). Cambridge, MA: Oelgeschlager, Gunn & Hain.

Harvey, J. H., Wells, G. L., & Alvarez, M. D. (1978). Attribution in the context of conflict and separation in close relationships. In J. H. Harvey, W. J. Ickes, & R. F. Kidd (Eds.), *New directions in attribution research* (Vol. 2, pp. 235–260). Hillsdale, NJ: Erlbaum.

Holtzworth-Munroe, A., & Jacobson, N. S. (1985). Causal attributions of married couples: When do they search for causes? What do they conclude when they do? *Journal of Personality and Social Psychology, 48*, 1398–1412.

Janoff-Bulman, R. (1979). Characterological versus behavioral self-blame: Inquiries into depression and rape. *Journal of Personality and Social Psychology, 37*, 1798–1809.

Jones, E. E., Kanouse, D. E., Kelley, H. H., Nisbett, R. E., Valins, S., & Weiner, B. (1972). *Attribution: Perceiving the causes of behavior*. Morristown, NJ: General Learning Press.

Leary, T. (1957). *Interpersonal diagnosis of personality*. New York: Ronald.

Levenson, R. W., & Gottman, J. M. (1983). Marital interaction: Physiological linkage and affective exchange. *Journal of Personality and Social Psychology, 45,* 587–597.

Levenson, R. W., & Gottman, J. M. (1985). Physiological and affective predictors of change in relationship satisfaction. *Journal of Personality and Social Psychology, 49,* 85–94.

Madden, M. E., & Janoff-Bulman, R. (1981). Blame, control, and marital satisfaction: Wives' attributions for conflict in marriage. *Journal of Marriage and the Family, 43,* 663–674.

Newman, H. M. (1981a). Communication within ongoing intimate relationships: An attributional perspective. *Personality and Social Psychology Bulletin, 7,* 59–70.

Newman, H. M. (1981b). Interpretation and explanation: Influences on communicative exchanges within intimate relationships. *Communication Quarterly, 29,* 123–131.

Noller, P. (1980). Misunderstandings in marital communication: A study of couples' nonverbal communication. *Journal of Personality and Social Psychology, 39,* 1135–1148.

Noller, P. (1981). Gender and marital adjustment level differences in decoding messages from spouses and strangers. *Journal of Personality and Social Psychology, 41,* 272–278.

Noller, P. (1984). *Nonverbal communication and marital interaction*. Oxford: Pergamon Press.

Noller, P. (1986). Sex differences in nonverbal communication: Advantage lost or supremacy regained? *Australian Journal of Psychology, 38,* 23–32.

Noller, P. (1988). Overview and implications. In P. Noller & M. A. Fitzpatrick (Eds.), *Perspectives on marital interaction* (pp. 323–344). Cleveland & Philadelphia: Multilingual Matters.

Noller, P., & Fitzpatrick, M. A. (Eds.) (1988). *Perspectives on marital interaction*. Cleveland & Philadelphia: Multilingual Matters.

Noller, P., & Venardos, C. (1986). Communication awareness in married couples. *Journal of Social and Personal Relationships, 3,* 31–42.

Raush, H. L., Barry, W. A., Hertel, R. K., & Swain, M. A. (1974). *Communication conflict and marriage*. San Francisco: Jossey-Bass.

Revenstorf, D. (1984). The role of attribution of marital distress in therapy. In K. Hahlweg & N. S. Jacobson (Eds.), *Marital interaction: Analysis and modification* (pp. 325–336). New York: Guilford Press.

Rubin, M. E. Y. (1977). Differences between distressed and nondistressed couples in verbal and nonverbal communication codes. *Dissertation Abstracts International, 38,* 1902.

Ruzzene, M. (in preparation). *Attributional processes in marriage: Judgments of cognition, affect and causality in conflict interactions*. Doctoral dissertation in preparation, University of Queensland.

Thompson, S. C., & Kelley, H. H. (1981). Judgments of responsibility for activities in close relationships. *Journal of Personality and Social Psychology, 41,* 469–477.

Zuckerman, M., Lipets, M., Koivumaki, J. A., & Rosenthal, R. (1975). Encoding and decoding nonverbal cues of emotion. *Journal of Personality and Social Psychology, 32,* 1068–1076.

9 Interaction in Close Relationships and Social Cognition

Garth J. O. Fletcher
Leah Kininmonth
University of Canterbury

One of the most obvious and oft-cited central defining characteristics of close relationships, especially sexual relationships, concerns the way that the participants' interactive behavior is profoundly enmeshed in organized sequences and patterns. It may strike one as surprising, therefore, that, in spite of the burgeoning research interest concerning cognition in close relationships, psychologists have given relatively little attention to the role played by cognition in interactive behavior per se. Instead, most research attention has been focused on the relations between cognitive or affective processes and general constructs such as relationship satisfaction or depression.

One major reason for this glaring lacuna is almost certainly the difficult theoretical and methodological problems involved when measuring cognitive activity that occurs during dyadic interaction. However, although the research literature is not voluminous, psychologists (including social psychologists) have developed several techniques to examine cognitive processes in the context of interactive behavior. Like all methodologies, they have their strengths and weaknesses. However, the central message of this chapter is that the interaction between on-going cognition and social behavior is not only eminently researchable, but that this area should occupy center stage if we wish to examine close relationships from a truly social-psychological perspective.

Initially, in this chapter, we provide a brief overview of the relevant work, from the behavioral literature, that has dealt with the behavioral interaction of couples. Second, we discuss the research that has directly examined cognitive or affective processes in the course of interactive behavior, including more recent research that has adopted a social-psychological perspective. Third, we describe a recent study, in some detail (Fletcher & Fitness, 1990), that develops and tests a method for accessing and recording the social cognitive flow as it occurs *in vivo,* in the context of interaction between couples in close relationships. Finally, we review the problems and prospects for future research in this area.

THE BEHAVIORAL TRADITION

Most work in the 1970s concerned with close relationship interaction was rooted in behavioral theory and adopted a clinical orientation. Hence, the central thrust of this work has been toward describing the behavioral, interactional patterns of couples in relation to marital satisfaction. Although a variety of self-report techniques have been utilized, undoubtedly the most influential body of research has involved the filming or videotaping of marital interactions, usually problem-resolution discussions, with the verbal and nonverbal behavior coded by observers using one of several standardized techniques.

Reviews of this observational research (e.g., Gottman, 1979; Schaap, 1982; Weiss & Heyman, 1990) have shown that certain findings have been well replicated. However, although these research findings were grounded in behavioral theory, researchers have often interpreted the results with explanations that have a distinctly cognitive hue. For example, the finding that unhappily married couples, compared to happy couples, appear to be particularly susceptible to the rapid escalation of negative conflict has typically been explained in terms of ability deficits, presumably cognitive in nature, related to communication or problem solving (e.g., Gottman & Porterfield, 1981). To take another example, the finding that nonverbal behavior is more strongly related to relationship satisfaction than verbal behavior is often explained by the simple proposition that nonverbal behavior is more closely tied to underlying affect than verbal behavior (e.g., Gottman, 1979).

In addition, some psychologists working from within a traditional behavioral approach have investigated the subjective perceptions and judgments of the relationship members. For example, some researchers have examined the consistency between observer-coded behavior of dyadic interaction and the private judgments of the participants (e.g., Birchler, Clopton, & Adams, 1984; Haynes, Follingstad, & Sullivan, 1979), and others have investigated subjects' intentions in the context of behavioral interaction (e.g., Gottman et al., 1976).

This interest in cognition has sometimes resulted in important shifts in theoretical perspective. For example, Fitzpatrick and her colleagues (1984) have postulated three prototypical relationship styles: traditional, independent, and separate. Traditionals adopt a relationship style that stresses traditional societal values related to marriage, independents value freedom and independence within a relationship, and separates tend to hold traditional values by maintaining psychological distance from their partners. The earlier work by Fitzpatrick concentrated on the behavioral correlates of these styles during dyadic interaction sequences (for a review, see Fitzpatrick, 1984). More recently, Fitzpatrick (1988) has relocated these three behavioral/personality styles inside the skull, and reconceptualized them as marital schemata which can influence the processing of information.

Doubtless, this shift to a more cognitive stance is simply a part of the general cognitive zeitgeist in psychology. However, the critical point here is that very little of this work has been informed by, or conceptualized in terms of, modern social cognitive theory or even a thorough-going social psychological approach, although this work does provide some provocative clues concerning the underlying cognition involved in dyadic interaction (see, e.g., Bradbury & Fincham, 1987). We refer to some of these clues in the following sections, where we will describe the research that has been directly concerned with social cognition in the context of dyadic interaction. In so doing, we also cast doubt on some of the cognitively oriented explanations, cited above, that have emanated from psychologists working from within a behavioral framework.

RESEARCH DEALING WITH
THE COGNITION/INTERACTION INTERFACE
IN CLOSE RELATIONSHIPS

In this section we deal with research that has directly examined cognitive or affective processes in the context of dyadic interactive behavior. The three main methodologies that have been used reflect the three possible ways of measuring cognition in dyadic interaction: before, during, or after the interaction sequence. The first approach relies on questionnaires dealing with cognitions, such as attributions, concerning the problem to be discussed or the interaction itself. The second approach focuses on the behavioral intentions behind specific behaviors and typically uses the "talk-table" technique (described later) developed by Gottman (Gottman et al., 1976). The third approach uses videotape-reviewing techniques to gather subjects' recollections of their thoughts during the dyadic interaction. We will briefly discuss each set of studies, point out the strengths and weaknesses of each approach, and analyze some of the issues raised by how the results from these studies should be interpreted or explained.

Measuring Cognition Prior to the Interaction

As previously indicated, the usual research procedure has been to relate distal variables, such as marital satisfaction, to dyadic behavior. A much smaller number of studies have examined expectations or attributions that are prior to, and specifically focused on, the upcoming interaction.

The importance of subjects' cognition or affect immediately prior to a dyadic sequence was signaled by Levenson and Gottman's (1985) finding that higher levels of physiological arousal, while couples were waiting for an interaction sequence, were strongly related to decreases in relationship satisfaction over a 3-year period. The implication is that subjects' attitudes, expectations, or other cognitions existing prior to an interaction episode are related in a fundamental way to broader relationship processes.

There is good evidence that attributions for specific marital problems are related to behavior during discussions of the same problems. Fincham and Bradbury (1988) found that relationship-positive attributional patterns (e.g., internal attributions for positive behavior and external attributions for negative behavior) for specific relationship problems were positively correlated with positive behavior and negatively correlated with negative behavior emitted during discussions of the same problems (statistically controlling for marital satisfaction). Moreover, these authors found evidence that reciprocation of behaviors was related to the attributions for these marital problems. For example, wives were less likely to reciprocate positive behavior if they viewed the cause of the problem as global and if they saw the husbands' contribution as being intentional and selfishly motivated (Bradbury & Fincham, 1988).

In an interesting study, Sillars, Pike, Jones, & Murphy (1984) had married subjects rate the importance of various marital problems for both themselves and their partners. The accuracy of subjects' assessments of their partners' positions was then calculated by correlating the subjects' estimates of their partners' attitudes with the self-ratings of the partners themselves, but partialing out the subjects' self-estimates of importance. This latter step removes the possibility that accuracy is an incidental by-product of the projection of self-judgments (Cronbach, 1955). These accuracy scores (referred to as understanding scores by Sillars et al., 1984) were then correlated with behavioral indices coded from audiotaped discussions of couples discussing the same marital problems. More accurate perceptions of partners' judgments of the importance of the problems were positively correlated with their partners producing more negative vocal tone and more verbally negative acts (faulting, rejection, hostile questions, etc.). We will further discuss some of the methodological issues in measuring the accuracy of social judgments at a later point. For the moment, we note that these findings imply that those who strongly communicate negative feelings about marital problems to their partners also enable their partners to obtain more veridical understandings of their own views.

In the most comprehensive study to date, Bradbury (1990) examined a variety of prior cognitions in relation to the behavior and affect of 47 married couples' discussions of major marital problems. The results varied according to gender and the kinds of behavior evinced, but generally (statistically controlling for the effect of marital satisfaction) it was found that (a) subjects who produced more relationship-positive attributions for the problem showed more effective problem-solving behavior and fewer negative emotional displays (such as anger and contempt), (b) subjects who judged the problem as more readily solvable produced more effective problem-solving behavior and fewer negative emotional displays, and (c) subjects who had more positive expectations for the discussion displayed more effective problem-solving behavior and less anger and contempt. In addition, consistent with Levenson and Gottman's (1985) findings noted above, declines in marital satisfaction over a 12-month period were associated with some of the pre-interaction expectations measured; for example, wives with higher expectations of tension and husbands with lower expectations of positive behavior reported lower levels of marital satisfaction 12 months later.

These studies suggest that expectations or other cognitions concerning a particular interaction episode may have an important influence on the behavior occurring in a dyadic sequence, over and above the variance explained by relationship satisfaction. Moreover, the findings that such pre-interaction cognitions predict changes in relationship satisfaction over long periods of time, suggest that such cognitions are strongly related to distal variables that capture the history of relationship interactions, such as general relationship accounts, or general expectations and predictions concerning the future of the relationship.

One obvious task for further research in this area is to relate pre-interaction cognition to *both* cognition and behavior that occur during the interaction. In the next two sections we deal with research that attempts to measure social cognition that occurs concurrently with dyadic behavior.

Measuring Cognition During Interaction

Attempting to measure on-line cognition during unstructured dyadic interaction is fraught with methodological difficulties. Indeed, the only technique we know of that has attempted such a feat is the talk-table procedure developed by Gottman and his colleagues (Gottman et al., 1976). The talk-table is a double-sloping table with switches for each partner to indicate who has the floor (only one person may speak at one time). Each partner rates each verbal message on a positive–negative dimension in terms of its intended impact (if the message is sent) or its perceived impact (if the message is received). These ratings are made on a set of buttons, which are hidden from the view of the partner.

The first study to use this technique (Gottman et al., 1976) found that happily married spouses judged the impact of their spouses' messages as more positive than distressed spouses, whereas Schachter and O'Leary (1985) found that happily married spouses were more positive for both their own intentions and impact ratings than distressed spouses. Kowalik and Gotlib (1987) also reported that married couples in which one partner was clinically depressed, compared to couples in which both partners were nondepressed, judged both their own intentions and the impact of their partners' messages as more negative. These findings are consistent with research that has used questionnaires or hypothetical scenarios to measure cognitions (see Fletcher & Fincham, this volume).

The talk-table technique has also been used to assess the degree of agreement between the judgments of relationship members and those of observer raters who rate the positivity of each message (Floyd, 1988; Gottman, 1979; Kowalik & Gotlib, 1987). The findings have suggested that unhappy couples are in closer agreement with outside raters than are happy couples. One popular explanation for these findings, first advanced by Gottman (1979), is that happy couples tend to have a more private message system, compared to distressed couples, that is opaque to observers. However, in our view, given that the participants and the observers are producing judgments that are demonstrably for different things (private intentions vs. observed behavior) less exotic explanations seem plausible. For example, perhaps happy partners are inclined to tone down their negative behaviors (even when they have negative intentions), whereas unhappy partners may be more likely to give full behavioral vent to their negative intentions. Now, given the well-replicated finding that negative behavior is more strongly related to relationship satisfaction than positive behavior, these two factors combined would explain the findings that the intentions of happy couples are less consistent with their externally observable behavior than the intentions of unhappy couples.

The talk-table technique exemplifies the difficulties in assessing on-line cognition during dyadic interaction. First, this technique is limited in its application because it is clearly only practical to require subjects to make fast and simple judgments so as not to unduly interfere with the communicative process. Second, even the gathering of relatively simple affective or evaluative judgments will almost certainly heavily prime the occurrence of explicit and conscious judgments of the sort that are being measured (such as the positivity of intentions). In short, the process of measuring a class of cognitions may substantially influence or alter both the cognitions themselves and also the associated behavior. Perhaps for both of these reasons (social) psychologists have usually resorted to measuring cognition in the context of dyadic interaction by gathering retrospective accounts or judgments concerning the dyadic interaction. We now turn to a review and discussion of this genre of research.

Measuring Cognition After Interaction

The research in this domain requires subjects to review videotapes of dyadic interaction. One approach is to require subjects to choose particular interactional events from the entire dyadic interaction (usually a 10- to 15-minute discussion) that are important or significant, and provide ratings or descriptions of their thoughts or feelings concerning the particular events. Judgments can thus be obtained from *both* participants concerning the same events. The second method that has been used attempts to gather a general profile of thoughts and feelings across the entire dyadic sequence. We briefly review and discuss the relatively few studies that have been carried out using these techniques, beginning with the former approach.

In one of the first studies of its type, Knudson, Sommers, and Golding (1980) had married couples role play discussions of an important marital problem, which were videotaped. Observer raters selected three short sections of the discussion that represented three stages of the conflict: pre-conflict, mid-conflict, and termination of conflict. Both partners then independently viewed the videotapes and provided open-ended accounts of their own thinking and the thinking attributed to their partners for the three stages of the conflict discussion. The couples were also classified by independent observers, on the basis of viewing the videotapes, as either avoiding problem resolution or directly engaging the issue. Analysis of the subject-provided accounts suggested that couples who attempted to resolve the issue in a direct fashion, compared to couples who avoided resolving the problem under discussion, displayed an increasingly accurate understanding of each other's thoughts and feelings across the evolution of the discussion from the beginning to the end.

The findings from the Knudson et al. (1980) study are intriguing and based on an admirably rich set of data. We have some qualms about the results, however. The method for obtaining the verbal accounts of the couples was not standardized, and the coding of these accounts was of labyrinthine proportions (with subsequent reliability problems). In addition, the results are obviously open to several interpretations. For example, it is possible that couples who directly confronted the problem increased their understanding because more useful information became available, compared to couples who adopted an avoidant style of conflict resolution. Such an interpretation is consistent with Sillar et al.'s (1984) findings, which we have previously described: namely, that partners who clearly communicate their negative feelings about marital problems to their partners also enable their partners to develop a more veridical understanding of their own attitudes to those problems. On the other hand, it is possible that the different behavioral styles were related to dispositional variables that could explain the differences in accuracy (e.g., relationship satisfaction).

Gaelick, Bodenhausen, and Wyer (1985) also required married couples to review selected videotaped segments of interaction sequences, but used a standardized procedure and a set of experimenter-supplied, structured measures. In this study, which focused on emotional communication, each partner independently reviewed tapes of a 10-minute problem discussion and selected three verbal statements that were judged to have important effects on the interaction. Subjects rated the statements they selected and those chosen by their partners on a range of dimensions including the emotional flavor of the message, the feelings that the communicator intended to convey, the recipient's perception of the communicator's feelings and intentions, and so forth.

The main advantage of this technique is that perceived similarity between the judgments across couples can be compared to the actual similarity between judgments. Gaelick et al. (1985) found that subjects believed there was substantial correspondence between their own feelings and the feelings they attributed to their partners for each behavior, regardless of whether they were the speaker or the listener. However, correlations across couples for each behavior on the relevant ratings (e.g., the correlation between the speaker's self-rated feelings and the feelings their partners, the listeners, attributed to them for the same behaviors) showed that couples were completely inaccurate for emotionally positive messages, but moderately accurate for emotionally negative behaviors. This latter result confirms the point that negative behavior appears to play a more important role in dyadic interaction than positive behavior. One methodological problem with the Gaelick et al. study is that the videotapes were reviewed in two separate sessions, 1–2 days and 1 week after the original videotapings took place. This procedure may have unwittingly forced the participants to reconstruct their memories on the basis of observing their interaction anew, rather than allowing subjects to provide veridical accounts of their own judgments experienced during the interaction (we deal with this general issue later).

A similar technique has been utilized by Ruzzene (1990), who examined married couples' discussions of long-standing problems in their relationships. This study is described in detail in Noller and Ruzzene (this volume), and so will not be covered in any depth here. The main differences between Ruzzene's study and the Gaelick et al. study (1985) are that in the Ruzzene study six behaviors (rather than three behaviors) were chosen by the subjects, and perceived or self-reported intentions were written down by subjects in a free-response format; estimates of affect were recorded using rating scales (as per the Gaelick et al. study). Their general finding was that people in happy marriages, compared to those in unhappy marriages, tended to be more accurate in some of their affective and intentional judgments of their spouses. This general finding is consistent with the conventional wisdom that happy relationships, compared to unhappy relationships, are characterized by good communication and accurate interpersonal perception.

We have talked rather glibly of the accuracy of judgments in describing some of these research findings. However, we think caution should be exercised in interpreting accuracy correlations (in the studies above represented by the correlation between A's judgment of partner B, and B's self-judgment). As pointed out earlier, significant levels of accuracy may be incidental products of people simply projecting their own attitudes or judgments onto others. Given the evidence that couples in happy relationships tend to assume that they are more similar to each other than those in unhappy relationships (Sternberg & Barnes, 1985), then the possibility exists that higher accuracy for those in happy relationships may be a function of the *actual* similarity between couples in terms of their thoughts, their attitudes, or their beliefs.

Indeed, there is evidence that accuracy correlations for at least some kinds of judgment are products of self-projection. In the study mentioned previously, Sillars et al. (1984) had spouses rate the importance of various conflict issues in marriages for themselves and also how their partners' would rate the same issues.

The accuracy correlations were all significant (between .3 and .4), but when the subjects' own ratings were statistically controlled the correlations dropped to nonsignificant levels. We would recommend that similar procedures be carried out in future studies dealing with the accuracy of interpersonal judgments.

In general, research and theory concerned with the link between interpersonal accuracy or bias and relationship satisfaction point in different directions. One general argument, backed up by several research findings, is that people who are deeply in love or have the fortune to be in very happy intimate relationships, tend toward an overoptimistic, Pollyannaish mental set that systematically distorts relationship judgments in a positive direction (e.g., Fincham, Beach, & Baucom, 1987; Hendrick & Hendrick, 1988). In contrast, those who are disillusioned or unhappy with their relationships may perceive their relationships in a realistic, even-handed, and hence, pessimistic fashion. This disquieting possibility is supported by a few scattered findings, some mentioned above, suggesting that high levels of marital satisfaction are associated with less accurate interpersonal judgments. Moreover, this account is theoretically consistent with the research literature suggesting that normal human cognition is characterized by unrealistically positive views of the self, exaggerated perceptions of personal control, and unrealistic optimism, whereas those who view the social world in a more even-handed and balanced fashion tend to suffer from mild depression (see Taylor & Brown, 1988, for a review).

However, this thesis stands in stark contrast to the findings reported by Noller and her colleagues (see Noller & Ruzzene, this volume), which suggest that happily married spouses tend to produce more accurate interpersonal judgments than unhappy spouses. One difficulty in reconciling these competing sets of findings is that the different studies use different methodologies and techniques for assessing accuracy. Combined with the methodological problems mentioned above, it is perhaps not surprising that the findings differ from study to study. Perhaps further progress would be made in this area if the assessment of accuracy was combined with more rigorous attempts to evaluate explanations in terms of the cognitive processes hypothesized to underlie differences in accuracy between those in happy and unhappy relationships.

To sum up, the few studies using the technique described above have reported some interesting results, and there are many ways in which this technique could be expanded or developed. However, a major problem with any procedure that asks direct questions concerning specific cognitions is whether the cognitive products or processes revealed may be different from the cognition that would occur in the absence of such questions. A more nightmarish possibility is that such cognitions may simply be absent in their natural environments. Dealing with this problem presents one of the sharpest challenges to the methodological ingenuity of social psychologists.

One particularly promising method, pioneered by Ickes and his colleagues (Ickes, Robertson, Tooke, & Teng, 1986), that measures the occurrence of *spon-*

taneous social cognition in the context of dyadic interaction, combines the tape-reviewing technique with a thought-listing procedure to gather a profile of thoughts and feelings over an entire dyadic sequence. In this approach, subjects independently review videotapes of a previous short conversation, stop the tape whenever they can remember having experienced specific thoughts or feelings, and write them down. Ickes et al. (1986) provided evidence for the reliability and validity of this technique using pairs of strangers who were unknowingly videotaped while supposedly waiting for an experimental session. The results suggested that the positivity of subjects' private thoughts and feelings during the interaction were related to personality factors (such as private self-consciousness), as well as the behavior occurring during the dyadic interaction. In the study we describe next, carried out by Fletcher and Fitness (1990), the Ickes et al. technique was adapted for use in the context of discussions concerning relational problems experienced by couples in long-term unmarried relationships.

The Fletcher and Fitness Study

This research had two general aims. First, we wanted to further develop and test a method for accessing and recording social cognition as it occurs *in vivo*, in the context of behavioral interaction of couples in close relationships. Second, we intended to use the technique to examine ongoing social cognition in relation to both distal variables and also the behavior evinced during the interaction. We describe this research and the results in some detail, because this research pioneers this methodology in a close relationship context, and is one of the only studies we know of that simultaneously examines the relations between distal variables (e.g., relationship satisfaction), dyadic behavior, and ongoing social cognition.

Method.   Thirty-eight couples had 10-minute discussions of important problems in their relationships, which were videotaped. Each partner then immediately reviewed a copy of the videotape in separate rooms without the experimenter (subjects had no prior knowledge of the review procedure). Subjects were instructed to stop the tape with the remote control when they could remember experiencing a specific thought or feeling, and to verbally state what that thought or feeling was. These open-ended responses were recorded on an audiotape. Subjects finally completed rating scales concerning the positivity of the verbal and nonverbal behavior during the discussion.

The verbal and nonverbal behavior of the subjects was also rated by observers who judged the positivity of the verbal content, voice tone, facial expressions, and posture. In addition, observers coded transcriptions of the thought/feeling protocols provided by subjects when reviewing the videotapes. Using the emotion coding taxonomy specifically developed by Fitness and Fletcher (in press) for application to close relationships, emotional expressions were first coded from the thought/feeling protocols. The remaining units from the thought/feeling protocols were counted as cognitions and coded as positive, negative, neutral, or unrelated to the relationship. Reliability levels for all coding were good with coefficients between .8 and .9.

Descriptive results and correlations between the distal and proximal variables. Subjects stopped the videotape on 10.23 occasions on average. Not surprisingly, given that problems were being discussed, subjects reported more negative cognitions ($M = 13.6$) than positive cognitions ($M = 6.3$), and fewer positive emotions ($M = .7$) than negative emotions ($M = 3.7$). The thought/feeling protocols were consistent with what might have been expected if we were accessing the stuff of conscious mental life: Subjects self-reports were composed of a jumbled set of ideas, shot through with attributions and feelings, and the occasional thought that was quite irrelevant to the relationship or the observed behavior. Here are a few representative examples to give a flavor of these accounts: "I was thinking how often he can only see what he thinks is right, and he can only see his way of thinking, and, it's something that annoys me sometimes, and, I was thinking, this is what he is doing at the moment"; "I felt a bit of frustration"; "I was starting to feel a bit tense here"; "I felt, well it's not fair because he's laying the blame on me. I started to get a bit angry"; "For a second I felt like giving him a big hug"; "I was thinking, when I said that, something that I really like about him, he stops me getting too confused about something that's not really worth it"; "It's really infuriating because I've heard it so many times before"; "I thought, what an excuse!"; "Very angry at this point, could have exploded"; and "Believe it or not but at that time I was thinking about John Lennon."

A major difficulty with computing correlations between variables from close relationship studies is that many such variables are nonindependent at the dyadic level. This study was no exception, with many of the variables attaining high and positive correlations between partners (e.g., .84 for verbal content and .53 for relationship satisfaction). As pointed out by Kenny and La Voie (1985), with these sorts of data, correlations calculated across individuals ignore the fact that shared variance might be an emergent product of the dyad rather than produced by intra-individual psychological processes. Conversely, correlating variables at the dyadic level, which takes into account the nonindependence of data, ignores the possibility that the resultant correlations may be a function of intra-individual processes rather than purely a product of dyadic interaction or other psychological processes that may operate at the group level.

In accordance with the analytical procedures Kenny and La Voie (1985) have recommended to deal with this problem, we calculated two types of correlation: dyad-level and individual-level correlations. At the dyad level, each dyad is treated as a single case, and the data are summed scores of each dyad pair. The

TABLE 9.1
Correlations Between Relationship Satisfaction, Depression and Selected Variables

Variables	Relationship Satisfaction		Depression	
	Dyad	Ind-Adj	Dyad	Ind-Adj
Observer Behavioral Ratings				
% positive verbal content	.02	.02	-.05	.00
positive voice tone	.43[b]	.35[a]	.41[b]	-.29
positive facial expression	.49[b]	.35[a]	-.41[b]	-.23
positive posture	.29	.04	.00	.07
Thought/Feeling Protocols				
% positive cognitions	.54[c]	.13	-.34[a]	-.01
% positive emotions	-.02	.00	-.38[a]	-.27
Individual Differences				
relationship satisfaction	–	–	-.48[b]	-.43[b]

Note. Dyad = dyad-level correlations, df = 36; Ind-Adj = adjusted individual-level correlations, df = 37.
[a] $p < .05$.
[b] $p < .01$.
[c] $p < .001$.

adjusted individual-level correlation represents the residual covariance between individuals that remains when the variance for the dyad-level correlation is partialed out of the variance for the ordinary individual-level correlations. This is done for a given pair of variables simply by subtracting the dyad-summed scores from each individual data point and correlating the subsequent adjusted scores (see Kenny & La Voie, 1985, for more details).

Table 9.1 shows the dyad-level and adjusted individual-level correlations between the distal variables of relationship satisfaction and depression and other selected variables. As expected, replicating previous research with married couples, couples who reported higher levels of relationship satisfaction and were less depressed displayed significantly more positive nonverbal behavior, whereas the relations between relationship quality and depression and the positivity of verbal content were nonsignificant. In addition, as predicted, according to the dyad-level correlations, subjects reporting more relationship satisfaction also produced more positive cognitions (and fewer negative cognitions) in the thought/feeling protocols, whereas less depressed subjects produced more positive cognitions and more positive emotions. Finally, replicating the welter of findings with married couples, we found that subjects with lower levels of relationship satisfaction also reported being more depressed.

The adjusted individual-level correlations make interesting reading. As can be seen in Table 9.1, these are nonsignificant for the correlations with variables coded from the thought/feeling protocol variables. Examining the entire pattern of correlations, only some of which are shown in Table 9.1, it was found that of the 7 dyad-level correlations that were significant with the percentage of positive cognitions and emotions, 6 of the associated adjusted individual-level correlations were nonsignificant. In contrast, of the remaining 10 significant dyad-level correlations only 2 were nonsignificant at the adjusted individual level. This pattern of findings strongly suggests that the cognitions and emotions reported by people in this interaction context were a product of dyadic interaction processes, rather than simply tied to intra-individual psychological processes. Spontaneous social cognition that occurs in the course of dyadic interaction appears to be truly a social phenomenon.

Agreement between subject and observer ratings of behavior. As noted previously, subjects rated the positivity of verbal behavior that occurred, on standard rating scales after they had reviewed the videotapes. Interestingly, the assessed incidence of positive and negative verbal behaviors was not significantly related within subjects, thus showing that subjects perceived the incidence of positive and negative behaviors across the 10-minute interaction as independent. Subject ratings of positive verbal content (summed across self and partner) were not significantly related to the percentage of positive verbal behaviors coded by the observers. However, subjects' ratings of the incidence of negative verbal content were significantly related to the percentage of positive verbal behaviors coded by observers ($r = -.53$, $p < .001$). That is, subjects' assessments of the incidence of verbal behavior were more accurate for negative behavior than for positive behavior.

This result is consistent with the research results already mentioned, concerning the importance of negative behaviors, and further supports the notion that positive and negative behaviors may be differentially encoded, stored, or retrieved. For example, if negative behaviors are typically more salient and accordingly processed in a more in-depth fashion than positive behaviors, then this could account for the typically stronger relations found to exist between negative behavior and relationship satisfaction than between positive behavior and relationship satisfaction.

The tendency to give greater weight to negative information than positive information is in fact a well-established finding in social psychology in relation to the formation of person impressions. This phenomenon has been explained in a number of ways, including the notion that negative cues are less frequent than positive cues and are hence more novel and salient (Fiske, 1980), that negative cues are less ambiguous in terms of their implications concerning traits or other categories of attribution (Wyer, 1973), or that negative cues are more discrepant than positive cues from our expectations which tend to be positive (Simpson & Ostram, 1976). All these explanations would account for the finding that subjects were more accurate in assessing the incidence of negative behavior than positive behavior in close relationships.

However, the work by Reeder and his colleagues (Reeder, 1985; Reeder & Brewer, 1979) has suggested that positive and negative behaviors also differ in relation to schemata that relate dispositions to behaviors. Such schemata often take asymmetrical forms, such that negative behaviors will be more diagnostic than positive behaviors. For example, people tend to assume that moral people are unlikely to perform immoral acts, whereas immoral people are likely to perform moral acts, along with the occasional heinous action (Coovert & Reeder, in press). To use a close relationship example, one untrustworthy action may well demolish the trust held for one's partner, whereas a trustworthy behavior will probably have little impact on a prior judgment that the partner is untrustworthy.

None of this theorizing in social psychology has been extended to close relationship settings. However, the implications of applying schema theory to relationship settings imply that negative relationship attributions (e.g., we don't communicate well) or negative partner attributions (e.g., my partner is insecure) will be relatively resistant to change compared to positive attributions, which will be more susceptible to attack. Perhaps overoptimistic, rose-tinted views of our own relationships are necessary to prevent such schemata from wreaking havoc in our personal lives. Regardless of such speculations, social cognitive theorizing provides a valuable, and hitherto unused, theoretical source for the further investigation of the processing of positive and negative behavior in close relationship contexts.

Regression analyses. One difficulty with interpreting the correlations already reported is the fact that several key measures share variance (such as relationship satisfaction and depression). In addition, an important question is whether the relations between variables at the proximal level (e.g., behaviors and cognitions) can be accounted for by the prior distal variables. For example, it is possible that the correlation between cognition and behavior is spurious because both cognition and behavior are caused by prior levels of depression and relationship satisfaction. Hierarchical multiple regression is an appropriate technique that effectively deals with these issues (Cohen & Cohen, 1983).

In this analysis (shown in Table 9.2), the distal variables were entered first as one set and the proximal variables were entered second. The regression coefficients for the Set 1 variables represent the unique variances associated with the dependent variable, controlling for the influence of all other variables in Set 1. The Set 2 regression coefficients represent the unique variances associated with the dependent variable, controlling for all the variables from Set 1 and Set 2. Because many of the variables were highly correlated across partners, all analyses used the variables calculated at the dyad level.

Controlling perceived problem seriousness as the first variable in Set 1 rules out one obvious artifactual explanation for any relation found to exist between the dependent and independent variables. For example, it is possible that the relation between nonverbal behavior and relationship satisfaction is a function of

TABLE 9.2
Standardized Regression Coefficients from Hierarchical Regressions with Dyad-Level, Observer
Rated Behavior as the Dependent Variables

Independent Variables	Dependent Variables			
	Verbal Content	Voice Tone	Facial Expression	Posture
Set one: Distal variables				
Problem seriousness	.23	-.01	.05	.21
Relationship satisfaction	.04	.31	.39[a]	.42[a]
Depression	-.11	-.26	-.24	.13
R^2 Increase in set one over problem seriousness	.02	.20[a]	.26[b]	.13
Set two: Proximal variables				
% positive cognitions	.44[a]	.63[b]	.12	.02
% positive emotions	.32	-.03	-.12	-.16
R^2 increase in set two	.27[b]	.27[b]	.02	.02
Multiple R^2	.32[a]	.51[b]	.30[a]	.17

Note. The R^2 increase for set one variables represents the increased variance over problem seriousness.
The set two coefficients were obtained with all variables entered into the equation. The set two R^2 is the
increase in variance over the set one variables. The final multiple R^2 is the total variance explained with
all variables entered (including problem seriousness).
[a] $p < .05$.
[b] $p < .01$.

the fact that those who were more satisfied with their relationships discussed less serious or less intractable problems.

The results show an intriguingly different pattern of results for the verbal material (verbal content and voice tone) and the other two nonverbal measures (facial expression and posture). The verbal material (voice content and tone) was not related to relationship satisfaction or depression, but was related to the production of positive cognitions during the interaction. In contrast, facial expression and posture were related to relationship satisfaction, but not to the occurrence of cognitions or emotions during the interaction.

As previously noted, the finding that nonverbal behavior is more strongly related to relationship satisfaction than is verbal behavior has often been explained in terms of the greater affective significance of nonverbal behavior. However, our results suggest an alternative explanation that is related to the distinction between *controlled* and *automatic* processing, a distinction outlined in detail in the chapter by Fletcher and Fincham (this volume): namely, that verbal material (content and voice tone) is typically monitored more closely and is under tighter intentional control than nonverbal behavior. On the one hand, this would allow the influence of distal variables, such as depression and relationship satisfaction, to leak through into nonverbal but not verbal behavior. On the other hand, because people are concentrating their attention on the verbal content and associated voice tone, the thoughts they can readily remember and verbalize will be tied more closely to the verbal material than nonverbal behavior such as posture.

This explanation is consistent with Vincent, Friedman, Nugent, and Masserly's (1979) study in which happily married people were asked to fake the interaction characteristics of unhappily married couples, and vice versa for couples who reported being unhappily married. According to observer coders, both couples were successful in faking verbal behavior, but neither group was able to alter its nonverbal behavior.

In contrast to the other nonverbal channels, voice tone was quite strongly related to the proportion of positive cognitions reported by subjects. This may not be surprising, given that voice tone is more obviously intertwined with verbal content than with the other nonverbal indices. That voice tone appears to perform a different function to the other nonverbal channels is consistent with Noller's (1985) findings in the marital interaction area that different behavioral channels are often inconsistent, the most common pattern being that partners smile when they say something nasty. The evidence from this research is that, when such inconsistency occurs, partners consciously attend to the verbal message rather than the smile.

It is not possible, of course, to know from our correlational results whether the social cognitive flow is causing behavior, or whether the behavior is causing the occurrence of cognitions and affect, or both. Our best guess is that the causal influence flows in both directions. One important goal of further research will be to tease out the extent to which cognitions and emotions either precede or are elicited by behavior, one possible method being to combine the technique used here with the type of sequential analyses popular in marital interaction research (Bakeman & Gottman, 1986; Bradbury & Fincham, in press).

One noteworthy feature concerning the present results is that the coded material from the thought/feeling protocols obtained substantial relations with the observer-coded measures of the actual behavior: The percentage of cognitions and emotions accounted for 27% of the variance for both verbal content and voice tone. If this does not seem overly impressive, consider that both independent and dependent variables contained measurement error (which lowers correlations), and that there was no shared method variance (unlike studies that rely solely on self-reports). Overall, our findings suggest that the videotape-reviewing technique, adapted for use in this study, is a useful tool available for the task of examining cognition as it occurs naturalistically in the context of dyadic interaction.

PROBLEMS AND PROSPECTS

The most obvious problem with the videotape-reviewing technique, invariably latched onto by manuscript reviewers, is that subjects may be constructing reports of their own cognitions and emotions on the basis of their observations of behavior during the videotape-reviewing session, rather than providing veridical descriptions of their thoughts and feelings experienced at the time of the interaction. If various methodological niceties are observed, this tendency may by reduced; namely, the instructions should stress to subjects not to construct new thoughts or ideas, and the time gap between the videotaping and reviewing of the discussions should to be kept as short as possible to maximize the veridicality of the subsequent reports (see Ericcson & Simon, 1984). In the Fletcher and Fitness (1990) study, material in the thought/feeling protocols were almost always in the past tense, usually being prefaced by such phrases as "I remember," a feature that gives the accounts some face validity. In addition, subjects frequently cited cognitions that were not related to the relationship or the observed behavior ($M =$ 4.2 units per protocol). If subjects were reconstructing their reports of cognition purely on the basis of their observations of behavior during the videotape-reviewing session, one would not expect to find so many reports of thoughts and feelings that were irrelevant to the relationship or the interactive behavior.

Clearly, it would be foolish to deny that some reconstruction of cognition or affect may not occur during observation of behavior on the videotapes. However, based on the face validity of the accounts, our own experiences of going through the procedure, and those of our subjects, we think if these methodological guidelines are followed the technique can be reasonably considered a powerful mnemonic device.

A second issue that affects the use of *any* self-report method, and one that is oddly rarely mentioned, is that such methods access cognitions that subjects are *consciously aware* of; hence, self-report methods miss out on the unconscious cognitive activity that presumably bulks large in the course of dyadic interactive behavior (see Fletcher & Fincham, this volume). Almost by definition, unconscious cognitive activity cannot be directly measured by using self-reports. This does not mean that unconscious processes are not researchable, but that methods other than those described in this chapter will need to be utilized to investigate the role of unconscious cognitive activity (see Uleman & Bargh, 1989).

One advantage of the sort of tape-reviewing technique adopted by Fletcher and Fitness (1990) is that it enables researchers to get closer to social cognition as it actually occurs in the context of dyadic interaction. However, although ecological validity issues are important, we think it unwise, for several reasons, to become obsessive about the external validity or generalizability of research findings in relation to any research procedure. First, we are impressed with the fact that the results from attribution research in the close relationship arena have shown a consistent pattern of findings produced by procedures varying from reactive questionnaires to relatively unobtrusive measures of unsolicited cognitions (see Fletcher & Fincham, this volume).

Second, this issue turns on deeper questions connected to the philosophy of psychology. If social psychology is understood simply to be in the business of documenting relations between variables and generating lawlike generalizations (a rather old-fashioned empiricist approach), then the question of whether findings from artificial experimental contexts generalize to real-life settings becomes of paramount importance. On the other hand, if our research findings are intended to help generate or test *theories* concerned with how human cognition and social behavior are generated, then it is the generalizability of the theories or the understanding gained that counts rather than the empirical findings themselves (see Mook, 1983).

The second option sketched above is likely to be embraced by those social psychologists who regard their central aim as building theories that link our cognitive machinery to the generation of social behavior. Most of the studies reviewed above, like much research in close relationships we hasten to add, have an atheoretical feel to them. There is nothing wrong, in our view, with exploratory research aimed at theory generation. Nevertheless, perhaps it is time for social psychologists working in the close relationship field to generate and test social-psychological theories that explain in greater detail how distal variables, such as relationship satisfaction or relationship accounts, are related to affect and cognition. We have attempted to provide a few theoretical suggestions in this chapter concerning the processing of information within close relationship interaction settings, but have gladly left the bulk of this task to those writing chapters in the first section of this book.

Finally, some comments are called for concerning the methodological and statistical problems facing researchers working in this area. The main difficulty with analyzing data from couples is that the data at the individual level are often not independent. Kenny (1988) has pointed out that the first step in data analysis should be to test whether the data from couples are independent. When the sample is composed of heterosexual couples, this can simply be done by calculating the familiar product moment correlation across couples. However, where dyads are used that cannot be separated into two groups, such as same-sex friends, then a correlation known as the *intraclass* correlation can be calculated using standard computer packages (see Kenny, 1988, for details). Where the data from the dyads are independent, the sample can be treated as individual subjects. However, where the data are nonindependent, as is often the case, this creates problems, as we noted previously when reporting the results from the Fletcher and Fitness (1990) study. One solution to this problem, and the one used in the Fletcher and Fitness (1990) study, is to calculate correlations at both the dyad level and at the individual level but controlling for the effect of the group.

There has been considerable development in data-analytic techniques concerned with dyadic data over the past decade, with a rash of articles appearing over the past few years. This development is a double-edged sword for the practicing researcher. First, many of the statistical techniques are not available in standard computer packages. Second, the researcher is faced with the need to master more statistical jargon, understand the problems and restrictions involved, and so on. Perhaps we need to remind ourselves occasionally that fancy statistics are no substitute for good theorizing, powerful explanations, or sound methodologies.

The practicing researcher also faces practical problems in carrying out the kind of research we have reviewed in this chapter. The research is often expensive and time consuming and sample sizes are frequently on the low side, which considerably reduces the power of the research designs, especially when a number of independent variables are being measured. However, for those (social) psychologists wishing to take the plunge, there are a number of promising research methodologies available that we have described in this chapter. Of course, such methods have their weaknesses, as well as their strengths, but this is not peculiar to this area of work, being true of all research methods in any arena in psychology.

To conclude, as will be obvious by now, we are favorably disposed toward the cognitive approach adopted in modern-day social psychology. However, *social* psychologists must study social cognition in the context of *real* social behavior at some point, if social psychology is to be anything other than the study of the socially isolated mind.

REFERENCES

Bakeman, R., & Gottman, J. M. (1986). *Observing interaction.* New York: Cambridge University Press.

Birchler, G. R., Clopton, P. L., & Adams, N. L. (1984). Marital conflict resolution: Factors influencing concordance between partners and trained coders. *American Journal of Family Therapy, 12,* 15–28.

Bradbury, T. N. (1990). *Cognition, emotion, and interaction in distressed and nondistressed couples: Towards an integrative model.* Unpublished manuscript, University of California, Los Angeles.

Bradbury, T. N., & Fincham, F. D. (1987). Affect and cognition in close relationships: Towards an integrative model. *Cognition and Emotion, 1,* 59–87.

Bradbury, T. N., & Fincham, F. D. (1988). *The impact of attributions in marriage: Attributions and behavior exchange in marital interaction.* Paper presented at the 22nd Annual Convention of the Association for the Advancement of Behavior Therapy, New York.

Bradbury, T. N., & Fincham, F. D. (in press). The analysis of sequence in social interaction. In D. G. Gilbert & J. J. Conley (Eds.), *Personality, social skills, and psychopathology: An individual differences approach.* New York: Plenum.

Cohen, J., & Cohen, J. (1983). *Applied multiple regression/correlation analysis for the behavioral sciences* (2nd ed.). Hillsdale, NJ: Erlbaum.

Coovert, M. D., & Reeder, G. D. (in press). Negativity effects in impression formation: The role of unit formation and schematic expectations. *Journal of Experimental Social Psychology.*

Cronbach, L. J. (1955). Processes affecting scores on "understanding of others" and "assumed similarity." *Psychological Bulletin, 52,* 177–193.

Ericcson, K. A., & Simon, H. A. (1984). *Protocol analysis: Verbal reports as data.* Cambridge, MA: MIT Press.

Fincham, F., Beach, S. R., & Baucom, D. H. (1987). Attribution processes in distressed and nondistressed couples: 4. Self-partner attribution differences. *Journal of Personality and Social Psychology, 52,* 739–748.

Fincham, F. D., & Bradbury, T. N. (1988). The impact of attributions in marriage: Empirical and conceptual foundations. *British Journal of Clinical Psychology, 27,* 77–90.

Fiske, S. T. (1980). Attention and weight in person perception: The impact of negative and extreme behavior. *Journal of Personality and Social Psychology, 38,* 889–906.

Fitness, J., & Fletcher, G. J. O. (in press). Emotion labelling in close relationships. *New Zealand Journal of Psychology.*

Fitzpatrick, M. A. (1984). A typological approach to marital interaction: Recent theory and research. In L. Berkowitz (Ed.), *Advances in experimental social psychology* (Vol. 18, pp. 1–47). Orlando, FL: Academic Press.

Fitzpatrick, M. A. (1988). Approaches to marital interaction. In P. Noller & M. A. Fitzpatrick (Eds.), *Perspectives on marital interaction.* Clevedon, Eng.: Multilingual Matters.

Fletcher, G. J. O., & Fitness, J. (1990). Occurrent social cognition in close relationship interaction: The role of proximal and distal variables. *Journal of Personality and Social Psychology, 59,* 464–474.

Floyd, F. J. (1988). Couples' cognitive/affective reactions to communication behaviors. *Journal of Marriage and the Family, 50,* 523–532.

Gaelick, L., Bodenhausen, G. V., & Wyer, R. S. (1985). Emotional communication in close relationships. *Journal of Personality and Social Psychology, 49,* 1246–1265.

Gottman, J. M. (1979). *Marital interaction: Experimental investigations.* New York: Academic Press.

Gottman, J., Notarius, C., Markman, H., Bank, S., Yoppi, B., & Rubin, M. E. (1976). Behavior exchange theory and marital decision making. *Journal of Personality and Social Psychology, 34,* 14–23.

Gottman, J. M., & Porterfield, A. L. (1981). Communicative competence in the nonverbal behavior of married couples. *Journal of Marriage and the Family, 43,* 817–824.

Haynes, S. N., Follingstad, D. R., & Sullivan, J. C. (1979). Assessment of marital satisfaction and interaction. *Journal of Consulting and Clinical Psychology, 34,* 14–23.

Hendrick, C., & Hendrick, S. S. (1988). Lovers wear rose colored glasses. *Journal of Social and Personal Relationships, 5,* 161–184.

Ickes, W., Robertson, E., Tooke, W., & Teng, G. (1986). Naturalistic social cognition: Methodology, assessment, and validation. *Journal of Personality and Social Psychology, 51,* 66–82.

Kenny, D. A. (1988). The analysis of data from two-person relationships. In S. Duck (Ed.), *Handbook of personal relationships* (pp. 57–78). London: Wiley.

Kenny, D. A., & La Voie, L. (1985). Separating individual and group effects. *Journal of Personality and Social Psychology, 48,* 339–348.

Knudson, R. M., Sommers, A. A., & Golding, S. L. (1980). Interpersonal perception and mode of resolution in marital conflict. *Journal of Personality and Social Psychology, 38,* 751–763.

Kowalik, D. L., & Gotlib, I. H. (1987). Depression and marital interaction: Concordance between intent and perception and communication. *Journal of Abnormal Psychology, 96,* 127–134.

Levenson, R. W., & Gottman, J. M. (1985). Physiological and affective predictors of change in relationship satisfaction. *Journal of Personality and Social Psychology, 49,* 85–94.

Mook, D. G. (1983). In defense of external invalidity. *American Psychologist, 38,* 379–387.

Noller, P. (1985). Negative communication in marriage. *Journal of Social and Personal Relationships, 2,* 289–301.

Reeder, G. D. (1985). Implicit relations between dispositions and behaviors: Effects on dispositional attribution. In J. H. Harvey & G. Weary (Eds.), *Attribution: Basic issues and applications* (pp. 87–116). New York: Academic Press.

Reeder, G. D., & Brewer, M. B. (1979). A schematic model of dispositional attribution in interpersonal perception. *Psychological Review, 86,* 61–79.

Ruzzene, M. (1990). *Attributional processes in marriage: Judgments of cognition, affect, and causality in conflict interactions.* Unpublished manuscript, University of Queensland, Australia.

Schachter, J., & O'Leary, K. D. (1985). Affective intent and impact in marital communication. *American Journal of Family Therapy, 13,* 17–22.

Schaap, C. (1982). *Communication and adjustment in marriage.* The Netherlands: Swets & Zeitlanger, B. V.

Sillars, A. L., Pike, G. R., Jones, T. S., & Murphy, M. A. (1984). Communication and understanding in marriage. *Human Communication Research, 10,* 317–350.

Simpson, D. D., & Ostram, T. M. (1976). Contrast effects in impression formation. *Journal of Personality and Social Psychology, 34,* 625–629.

Sternberg, R. J., & Barnes, M. L. (1985). Real and ideal others in romantic relationships: Is four a crowd? *Journal of Personality and Social Psychology, 49,* 1586–1608.

Taylor, S. E., & Brown, J. D. (1988). Illusion and well-being: A social psychological perspective on mental health. *Psychological Bulletin, 103,* 193–210.

Uleman, J. S., & Bargh, J. A. (Eds.). (1989). *Unintended thought.* New York: Guilford Press.

Vincent, J. P., Friedman, L. C., Nugent, J., & Masserly, L. (1979). Demand characteristics in observations of marital interaction. *Journal of Consulting and Clinical Psychology, 47,* 557–556.

Weiss, R., & Heyman, R. (1990). Observation of marital interaction. In F. D. Fincham & T. N. Bradbury (Eds.), *The psychology of marriage* (pp. 87–117). New York: Guilford Press.

Wyer, R. S. (1973). Category ratings as "subjective expected values": Implications for attitude formation and change. *Psychological Review, 80,* 96–112.

10

How Can We Know What Love Is? An Epistemological Analysis

Robert J. Sternberg
Anne E. Beall
Yale University

> "My God, don't be silly. That's not love, and you know it," Mel said. "I don't know what you'd call it, but I sure know you wouldn't call it love."
>
> "Say what you want to, but I know it was," Terry said. "It may sound crazy to you but it's true just the same. People are different, Mel. Sure, sometimes he may have acted crazy. Ok. But he loved me. In his own way maybe, but he loved me. There was love there, Mel. Don't say there wasn't." (Carver, 1985, p. 175)

Many laypeople believe that they know what love is. Our experience is that, if they know at all, it is at the level that Supreme Court Justice Potter Stewart knew what pornography was when he commented, "I know it when I see it and this isn't it." Many people believe they know what love is, but they would have trouble saying what it is.

Psychologists interested in the study of love, in contrast, wish to know what love is at a level that lends itself to verbal, and sometimes quantitative, description. Numerous theories have been proposed to account for the nature of love (see, e.g., Sternberg, 1987; Sternberg & Barnes, 1988, for reviews of recent theories of love). In this chapter, our concern is not with what love is, but with how we would know what love is. In other words, our goal is an epistemological analysis of the concept of love. We consider alternative theoretical approaches to understanding the nature of love, and discuss some of the advantages and disadvantages to each. The approaches we shall consider are (a) the implicit-theories approach, (b) the clinical approach, (c) the learning approach, (d) the social-psychological approach, (e) the developmental approach, (f) the cognitive approach, (g) the sociobiological approach, and (h) the psychometric approach.

We think it worth saying at the outset that our goal is not to demonstrate that one of these approaches is right, and that the others are wrong, or to demonstrate that one approach is clearly superior to the others. We do not believe that there is any one right approach to the study of love, or anything else for that matter. Rather, a given theoretical or methodological approach has both advantages and disadvantages. Ideally, researchers studying love will use converging operations (Garner, Hake, & Eriksen, 1956) in order to study love in a way that compensates for the inadequacies of any single methodology, and will use a theory-knitting approach (Kalmar & Sternberg, 1988) in order to formulate a theory of love that circumvents the shortcomings of any single type of theorizing. If scholars wish fruitfully to combine methodological or theoretical approaches in order to capitalize on the strengths and to compensate for the weaknesses of each of these approaches, then they need to know what their strengths and weaknesses are. Our goal in this chapter is to review these.

THE IMPLICIT-THEORIES APPROACH

In the implicit-theories approach, one seeks to understand the nature of love by investigating what people believe love to be. Thus, this approach involves the investigation of folk theories of love.

There are a number of subapproaches to the implicit-theories approach, but we consider just two. One is an approach that involves examining the natural history of love (Hunt, 1959; Singer, 1984). In this subapproach, one analyzes historical records, as well as the literature, art, and even music of the time, in order to understand what people's conceptions of love were throughout the ages. The second subapproach is a more strictly psychological one, in which one does empirical investigations, using quantitative techniques, of current folk conceptions of the nature of love. We consider each of these subapproaches in turn.

The Historical Subapproach

The historical subapproach shows how dominant conceptions of love during a particular period of history reflect the sociocultural mores of the time. One can see how dominant ideas during a time period have influenced conceptions of love when one reviews the various time periods.

For example, the dominant conception of love during the Enlightenment was that love is a primarily rational experience that can be controlled, at least to some extent, by those who experience it. The Enlightenment was a period during the 18th century when people believed that humans were completely rational beings. Love was not exempt from this idea. For example, in *The History of Tom Jones, a Foundling* (Fielding, 1952), an Enlightenment novel, a magistrate reproaches one of the characters, Jenny, for losing her chastity. The magistrate informs her that she should not use love as an excuse for this behavior because "love is a rational passion" (p. 9). At least some individuals who lived during this time apparently conducted their love affairs according to these beliefs. When Madame D'Esparbes told her lover that she wanted to end their affair, she calmly stated: "Believe me, little cousin, being romantic does not succeed, but makes one ridiculous and nothing more. . . . Be convinced that the loss of love can always be repaired by another" (Hunt, 1959, pp. 256–257).

In the 18th and 19th centuries, during the age of Romanticism, people believed that love was difficult to control because it was not a completely rational experience. Boswell (1952) claimed that love is "not a subject of reasoning, but of feeling and therefore there are no common principles upon which one can persuade another concerning it" (p. 64). Some typical comments that we have been able to find of people during this era were like those of Henry Poor, who described love as a "sentiment which excites such a tumult in our hearts and such overpowering sensations through our whole frames" (Rothman, 1984, p. 104), and the statement of Elizabeth Prentiss that "if I ever fall in love I dare say I shall do it so madly and absorbingly as to become in a measure and for a season forgetful of everything and everybody else" (see Rothman, 1984, p. 104).

History shows how conceptions of love often derive, at least in part, from sex-role stereotypes of a given era. For example, during the Middle Ages, it was believed that true love should be largely reserved for God. Indeed, it is not clear why men would wish to love women, given women's perceived evil nature. Drawing upon the story of Adam and Eve in the Bible, church leaders attacked women as the reason for the downfall of men. As one church leader said of women: "You are the gate of hell, the unsealer of that forbidden tree, the first deserter of the divine law" (Hunt, 1959, p. 109). Sometimes, church leaders went to lengths that by almost any standard would be considered extreme, at least today. One bishop proposed that women do not have souls, another that women had to become sexless so that they could appear before God in heaven (Hunt, 1959). Clearly, these conceptions of women influenced Medieval conceptions of love in a way that rendered women as unworthy of men's love.

Of course, in other periods of time, exactly the opposite was true. During the Victorian era, it was believed that women are innately good and pure, and hence the love of a man for a woman was believed to be an ennobling experience for the man. Men were viewed as morally lost, and in need of women's succor (Rothman, 1984). As said by William Lloyd Garrison, "men would be much better if they acted always as if [women] were looking at them" (Rothman, 1984, p. 92). According to Rothman, a man of the Victorian era told his fiancee: "the true female character was perfectly adapted and designed by its influence often exerted to soften and beautify the wild rough and turbulent spirit of man" (p. 92).

Just as some people believe that evolution has stopped with the assent of humankind, others believe that the sociocultural processes that have affected cultural conceptions of love from the past no longer apply. Nothing could be further from the case. For example, during the 20th century, as well as in many earlier times, it was commonly believed that men are essentially active, and women essentially passive (Broverman, Vogel, Broverman, Clarkson, & Rosen-krantz, 1972). Men are characterized as individuals who initiate events in their lives, whereas women are often characterized as individuals who wait for events to happen to them. Romantic relationships have reflected this distinction. Men in today's literature are often portrayed as the individuals who actively initiate relationships with women to whom they are attracted.

For example, in the novel *Love in the Time of Cholera* (Garcia-Marquez, 1988/1985), the female protagonist, Fermina, is depicted in two different hetero-sexual love relationships in her lifetime. In both situations, the men initiated the romantic relationship, with her role being essentially passive. She receives letters from the men, is visited by the men, and is proposed to by the men. She either accepts or rejects these offers, but does not initiate any offers herself. In *A Farewell to Arms* (Hemingway, 1957), the male protagonist, Henri, also has the active role in his relationship with Kathryn. He visits her at her home and initiates all of their sexual activity. When she becomes angry about the infrequen-cy of his visits, she simply waits for him to visit again. She does not attempt to visit him or to send a message to him about her feelings.

One could cite many other examples of how the sociocultural context affects conceptions of love, but we hope that our point is made. It is difficult, and arguably impossible, to study love without understanding it in a sociocultural context. One can propose psychological theories of love ad infinitum, but one cannot divorce oneself from one's sociocultural context. These theories will reflect the time and place in which they are proposed, and in order to show their universality, one needs to show their validity across time and space.

Empirical Psychological Research

Sternberg and Barnes (see Sternberg, 1988) asked adults from the New Haven area (excluding college students) what kinds of behavior they believed charac-terized romantic love. After breaking down a long list of items into 140 distinct behaviors, they asked 114 New Haven area adults—again, excluding students—to rate each behavior on a scale of one to nine with respect to the importance of each to the concept of romantic love. Using factor analysis, they found four basic dimensions underlying people's notions.

The first dimension looked pretty much like an intimacy factor. Some of the core behaviors were (a) feeling loved by your partner, (b) feeling certain that your partner would always be there for you when you needed him or her, (c) believing in the excellence of the other and supporting each other when needed, (d) making each other happy, and (e) having a partner who is considerate of and sensitive to your needs.

The behaviors in this factor emphasize communication, sharing, acceptance, and support. These attributes characterize intimacy, in general. But people dis-tinguish among different aspects of intimacy because the second factor, although similar to the first, appears to be a special aspect of intimacy: namely, having a partner who is good for you in particular. Typical behaviors at the core of this factor are (a) having a partner who understands your feelings and personality, (b) having a partner who stimulates you intellectually, (c) having a partner who brings out your strengths and helps your weaknesses, (d) having a partner who is observant of your needs, and (e) liking the way you feel around your partner. Another dimension that is specific to intimacy is having a partner in a truly special relationship. The core behaviors are (a) thinking your partner is special, (b) respecting your partner, (c) having a partner who makes you feel special, (d) being needed by your partner, and (e) having a partner who is gentle and kind.

A further dimension was that of passion, and particularly sexual passion, including behaviors such as (a) having a partner who is good sexually, (b) being sexually attracted to your partner, (c) wanting to be with your partner more than anyone else, (d) having a partner who stimulates you sexually, and (e) being close to your partner sexually.

A prototype study of love and commitment was performed by Fehr (1988). Fehr was interested in the relation between love and commitment, and in a series of studies had subjects perform tasks that addressed this question. She concluded from the several studies that the layperson's view of how love and commitment are related is one of overlapping constructs that are partially independent, along the lines suggested by Kelley (1983).

Evaluation of the Implicit-Theories Approach

It would be easy for one to summarily dismiss the implicit-theories approach with the argument that this approach tells us not what love is but what people think it is. However, we believe that there are at least three good reasons why this approach should not be dismissed out of hand.

First, the boundary between the construct and what people believe the construct to be is not as clearly drawn in the study of love as it is in the study of many other constructs. For example, it would be relatively straightforward to distinguish between people's conceptions of memory and memory itself. People can believe whatever they want about memory; the construct will not change as a function of their beliefs. But in the case of love, the way people will relate to each other in loving relationships may largely be determined by what those people believe love to be. Romantic relationships may differ as a function of people's beliefs in the nature of love, and indeed, loving relationships have differed radically in kind as a function of time and place, as beliefs about the nature of love differ spatiotemporally. Moreover, countless relationships have failed because the couple have had different conceptions of what it means to love each other, and have been unable to compromise about such differences. One could reasonably argue that there is not and can never be a content-based theory of love, because what love is will be determined in large part by the contextual milieu in which people live. Thus, from this point of view, to understand love, we need to understand people's folk theories of the construct.

Second, implicit theories clearly help shape explicit theories. Psychologists' (or others') explicit theories of love do not arise in a vacuum. Although some would like to believe that science can be understood without context and that scientific theories originate from some kind of spontaneous generation, this view is not realistic. Scientists themselves live in a sociocultural milieu, and their views of love will inevitably be shaped by the context in which they live. Thus, if only to understand the origin of explicit theories of love, we need to understand implicit theories of love. For example, Maslow's (1962) theory of love, with his emphasis on self-actualization in what he calls being-love (B-love), sounds strangely reminiscent of the 1960s. During the 1960s, many people seemed to be busily running around trying to self-actualize in a variety of ways; today, this goal seems somewhat less evident and more elusive, at least on the surface. Times change, and so do people's conceptions of what life and love are about.

Third, we need to take implicit theories seriously, if only because it is through such theories that the large majority of people who have thought about love have sought to understand it. The philosophers, literary writers, and historians, among others, who have speculated on the nature of love have basically used an implicit-theories approach, as have some psychologists. To understand their theorizing, we need to understand the nature of implicit theories, as well as their strengths and limitations. Learning about these implicit theories through the ages helps us understand not only how people have conceived of love at various times, but how limited our own present theories may be. Thus, implicit theories across time and place can be useful in pointing out the limitations in scope, and sometimes in depth, of present theories of love.

For all its strengths, however, the implicit-theories approach has limitations. Consider two of them. First, implicit theories may reflect an idealistic view of love that does not correspond to any real experience of love. Ideas of love may represent what a time period or society desires in terms of human relationships and feelings, but not how people actually live and love. For example, during the Middle Ages, love was viewed as an emotion that involved ritualized courting behavior among knights and ladies. This type of love was called courtly love (Hunt, 1959). It was inaccessible to the majority of people who lived during this time period. Because only the nobility had the resources and the time to practice courtly love, one cannot conclude that the other members of the society did not experience love.

Second, it is possible that implicit theories of love from different time periods simply reflect how societies label different experiences. What one society may label *love,* another may label *infatuation.* Thus, love may have existed in every society but may have been called by different names. For example, during the Middle Ages, people believed that one could not love one's spouse (Hunt, 1959). Instead, people labeled feelings that occurred between marital partners as feelings of attachment or affection. Thus, feelings of love may change only in name through different time periods.

We have devoted a considerable amount of space to implicit theories because they represent one of two major kinds of theorizing. In the remainder of the chapter, we discuss the various kinds of explicit theories that have been proposed to account for love. We have grouped these theories into a taxonomy that we thought would be useful. However, this taxonomy is not the only one that could be used to group these theories. There are undoubtedly many ways to view this work.

CLINICAL THEORIES

Theories can be clinical by virtue of their derivation from the clinical experience of the theorists. For example, Freud's theory was derived from his treatment of many patients exhibiting a variety of clinical syndromes.

Freud (1955/1922) viewed love in terms of sublimated sexuality, whereas Reik (1944) viewed love as arising out of dissatisfaction with oneself and one's lot in life. Related to this latter view is that of Klein and Riviere (1953), according to whom love arises from one's dependency on others for the satisfaction of one's needs. Maslow's (1954) D-love, or deficiency love, is also of this kind, arising from one's needs for security and belongingness. Indeed, the term *deficiency* provides an apt characterization of most of these theories, in that they view love as arising from some lack or a feeling of something missing within the person. Maslow's B-love, or being love, arises out of a person's higher level emotional needs, especially the desire for self-actualization and actualization of another. Similarly, Fromm (1956) viewed love as arising from care, responsibility, respect, and knowledge of another. More recently, Peck (1978) has suggested that love is largely a decision and the commitment to that decision. Peele and his colleagues (Peele, 1988; Peele & Brodsky, 1976) have suggested that love is fundamentally an addiction.

The greatest strength of an approach is often simultaneously its greatest weakness. This dual status would seem to apply to clinical views. On the one hand, their derivation from the clinical experience of their originators gives them a certain immediacy, face validity, and even richness, that certain other kinds of theories may not have. On the other hand, these theories have not withstood rigorous empirical testing, and hence have proliferated without viable attempts to confirm or disconfirm them empirically. This is not to say that these theories could not, in principle, be subject to empirical tests, only that they have not as yet been empirically tested.

Clinical theories may be particularly influenced by context, including ones that go beyond the sociocultural milieu in which typical people live. Clinicians generally do not treat a random sample of patients drawn from a typical cross-section of the population. Rather, they typically treat people who have identified, or who seek to identify, problems in their behavior. Thus, emphases on love as arising out of dissatisfaction, or as representing an addiction, may better characterize certain clinical populations than the population at large. Moreover, even psychological ailments have no privileged universal status across time and space. Hysteria, a common ailment in Freud's day, is extremely uncommon at the present time.

Several clinical theories of love are special cases of the more general theories. These theories generally address other domains before they address love. Again, this is both a strength and a weakness of these theories. The strength is that these theories of love are part of a larger, comprehensive theoretical framework, unlike theories of love developed in isolation. The downside is that one wonders whether the clinical view of love is not overly colored by the theorist's world views rather than with love as a phenomenon. For example, sexuality and sublimation were both key concepts in Freud's theory, and so it makes sense in terms of his theory that love would be viewed in terms of sublimated sexuality. But it may make less sense when one attempts to view love in all its richness. Similarly, Maslow's (1954) theory of love makes sense in terms of his theory of motivation, which places needs on a hierarchy and hence would view D-love as being based on needs lower in the motivational hierarchy than B-love. Then again, one wonders whether the concept of love is being molded to fit a theoretical framework in a way that does not do full justice to the construct.

LEARNING THEORIES

Learning theories have been applied to understanding attraction, a concept related but not identical to love. According to Lott and Lott (1961, 1974), for example, attraction for a person results when one experiences reward in the presence of that person (thereby enabling him or her to become the secondary reinforcer). Both classical and instrumental conditioning can play a role in the development of attraction. An interesting implication of this view is that someone can become attracted to someone else not because of who he or she is, but because one just happens to experience positive reinforcement in the presence of the person—reinforcement that may have nothing to do with the person to whom one is attracted. Similarly, one can come to view people around whom one is punished as unattractive.

Another view based on Byrne's (1971) learning theory depends on the notion that attitudinal similarity is a potent source of attraction. According to Byrne, attitudinal similarity leads to attraction because it provides an individual with independent evidence for the correctness and value of his or her opinions. Byrne has found that the proportion, rather than the number, of attitudes that are shared with an individual leads to attraction. The amount of attraction is a positive linear function of the sum of the weighted positive reinforcements associated with the other, divided by the total number of weighted positive and negative reinforcements associated with the other. Clore and Byrne (1974) have proposed an associational-affect model that extends some of these ideas.

The learning-theory approach seems to apply more to attraction, which most people believe to be an important component of love but not its sole component, than it does to love itself. Nevertheless, we sometimes refer to people as "learning to love each other," and indeed, in societies in which matchmaking is routine, couples may have little choice.

Reinforcement theory is useful for explaining certain phenomena that occur in the context of love and close relationships. One of these phenomena, mentioned earlier, is the value of engaging in rewarding activities with another person: Positive feelings, and perhaps love, can result at least in part from secondary reinforcement through engagement in pleasurable activities. Another phenomenon well explained by reinforcement theory is the seemingly senseless clinging to feelings of love that sometimes occurs in the presence of intermittent reinforcement. When one person is intermittently reinforced by another—with rewards and punishments administered in varying alternating sequences—feelings of love may persist in the absence of an opportunity for a viable relationship. If nothing else, it is sometimes useful for a person to understand that his or her feelings are being maintained by another, inadvertently or otherwise, through intermittent reinforcement.

We believe that the greatest weakness of learning-theory approaches to love is simply their narrowness: There are a lot of phenomena for which they cannot account. One of those phenomena, about which much has been written in song, is that of a person's love for people who are not good for or to them. People sometimes find themselves in love with individuals who are punishing, and not in love with those who are rewarding. The latter may merely be liked. Of course, it is possible to stretch reinforcement theory on an ad hoc basis to state that, in these cases, the punishment is somehow reinforcing, and the kindly behavior either nonreinforcing or even punishing. But once we stretch reinforcement theory in this way, it seems that there is little for which it could not account in an ad hoc, and hence uninteresting, way.

Finally, reinforcement theories say nothing about what goes on in the head, or, metaphorically, in the heart, when one person loves another. This kind of theorizing was popular during the early 20th century when psychologists were content to view the organism as a black box, with psychology as merely the study of the behavior that results from stimuli that impinge upon the organism from the environment. Relatively few people today are happy to view the organism as nothing more than a black box, and hence want something more of a cognitive theory than reinforcement theory is able to provide.

SOCIAL PSYCHOLOGICAL THEORIES

Four fairly well known theories of love are those of Lee (1977), Davis (1985), Hatfield (1988), and Sternberg (1986). These theories address both the components and the types of love.

Lee (1977) used the metaphor of colors as the basis for his proposal for a typology of kinds of love. He derived his typology from a number of sources, including literature and a card-sorting task in which individuals were asked to sort about 1,500 cards containing brief descriptions of love-related events, ideas, or emotions. The results of the sorting were then subjected to factor analysis, which generally supported the theory. More recently, Hendrick and Hendrick (1986) have done a fairly exhaustive factor-analytic study testing the theory, with generally positive results.

Lee's (1977) typology distinguished among six major kinds of love: (a) eros, characterized by the search for a beloved whose physical presentation of self embodies an image already held in the mind of the lover; (b) ludus, which is Ovid's term for playful or gamelike love; (c) storge, based on slowly developing affection and companionship; (d) mania, characterized by obsession, jealousy, and great emotional intensity; (e) agape, or altruistic love, in which the lover views it as his or her duty to love without expectation of reciprocation; and (f) pragma, a practical style involving conscious consideration of the demographic and other objective characteristics of the loved one.

Davis (1985) proposed that loving is an extension of liking. According to Davis, liking consists of eight main elements: enjoyment, mutual assistance, respect, spontaneity, acceptance, trust, understanding, and confidence. Love is found when two more feelings are added to this space: passion, which involves fascination with the other, sexual desire for the other, and exclusiveness of one's relationship with the other; and caring, which involves championing or being a primary advocate for the other and giving the utmost of oneself to the other.

Hatfield (1988) distinguished between passionate and companionate love. She defined passionate love as "a state of intense longing for union with another. Reciprocated love (union with the other) is associated with fulfillment and ecstasy. Unrequited love (separation) [is associated] with emptiness, anxiety, or despair. [Unrequited love causes] a state of profound physiological arousal" (p. 191). She defined companionate love as "the affection we feel for those with whom our lives are deeply entwined" (p. 191) (see also Hatfield & Walster, 1978). Hatfield has developed a passionate love scale that appears effectively to measure the degree of passion an individual feels in a given close relationship.

Sternberg (1986, 1988) has proposed a triangular theory of love, according to which love can be viewed in terms of three components: intimacy, passion, and decision/commitment. These three components are viewed as forming the vertices of a triangle. In the context of this theory, the intimacy component refers to

266

those feelings in a relationship that promote closeness, bondedness, and connectedness. The passion component of love consists of those motivational and other sources of arousal that lead to the experience of passion. The decision/ commitment component of love consists of two aspects, the decision that one loves a certain other and the commitment to maintain that love over time. These three components, in various combinations, give rise to seven different kinds of love. For example, infatuated love is the presence of passion and the absence of intimacy and commitment. Romantic love is the presence of intimacy and passion and the absence of commitment. Companionate love is the presence of intimacy and commitment and the absence of passion. Consummate love involves all three components.

The social-psychological theories have several strengths and weaknesses. These theories deal directly with love and bring a neat theoretical framework to the study of love. However, these theories exist in isolation, and do not relate love to broader social-psychological phenomena, except on an ad hoc basis. In some cases, these independently existing theories seem to combine within their purview both kinds of love and other kinds of things that are labeled as love. For example, is pragma, in Lee's (1977) theory, really a style of love, or a decision to go after a mate who scores the most points on demographic characteristics, such as finances, social status, upward mobility, or whatever? Is empty love in Sternberg's (1986) theory—the presence of commitment without either intimacy or passion—really love, or merely nothing more than commitment, which some see as separable from love (Fehr, 1988; Kelley, 1983)?

The styles in Lee's (1977) theory and the kinds of love in Sternberg's (1986) theory are rather neatly delineated, but we question whether such pure cases exist, or at least exist often. A person may be primarily pragmatically motivated in finding a partner, but may still look for some of the eros that would separate the eventual spouse from other well-heeled individuals who might not be suitable for marriage. Similarly, a person who is susceptible to ludic affairs may gradually find himself or herself falling in love with someone with whom he or she was initially playing a game, and thus go through a series of transitional stages between ludus and eros, or perhaps between ludus and mania. The kinds of love in Sternberg's theory are based on the presence of some components in the absence of others, but clearly these components are present in degrees, and only rarely either totally absent or present to the maximal extent. Thus, the kinds of love proposed are more realistically viewed as limiting cases than as kinds of love typically found in close relationships. Moreover, the statistical evidence is only moderately supportive of the triangular theory, in that the scales constructed to date have shown relatively high correlations between intimacy, passion, and commitment (Sternberg, 1987). Of course, the problem may be in the scales rather than in the theory, but the true locus of the problem remains to be shown.

A DEVELOPMENTAL THEORY

Hazan and Shaver (1987) (see also Shaver, Hazan, & Bradshaw, 1988) have drawn upon the attachment concept in the infancy literature developed by Bowlby (1969) and Ainsworth (1973) in order to understand attachment styles in adult love relationships. Following Ainsworth, Hazan and Shaver have proposed that romantic lovers, like infants, tend to have one of three attachment styles in their relationships. Styles are an individual-difference characteristic, which is alleged to derive in part from the kind of attachment people had to their mother when they were young.

Secure lovers find it relatively easy to get close to others. They also find they can be comfortable in depending on others and in having others depend on them. They do not worry about being abandoned or about someone getting too close to them. Avoidant lovers, in contrast, are uncomfortable being close to others. They find it difficult to trust others completely and difficult to allow themselves to depend on others. They get nervous when anyone gets too close, and often, they find that their partners in love want to become more intimate than they find comfortable. Anxious-ambivalent lovers find themselves in a situation, in some respects, diametrically opposed to avoidant lovers. They find that others are reluctant to get as close as they would like. They often worry that their partners do not really love them or will not want to stay with them. They want to merge completely with another person, and this desire sometimes scares others away. We appreciate the innovation behind the attachment theory of love, and also like the extension of social-developmental theory across the life span. Moreover, we are impressed by at least some of the data that have been collected to test this theory. At the same time, our enthusiasm for the theory is rather limited, for several reasons.

First, Shaver and his colleagues base their support for the idea that attachment styles in infancy carry over into adulthood on retrospective data. These data are self-reports of how people view themselves relating to heterosexual love partners and how they remember themselves as having related to their mothers. In our opinion, a purer example of a correlation caused by demand characteristics would be hard to find. Retrospective reports, even of recent events, have been found to be highly questionable, but retrospective reports of happenings of attachment phenomena in infancy are probably worth next to nothing; almost no one remembers their infancy, and most people have difficulty remembering much that happened even when they were 4 or 5 years old (Zechmeister & Nyberg, 1982). It seems dubious, in light of our present knowledge about memory, to accept retrospective reports of the kind of relationship that an individual recalls having had with his or her mother as an infant. Given the experimental context, it seems likely that people either have constructed implicit theories whereby their relations in the present have derived from their relations in the past, or else are assuming, within the context of the experiment, that their relations now should reflect their relations earlier. This is not to say that infant attachment styles fail to persist into adulthood, but only that the evidence for this persistence is still very weak.

We also believe that this theory fails to take into account the increasingly large literature on person-situation interactions (see Magnusson & Endler, 1977). Whereas attachment style may well be a stable individual-differences characteristic in infancy, we doubt that it is particularly stable in adulthood. Both authors of this chapter can think of relationships we have been in that correspond to each of the three attachment styles, and we believe that if Shaver and his colleagues, or anyone else, conducted research in which subjects were queried on multiple past relationships, it would be found that they show at least some distribution across attachment styles for the various relationships. It is only when they are asked to generalize that people give the experimenters what the experimenters want, namely, a generalization. This is not to say that people do not have a preferred attachment style or an attachment style that is characteristic of a plurality or even majority of their relationships; but rather it is to say that we believe it unlikely that the same attachment style pervades all or even almost all of the adult romantic relationships in which a person participates. The same person who is anxious-ambivalent in one relationship may well be avoidant in another, and secure in yet another. What we believe may differ most is the extent to which individuals are satisfied with each of these kinds of relationships. Some may find greatest fulfillment in one kind, others in another kind. Thus, some people, finding themselves in an avoidant relationship, may find it totally unsatisfactory and wish to leave it quite rapidly, whereas other people may find themselves quite comfortable with this mode of relating, and find themselves becoming uncomfortable when they are either secure or anxious-ambivalent.

Finally, we view attachment theory as a theory more of tendencies toward three ways of relating to people in general than we do as a theory of love. It is probable that some people are just more secure than other people in their relations. All of us are acquainted with people who tend to be avoidant, whether it is in love or in work relationships. With empirical testing, this work may contribute substantially by showing that Ainsworth's three attachment styles generalize to relationships beyond the infant's relationship with his or her mother. This generalization may not be peculiar to adult romantic relationships.

COGNITIVE THEORIES

A series of cognitively based theories are the cognitive consistency theories. Following Festinger and Carlsmith (1959), if a person finds herself or himself doing things for someone that are not very rewarding, she or he is liable to come to the conclusion that she or he must like or possibly love that person, and that she or he would not do the things for their own sake. Through this construal of the situation, one achieves cognitive consistency. One sees oneself as doing those things not because one likes doing them but because one likes (or loves) the person for whom one is doing them.

Walster and Berscheid (1974) view love in terms of the way people understand or label their feelings. They drew on Schachter and Singer's (1962) cognitive theory of emotion. According to this theory, people feel emotions as a function of how they label, in a situationally appropriate way, the arousal that they experience (see also Lange, 1922/1885). According to Walster and Berscheid (1974), people should be vulnerable to experiencing love whenever they are intensely aroused physiologically. People then cognitively label this arousal as love. In other situations, the same arousal might be labeled as fear, anger, loathing, or whatever. Although this theory might seem a bit simplistic to some, there is actually some evidence to support it in the context of interpersonal attraction (e.g., Dutton & Aron, 1974).

We suspect that there is more to love, and even to passionate love, than the desire to maintain consistency between one's thoughts and actions or the labeling of the unitary form of arousal. Indeed, recent evidence suggests that arousal is not of a single kind, but does differ as a function of the emotion involved (Schwartz & Weinberger, 1980). Thus, labeling may be based on differentiated experiences of arousal. Current theories of emotion also tend to be more complex than the Schachter–Singer theory (e.g., Mandler, 1980; see Fitness & Strongman, this volume). From the standpoint of both emotion and arousal, these cognitive theories seem to be oversimplifications. Nevertheless, they do point out an important role that cognitions play in love. People may have a desire to label their feelings and maintain a consistency in their actions and thoughts.

Another cognitive theory is social exchange theory (Homans, 1974), which proposes that people try to maximize their rewards and minimize the amount of punishment they experience. Thus, people will seek out others who reward them the most. However, the more of something that one has, the less rewarding it will seem. For example, a millionaire will value $1,000 less than a pauper. The theory predicts that people will make these appraisals of one another and will be most interested in people who have scarce resources. If one applies this theory to love, it predicts that you will love the person who rewards you with scarce resources more frequently than he or she punishes you.

Equity theory can be seen as deriving most immediately from social exchange theory. Equity theory predicts that people try to maximize their rewards and minimize their punishments. People have a standard for what is equitable and fair for all people to achieve this outcome. However, if people discover that they are in inequitable relationships, they will become distressed. The more inequitable the relationship appears, the more upset the person will become. The person will attempt to relieve his or her distress by restoring equity to the relationship. If one applies this theory to love, equity theory predicts that people will love those with whom they have equitable relationships and will become upset by inequitable relationships. On this view (Walster, Walster, & Berscheid, 1978), (a) individuals try to maximize their outcomes (i.e., the rewards minus the punishments received); (b) when an individual finds himself or herself in an inequitable interpersonal relationship, the person becomes distressed, with the amount of distress increasingly monotonically in proportion to the amount of inequity experienced; (c) such an individual attempts to eliminate his or her distress by restoring equity to the relationship; the greater the experienced inequity, the greater will be the effort to restore equity. In the present context, people will be more attracted to those with whom they have a more equitable relationship.

Social exchange theories are very interesting because they provide an insight into the kinds of evaluations that people have of their romantic relationships and partners, especially during certain periods of the relationship. These theories may explain why a person loves one person over another. However, these theories have certain limitations when they are applied to the study of love. First, it is not clear that people keep track of the amount of rewards or equity they experience in a romantic relationship. People do not seem to approach their romantic relationships in the same way that they approach their checking accounts. Otherwise, we would not see so many people in inequitable relationships. Researchers have found that romantic relationships, known as communal relationships, are characterized by a lack of record keeping as compared to the level that commonly occurs in friendships or exchange relationships (Mills & Clark, 1982). Second, exchange theories do not include the role of affect, which could influence one's cognitive appraisals of another person. Exchange theories seem to assume that people make a rational appraisal of each other and then accept or reject the person or relationship. However, one's initial affective response to a person could influence the kinds of appraisals one makes. Cognitive appraisals may not always determine affect.

SOCIOBIOLOGICAL THEORIES

Wilson (1981) has proposed an evolutionary account of love that uses a sociobiological framework. Wilson has suggested that adult love is an outgrowth of at least three main instincts (see also Buss, 1988). The first is the need of the infant to seek protection through its parents or substitutes for its parents. Wilson has suggested that the evolutionary function of attachment is primarily protection from predators and that, indeed, people—whether children or adults—tend to seek attachments most when they are somehow threatened from the outside. Wilson, like Shaver and Hazan in their later work, has argued that there is a close analogy between the kind of attachment that Bowlby (1969) studied in infants and the kind of attachment that can be observed in adult lovers. He believes that a certain kind of imprinting occurs with respect to one's parents and that people later tend to seek lovers who resemble their parents in certain critical respects.

The second basic instinct—in some respects, the flip side of the coin—is the parental protection instinct. People seek not only to be protected by their lovers but to protect them as well. The evolutionary function is the protection that one gives to the other and, thereby, to the child of any pair relationship, who will need the other as parent. The third kind of instinct is sexual. Wilson has claimed that sexual imprinting develops around the age of 3 or 4 years and that sexual orientation arises at that time.

Buss (1988) also proposed a sociobiological theory of love. He contended that love manifests itself in different love acts that have certain evolutionary functions. Buss claimed that males and females display different types of acts due to the different resources and concerns that are typical of each sex. He claimed that, because females have a small number of offspring, they will be interested in males who can protect their young. Thus, male love acts will consist of displaying resources that could potentially be invested in future offspring. In contrast, males' reproductive capabilities are constrained by the number of reproductively viable women they can inseminate. Therefore, males will be interested in females who display their reproductive capabilities. Thus, female love acts will consist of various appearance-enhancing acts that are designed to show their reproductive viability.

Wilson's and Buss' theories are intriguing for some of the same reasons that Hazan and Shaver's theory is intriguing. All seek to understand love in a broader context of development. In Hazan and Shaver's case, this broader context is the development of the organism, whereas in Buss' and Wilson's case, the broader context is the development of the species.

The sociobiological account is an attractive one in its integration of disciplines, and it makes intuitive sense; at the same time, it is problematic in some respects. For example, it is very difficult to disagree with the theory at some level. Who could disagree that attachment serves to prevent the young of the species from predators, or that many species show sexual instincts? But a theory loses interest if its main tenets are ones that almost anyone would accept. In addition, it should be stated that Wilson and Buss make claims that are contentious, for example, that men are fundamentally polygynous, "harem builders." But one could easily accept the sociobiological approach without accepting this or similar tenets.

Second, even if one were to disagree it is difficult to see what kind of empirical operations could be designed to disconfirm this or similar theories. Sociobiology is remarkably flexible because it can be used to account for almost anything in terms of evolution. One is reminded of the principle of sufficient reason, used by Leibniz and mocked by Voltaire, which can account for anything by stating that if a thing has happened there must have been sufficient reason for it to have happened.

Third, sociobiological theory seems to be more concerned with the origins of love or attachment than with what love is itself. There is nothing wrong with this, per se. We merely point out, as we have before, that many theories that are nominally theories of love are actually theories of something else, whether it be of the origins of love or of attachment, or of the ways in which love is expressed in relationships or of attraction whether or not within the context of a loving relationship.

Fourth, views of love as a concept have changed so greatly over time that it is difficult to find a sociobiological theory that can account for all these changes. At different times in the history of Western civilization, love has been associated with chastity or with sexual promiscuity. Theories that claim that the function of love is to reproduce one's genes cannot account for this large variation in the activities that have been associated with love. Indeed, if there is some underlying function of love, it has been very difficult to find it in the history of this concept.

PSYCHOMETRIC THEORIES

The first psychometrically based theory of love was that of Rubin (1970, 1973). Rubin used factor analysis and related methods to derive a love scale (as well as a liking scale). Rubin (1970) suggested that the 13 items on his love scale could be viewed as falling into three distinct clusters—affiliative or dependent need, predisposition to help, and exclusiveness and absorption—although these three clusters did not clearly emerge from factor analysis. The Rubin scales are something of a psychometric tour de force, in that they have been shown to be psychometrically reliable and to exhibit convergent and discriminant validity with respect to a variety of external measures. For example, Rubin found their reliability to be about .85, and he found that scores on the love scale are predictive of how much two individuals in a close relationship will gaze at each other. Moreover, although men and women both love and like their romantic partners more than they do their friends, the difference between romantic partners and friends is greater for the love scale than for the liking scale scores. Rubin (1970) found only moderate correlations between the liking and loving scales, although Sternberg and Grajek (1984) found correlations that were considerably higher.

Sternberg and Grajek (1984) also proposed a psychometrically based theory of love. They based their theory on Thomson's (1939) psychometric theory of intelligence. According to Thomson, intelligence could be understood in terms of the mind's possessing an enormous number of bonds, including reflexes, habits, learned associations, and the like. Performance on any one task would activate a large number of these bonds. Related tasks, such as those used on mental tests, would sample overlapping subsets of bonds. In terms of a structural theory of love, one might conceptualize love in terms of affects, cognitions, and motivations that, when sampled together, yield a composite experience that people label as love. Thus, although love might feel like a unitary experience, underlying it would be the sampling of a sufficient number of bonds to yield an epiphenomenally unitary experience. Sternberg and Grajek chose this theory over two alternative psychometric approaches (based upon Spearman's, 1927, and Thurstone's, 1938, theories of intelligence), based on factor analysis and hierarchical cluster analyses used to distinguish among the various psychometric theories.

The theories of Rubin (1970, 1973) and Sternberg and Grajek (1984) were both psychometrically derived and tested and, hence, have at least some empirical base to support them. The strength of these theories is in their structural models of the nature of love, and in their use of quantitative operations for theory testing. Rubin's theory, especially, as operationalized in his love scale, has been extensively tested empirically. Nevertheless, neither of these theories is totally satisfying.

First, the love scales seem, in a sense, to do to love what intelligence tests do to intelligence. They leave it somewhat bloodless. The relatively high correlation between liking and loving scales is not surprising, given that the love scales seem to measure those aspects of love that are most akin to liking. They certainly do not fully measure the hot, passionate aspects of love dealt with in the theories of Freud (1962/1905), Reik (1944), and others of the clinical psychologists discussed earlier. Indeed, the Sternberg and Grajek (1984) results suggest that love is the same from one close relationship to another, but certainly this finding seems like an oversimplification if one considers love in all its richness.

Second, the psychometric theories are rather weak on mechanism and especially development, as tends to be the case for psychometric theories of other constructs as well. Although the theories specify in some detail the structure of the constructs under consideration (a strength of psychometric theories), they have little to say about the development of those constructs. Reinforcement theory, in contrast, has quite a bit to say about the development of the constructs. Thus, the psychometric theories are less complete than one might like.

Third, and again like other psychometric theories, the psychometric theories of liking and loving have a certain ad hoc quality about them. Because they are not only tested by psychometric analysis but are also based on it, the theories largely follow from the data rather than the other way around. These theories probably come closest, of all the theories thus far considered, to being restatements of the data, in that factor analysis essentially transforms data from one form (the original form) to another (a reduced form).

Finally, these theories, unlike some of those considered earlier, do not tie into more general theories of psychological functioning. The reinforcement, cognitive consistency, two-component, attachment, and interruption theories are special cases of more general psychological theories. The theories of Rubin (1970, 1973) and of Sternberg and Grajek (1984) are not. Of course, there is no a priori reason why a theory of liking and loving should have to be a special case of a more general psychological theory. And we need to show that general theories can yield true theories of love. At the same time, it remains to be seen how the psychometric accounts of love can be tied into more general theories of psychological functioning.

CONCLUSION

In this chapter, we have reviewed alternative approaches to theorizing about love, and have assessed some of the strengths and weaknesses of each approach. We may have seemed overly critical, but we wished to emphasize that our main point is that any approach has both strengths and weaknesses. What is important is that the strengths and weaknesses of the various theoretical as well as methodological approaches are largely complementary, so that by using converging operations of theory knitting one can alternately study love in a way that transcends the limitations of any one approach.

Theorists, ourselves included, tend to become overly accepting of their own theories and approaches, and can easily become blind to the limitations that inhere in their own work. Indeed, it is always easier to point out the limitations of the work of others than of one's own work. Even worse, in the desire to prove that their own theory is best, theorists often start comparing theories that may well purport to be theories of the same thing but that are actually theories of different things. For example, Hendrick and Hendrick (1986) have compared several theories of love, those of Lee, Sternberg, Davis, and Hatfield, in an effort to choose among the theories. On the one hand, a development such as this one is salutary because it is an attempt to pit theories against one another and let the best of them win. On the other hand, we have a reservation about their approach, because as we have seen, these theories are not theories of identical things. Lee deals with styles of loving, Sternberg's and Hatfield and Walster's with kinds of loving, Davis' and Sternberg's with components of loving, and Hazan and Shaver's with attachment styles in love. Clearly, there is overlap in the ground covered by the various theories, but this overlap is not complete. A comparison among theories is therefore hazardous, at best.

We do not want to suggest that theories should not be tested against one another, because we would then end up with a large potpourri of theories, none of which has been challenged by any other. But we must recognize the limitations of comparative theory testing and be aware that some of our comparisons will be among theories that are not, strictly speaking, comparable. Most importantly, we believe, is the need to recognize the sociocultural constraints on any theory of love, whether implicit or explicit. Both implicit and explicit theories are products of their contexts.

In this chapter, we reviewed theoreticians of love only from the 19th and 20th centuries. One could compare these theories and pit one against the other. However, we believe that it would be more beneficial to compare theories of this society and time period with those of other societies and other time periods in order to understand the nature of love. Ideas about what constitutes love have changed so drastically over time that modern theorists of love might even be unable to recognize love in certain other time periods. What is perceived as loving at one time may be perceived as infatuation at another, or what is perceived as liking at one time may be perceived as love at another. At some times, heterosexual love of the kind we have been discussing has not even been perceived as something of any real consequence. During the time of Plato, for example, homosexual love between men was of much greater importance, and the most valued love of all was the love of an idea. But whereas Plato discussed at some length his views on love for ideas, how much is this kind of love discussed today? Truly we need to recognize just how limited our theories can be when viewed in the full context of space and time.

In conclusion, we reiterate that there is not one answer to the question: What is love? There are many ways to approach this question. We have reviewed these theories and have discussed their strengths and their weaknesses. All of these theories contribute to the study of love, especially when they are viewed as a group. We suggest that theorists begin to study love in this eclectic way. Some of the most informative theories are ones that address love from a variety of perspectives. Shaver et al.'s (1988) theory is an example of this kind of work because it incorporates attachment and developmental work with the study of love. The triangular theory of love (Sternberg, 1988) is also a step in this direction because it includes cognitive, motivational, and emotional components. Because theorists are beginning to address the numerous facets of love and are breaking down the boundaries between theories, this field is embarking on an exciting time that we look forward to with enthusiasm.

REFERENCES

Ainsworth, M. D. S. (1973). The development of infant–mother attachment. In B. M. Caldwell & H. N. Ricciuti (Eds.), *Review of child development research* (Vol. 3, pp. 1–94). Chicago: University of Chicago Press.

Boswell, J. (1952). The life of Samuel Johnson, L.L.D. In *Great books of the western world* (Vol. 44, pp. 1–587). Chicago, IL: Encyclopedia Brittanica.

Bowlby, J. (1969). *Attachment and loss: Vol. 1. Attachment.* New York: Basic Books.

Broverman, I., Vogel, S. R., Broverman, S. M., Clarkson, F. E., & Rosenkrantz, P. S. (1972). Sex role stereotypes: A current appraisal. *Journal of Social Issues, 28,* 59–78.

Buss, D. (1988). Love acts: The evolutionary biology of love. In R. J. Sternberg & M. Barnes (Eds.), *The psychology of love* (pp. 100–118). New Haven, CT: Yale University Press.

Byrne, D. (1971). *The attraction paradigm.* New York: Academic Press.

Carver, R. (1985). What we talk about when we talk about love. In J. F. Trimmer & C. W. Jennings (Eds.), *Fictions* (pp. 175–183). New York: Harcourt Brace Jovanovich.

Clore, G. L., & Byrne, D. (1974). A reinforcement-affect model of attraction. In T. L. Huston (Ed.), *Foundations of interpersonal attraction* (pp. 143–170). New York: Academic Press.

Davis, K. E. (1985, February). Near and dear: Friendship and love compared. *Psychology Today*, *19*, 22–30.

Dutton, D. G., & Aron, A. P. (1974). Some evidence for heightened sexual attraction under conditions of high anxiety. *Journal of Personality and Social Psychology*, *30*, 510–517.

Fehr, B. (1988). Prototype analysis of the concepts of love and commitment. *Journal of Personality and Social Psychology*, *55*, 557–579.

Festinger, L., & Carlsmith, J. M. (1959). Cognitive consequences of forced compliance. *Journal of Abnormal and Social Psychology*, *58*, 203–210.

Fielding, H. (1952). The history of Tom Jones, A foundling. *In Great books of the Western World* (Vol. 37, pp. 1–405). Chicago, IL: Encyclopedia Brittanica.

Freud, S. (1962/1905). *Three contributions to the theory of sex*. New York: Dutton.

Freud, S. (1955/1922). Certain neurotic mechanisms in jealousy, paranoia, and homosexuality. In *Collected Papers* (Vol. 2, pp. 235–240, 323). London: Hogarth.

Fromm, E. (1956). *The art of loving*. New York: Harper.

Garcia-Marquez, G. (1988/1985). *Love in the time of cholera*. (E. Grossman, Trans.) New York: Penguin Books.

Garner, W. R., Hake, H. W., & Eriksen, C. W. (1956). Operationism and the concept of perception. *Psychological Review*, *63*, 149–159.

Hatfield, E. (1988). Passionate and companionate love. In R. J. Sternberg & M. Barnes (Eds.), *The psychology of love* (pp. 191–217). New Haven, CT: Yale University Press.

Hatfield, E., & Walster, G. W. (1978). *A new look at love*. Lantham, MA: University Press of America.

Hazan, C., & Shaver, P. (1987). Romantic love conceptualized as an attachment process. *Journal of Personality and Social Psychology*, *52*, 511–524.

Hemingway, E. (1957). *A farewell to arms*. New York: Macmillan.

Hendrick, C., & Hendrick, S. (1986). A theory and method of love. *Journal of Personality and Social Psychology*, *50*, 392–402.

Homans, G. C. (1974). *Social behavior: Its elementary forms* (rev. ed.). New York: Harcourt Brace Jovanovich.

Hunt, M. M. (1959). *The natural history of love*. New York: Knopf.

Kalmar, D. A., & Sternberg, R. J. (1988). Theory knitting: An integrative approach to theory development. *Philosophical Psychology*, *1*, 153–170.

Kelley, H. H. (1983). Love and commitment. In H. H. Kelley, E. Berscheid, A. Christensen, J. Harvey, T. L. Huston, G. Levinger, E. McClintock, A. Peplau, & P. R. Peterson. (Eds.), *Close relationships* (pp. 265–314). New York: Freeman.

Klein, M., & Riviere, J. (1953). *Love, hate, and reparation*. London: Hogarth.

Lange, C. G. (1922/1885). *The emotions*. Baltimore: Williams & Wilkins.

Lee, J. A. (1977). A typology of styles of loving. *Personality and Social Psychology Bulletin*, *3*, 173–182.

Lott, A. J., & Lott, B. E. (1961). Group cohesiveness, communication level, and conformity. *Journal of Abnormal and Social Psychology*, *62*, 408–412.

Lott, A. J., & Lott, B. E. (1974). The role of reward in the formation of positive interpersonal attitudes. In T. L. Huston (Ed.), *Foundations of interpersonal attraction* (pp. 171–189). New York: Academic Press.

Magnusson, D., & Endler, N. S. (Eds.). (1977). *Personality at the crossroads: Current issues in interactional psychology*. Hillsdale, NJ: Erlbaum.

Mandler, G. (1980). The generation of emotion: A psychological theory. In R. Plutchik & H. Kellerman (Eds.), *Emotion: Theory, research, and experience* (Vol. 1, pp. 219–243). New York: Academic Press.

Maslow, A. H. (1954). *Motivation and personality*. New York: Harper & Row.

Maslow, A. H. (1962). *Toward a psychology of being*. Princeton, NJ: Van Nostrand.

Mills, J., & Clark, M. S. (1982). Exchange and communal relationships. In L. Wheeler (Ed.), *Review of personality and social psychology* (Vol. 3, pp. 121–144). Beverly Hills, CA: Sage.

Peck, M. S. (1978). *The road less traveled: A new psychology of love, traditional values, and spiritual growth.* New York: Simon & Schuster.

Peele, S. (1988). Fools for love: The romantic ideal, psychological theory, and addictive love. In R. J. Sternberg & M. Barnes (Eds.), *The psychology of love* (pp. 159–188). New Haven, CT: Yale University Press.

Peele, S., & Brodsky, A. (1976). *Love and addiction.* New York: New American Library.

Reik, T. (1944). *A psychologist looks at love.* New York: Farrar & Rinehart.

Rothman, E. K. (1984). *Hands and hearts.* New York: Basic Books.

Rubin, Z. (1970). Measurement of romantic love. *Journal of Personality and Social Psychology, 16,* 265–273.

Rubin, Z. (1973). *Liking and loving: An invitation to social psychology.* New York: Holt, Rinehart, & Winston.

Schachter, S., & Singer, J. E. (1962). Cognitive, social, and physiological determinants of emotional state. *Psychological Review, 69,* 379–399.

Schwartz, G. E., & Weinberger, D. A. (1980). Patterns of emotional responses to affective situations: Relations among happiness, sadness, anger, fear, depression, and anxiety. *Motivation and Emotion, 4,* 175–191.

Shaver, P., Hazan, C., & Bradshaw, D. (1988). Love as attachment: The integration of three behavioral systems. In R. J. Sternberg & M. Barnes (Eds.), *The psychology of love* (pp. 68–99). New Haven, CT: Yale University Press.

Singer, I. (1984). *The nature of love* (Vol. 1). Chicago, IL: University of Chicago Press.

Spearman, C. (1927). *The abilities of man.* New York: Macmillan.

Sternberg, R. J. (1986). A triangular theory of love. *Psychological Review, 93,* 119–135.

Sternberg, R. J. (1987). Liking versus loving: A comparative evaluation of theories. *Psychological Bulletin, 102,* 331–345.

Sternberg, R. J. (1988). *The triangle of love.* New York: Basic Books.

Sternberg, R. J., & Barnes, M. (Eds.). (1988). *The psychology of love.* New Haven, CT: Yale University Press.

Sternberg, R. J., & Grajek, S. (1984). The nature of love. *Journal of Personality and Social Psychology, 47,* 312–329.

Sterne, L. (1952). Tristram Shandy. In *Great books of the western world* (Vol. 36, pp. 191–556). Chicago, IL: Encyclopedia Brittanica.

Thomson, G. H. (1939). *The factorial analysis of human ability.* London: University of London Press.

Thurstone, L. L. (1938). *Primary mental abilities.* Chicago: University of Chicago Press.

Walster, E., & Berscheid, E. (1974). A little bit about love: A minor essay on a major topic. In T. L. Huston (Ed.), *Foundations of interpersonal attraction* (pp. 355–381). New York: Academic Press.

Walster, E., Walster, G. W., & Berscheid, E. (1978). *Equity: Theory and research.* Boston: Allyn & Bacon.

Wilson, G. (1981). *The Coolidge effect: An evolutionary account of human sexuality.* New York: Morrow.

Zechmeister, E. B., & Nyberg, S. E. (1982). *Human memory: An introduction to research and theory.* Monterey, CA: Brooks/Cole.

III

APPLICATIONS AND EXTENSIONS

Close relationships occupy a central position in people's lives. They have the capacity to psychologically cripple people or substantially contribute to their well-being. Accordingly, one of the central features of close relationship research has always been its potential for application to real-world concerns. These final chapters extend and apply some of the ground covered in the prior sections of the book, and also summarize and integrate what we have learned concerning the role of cognition in close relationships.

In the first chapter of Part 3, *The Development of Close Relationships: A Cognitive Perspective,* Surra and Bohman analyze a central task in the social psychology of close relationships that has been touched on in many of the prior chapters—explaining the development of close relationships over long periods of time. Consistent with the theme of this book, Surra and Bohman argue that understanding the formation, maintenance, and breakdown stages of relationship development necessitates attention being given to cognitive structures and processes. Indeed, Surra's analysis relies heavily on some of the theories and ideas expounded in the first section of the book.

Chapter 12, *Social Cognition and the Relationship Repair Process: Toward Better Outcome in Marital Therapy,* deals with the application of close relationship research and theory to marital therapy. Beach notes that marital therapy is unsuccessful for many couples, and suggests that one answer is the appropriate application of (cognitive) social psychological theories to the relationship repair process, combined with the specification and measurement of important mediating goals and moderating variables in therapy.

11

The Development of Close Relationships: A Cognitive Perspective

Catherine A. Surra
Thomas Bohman
The University of Texas at Austin

For years, research on close relationships was dominated by the behaviorist tradition and the belief that the meaning of behavior is transparent. A corollary of this belief is that observers of behavior should agree on its interpretation, outside observers should agree with partners, and coupled partners should agree with each other. Faced with a barrage of evidence to the contrary (see Surra & Ridley, 1991, for a review), some researchers have reevaluated these assumptions and have set out to understand how partners in close relationships interpret the meaning of each other's behaviors. The purpose of this chapter is to take this work a step further by analyzing cognitive processes in close relationships from a developmental perspective. We also examine how cognitive activity during interaction contributes over the long run to the subjective experience of being close.

To lay the groundwork for the developmental analysis, we discuss from a cross-sectional perspective the role of cognition in close relationships. Transient cognitive activity as a manifestation of influence during interaction is examined first. We draw on interdependence models of close relationships (Kelley et al., 1983) and models of social information processing (Bradbury & Fincham, 1987; Wyer & Srull, 1986) to describe how cognitive activity links partners to each other during interaction. Second, we define three knowledge structures or memory stores that are especially relevant to a particular close relationship: (a) prototypical conceptions of relational constructs and the assessments of these constructs within a particular close relationship; (b) causal accounts, or organized representations concerning why interaction events and other relationship-relevant events occur; and (c) relationship-specific schemas, or knowledge about the self, the other, and the relationship.

The connections between cognitive activity and larger knowledge structures are explored in the sections on relationship development. We distinguish between two periods of development: instability, which includes the formation, growth, and deterioration of relationships, and stability or maintenance of the status quo. Cognitive activity during interaction and relational knowledge structures are analyzed for each type of developmental period.

A CROSS-SECTIONAL VIEW OF COGNITION
IN CLOSE RELATIONSHIPS

In close relationships, cognition plays a dual role. The first concerns the relatively transient thoughts and related cognitive processes that result from interaction between partners. In this instance, partners' cognitions are interconnected by virtue of the actions that occur between them (Wegner, Giuliano, & Hertel, 1984). Second, over time, partners develop more permanent knowledge structures or cognitive representations specific to a close relationship.

Cognitive Activity During Interaction
as an Indicator of Mutual Influence

Interaction can be viewed as a multi-event process that involves the connections between each partner's observable behaviors and the other's subjective responses (i.e., thoughts and feelings). The interdependence between partners' behaviors, thoughts, and feelings is mutual influence, the fundamental defining feature of relationships (Kelley et al., 1983). One partner's cognitive response to another's action constitutes one indicator of the impact the other has.[1]

Illustrations of the way in which partners' behaviors influence subjective responses are abundant in the empirical literature (See Fletcher & Kininmonth, this volume). Here, we mention a few examples simply to illustrate what we mean by mutual influence. Levenson and Gottman (1983) demonstrated that spouses' ongoing physiological responses during interaction were linked. The degree of linkage was stronger for distressed spouses than nondistressed spouses, suggesting that distressed spouses have more influence over each other's subjective responses than do nondistressed spouses.

Another example of influence is intersubjectivity, or the similarity between the thoughts and feelings partners experience during interaction (Ickes, Tooke, Stinson, Baker, & Bissonnette, 1988). Ickes and his colleagues found that previously unacquainted partners who interacted for 5 minutes evidenced intersub-

---

[1]In this chapter we are particularly concerned with how one partner's behavior affects the other's cognitions. Thoughts are closely linked to feelings, however, and it is often difficult to separate these two subjective responses during the flow of interaction.

jectivity, whereas pseudodyads (formed by randomly pairing data from different partners) did not. These findings indicate that intersubjectivity between strangers develops quickly and probably results from interaction rather than from the context or from more general beliefs about relationships. Similarly, Fletcher and Fitness (1990) found that the positive thoughts and feelings daters experienced during interaction were more a function of dyadic interaction than of intrapersonal psychological processes.

Although we know that behavior affects cognitive and affective responses during interaction, we know relatively little about the process by which this occurs. In the next section, we analyze this process in more detail by utilizing an information-processing approach to interaction.

An Information-Processing Approach to Cognition During Interaction

Information-processing models of social cognition greatly enrich the view of influence just described. Wyer and Srull's (Scott, Fuhrman, & Wyer, this volume; Wyer & Srull, 1986) model of social information processing is especially applicable because it is consistent with what we know about cognitive activity in response to behavior during interaction (see Fletcher & Kininmonth, this volume) and because it conforms to some current models of cognition in relational communication (Bradbury & Fincham, 1987; Noller & Guthrie, in press).

According to information-processing models, one partner's behavior during interaction is input that stimulates behavioral responses or output on the part of the other. Cognitive processes and structures stored in memory mediate the connections between inputs and outputs, and permit partners to recognize, interpret, and act on each other's actions. Initially, information from one partner's behavior is processed by the other at a very low level of abstractness to extract its semantic meaning (Wyer & Srull, 1986). At this level, for example, a father simply hears the meaning of his son's words "I need some money for the video arcade tonight." According to Wyer and Srull's (1986) model, initial processing is accomplished by a processor called the Comprehender, which extracts semantic meaning automatically by drawing on prior knowledge. Encoding at this level is independent of any processing goal the individual has. The activity of the Comprehender has its parallel in the primary processing feature of Bradbury and Fincham's (1987) model of marital interaction.

In some cases, higher order or secondary processing of information is necessary (Bradbury & Fincham, 1987; Wyer & Srull, 1986). Processing at this level relies on information contained in the Comprehender as well as information contained in long-term memory. New information in the Comprehender is weighed against previously acquired information in order to form a subjective evaluation or abstraction. Dad, for example, trying to figure out why his son needs more money, may recall that he bought his son new designer sneakers and a tennis racket just last week. Drawing on all of this information may lead dad to conclude, "He is such a spendthrift." In Wyer and Srull's (1986) model, higher order processing is accomplished by a processor called the Encoder/Organizer. Higher order processing is undertaken when processing goals require it (Wyer & Srull, 1986) or when the results of initial processing demand it (Bradbury and Fincham, 1987).

Based upon the results of higher order processing, the other selects a behavioral response (Bradbury & Fincham, 1987; Wyer & Srull, 1986). This response then serves as informational input for the partner's next action.

Two storage units in Wyer and Srull's (1986) model are especially important to understanding relational communication. First, the Work Space is a temporary storage place for all information currently in use to attain processing goals. It holds information about the stimulus behavior, abstract encodings of this information based on previously stored concepts, subjective judgments, and the like (Wyer & Srull, 1986). The Work Space has a limited capacity and is cleared whenever processing goals have been obtained or when the information load is high. When it is cleared, information not stored permanently is lost.

The second storage unit discussed by Wyer and Srull that is relevant to our purposes is long-term memory, or the Permanent Storage Unit. This consists of a set of storage bins that are addressed according to their content. Two categories of bins are pertinent here: semantic and referent. The semantic bin is like a mental dictionary; it contains information about concepts and their related features. With respect to close relationships, for instance, the semantic bins might hold the meaning of nouns such as love and trust, actions such as kissing and arguing, and emotions like anger and joy. Although the semantic bin can be accessed by either the Comprehender or the Encoder/Organizer, it is frequently accessed early during processing by the Comprehender to interpret the semantic meaning of sensory information. Referent bins are used to attain higher order processing objectives. Referent bins hold encyclopedic knowledge and personally relevant information about particular people, categories of people, objects, and events. A referent bin specific to a close other, for example, might contain information about the attributes of the other, activities engaged in with the other and procedures for doing so, interaction scenarios, affective reactions to the other, visual representations of the other, and so on. The content of different bins overlaps such that the same information might be stored in different places.[2]

An individual's processing goals are a pervasive determinant of how information is encoded, organized, stored, and retrieved (Wyer & Srull, 1986). Laboratory research has shown, for instance, that information about the traits and behaviors of a person is stored and used differently depending upon whether

---

[2]The concept of the Permanent Storage Unit shares some features in common with Bradbury and Fincham's (1987) description of the distal context of interaction, although the latter is much broader. It also includes such individual difference variables as processing style and chronic mood states.

subjects have been instructed to form an impression of the person or simply to remember information about the person (Wyer & Srull, 1986). Two common processing goals spouses have are to ascertain the causes of negative marital events and who is responsible for such events (Fincham, Bradbury, & Scott, 1990; Fincham & Bradbury, in press). Goals come into play during active processing and in permanent storage. During active processing, the Goal Specification Box contains immediate processing objectives and instructions and procedures for how to attain them. In Permanent Storage, goal bins are a particular type of referent bin: one that contains information about how to attain particular objectives. We discuss below what processing goals and goal schema are especially pertinent to close relationships and how the relevance of processing goals changes over time.

The Executor is a processing unit that directs and organizes the flow of information among other processing and storage units (Wyer & Srull, 1986). The activities of the Executor are goal directed and conscious, whereas those of other processing units are subconscious. Hence, individuals are usually aware of such activities as accessing memory, transmitting information from memory to the Work Space, and returning information to storage from the Work Space. They also tend to be conscious of the output of processing units (e.g., semantic meaning or information from memory). As discussed below, the distinction between conscious and subconscious processing is an important determinant of the degree of influence during interaction.

The amount and type of processing required to interpret, evaluate, and respond to another's behavior are good indicators of the degree of one partner's influence on the other. Processing is more demanding when it is conscious and goal directed and when it requires searching memory. Cognitive work also is greater when the information relevant to interpreting the behavior is not available in memory and when the relevant information is stored in different places. Similarly, the selection of an appropriate behavioral response is more difficult when the evaluative or descriptive implications of the other's behavior are unknown (see Srull & Wyer, 1989). For all of these reasons, the influence of one partner's behavior on another is greater the more difficult it is for the other to encode the partner's behavior.

As the preceding discussion indicated, knowledge structures stored in long-term memory play a significant role in the link between behavior and cognition. In the next section, we describe knowledge structures that are especially relevant to close relationships.

Relational Knowledge Structures

Cognition plays a second role in the development of close relationships, one that concerns the formation and operation of permanent knowledge structures. Knowledge structures are organized, structured stores of information that result from prior information processing and that affect the subsequent interpretation and organization of information (Markus & Zajonc, 1985). We discuss three knowledge structures important in close relationships: prototypical conceptions and assessments of relational constructs, causal accounts, and relationship-specific schemas. Throughout the remainder of the chapter, we refer to these three representations as relational knowledge structures.

Prototypical conceptions and assessments of relational constructs.   Prototypical conceptions of relational constructs are laypersons' understandings of the meaning of love, commitment, trust, and other concepts important in close relationships generally. Prototypical conceptions consist of interrelated sets of attributes commonly ascribed to the construct (Fehr, 1988; Shaver, Schwartz, Kirson, & O'Connor, 1987). Partners use their prototypical definitions, in combination with other knowledge, to assess whether and how much the construct applies to their relationships (e.g., "How committed are we?"). Prototypical conceptions are semantic bins (Wyer & Srull, 1986) that contain definitional information about relationship constructs. We will review the research on love and commitment as prototypes (Fehr, 1988; Shaver et al., 1987) to illustrate the nature of these knowledge structures. In these studies, laypersons' accounts and definitions are investigated to examine the nature of the prototype.

With regard to the content of prototypes, studies agree that the meaning of love is defined by features of the relationship, such as caring, liking, affection, and honesty; behaviors (e.g., gazing at the other or doing things for the other); emotional responses that are both positive and negative (e.g., feeling warm, joyful, or scared); and even physiological reactions (e.g., fast heartbeat) (Fehr, 1988; Shaver et al., 1987). Cognitive activities, such as thinking about the other all the time, are also characteristic of love. Laypersons' definitions of love include such admitted distortions as seeing only the other's good qualities or the positive side. Likewise, commitment is defined by beliefs, behaviors, and descriptions of cognitions and emotions (Fehr, 1988).

Although love and commitment are broadly defined, like other prototypes they each have a core content most central to their meaning. Caring, affection, and other attributes of companionate love constitute the core meaning of love (Fehr, 1988; Shaver et al., 1987). The peripheral features of love concern its passionate aspects, such as sexual attraction and lust (Fehr, 1988; Shaver et al., 1987). Commitment's core attributes include loyalty, responsibility, living up to one's word, and faithfulness, whereas security, feeling trapped, and other features are more peripheral (Fehr, 1988). As we shall see below, the presence of central features is probably related to the extent to which people judge themselves to be in love and committed in their close relationships.

Studies also suggest that prototypical conceptions are horizontally and vertically organized. With respect to the former, accounts of love contain tightly interrelated subclusters of attributes and responses that distinguish love from other emotions (Shaver et al., 1987). Similarly, love has sets of features that distinguish it from commitment (Fehr, 1988).

The vertical structure of love is apparent in the results of Shaver et al.'s (1987) study of love and other emotions. They found that love and other emotions fall into two superordinate categories: positive and negative. At best, though, fuzzy boundaries separate one construct or emotion from another (see Kelley, 1983; Shaver et al., 1987). Fehr (1988) found, for instance, that love shares about a third of its features, especially its core companionate features, with commitment, whereas commitment shares about half of its features with love. Both love and commitment also have unique attributes that distinguish them from each other.

The organization of attributes within constructs and the degree of separation or overlap between constructs affect whether people ascribe the constructs to their own relationships and to what degree they do so. The observation, for example, that the relationship possesses some of the core attributes of love may result in attributing love and its other features to the relationship. The fuzzy boundaries between constructs explains why attributing love to a relationship may also stimulate attributing commitment or other constructs.

Causal accounts.   Another type of relational knowledge structure is causal accounts. Causal accounts are products of inferential processes, whereby partners seek to understand and explain why events occur as they do in a relationship. Causal accounts are not composed of single, momentary attributions about behaviors during interaction; rather, they are organized, stored representations of how and why events happen that persist long after the events themselves (Harvey, Weber, Galvin, Huszti, & Garnick, 1986; Surra & Huston, 1987; Weiss, 1975). Different accounts are developed, for instance, to explain how I met Bob, how we became committed, why Bob behaves as he does, and why we split up. Accounts are an event bin, a type of referent bin (see Wyer & Srull, 1986) that contains information about the interrelated people, occurrences, and episodes surrounding a relationship-relevant event.

Research on the content of accounts universally shows that respondents use a wide variety of internal, interpersonal, and external attributions to explain events (Fletcher, 1983a, 1983b; Harvey, Wells, & Alvarez, 1978; Lloyd & Cate, 1985; Surra, 1987; Surra, Arizzi, & Asmussen, 1988). Internal or individual attributions include explanations that concern self-dispositions or preexisting expectations for what relationships should be like. Interpersonal or dyadic attributions are statements about the character of the relationship itself, the self relative to the partner, or the behaviors transacted between partners. Attributions about partner dispositions are treated in some studies as internal or individual attributions (Cupach & Metts, 1986; Fletcher, 1983a) and in other studies as dyadic attributions (Surra, 1987; Surra et al., 1988). External attributions include references to the social network, life events or circumstances, institutions, or uncontrollable forces (Surra et al., 1988). As one might expect, attributions to the partners or the relationship predominate in causal accounts; yet a substantial percentage of attributions concern network or other external events, roughly 25% to 30% in several studies (Fletcher, 1983a; Lloyd & Cate, 1985; Surra et al., 1988; Surra & Huston, 1987). Studies of causal accounts demonstrate that participants have broad and complex causal understandings of relationship events.

Attributions to the various internal, dyadic, and external causes are structured as networks of inferences. With regard to relationship breakup, accounts are storylike and contain descriptions of the context of the event, the characters involved, and behavioral episodes (Harvey et al., 1986; Harvey et al., 1978; Weber, Harvey, & Stanley, 1987). Imposing a plot or story line on a breakup may make it more comprehensible (Harvey et al., 1986). In accounts of changes in commitment, attributions form spatial, temporal, or logical sequences that vary in their length and complexity (Surra & Planalp, 1990).

Differences between the two types of accounts undoubtedly are due partly to the events people are asked to account for. When accounting for provocative relationship events like breakups, there is a great need to produce functional accounts that explain or justify why events happened as they did (Harvey, Agostinelli, & Weber, 1989). The content of such accounts must be coherent, justifying, face saving, and evidential. It may be necessary to construct a comprehensive story to meet all these demands. However, when accounting for changes in commitment, the motivational demands are lower and accounts may mostly reflect people's actual reasons for behaving as they did (Surra, 1987; Surra et al., 1988; Surra & Huston, 1987).

Relationship-specific schemas.   The third type of knowledge structure is what we call relationship-specific schemas. A relationship-specific schema is an organized representation of traits, beliefs, behaviors, and action sequences that are relevant to a particular other person and to one's relationship with that person. Relationship-specific schemas are a type of referent bin (see Wyer & Srull, 1986) that is organized around the relationship rather than the other person, but it includes characteristics of the other person.

The content of relationship-specific schemas shares much in common with person schemas. A schema of a real person contains descriptions of the other's physical appearance, personality traits, and behaviors (Fiske & Cox, 1979; Markus & Zajonc, 1985; Park, 1986). In addition, relationship-specific schemas contain interpersonal knowledge about the target relationship (Surra, 1987; Surra et al., 1988). This includes references to the qualities of the relationship (e.g., "We have the same goals"); to the self in relation to the partner (e.g., "I am more insecure than she is"); to the target relationship compared with other relationships (e.g., "I felt more comfortable with him than I ever had with anyone before"); and to typical interaction or action sequences (e.g., "Everything we talk about ends in a fight").

Research on relational schemas verifies the notion that schema content is specific to particular relationships and varies across relationships. Davis and Todd (1985) identified characteristics common to friendship, such as intimacy and enjoyment, then demonstrated that participants differentially attributed the characteristics to best friends, close same- and opposite-sex friends, acquaintances, and former friends. Different close relationships, however, share some knowledge in common, knowledge that helps to define them as close. The primary content of beliefs about dating relationships and close friendships, for example, are trust (e.g., honesty, willingness to confide in another), involvement (e.g., closeness, companionship), and relationship rules (e.g., duties, freedoms, responsibilities) (Planalp & Honeycutt, 1985; Planalp, Rutherford, & Honeycutt, 1988).

The various elements of schematic content are linked and organized, perhaps hierarchically. The interconnectedness of schematic knowledge is apparent in studies showing high intercorrelations among different beliefs about relationships (Davis & Todd, 1985; Planalp & Honeycutt, 1985; Planalp et al., 1988). Fiske and Cox (1979) found that the content of written descriptions of others varied over the time it took to write them, suggesting that content is differentially available or accessed from memory. Early on, the other's physical attributes and one's relationship to the other predominate; apparently, the latter serves as an overarching label or organizing cue. Next, behaviors, then personality traits, predominate. In their qualitative study of schema change, Planalp and Rivers (1988) also found that the relationship as a whole forms the top of the organizing hierarchy, with concrete behaviors at the lowest level, and attributes in between. Invariably, concrete behavioral occurrences or their absence triggered changes in relational attributes, supporting the notion that behaviors are encoded before relational attributes.

As in the case of other knowledge structures, the organization of relationship-specific schemas has implications for relationship maintenance and change. As discussed previously, schematic knowledge of various types affects what information is perceived from interaction and how new information is integrated, the retrieval of information from memory, interpretations and judgments, and the selection of behavioral responses. Consistent with this view, Weiss (1984) found that spouses' expectations for how their interactions typically proceed predicted not only their interpretation of interaction events, but also their behavior. Likewise, attributions for why spouses perform negative and positive behaviors maintain established beliefs about how satisfying the marriage is (see Bradbury & Fincham, 1990, for a review). With regard to the impact of schemas on memory, Planalp (1985) found that accuracy and types of errors were strongly biased in ways consistent with schema for professor–student relationships. Thus, schemas bring a coherence and understanding to events that go beyond the information available in the environment (Markus & Zajonc, 1985).

Up to this point, we have examined two ways that cognition operates in relationships, cognitive activity during interaction, and relational knowledge structures. The analysis so far has been limited to describing how the phenomena operate at a single point in time. In the next sections, we turn our attention to cognition and the development of relationships.

COGNITION DURING PERIODS
OF RELATIONSHIP INSTABILITY AND STABILITY

To understand how cognition in relationships changes over time, we distinguish between periods of stability and instability. Periods of instability occur when partners are becoming more or less involved. When relationships are unstable, such dimensions as attraction, liking, commitment, closeness, behavioral interdependence, and the like are in a state of flux. During periods of stability, in contrast, the dimensions of involvement are maintained at a relatively stable state. Three periods of instability can be identified: the formation of new relationships, the deterioration of established relationships, and the growth of established relationships. We recognize that periods of stability and instability are relative, and depend in part on how much change is evident and over what time span. Yet we find it useful to separate the two periods in order to examine cognition developmentally and to emphasize the point that relationships oscillate between times of instability and stability.

In the remaining sections of this chapter, we examine cognitive processing and knowledge structures in relation to periods of instability and stability.

Cognitive Processing During Periods of Instability

During periods of instability, cognitive activity during interaction is extensive and processing demands are great. Processing is also likely to be higher order, that is, to rely upon information in permanent storage and on several different knowledge stores, and to be conscious, effortful, and goal driven.

There are several reasons why this is so. Most importantly, when relationships are unstable, uncertainty about them is high. Uncertainty can be reduced by means of increased knowledge and understanding about the partnership, which renders behavior more predictable. As a result, behaviors exchanged during times of instability are replete with potential meaning. Hence people must be careful about extracting meaning from the other's behaviors, as well as conveying meaning in their own behaviors.

Several lines of evidence support the idea that cognitive activity is more extensive during periods of instability. Descriptions of the experience of falling in love (Shaver et al., 1987) and of ending a marriage (Weiss, 1975) have in common references to excessive cognitive activity in the form of thinking about the other, analyzing and rehashing past interactions, and rehearsing future ones. Weiss (1975) noted that relational loss is characterized by obsessive review of past events, or "a constant, absorbing, sometimes maddening preoccupation that refuses to accept any conclusion" (p. 79). Cognitive activity in dating relationships also is greater when the relationship is changing. In one study, daters' ratings of the time they spent thinking about their relationships were higher when the relationships were shorter, when they spent more time thinking about separation and increased commitment, and when the relationship was perceived as unstable (Fletcher, Fincham, Cramer, & Heron, 1987). These findings suggest that conscious cognitive activity that respondents are aware of and can verbalize is greater when the degree of involvement in relationships is increasing or decreasing.

The deterioration of relationships may be especially characterized by attributional cognitive activity. Fletcher et al. (1987) found that spontaneous causal attributions in free-response descriptions of dating relationships were more likely the more time daters reportedly thought about separating and the more they perceived their relationships as unstable (measured as a summary of ratings of uncertain, changeable, and unpredictable). Spontaneous attributions, however, were not associated with the length of the dating relationship or with time spent thinking about commitment. Investigations of the breakup of relationships further indicate that women do more attributional analysis than men during this type of instability (Baxter, 1986; Cupach & Metts, 1986; Fletcher, 1983b; Harvey, et al., 1978). As we noted previously, attributional activity may be greater during periods of relational decline than during other types of instability because of the need to make sense of socially undesirable events. The functional and motivational demands of accounting for breakups may be stronger for women than men.

Uncertainty of behavior.   Uncertainty is high during instability because of the peculiar nature of close relationships. In a close relationship, one partner controls the affective outcomes the other derives from interaction (Kelley, 1979). People are aware of the fact that closeness means giving another the power to inflict pleasure or pain and that they have the same power over the other. They also recognize that this interdependence of outcomes means that closeness can be exceedingly pleasurable or exceedingly painful. During periods of instability, uncertainty and ambivalence about closeness are high because partners are dependent on each other for rewards, but they are unclear about whether, when, and to what extent positive outcomes will be forthcoming. During relationship formation, partners are aware of the potential rewards the other might deliver, but they are unsure about whether they can be obtained. In addition, individuals are hopeful about the long-term promise of closeness, and they are concerned about managing their own behavior so that the promise can be fulfilled. Relationship deterioration is characterized by uncertainty about future rewards, doubts about whether a relationship that presumably once was rewarding will continue to be so, confusion about how one should behave toward the other, and the costliness of the negative behaviors, conflicts, and tensions that accompany deterioration. Even the growth of closeness may engender ambivalence (Braiker & Kelley, 1979), as partners who interact more frequently and in more diverse ways question just how much they want their outcomes to depend on the actions of another (Surra & Milardo, in press).

Relational knowledge and uncertainty reduction.   The uncertainty and vulnerability that accompany instability are costly. They can be partially mitigated, however, if partners acquire knowledge about the character of the other and their relationship (Berger, 1979; Surra & Milardo, in press). Relational knowledge affects the costliness of outcome interdependence in four ways. First, relational knowledge may reduce costliness because it decreases uncertainty about the motives and intent of the other during interaction. Second, it will typically increase the predictability of the other's future actions, thereby decreasing uncertainty. Third, it will decrease the extent to which individuals feel vulnerable because it increases their sense of control over the other. The acquisition of relational knowledge during times of instability also may enable people to gain some predictability and control over their own welfare, which otherwise will seem dependent on the capriciousness of another (see Heider, 1958). Fourth, relational knowledge may increase the efficiency of joint behavior (see Thibaut & Kelley, 1959) because it can simplify the interpretation of the other's behavior and ease the selection of an appropriate behavioral response. A wife's knowledge, for example, that housecleaning is shared can render her husband's comment that "the house is a mess" to be easily interpreted as "it needs to be cleaned," rather than "you are a bad housekeeper." It also simplifies the task of choosing an appropriate behavioral response, which in this case might be, "Well, I guess I know what we'll be doing this weekend."

Direct evidence that increases in cognitive activity stem from outcome interdependence comes from an experimental investigation by Berscheid and Graziano (1979). Unattached subjects agreed to have the researchers take over their dating lives for the next 5 weeks. Outcome dependency was manipulated by telling some subjects that they would be dating the same person for 5 weeks (high exclusivity), other subjects that they would be dating five different people over the 5 weeks (low exclusivity), and still other subjects that they would be dating five different people but the prospective date was not seen in a videotape subsequently viewed by the subjects (zero exclusivity). Participants received the names and telephone numbers of their dates. Then, ostensibly to get data on the dating problems of the opposite sex, participants viewed a videotape of a discussion among three opposite-sex persons, who mentioned their names during the conversation. One of the conversants was the subject's date. Amount of attention paid to the other (measured as the amount of time the participant pushed a switch to view the date on the videotape) and recall about the other increased with outcome dependence. The results suggest that cognitive activity increases with outcome dependence in the context of relationship formation, presumably in response to the motivation to predict and control the social environment (Berscheid & Graziano, 1979).

Conscious and goal-directed processing.   Because the acquisition of relational knowledge and the selection of appropriate behavioral responses are especially important and difficult during times of instability, information processing will tend to be conscious and goal directed. Three processing goals appear to be salient during periods of instability. One goal, common to many social situations, is to acquire information about the personality of the other, such as how cooperative or selfish the partner is. Information about another's personality is needed to identify the stable traits that are likely to influence the other over time and situations. In close relationships, information about O's personality is also needed to ascertain what behavioral response might be pleasing or displeasing to O. A second goal, unique to close relationships, is to identify the character of the relationship and to evaluate the interpersonal qualities and abilities present in the relationship. Interpersonal knowledge and assessments are necessary because close relationships involve not only attending to how the other's behavior affects the self, but also how the self affects the other. Interpersonal qualities and assessments involve, for instance, estimating how loving, committed, or marriageable the relationship is; weighing how much the partner likes the self; and knowing how similar the other's personality and background are to the self. Finally, during instability, partners are motivated to explain why they behave as they do and why relationship-relevant events happen. This goal requires identifying the intentions and motivations underlying another's behavior. It also involves determining whether the causes of events and behaviors are rooted in the self, the partner, the relationship, or external sources.

As the result of efforts to acquire relational knowledge, relationship-specific schema, causal accounts, and assessments of relational constructs form and change during periods of instability. In the next section, we examine what these changes are and how they come about.

Changes in Knowledge Structures
During Periods of Instability

Behaviors exchanged during instability are often novel or inconsistent with prior relational knowledge. Such behaviors instigate an intensive search for meaning, which involves deeper processing; one's processing goals will typically require that information stored in memory be utilized. In addition, information will be interpreted at a higher level of abstraction in terms of descriptive or evaluative concepts. This is accomplished in part by the Encoder/Organizer, which interprets information from memory along with information already in the Work Space (Wyer & Srull, 1986). Because the information contained in different knowledge structures is interrelated (e.g., the same behavior may be coded in different structures), the search is likely to involve several different knowledge structures. During instability, the interpretation of novel or inconsistent behaviors result in the development of and change in relational knowledge structures.

The process by which this occurs during interaction is summarized in Figure 11.1. When a relationship is initiated, partners have no prior knowledge concerning that relationship. As a result, they must rely on structures already in place. The results of research on relational accounts (Planalp & Rivers, 1988; Surra et al., 1988; Surra & Milardo, in press; Wilkinson, 1987) suggest that four types of preexisting knowledge structures are important in newly forming relationships: generalized schema for a particular class of relationships, relationship-specific schema for other close relationships, self-schema, and prototypic conceptions of relational constructs. The other uses these knowledge structures initially to interpret the partner's behavior. Over time as the relationship becomes more established, relationship-specific knowledge structures are formed, including relationship-specific schema, assessments of relational constructs, and causal accounts (see Figure 11.1). The partner utilizes the same types of knowledge to evaluate the other's behavior and respond to it. During periods of growth and deterioration, structures specific to the target relationship are already in place, and partners use them as well as previously existing structures to interpret the other's behavior and to select an appropriate behavioral response.

Knowledge structures and the formation of relationships.   Research on impression formation in new relationships indicates that partners develop knowledge (or schema) about the other and the relationship fairly quickly (Park, 1986; Wilkinson, 1987). Park (1986) studied the development of impressions of real,

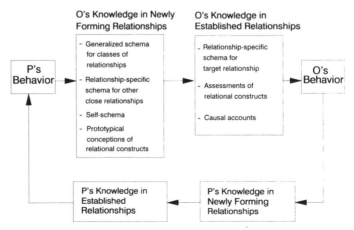

FIG. 11.1. Knowledge structures and the development of relationships (P = partner and O = other).

previously unacquainted individuals over a 7-week period. Categorization of the content of impressions showed that the most frequent description was of traits (65%), followed by behaviors (23%). Over the course of the study, the use of traits increased, whereas the use of behaviors decreased, suggesting that impressions become more abstract as people get to know each other. Descriptors initially used predominated in subsequent impressions. Thus, information about the other's attributes was acquired early, and once in place was relatively stable. Wilkinson's (1987) qualitative study of impression formation further suggests that interpersonal knowledge is acquired early. Interpersonal knowledge obtained early on includes information about how the self behaves compared with the other, how similar the self is to the other, and what each contributes to the relationship.

A generalized schema for a class of relationships is one source of prior knowledge that contributes to the development of relational knowledge. A generalized schema contains beliefs about what a relationship is typically like, normative beliefs about what makes a relationship good or bad, and rules for appropriate behavior. Schemas about friendship, for example, contain the beliefs that they are a source of enjoyment, assistance, companionship, authenticity, and intimate disclosure (Davis & Todd, 1985), and the rules that friends show emotional support, share news of success, strive to make each other happy, volunteer help, confide in each other, and stand up for the other (Argyle & Henderson, 1984). In order to draw conclusions about the target relationship, a person compares the other's behavior and characteristics of the target relationship with features of the generalized schema, such as what is typical or acceptable for that type of relationship (Planalp & Rivers, 1988; Surra et al., 1988; Surra & Huston, 1987). A woman's observation, for instance, that her partner has a stable job and a good income might lead to the conclusion that he would make a good husband or that the partners are ready to wed. Similarly, the observation that "we never fight" may result in the belief that the relationship is marriageable.

Other sources of preexisting knowledge employed during relationship formation are relationship-specific schemas for other close relationships, for instance, knowledge about my past romance with Bill, my former marriage to Allison, or my relationship with my brother. Judgments about the target relationship are made by comparing the target's behavior with characteristics of known close relationships (Surra & Milardo, in press). A man's observation that his girlfriend talks to his little brother like his mother talks to his little brother, for example, might lead to the conclusion that the girlfriend is "kind like his mother." Social comparison processes are particularly useful in close relationships for making assessments of valence, value, and ability, for which there are no physical yardsticks (Surra & Milardo, in press). Likewise, interpersonal beliefs are formulated on the basis of comparisons between qualities of known close relationships with the target relationship, as when an individual concludes that "I must have cared about her" because "I was spending as much time with her as with my brothers and sisters."

Self-knowledge may be used to form relational knowledge in the same way that knowledge about other close relationships is used: Information about the self is a standard by which the other and the relationship can be judged. Wilkinson (1987) found that comparisons involving the self come into play frequently in the formation of first impressions, and tend to decrease over time, supporting the notion that prior knowledge structures—in this case, self-schema—operate most powerfully during relationship formation.

Other memory stores that affect the formation of relationships are prototypical conceptions of the meaning of love, commitment, and other relational constructs. These conceptions undoubtedly influence the initial, semantic interpretations of another's behavior and assessments of whether and how the constructs apply to the target relationship. Fehr's (1988) research on love and commitment suggests several processes by which this occurs. As described previously, love and commitment both have a set of attributes that define them, and each has core attributes that are most central to its definitions. When behavioral data fit prototypical attributes well, especially the core attributes, people will judge their relationships as possessing the construct, even when the behavioral data are fairly limited. Consistent with this view, Fehr (1988) found that increases in love and commitment in different hypothetical relationships were associated with increases in the relevance of their attributes, especially their central attributes. In addition, for both love and commitment, violations of central attributes had a greater impact on hypothetical relationships than did violations of peripheral attributes (Fehr, 1988).

The relational constructs people ascribe to their relationships also may be affected by the interrelatedness among the prototypical features of each construct. Fehr (1988) found that, once the concepts of love and commitment were activated by presenting subjects with descriptors of each construct, subjects falsely remembered and recognized attributes that were not present. Such findings indicate that encountering only part of the defining attributes of a construct may lead partners to "fill in the blanks" by attributing related characteristics that may not be present in the other's behavior. Believing that a relationship possesses these features will, in turn, affect the selection of a behavioral response. The fact that prototypes for different constructs share some attributes in common further suggests that ascribing one construct may contribute to ascribing another. Experiencing the features of love may automatically be accompanied by increased commitment (or vice versa), even in the absence of other evidence indicative of commitment. Such inferential leaps may be especially hazardous when it comes to commitment, as its definitional qualities are much more global than those of love (Fehr, 1988; Kelley, 1983). Conversely, violations of the shared features of love and commitment may have unwarranted impact on both.

Knowledge structures and the growth and deterioration of relationships. Once they are in place, relational knowledge structures primarily guide the interpretation of the other's behavior and the selection of a response (see top right of Figure 11.1). During periods of growth and deterioration, the content and structure of relational knowledge change in response to behavioral data that are inconsistent with established relational knowledge. According to Srull and Wyer's (1989) model of person memory, inconsistent behaviors have either evaluative or descriptive implications that differ from the implications of concepts already in place. Inconsistent behaviors become associated in memory with other behaviors consistent with the concept and must be reconciled with them. The interbehavior associations mean that inconsistent behaviors are more likely than are consistent ones to be remembered later (Srull & Wyer, 1989). The recall advantage of inconsistent behaviors increases the likelihood that they will influence the interpretation and encoding of other, related inconsistent behaviors. In addition, the recall advantage of one inconsistent behavior means that subsequent recurrent instances of the same behavior will be associated with it (Planalp, 1987). The interpretation of inconsistent behaviors may require that information from knowledge structures other than relational structures be called into service, especially those that contain information about what close relationships should be like or usually are like (see top left of Figure 11.1).

How do inconsistent behaviors trigger change in relational knowledge? Two models of schema change are especially relevant to close relationships (see Crocker, Fiske, & Taylor, 1984; Planalp, 1987; Rothbart, 1981). The first is the bookkeeping model, in which gradual changes are made each time an incongruence arises. In the bookkeeping model, recurrent inconsistent behaviors result in slow changes in relational knowledge. The second, or conversion model, refers to sudden changes incorporated as the result of dramatic or salient events. In this model, change may stem from one behavior or a set of interrelated, co-occurring behaviors that are incompatible with existing knowledge.

Both the conversion and bookkeeping models have been observed in the development of relationships. Drawing on data from newlyweds' recollections of why their commitment increased or decreased over the course of their courtships, Surra and her colleagues (Surra et al., 1988) outlined two types of commitment processes: event-driven and relationship-driven. Relationship-driven commitments were based in such interpersonal attributions as spending (or not spending) time together, engaging (or not engaging) in particular activities, and disclosing (or not disclosing) information to each other. These sorts of reasons also were associated with moderate changes in commitment that occurred over longer periods of time. Relationship-driven commitments, in which positive or negative changes in commitment occur gradually, based on the exchange of behaviors, are akin to bookkeeping models of schema change. Event-driven commitments are similar to the conversion model of schema change. Event-driven commitments were rooted in salient or dramatic happenings that seemed to provide immediate, undeniable information about commitment. Most often the happenings involved the social network, such as finding out that parents approved of the partner or attending the wedding of two best friends. Events also concerned certain types of dyadic occurrences, however, as when one partner independently and voluntarily did something that altered the other's conception (e.g., giving up a summer vacation to be with the partner, the partner getting into a bloody fight at a ballgame) or a decision concerning a new stage of involvement (e.g., getting engaged or disengaged). Planalp and Rivers (1988) concluded that the conversion model best fit respondents' explanations for why their uncertainty increased about an established relationship. They also noted, however, that this model and the bookkeeping model were not entirely adequate for explaining uncertainty increase (also see Planalp et al., 1988).

During growth and deterioration, changes in relational schema are influenced by other schema pertinent to relationships, including generalized schema for classes of relationships, relationship-specific schema for other close relationships, self-schema, and prototypical conceptions of relational constructs. As we pointed out in our discussion of relationship formation, these schemas frequently provide interpretive information about the acceptability of novel behaviors. They operate similarly in the interpretation of inconsistent behaviors during growth and deterioration. Planalp and Rivers (1988) found, for example, that violations of relationship rules were common reasons for increases in uncertainty in already established relationships.

Causal accounts and changes in relational knowledge. Whether people will engage in the cognitive work required to encode information about inconsistent behaviors is influenced by a variety of factors, such as the limits of their attention, the accessibility of the schema, and their motivation to assess behavior accurately (Crocker et al., 1984; Srull & Wyer, 1989). One factor especially relevant to close relationships is causal accounts (see Figure 11.1). The content of some accounts makes it possible to explain away inconsistencies such that relational knowledge is unaffected (Planalp & Rivers, 1988). Attribution to nonrelational causes (e.g., causes external or internal to the partners) or to unstable or specific causes are two means of dismissing the impact of inconsistent behaviors. For example, attributing a friend's refusal to return telephone calls to a busy work schedule, rather than to the friend's desire to cool the relationship, leaves relational knowledge intact.

Discounting by attribution to nonrelational causes is especially common in dating relationships of poor quality. Fletcher et al., (1987) found that daters who reported more attributions to external causes for relationship maintenance had lower levels of happiness, love, and commitment. Surra et al. (1988) found that newlyweds who gave a higher proportion of social network reasons for being committed during courtship had lower levels of marital happiness four years later. In addition, studies of partners who wed (Surra et al., 1988; Surra & Huston, 1987) and those who broke up (Lloyd & Cate, 1985) have shown that positive changes in commitment were more likely to be attributed to interpersonal causes than to other causes, whereas negative changes were more likely to be attributed to social network, circumstantial, and intrapersonal causes than to interpersonal causes. Explaining away by means of attribution to nonrelational causes may be characteristic of partners in unhappy dating relationships or of partners whose commitment is declining because of the need to account for negative events and behaviors while preserving an idealized view of the relationship. Alternatively, some partners may simply attend more to external and intrapersonal events than to interpersonal ones in the first place and, therefore, may base their decisions about relationships on assessments that have little to do with the nature of the relationship. As a result, they may make poor relationship choices (Surra et al., 1988; Surra & Huston, 1987). (See Bradbury & Fincham, 1990, for a review of literature on how attributions affect the interpretation of behavior.)

The tendency to ignore or discount the impact of inconsistent information on relational knowledge will be affected by characteristics of the events, the partners, and the relationship. Certain kinds of events are more undeniable than others, as when one spouse finds his or her partner in bed with a lover. Similarly, sometimes the pattern or confluence of events (e.g., the dating partner's withdrawal combined with a friend's message that "I saw Jack sitting with another girl in the Union last night") clearly points to a cause that concerns relational knowledge (Planalp & Rivers, 1988). One characteristic that is apt to influence the explaining away of inconsistent behaviors is the extent of outcome dependence. Partners whose outcome dependence is high, perhaps because they perceive few alternatives, should be more likely to discount the impact of inconsistent behaviors than partners who have low outcome dependence. Finally, the stage of the relationship itself will influence the kinds of attributions that are likely to occur. Attributions to the self or the partner tend to predominate once relationships are over (Cupach & Metts, 1986; Fletcher, 1983a; Lloyd & Cate, 1985), perhaps in order to separate oneself from the relationship and to gain a sense of control over its ending. Interpersonal attributions may dominate when partners are focused on maintaining a well-functioning relationship (see Fletcher et al., 1987).

Cognitive Processing During Periods of Stability

During times of stability, information processing frequently is lower order; partners process information subconsciously and automatically, without attention to processing goals. In some cases, partners may have goals that require calling up information from memory, but even this is easily accomplished because the other's behaviors are readily interpretable and behavioral responses are effortlessly chosen according to existing relational knowledge. This situation exists because, during maintenance, behavioral patterns are routinized and their meaning is known. Certainty about how to interpret behaviors is high.

During stability, the other's behavior typically is interpreted at a low level of abstraction in terms of its semantic meaning by the Comprehender (see Wyer &

Srull, 1986). Thus, in a long-term marriage, much of the conversation that transpires may be meaningful only with respect to the content it conveys. The end-of-the-day conversation, for instance, may simply reveal, "John picked up the dry-cleaning" and "Mary will be late coming home tomorrow." In many instances, processing is at such a low level that partners may become quite adept at holding up their end of a conversation while half attending to the other's behavior. At these times, partners attend enough to keep informed about the general nature of what is transpiring (see Wyer & Srull, 1986). This type of processing is automatic: It does not require a goal for activation, it makes minimal demands on capacity, and its activation is uncontrolled (Bargh, 1984).

When processing objectives require it, the Encoder/Organizer may be called upon to interpret information at a higher level, but during stability, it readily does so by utilizing previously encoded abstractions (Wyer & Srull, 1986). Thus, John may say to himself, "What did Mary mean by that remark?" but a casual search of his memory provides the answer to his question and an appropriate response. The search can be casual because it has been done many times before: Similar behaviors have been observed, their links to other behaviors have been noted, and the abstract concept that applies has been ascribed. According to Srull and Wyer (1989), the likelihood of recalling a representation increases according to the recency with which the representation was used and stored in the past. In addition, the probability of recalling specific behaviors is a function of the frequency with which various associations (e.g., between behaviors or between behaviors and concepts) have been traversed in the past. Over time, the mental search becomes increasingly localized. This is why in established relationships, where the same behavioral sequences are repeated again and again, even drawing upon memory stores does not demand much cognitive work.

Compared with instability, where partners are motivated to gather specific types of information about the partner and the relationship, processing goals during stability are simple and easily achieved. The two goals that apply during stability are common to communication in many social situations: the transmission of descriptive or factual information and the sending of an appropriate behavioral response (Scott, Fuhrman, & Wyer, this volume). The procedures that will accomplish these goals are already available in memory in goal schema. Thus, enacting the procedures that will achieve processing goals becomes automatic (Wyer & Srull, 1986).

Knowledge Structures During Periods of Stability

During periods of relationship stability, relational knowledge structures (see top right of Figure 11.1) exert the most powerful influences on behavior and its interpretation. In addition, the content and structure of relational knowledge are unchanging. One reason is that, during stability, most behaviors will be consistent with previously existing relational knowledge. Moreover, causal accounts of why interaction events happen as they do are already in place and are utilized to interpret consistent behavioral events (see Fletcher & Fincham, this volume). When behaviors are consistent with prior knowledge, they are easily assimilated into it (Markus & Zajonc, 1985; Planalp, 1987).

Another, more interesting feature of stability is that even inconsistent behaviors are assimilated into prior knowledge. As discussed previously, the encoding, retrieval, and judgment of behaviors are skewed in a way that confirms what is already known, even in the face of considerable data to the contrary (Planalp, 1987; Rothbart, 1981). When faced with an inconsistent behavior, partners may engage in bolstering, or the reviewing of consistent behaviors to reaffirm established knowledge (Srull & Wyer, 1989). One example of the skewing of behavioral information in close relationships is sentiment override, which refers to the tendency of spouses to interpret each other's behaviors to be consistent with their subjective assessments of their marriages, such as how happy or in love they are, but inconsistent with the way an objective outsider would interpret behaviors (see Surra & Ridley, 1991, for a review). Sentiment override suggests that partners are ignoring or misinterpreting the meaning of behavioral data and, instead, are relying upon what they already know.

Inconsistent behaviors will have little impact during relationship stability because of the features of relational knowledge structures that make them resistant to change (see Crocker et al., 1984). They are detailed (i.e., they contain a lot of information); they are complex (i.e., their content is highly interrelated); they are closely linked to other important knowledge structures (e.g., about the self and other close relationships); and they are distinctive and unique (i.e., considerable knowledge about a close relationship is specialized).

One characteristic that makes relational knowledge structures particularly unyielding is that they are interdependent, or shared to some extent between partners. Interdependence of relational knowledge means that it is reinforced not only by intrapersonal processes (e.g., frequency and recency of use), but also by the content of information exchanged during interaction.

Relational knowledge is interdependent in two ways: differentiated memory and integrated memory (Wegner et al., 1984). Integrated memory refers to knowledge shared between partners or the degree of congruence between partners' knowledge. Through the processes of dyadic interchange, partners share knowledge and their interpretations of events. Communicating about events increases the likelihood that partners will develop similar knowledge structures and that, once encoded, the similarity will be updated and reinforced during future interactions. Differentiated memory refers to the unshared knowledge each partner has (Wegner et al., 1984). Although differentiated knowledge is not shared, each partner has access to it by means of communication. In order to access the other's differentiated knowledge, the partner must know the kind of information possessed by the other and how it is structured (Wegner et al., 1984). A husband, for example, may rely on the wife to store information about significant relationship events: the day they met, where they went on their first date, and even the date of their wedding. Even though the husband does not have this information, he knows where and how to get it. Repeated interchanges in which partners assess each other's differentiated memories reinforce the status quo, and help to explain why existing relational knowledge is so intransigent.

CONCLUSION

This chapter provides a framework for understanding how cognition affects the development of close relationships. Cognitive activity in response to behavior during interaction was conceived in terms of an information-processing approach. We also examined how knowledge structures specific to a close relationship develop and, once developed, how they change over time. The ideas presented here are the products of two divergent research traditions, one on social cognition and the other on personal relationships. The two traditions diverge in several respects. Social cognition research usually relies on experimental methods in which standardized materials about hypothetical people, interactions, or relationships are used as stimuli. Scholars who study cognition in close relationships, in contrast, often utilize field research in which self-reports or qualitative case studies are gathered. Even studies of close relationships in laboratory contexts are comparatively uncontrolled. The fact that approaches with such different starting points have converged in their views of close relationships is testimony to the usefulness of each approach.

Is cognition in close relationships different from cognition in impersonal relationships? We believe that it is. Interaction in close relationships tends to reify knowledge structures in ways that other social interactions do not. This is because conversations between intimates often concern the very structure and content of each individual's memory, especially their relational knowledge. Communication enables partners to develop accurate relational knowledge (e.g., Does he still care about me?), to ensure that they share the same relational knowledge, and to discover the limits of their common knowledge and each one's specialized knowledge. In close relationships, cognitions frequently are the substance of communication, and interaction, in turn, solidifies relational memories.

REFERENCES

Argyle, M., & Henderson, M. (1984). The rules of friendship. *Journal of Social and Personal Relationships, 1,* 211–237.
Bargh, J. A. (1984). Automatic and conscious processing of social information. In R. S. Wyer, & T. K. Srull (Eds.), *Handbook of social cognition* (Vol. 3, pp. 1–43). Hillsdale, NJ: Erlbaum.
Baxter, L. A. (1986). Gender differences in the heterosexual relationship rules embedded in break-up accounts. *Journal of Social and Personal Relationships, 3,* 289–306.

Berger, C. (1979). Beyond initial interaction: Uncertainty, understanding, and the development of interpersonal relationships. In H. Giles & R. St. Clair (Eds.), *Language and social psychology* (pp. 122–144). Baltimore: University Park Press.

Berscheid, E. (1983). Emotion. In Kelley, H. H., Berscheid, E., Christensen, A., Harvey, J. H., Huston, T. L., Levinger, G., McClintock, E., Peplau, L. A., & Peterson, D. R. (Eds.), *Close Relationships* (pp. 110–168). NY: W. H. Freeman.

Berscheid, E., & Graziano, W. (1979). The initiation of social relationships and social attraction. In R. L. Burgess and T. L. Huston (Eds.), *Social exchange in developing relationships* (pp. 31–60). New York: Academic Press.

Bradbury, T. N., & Fincham, F. D. (1987). Affect and cognition in close relationships: Towards an integrative model. *Cognition and Emotion, 1,* 59–87.

Bradbury, T. N., & Fincham, F. D. (1990). Attributions in marriage: A review and critique. *Psychological Bulletin, 107,* 3–33.

Braiker, H. B., & Kelley, H. H. (1979). Conflict in the development of close relationships. In R. L. Burgess and T. L. Huston (Eds.), *Social exchange in developing relationships* (pp. 135–168). New York: Academic Press.

Crocker, J., Fiske, S. T., & Taylor, S. E. (1984). Schematic bases of belief change. In J. R. Eiser (Ed.), *Attitudinal judgment* (pp. 197–226). New York: Springer-Verlag.

Cupach, W. R., & Metts, S. (1986). Accounts of relational dissolution: A comparison of marital and non-marital relationships. *Communication Monographs, 53,* 311–334.

Davis, K. E., & Todd, M. J. (1985). Assessing friendship: Prototypes, paradigm cases and relationship description. In S. Duck & D. Perlman (Eds.), *Understanding personal relationships: An interdisciplinary approach* (pp. 17–38). Beverly Hills, CA: Sage.

Fehr, B. (1988). Prototype analysis of the concepts of love and commitment. *Journal of Personality and Social Psychology, 55,* 557–579.

Fincham, F. D., Bradbury, T. N., & Scott, C. K. (1990). Cognition in marriage. In F. D. Fincham & T. N. Bradbury (Eds.), *The psychology of marriage* (pp. 118–149). New York: Guilford Press.

Fincham, F. D., & Bradbury, T. N. (in press). Cognition in marriage: A program of research on attributions. In D. Perlman & W. Jones (Eds.), *Advances in personal relationships* (Vol. 2). London: Kingsley.

Fiske, S. T., & Cox, M. G. (1979). Person concepts: The effect of target familiarity and descriptive purpose on the process of describing others. *Journal of Personality, 47,* 137–161.

Fletcher, G. J. O. (1983a). The analysis of verbal explanations for marital separation: Implications for attribution theory. *Journal of Applied Social Psychology, 13,* 245–258.

Fletcher, G. J. O. (1983b). Sex differences in attributions for marital separation. *New Zealand Journal of Psychology, 13,* 82–89.

Fletcher, G. J. O., & Fitness, J. (1990). Occurrent social cognition in close relationship interaction: The role of proximal and distal variables. *Journal of Personality and Social Psychology, 59,* 464–474.

Fletcher, G. J. O., Fincham, F., Cramer, L., & Heron, N. (1987). The role of attributions in close relationships. *Journal of Personality and Social Psychology, 53,* 481–489.

Harvey, J. H., Agostinelli, G., & Weber, A. L. (1989). Account-making and the formation of expectations about close relationships. In C. Hendrick (Ed.), *Review of personality and social psychology: Close relationships* (Vol. 10, pp. 39–62). Newbury Park, CA: Sage.

Harvey, J. H., Weber, A. L., Galvin, K. S., Huszti, H. C., & Garnick, N. N. (1986). Attribution and the termination of close relationships: A special focus on the account. In R. Gilmour & S. Duck (Eds.), *The emerging field of personal relationships* (pp. 189–201). Hillsdale, NJ: Erlbaum.

Harvey, J. H., Wells, G. L., & Alvarez, M. D. (1978). Attribution in the context of conflict and separation in close relationships. In J. Harvey, W. Ickes, & R. Kidd (Eds.), *New directions in attribution research* (Vol. 2, pp. 235–259). Hillsdale, NJ: Erlbaum.

Heider, F. (1958). *The psychology of interpersonal relations.* New York: Wiley.

Ickes, W., Tooke, W., Stinson, L., Baker, V. L., & Bissonnette, V. (1988). Naturalistic social cognition: Intersubjectivity in same-sex dyads. *Journal of Nonverbal Behavior, 12*, 58–84.

Kelley, H. H. (1979). *Personal relationships.* Hillsdale, NJ: Erlbaum.

Kelley, H. H. (1983). Love and commitment. In H. H. Kelley, E. Berscheid, A. Christensen, J. H. Harvey, T. L. Huston, G. Levinger, E. McClintock, L. A. Peplau, & D. R. Peterson (Eds.), *Close relationships* (pp. 265–311). New York: Freeman.

Kelley, H. H., Berscheid, E., Christensen, A., Harvey, J. H., Huston, T. L., Levinger, G., McClintock, E., Peplau, L. A., & Peterson, D. R. (Eds.). (1983). *Close relationships.* New York: Freeman.

Levenson, R. W., & Gottman, J. M. (1983). Marital interaction: Physiological linkage and affective exchange. *Journal of Personality and Social Psychology, 45*, 587–597.

Lloyd, S. A., & Cate, R. M. (1985). Attributions associated with significant turning points in premarital relationship development and dissolution. *Journal of Social and Personal Relationships, 2*, 419–436.

Markus, H., & Zajonc, R. B. (1985). The cognitive perspective in social psychology. In G. Lindzey & E. Aronson (Eds.), *The handbook of social psychology* (Vol. 1, pp. 137–230).

Noller, P., & Guthrie, D. (in press). Studying communication in marriage: An integration and critical evaluation. In W. H. Jones & D. Perlman (Eds.), *Advances in personal relationships* (Vol. 3). London: Kingsley.

Park, B. (1986). A method for studying the development of impressions of real people. *Journal of Personality and Social Psychology, 51*, 907–917.

Planalp, S. (1985). Relational schemata: A test of alternative forms of relational knowledge as guides to communication. *Human Communication Research, 12*, 3–29.

Planalp, S. (1987). Interplay between relational knowledge and events. In R. Burnett, P. McGhee, & D. Clark (Eds.), *Accounting for relationships: Explanation, representation, and knowledge* (pp. 175–191). London: Methuen.

Planalp, S., & Honeycutt, J. M. (1985). Events that increase uncertainty in personal relationships. *Human Communication Research, 11*, 593–604.

Planalp, S., & Rivers, M. (1988). *Changes in knowledge of relationships.* Paper presented at the Interpersonal and Small Group Division, International Communication Association, New Orleans, LA.

Planalp, S., Rutherford, D. K., & Honeycutt, J. M. (1988). Events that increase uncertainty in personal relationships: II. Replication and extension. *Human Communication Research, 14*, 516–547.

Rothbart, M. (1981). Memory processes and social beliefs. In D. L. Hamilton (Ed.), *Cognitive processes in stereotyping and intergroup behavior* (pp. 145–181). Hillsdale, NJ: Erlbaum.

Shaver, P., Schwartz, J., Kirson, D., & O'Connor, C. (1987). Emotion knowledge: Further exploration of a prototype approach. *Journal of Personality and Social Psychology, 52*, 1061–1086.

Srull, T. K., & Wyer, R. S. (1989). Person memory and judgment. *Psychological Review, 96*, 58–83.

Surra, C. A. (1987). Reasons for changes in commitment: Variations by courtship type. *Journal of Social and Personal Relationships, 4*, 17–33.

Surra, C. A., Arizzi, P. & Asmussen, L. A. (1988). The association between reasons for commitment and the development and outcome of marital relationships. *Journal of Social and Personal Relationships, 5*, 47–63.

Surra, C. A., & Huston, T. L. (1987). Mate selection as a social transition. In D. Perlman & S. Duck (Eds.), *Intimate relationships: Development, dynamics, and deterioration* (pp. 89–120). Newbury Park, CA: Sage.

Surra, C. A., & Milardo, R. M. (in press). The social psychological context of developing relationships: Interactive and psychological networks. In W. H. Jones & D. Perlman (Eds.), *Advances in personal relationships* (Vol. 3). London: Kingsley.

Surra, C. A., & Planalp, S. (1990, July). *The structure of causal accounts of commitment.* Paper presented at the International Society for the Study of Personal Relationships. Oxford, England.

Surra, C. A., & Ridley, C. A. (1991). Multiple perspectives on interaction: Participants, peers, and observers. In B. Montgomery & S. Duck (Eds.), *Studying interpersonal interaction* (pp. 35–55). New York: Guilford Press.

Thibaut, J. W., & Kelley, H. H. (1959). *The social psychology of groups.* New York: Wiley.

Weber, A. L., Harvey, J. H., & Stanley, M. A. (1987). The nature and motivations of accounts for failed relationships. In R. Burnett, P. McGhee, & D. Clark (Eds.), *Accounting for relationships: Explanation, representation, and knowledge* (pp. 115–133). London: Methuen.

Wegner, D. M., Giuliano, T., & Hertel, P. T. (1984). Cognitive interdependence in close relationships. In W. Ickes (Ed.), *Compatible and incompatible relationships* (pp. 253–273). New York: Springer-Verlag.

Weiss, R. L. (1975). *Marital separation.* New York: Basic Books.

Weiss, R. L. (1984). Cognitive and behavioral measures of marital interaction. In K. Hahlweg & N. S. Jacobson (Eds.), *Marital interaction: Analysis and modification* (pp. 232–252). New York: Guilford Press.

Wilkinson, S. (1987). Explorations of self and other in a developing relationship. In R. Burnett, P. McGhee, & D. Clark (Eds.), *Accounting for relationships: Explanation, representation, and knowledge* (pp. 40–59). London: Methuen.

Wyer, R. S., & Srull, T. K. (1986). Human cognition in its social context. *Psychological Review, 93,* 322–359.

12

Social Cognition and the Relationship Repair Process: Toward Better Outcome in Marital Therapy

Steven R. H. Beach
University of Georgia

Approximately 20% of all married couples are experiencing marital discord at any given time (Beach, Arias, & O'Leary, 1987), and about half of all new-lyweds in first marriages will divorce (Glick, 1984). Marital discord, in turn, has been identified as an important variable in the etiology and treatment of a variety of psychological disorders (Beach, Sandeen, & O'Leary, 1990; Hafner, 1986; Jacobson, Holtzworth-Monroe, & Schmaling, 1989). However, it is only within recent years that the treatment of marital discord has received appropriate scrutiny through controlled outcome research (for reviews, see Baucom & Hoffman, 1986; Beach and O'Leary, 1985; Hahlweg & Markman, 1988; Weiss & Heyman, 1990). It is now apparent that there is considerable variability in response to treatment of marital discord and that the mean response to treatment is not optimal (Jacobson et al., 1984; O'Leary & Arias, 1983).

Beach and Bauserman (1990) noted that despite a number of attempts to enhance marital therapy outcome through the combination of treatment approaches, there is no evidence that these multifaceted interventions result in enhanced outcome. Indeed, we appear to be approaching an asymptote with regard to effectiveness in marital therapy with no breakthroughs being promised by the current approach to marital therapy outcome research (cf. Baucom, Sayers, & Sher, 1990). The purpose of this chapter, therefore, is to discuss other ways of improving marital therapy outcome. We argue that the greatest gains will occur when we (a) more clearly specify mediating goals of therapy, (b) identify moderator variables that identify couples who are not likely to achieve success on the mediating goals of therapy, and (c) use extant models from social psychology to provide guidance in identifying these moderators and designing interventions aimed at couples who would otherwise experience failure in current treatment programs. In particular, we show how the social-psychological liter-ature can help illuminate mechanisms that prevent couples from achieving max-imum benefit from currently used marital interventions.

PROCESS RESEARCH

Beach and O'Leary (1985) argued that before outcome in marital therapy could be enhanced, the reasons for nonresponse and less than optimal response to marital therapy need to be better understood. They suggested that greater atten-tion needed to be paid to mediating goals of therapy, that is, those goals of therapy whose attainment is hypothesized to produce improvement on the criteri-on of success. In other contexts, mediating goals of therapy have also been referred to as "points of intervention," that is, those areas best targeted for change in therapy (Beach, Abramson, & Levine, 1981). When tied together in integrated models, sets of mediating goals have been referred to as clinically relevant models of the problem to be addressed in therapy; that is, a roadmap for optimal clinical intervention for a given individual or couple (Beach et al., 1990). This variety of terms highlights the clinical importance and utility of having clearly specified mediating goals of therapy.

Beach and O'Leary (1985) argued that having clearly specified mediating goals of therapy was also important from the standpoint of clinical research. If variability in response to treatment is due to differential attainment of the mediat-ing goals of therapy, then it can be argued that treatment is on the right track but has not yet fulfilled its potential. In these circumstances, strategies for enhancing gains on mediating goals could be expected to result in greater average gains and a greater percentage of couples showing clinically significant change. On the other hand, to the extent that variability in response to treatment cannot be ascribed to differential attainment of mediating goals of therapy, this demon-strates a likely need to incorporate new mediating goals into the approach to therapy or else to revise the set of mediating goals proposed (cf. Gottman, 1979).

The two scenarios described have different implications. The first (i.e., vari-ability is related to nonattainment of mediating goals) would suggest that there should be a more in-depth examination of the reasons for nonattainment of the mediating goals of therapy. The second (i.e., variability is *not* related to nonat-tainment of mediating goals) would suggest a need to turn to more basic work on the structure of marital relationships and elaborate the set of mediating goals of therapy by including new constructs derived from this more basic work.

To clarify further the proposal made by Beach and O'Leary (1985), consider the logic of the proposal with regard to a particular set of mediating goals, for example, relationship skills. Given a standard outcome study with a treated and an untreated group, which have been assessed with regard to marital satisfaction and level of relationship skills, it should be possible to follow the logic outlined by Baron and Kenny (1986) and directly test the hypothesis that development of relationship skills mediates post-therapy marital satisfaction. Specifically, one could show that the treated group had superior outcome to the untreated group, that the treated group had superior levels of relationship skills to the untreated group, and that when outcome was regressed on relationship skills and treatment condition, the regression coefficient for treatment condition was reduced relative to its value when outcome was regressed on treatment condition alone. Complete mediation would be shown if all the above conditions held and, in addition, the regression weight for treatment dropped to zero when level of relationship skills was added to the regression equation. Complications involving less than completely reliable measurement and reverse causation may need to be considered in interpreting the results of a test of a hypothesized mediator (Baron & Kenny, 1986). In particular, because the mediator is likely to be measured with error, the regression analysis is likely to provide an underestimate of its role.

Once the mediational importance of relationship skills had been established in this way, it would be profitable to continue the examination. Mediational status would be assumed to have already been demonstrated, but the model could be subjected to a more intense test. Specifically, relationship skills assessed post-therapy could be used to predict post-therapy marital satisfaction within the treated group. It should be possible to determine to what extent the couple's attainment in relationship skills (the hypothesized mediating goal of therapy) accounts for post-therapy level of marital satisfaction (the criterion of successful outcome). To the extent that post-therapy relationship skill accounted for little variance in post-therapy marital satisfaction, other variables in addition to relationship skills would be needed if post-therapy marital satisfaction was to be explained adequately. This would justify the search for an expanded model of marital satisfaction, with additional possible points of intervention, along with a search for additional intervention components capable of producing change at the new points of intervention specified in the expanded model.

Although more complicated sets of mediating goals would produce more terms to include in a regression analysis, the fundamental logic would be the same. Thus, the same type of analysis could be repeated with a more complicated mediational model. Indeed, the logic would fail only if the therapy is very successful and if all couples are making relatively equivalent positive changes, or if the treatment is so inert that no gains are being made by anyone on the mediating goals of therapy. Stated differently, there will be problems for this approach to the validation of mediating goals when there is little variability in either the predictor variables (the mediating goals) or the dependent variable (the criterion of success).

In other situations, failure to find a strong relationship between attainment of mediating goals and the outcome of therapy suggests either problems of measurement or inadequacies in the proposed set of mediating goals. Because marital therapy technologies that currently possess documented effectiveness show good variability, both with regard to couple attainment of mediating goals of therapy and with regard to outcome of therapy, the process approach appears applicable to all mainstream marital therapy technologies. At present, however, considerable work is needed both to clarify the mediating goals of therapy, hypothesized to be important for successful change in marital therapy, and to specify particular models in social psychology that can be helpful in better understanding the nonattainment of mediating goals.

Once developed, is a well-formulated set of mediating goals of therapy useful? When a researcher is successful in formulating an integrated set of mediating goals of therapy, each of which constitutes an independent point of therapeutic intervention, the product is a clinically useful change model capable of guiding therapeutic intervention. At its best, a model of this type helps organize clinical activity in a natural and fluid manner, allowing the clinician to focus on tailoring specific interventions to fit the client couple, while keeping the clinician well grounded in the relevant research literature. It follows, then, that the mediating goals of therapy should be specified in a way that ties them to a literature capable of providing guidance about the production of change in each goal (Beach et al., 1990). In some cases this literature may be an applied literature dealing with particular marital techniques. In other cases, the literature may be more basic but provide suggestions or the broad outlines of potentially effective interventions. It is likely to be clinically unhelpful to propose as mediating goals of therapy facets of the relationship that cannot be changed directly, that are in no way tied to possible intervention strategies by the therapist, or that all imply the same intervention approach.

Elaboration of the Process Approach

As suggested previously, a process approach can lead in two directions, depending on the ability of the set of mediating goals proposed by the researcher to account for change. First, if the specified set of mediating goals of therapy *failed* to account for much of the variability in treatment response, it would be reasonable to conclude that some change in the proposed mediating goals of therapy was called for. The researcher might hypothesize that *additional* mediating goals of therapy were needed, or that a somewhat different formulation of the change process was necessary.

For example, if the researcher had specified previously a set of mediating goals of therapy that included only relationship skill attainment, the failure of these variables to account for a substantial portion of the variance in outcome might prompt the researcher to add, for example, cognitive variables or the ability to verbalize reasons for negative feelings as additional or alternative mediating goals of therapy. The utility of these additions could be tested directly by including measures of these constructs in the study along with the original set of hypothesized mediating goals of therapy. If the new variables both conformed to the requirements of true mediators, outlined above (Baron & Kenny, 1986), and accounted for additional variance in outcome beyond that already accounted for by the original set of mediating goals, this would be strong support for accepting the elaborated change model with its additional mediating goals of therapy. Alternatively, if the new variables failed to mediate the effect of treatment because the treatment produced no change in the new variables but accounted for significant additional variance in outcome, this would suggest the utility of adding interventions tied to each new mediating goal. A subsequent study using the logic outlined previously would be necessary to confirm that the variables were true mediators of effective treatment, and that the interventions tied to the new mediating goals were capable of producing change.

One important advantage of a change model, which identified several mediators of the effect of treatment on outcome, is the implication that some couples might be in need of change on only one or several, as opposed to all, of the mediating goals of therapy. A multifaceted change model, accordingly, provides some guidance in the task of tailoring treatment to match the needs of a given client couple. Couples could be provided with those interventions most directly related to the specific mediators on which they are deficient. In this way, process research should lead to technological diversification that is likely to be a useful addition to existing marital therapy programs. For example, if cognitive variables were found to be a useful addition to the change model in marital therapy, this would suggest that some couples may need intervention targeted primarily at cognition, whereas other couples may need change targeted only at relationship skills or perhaps at both cognition and marital skills (cf. Baucom et al., 1990). Assessment tied to each mediating goal of therapy, conducted prior to therapy, would indicate which couples should receive the interventions.

The second direction that might result from adopting a process approach would be the study of how to enhance the magnitude of change on particular mediating goals of therapy. Variability in gains in marital satisfaction may well be accounted for by couple differences in attainment of the hypothesized set of mediating goals of therapy. In this case, the researcher will be led to focus on finding methods for enhancing attainment of particular mediating goals, or reasons why some couples do not make sufficient progress with regard to the mediating goals of therapy. That is, the researcher is led to look for variables that *moderate* the effect of therapy on the mediating goals of therapy.

While many reasons for the nonattainment of mediating goals are possible, and the list of possible moderators of treatment effects seems likely to grow as the set of mediating goals of therapy grows larger, at present there is only one moderator of treatment effects that has general acceptance by marital therapists, namely, compliance. It seems clear that a directive component is present in all the effective marital therapies, including insight-oriented and experiential approaches (Beach & O'Leary, 1985). Accordingly, the propensity to comply with therapeutic directives is likely to emerge as a moderator variable that sets the stage for enhanced change in response to all the effective marital therapies. Research aimed at explicating compliance as a mediator in marital therapy should therefore prove useful in conjunction with almost any hypothesized set of mediating goals of marital therapy.

Testing moderators.   To clarify the first step in process research, aimed at identifying moderator variables in marital therapy, the example of relationship skills mediating treatment effects is elaborated to include a hypothesized moderating role for propensity to comply with therapist directives. Given a standard outcome study with a treated and an untreated group in which all participants have been assessed with regard to marital satisfaction, relationship skills, and propensity to comply with therapist directives, it should be possible to follow the logic of Baron and Kenny (1986) and directly test the hypothesis that compliance moderates the impact of treatment. Most germane is their discussion of mediated moderation. In particular, a 2 (treatment) × 2 (high vs. low compliance) analysis of variance should show a significant interaction effect. A regression of relationship skills on treatment, compliance, and their interaction should yield a significant beta weight for the interaction term. A regression of outcome on treatment, compliance, and their interaction should yield a significant beta weight for the interaction term. And, when post-therapy level of relationship skills is added to the regression of outcome on treatment, compliance, and interaction, the beta weight for the interaction term should be reduced to nonsignificance. If all the above conditions held, it would be possible to conclude both (a) that propensity to comply moderates the effect of treatment on outcome by moderating its effect on post-treatment level of relationship skills, and (b) that post-treatment relationship skills mediate the effect on outcome.

Once the propensity to be compliant (vs. noncompliant) was established as a true moderator of the effect of treatment on outcome, it would seem desirable to examine further the processes leading to propensity to comply or not comply. The assessment of reasons for compliance and noncompliance might be pursued fruitfully through clinical interview or intuition in the initial stages of investigation. However, it is likely that a clearer specification of processes leading to noncompliance would be forthcoming if researchers drew explicitly upon well-articulated models of social behavior. Whereas basic work in social psychology and the social-clinical interface is likely to be pertinent in all phases of process work, it is likely to be particularly so as researchers attempt to elaborate the processes implied by moderators of treatment effects in general, and the reasons for noncompliance in particular.

Because compliance seems likely to be important for most or all forms of effective marital therapy, an attempt will be made to develop the implications of three different models from the social-psychological literature, and show how testable implications for new marital therapy techniques might be forthcoming. The remainder of the chapter is devoted to the issue and occurrence of noncompliance in the context of clinically relevant models.

THREE EXAMPLES OF MODELS RELEVANT
TO NONCOMPLIANCE

We have selected three models that help illustrate some of the likely forces at work in noncompliance. The first model is Ajzen's (1985) theory of planned behavior, the second model is Fincham and Bradbury's (1987) attribution-efficacy model of conflict in close relationships, and the third model is Tesser's (1988) self-evaluation maintenance model. These models complement each other in highlighting different causes of noncompliance, as well as describing cognitive variables of potential importance to marital therapy. The theory of planned behavior addresses the common occurrence in therapy where one spouse does not intend to carry out the therapist's directives. Although this is not the most exciting reason for therapeutic failure, this may well be the most common. The attribution-efficacy model, on the other hand, helps explicate the commonly encountered problem of couples who are too locked into blame and retribution to listen to the therapist and to comply with treatment. Finally, the self-evaluation maintenance model helps explicate the problem of couples who cannot comply with therapist directives aimed at improving their problem-solving communication because their self-protective self-evaluation–maintenance strategies get in the way. It is important to note that these models are not the only ones that could be examined for relevance to compliance in marital therapy. They were chosen to illustrate the potential contribution of social-psychological models to therapy process research, and ultimately to marital therapy practice. Similarly, compliance is not the only variable of potential interest in accounting for the attainment of mediating goals in directive forms of therapy. Again, the purpose is to illustrate rather than exhaust the case for this type of process research.

The Theory of Planned Behavior

Finding a general model that might help guide clinical activity regarding the noncompliant client is particularly relevant to marital therapy. The current evidence suggests that, even at the outset of therapy, partners do not suffer from generalized skill deficits, but rather from a failure to implement commonly used interpersonal skills specifically with their spouse (Birchler, Weiss, & Vincent, 1975; Noller, 1984). Thus, many of the behaviors that couples are directed to perform are potentially available and largely voluntary in nature.

The model proposed by Ajzen (Ajzen, 1985; Ajzen & Madden, 1986) is designed to account for the occurrence of single, voluntary actions (see Fig. 12.1). Ajzen's model specifies a small set of predictor variables and describes the way in which they influence behavior. It is proposed that voluntary behavior is determined primarily by the intention to perform the behavior, in conjunction with any constraints in the environment on performing the behavior. When a clinician is confronted with noncompliance, therefore, Ajzen's model suggests looking at the intention to perform the behavior and the variables that influence

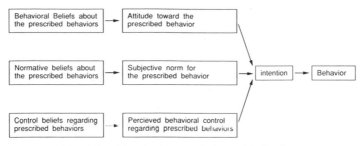

FIG. 12.1.   Ajzen's theory of planned behavior.

the intention to perform the given behavior. Three variables are hypothesized to influence intention to perform an act: (a) attitudes, (b) subjective norms, and (c) perceived behavioral control. The intention to perform the behavior is, in turn, hypothesized to be a powerful and immediate antecedent of actually attempting the behavior. Although other factors are presumed to influence the success of the attempt, the stronger the intent the more successful the outcome is expected to be. Indeed, to the extent that the individual has the opportunity and the resources to perform a behavior, the theory of planned behavior predicts that intent to perform the behavior is the primary variable determining extent of success. Clearly, Ajzen's model has something to tell clinicians about maximizing compliance.

The model also provides considerable guidance with regard to each of the antecedents of intent to perform the given behavior: behavioral beliefs, normative beliefs, and perceived behavioral control. Each antecedent potentially contributes to compliance and noncompliance in marital therapy. Behavioral beliefs are hypothesized to influence attitudes toward the behavior. Behavioral beliefs are those beliefs that link the behavior to some positive or negative outcome. The strength of each belief, along with the value of the expected outcome, is summed across all beliefs to result in a general attitude toward the behavior. For example, if a client spouse believes that complying with a particular therapeutic directive will result in negative consequences, either directly or indirectly, this would be expected to create a negative attitude toward complying, and in turn, decrease the intention to comply. Accordingly, Ajzen's model strongly implies the need for the careful assessment of behavioral beliefs in marital therapy. To the extent that the behaviors that are likely to be assigned in therapy can be predicted before marital therapy begins, behavioral beliefs about specific areas of change could be assessed pre-therapy. In conjunction with the other variables in Ajzen's model, pre-therapy behavioral beliefs should predict elevated levels of noncompliance in marital therapy, and so tend to moderate the impact of treatment on outcome of marital therapy.

Subjective norms are hypothesized to reflect the perceived approval or disapproval of important referent individuals or groups. Again, it is assumed that there may be a variety of normative beliefs, and the strength of each belief, along with the motivation to comply with the referent group, summed across all groups will give the valence and strength of the subjective norm. Typically, it is assumed that the therapist is one important referent individual, and that clients are motivated to gain the therapist's approval. In addition, to the extent that other important referent individuals are believed to disapprove of the behavior being prescribed by the therapist, the subjective norm for the behavior should become more negative and lead to the decreased intention to comply with the directive. For example, if the therapist directs the couple to try changing their division of household responsibilities, one or both spouses might believe that parents or peers would characterize the proposed changes negatively. As with behavioral beliefs, to the extent that behaviors likely to be assigned can be predicted before therapy, the perceived approval or disapproval of relevant others toward each behavior could be assessed and used to predict subsequent level of compliance in therapy.

Perceived behavioral control comprises the set of beliefs relevant to the proposition that the behavior can be successfully performed if it is attempted. That is, one of the sets of beliefs that influences compliance with therapist directives should be the belief that the requisite resources and opportunities to carry out the directive are present. It is assumed that beliefs about resources may reflect past experience, secondhand information, or other factors that influence perceived resources, opportunities, obstacles, and impediments. For example, to the extent that either spouse believes that there is no hope of performing the behavior assigned by the therapist, it should be expected that the intention to comply will be decreased. In therapy, this dimension of Ajzen's model may need to be assessed with each spouse for every assignment. Ajzen's model would predict correspondence between couple's stated beliefs that they have the requisite abilities and resources to carry out a given assignment and the probability that they actually attempt the assignment.

When no obvious constraints can be determined by the marital therapist (i.e., the individual appears able to comply, is not constrained by obvious negative consequences, and has had the opportunity to comply) and some lack of intention to comply with the therapist's directives can be inferred or has been directly stated, the model directs the therapist to examine each of the three areas influencing intention in turn: (a) the attitude toward the behavior, including both the connotations for the individual of engaging in the behavior and any perceived consequences of engaging in the behavior, (b) the social pressure felt by the individual, including the likely evaluations of significant others and the degree of motivation to conform to the expectations of these significant others, and (c) the individual's perception that he or she can perform the behavior, including perceptions of having the requisite skills, the necessary opportunities, and the required resources to comply. As can be seen, the theory of planned behavior provides a road map for the idiographic assessment of compliance-relevant cognition. Attitudes, connotations, self-perceptions, perceptions of the spouse, and predicted consequences are all germane to the compliance process. Ajzen's model, thus, provides a clear set of possible points of assessment and intervention in marital work with a noncompliant spouse. Although the model does not provide particular techniques relevant to each point of intervention, a number of options can be inferred from the literature on cognitive techniques (Baucom & Epstein, 1990).

First, if lack of intention to perform a given behavior is due to negative attitudinal factors, the model suggests that the therapist investigate the spouse's perception of the outcomes that would or could result from complying. The model suggests that the value of each possible outcome, in combination with its subjective probability of occurring, should determine the resulting attitude. Thus, if the therapist can help the spouse examine the expected negative consequences of complying, and find ways to avoid these consequences or help the spouse decrease the subjective probability that they will come to pass, the spouse's attitude should become more positive. This type of work may be particularly important in marital therapy that focuses on helping the husband to be more emotionally expressive or more accepting of intimacy (cf. Markman & Kraft, 1989). In particular, husbands are likely to have appraisals of the sharing of personal problems or of apologizing that involve strong images of personal powerlessness (Guthrie & Snyder, 1988). Thus, it should not be surprising if husbands' compliance with therapist directives for increased intimacy is less, on average, than their compliance with other aspects of marital therapy. In addition, exploration of negative attitudes toward the behaviors requested by the therapist may yield evidence that issues of blame and retribution are present. Problems of blame are explicated later in the discussion of the attribution-efficacy model.

Alternatively, it may be found that noncompliance is related to negative subjective norms for the prescribed behavior. In this case, the model suggests two alternative approaches. First, the cognition might be identified and treated as a dysfunctional relationship belief (cf. Baucom & Epstein, 1990). The therapist might then help the noncompliant spouse dispute the belief that important referent individuals or groups would in fact disapprove of the behavior assigned. The therapist might help the noncompliant spouse find evidence that would show that the belief was unlikely to be true. Alternatively, the therapist could help the spouse decrease his or her motivation to comply with the disapproving individual or group. In particular, the therapist might stress the dysfunctional results of conforming to the view of the referent group and highlight the possibility of choosing to decrease the influence of the referent group on this area. In either case, the influence of the disapproving individual or group should decrease because the strength of the normative beliefs is hypothesized to be a product of the normative beliefs and the motivation to comply.

Finally, the noncompliant spouse may perceive himself or herself as not being able to carry out the therapeutic directive. If further exploration of this area identified the problem as a perceived lack of opportunity or resources, the therapeutic response might be a straightforward problem-solving intervention. If this approach failed to alter the perception, despite what appeared to the therapist to be a workable plan, cognitive rehearsal could be used to increase the couple's perception of their own capacity to carry out the assignment. Alternatively, exploration of the perceived inability to carry out the assigned task might uncover other intrapersonal obstacles to change. Prominent among these is likely to be an inability to perform the behaviors because self-protective self-evaluation maintenance strategies present an obstacle to change. Because self-report may not always be the optimal way to assess such intrapersonal obstacles to change, their presence may need to be assessed through other approaches. The implications of self-protective self-evaluation processes are pursued further in the later discussion of Tesser's Self-Evaluation–Maintenance (SEM) model.

The theory of planned behavior suggests that the marital therapist should be ready to utilize a variety of cognitive techniques throughout the course of therapy (cf. Baucom, 1989). Furthermore, the theory of planned behavior provides a general framework for identifying circumstances when other models may provide additional clues about the optimal assessment and intervention for a particular couple. In addition, it provides a rich set of testable hypotheses about the role that intentions not to comply have on compliance in marital therapy and the many variables influencing the decision to not comply with the therapist.

From the standpoint of research strategies to be used in a process approach to enhancing marital therapy outcome, Ajzen's model provides guidelines for the development of a test that could be used to predict compliance and non-compliance in therapy. Spouses identified by such a measure, as being unlikely to comply with therapeutic directives, would be expected to respond poorly to marital therapy packages. Importantly, such a measure would also provide guidance in selecting the cognitive interventions most likely to enhance the couple's response to treatment. Thus, Ajzen's model advances the integration of marital therapy techniques.

The Attribution-Efficacy Model of Conflict

Partners may be so focused on blaming their spouse and exacting retribution for his or her perceived wrong-doing, that the discussion of constructive behavior seems irrelevant. Indeed, discordant couples are quite willing to attribute blame to each other (Fincham, Beach, & Baucom, 1987) and do so with high levels of certainty (Noller & Venardos, 1986). To the extent that this focus on blame renders engaging in healthy marital interaction a distasteful experience, one would expect to find partners endorsing negative behavioral beliefs about specific behaviors required in marital therapy. For example, extreme blame might lead a spouse to expect negative feelings to result from a communication exercise or an assignment to engage in a recreational activity with the spouse. The negative behavioral beliefs should, in turn, lead to decreased intention to comply with

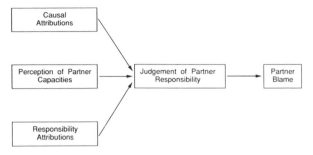

FIG. 12.2. Fincham and Bradbury's model of blame.

therapeutic directives, and ultimately to poorer overall compliance in accordance
with Ajzen's model. A framework that could guide research and intervention
regarding maladaptive blame in the dyad is the attribution-efficacy model
(Fincham & Bradbury, 1987, 1991; Fincham, Bradbury, & Grych, 1990).

The attribution-efficacy model highlights three stages in the process of attributing blame to the partner (see Fig. 12.2). First, an attribution that locates the
cause of an event in the partner must be made before any blame can be assigned.
Further, it is proposed that judgments of causal stability and globality will also
ultimately influence blame. Second, inferences relating to responsibility criteria
are critical. That is, consideration of the perceived motivation of the act, the
apparent voluntariness of the act, and the perceived intent of the act are hypothesized to influence blame profoundly. Third, judgments about the capacities of
the partner (e.g., his or her skills) can mitigate blame. By featuring these areas
the model draws our attention to such factors as potential points of intervention
and as variables that may account for less than optimal response to marital
therapy. A thorough review of the model and its implications for process research
would require a review of the very extensive literatures on causal attribution (see
Fletcher & Fincham, this volume), and the work on cognitive marital therapy
aimed at changing problematic causal attributions (e.g., Baucom & Epstein,
1990), in addition to a discussion of responsibility criteria. Discussions of techniques for addressing causal attributions are widely available elsewhere, however, and overlap with the earlier discussion of methods useful in disputing
dysfunctional beliefs, so here the focus is on responsibility criteria only.

The application of responsibility criteria after the cause has been located
within the spouse requires judgments regarding (a) motivation, (b) voluntariness,
and (c) intent, before any blame can be assigned. Each judgment represents an
opportunity for therapeutic intervention and is discussed in turn. Two processes,
discounting and augmentation (Kelley, 1972), are particularly relevant for changing perceived motivation. Discounting is the process that leads a person to
discount the importance of underlying motivation for a particular behavior because of the presence of other factors that could also account for that behavior.

For example, a wife might not ascribe her husband's behavior of spending more time at home as due to his unselfish motivation to show caring for her, if this behavior began only after his best friend and drinking buddy moved away. In contrast, augmentation is the process that leads a person to infer a strong motivational state because the behavior under consideration occurs in the face of powerful constraints that would be expected to inhibit its display. For example, if a husband spends less time at home despite considerable nagging on this point from his wife, this would be likely to strengthen his wife's conviction that he was deeply motivated to stay away from home.

To begin to work therapeutically on a particular negative, destructive motive that was ascribed to the spouse, the therapist would first examine the extent to which the perceived strength of the motive was a reflection of augmentation and discounting processes. In the above example, it might be possible to reinterpret what was previously seen as particularly strong evidence of a negative motive due to the operation of augmentation processes. By exploring the possibility that nagging actually worked to keep the husband away from the house rather than working as a powerful force to get him to come home, the therapist may reverse an augmented perception of motivation and allow it to be discounted entirely. Discordant spouses who are the most blaming of each other are also often those who have used the most coercive strategies to influence their partners behavior. Because the coercive behaviors are meant to control the partner's responses, but more commonly aggravate problem behaviors, one might expect the exploration of augmentation and discounting to be applicable in many cases.

A second responsibility criterion involves the ascription of voluntariness to the problem behavior. Indeed, a freely chosen action intended to bring about the outcome, which then actually occurs, is the quintessential act for which one can be held responsible (Hart, 1968). However, it is relatively easy for observers to see an actor's behavior as free and voluntary, even in the face of rather obvious constraints (cf. the "fundamental attribution error"; Ross, 1977). Thus, this may not represent a particularly ameniable point of therapeutic intervention. Interestingly, two strategies, which derive from different marital therapy traditions and which may appear markedly different to the practitioners within each tradition, seem remarkably similar when viewed from the framework of the attribution-efficacy model. On the one hand cognitive-behavioral marital therapists have often used a strategy of identifying skill deficits or poor learning because of dysfunctional parental modeling as the true cause of a problem behavior. Further, therapists may communicate this belief to their clients even though there often is reason to believe that this it is a partial explanation at best. Similarly, systems therapists may identify a need of the larger system as the true cause of a problem behavior. Both these interventions highlight limited capacity on the part of the offending spouse.

As Fincham et al. (1990) pointed out, stressing limited capacity to act otherwise is clearly one way to reduce the perceived voluntariness of the behavior.

Thus, if the behavioral marital therapist argues convincingly that the spouse could not foresee that the behavior would result in conflict, did not know any alternative behaviors, or simply did not have the ability to behave differently, then it should be difficult for the partner to ascribe blame (Fincham, 1983). Likewise, if a recurrent problem behavior is interpreted by a systems therapist as protecting the couple from too-rapid change, again, the problem behavior is not necessarily the voluntary decision of the individual performing it. Rather, the problem behavior is produced by the powerful constraint of the family system. In both approaches the naive view that individuals freely choose their own behavior is challenged through the presentation of a compelling alternative construction of reality. Thus, the therapist directly challenges the fundamental attribution error and highlights the role of the environment in controlling a person's behavior. When accepted by the couple this account of the constraints' operating on the previously blameworthy behavior should rapidly reduce perceived blameworthiness.

The third, and perhaps most central responsibility criterion is the ascription of intent. Basic research has shown that observers are more likely to attribute intent to produce a particular outcome when the actor is seen as having selected from among many alternatives the one behavior that would have produced that particular outcome (Ajzen & Holmes, 1976). Thus, to the extent that therapists can identify unique positive consequences of problem behavior, or reduce the perception of many unique negative effects of problem behavior, therapists may have a powerful impact on the ascription of intent.

Consider, for example, the case of Melissa and Jim. After dinner Melissa tells her husband, Jim, that she has not been able to balance the family checking account for the past six months; consequently, the check she wrote for the monthly mortgage payment bounced. Jim, in a fit of anger, calls her a "worthless incompetent" and then storms out of the house and does not return until morning. Melissa cries all night and reports to her therapist that Jim is simply a mean person because he wanted to punish her for making a mistake. Melissa bases her assertion on the fact that she cannot imagine being hurt by other things that Jim could have done, such as offering to help her balance the account, taking responsibility for the account himself, or getting annoyed but without calling her names and staying out all night. Thus, it seems to her that Jim chose the one option that produced the greatest upset possible to her. If the therapist is able to find other outcomes that are unique to the behavior Jim displayed, this should decrease the certainty with which Melissa holds her inference of negative intent. Thus, if Melissa had been abused physically by Jim in the past and she comes to view not being abused as a second unique outcome of Jim's leaving the house, she may change the intent she ascribes to his behavior.

Because most problem behavior is at least ambiguous with regard to its unique effects, and because discordant couples are likely to find the negative effects of a problem behavior more salient than any positive effects, it is likely that in many cases unique positive effects of problem behaviors that have been overlooked by the members of the discordant dyad can be found. Indeed, systems approaches routinely ascribe unique positive effects to problem behaviors by positive reframing of the problem behavior. For example, recurrent severe arguments may be ascribed to the couple's passion for each other and unwillingness to accept a less intense relationship. These interventions can be seen as explicit attempts to reduce self- and or partner blame by altering the perception of the extent to which the intended outcome of the problem behavior was positive rather than negative.

The attribution-efficacy model is a promising source of additional cognitive techniques in behavioral marital therapy. If it is found that compliance is central to improvement on important mediating goals of marital therapy and if extreme blame in the dyad is found to markedly reduce intention to comply with therapeutic directives, this model provides guidance for the development of clinically useful measurement and intervention strategies. Because both propositions seem plausible, this represents one avenue for future process research. Indeed, a potentially useful measure of the processes involved in extreme blame has already been put forward (Bradbury & Fincham, 1989). In addition, if supported empirically through process research, the attribution-efficacy model is capable of providing a framework that allows for the exploration and appropriate integration of systems therapy techniques with established directive approaches in marital therapy. Again, the goal of this type of process research would not be to build a new marital therapy package, but rather to help existing directive interventions reach couples who would otherwise be noncompliant early in therapy and be treatment failures at the end of therapy. By finding effective techniques to reduce noncompliance, it should be possible to help couples show enhanced gains on the mediating goals of therapy, and as a result show enhanced outcome.

The Self-Esteem Maintenance Model

Many marital therapy texts discuss couples in which spouses seem less interested in getting better than in being in control or dominant in some way (cf. Jacobson, 1989). These same couples might also tend to be noncompliant with therapist directives, and ultimately appear as treatment failures, because they are disposed to misconstrue the therapy situation as an opportunity to fight in front of a referee rather than an opportunity to learn new ways of cooperating with each other. Indeed, for some such couples, fights rapidly escalate out of control, effectively compromising the entire process of therapy (cf. Jacobson & Margolin, 1979). As Stuart (1980) pointed out, this type of power struggle can be particularly virulent in nature and has the potential to disrupt the course of therapy.

Power struggles may result from spouses' attempts to use the marital relationship for the purposes of self-esteem enhancement (cf. Weiss, 1989), albeit in a particularly maladaptive way. In particular, such battles may be interpreted as attempts to enhance the self by enlarging the domain of decision making controlled by the self. A model that describes self-evaluation maintenance processes could be helpful in understanding how such couples become noncompliant with therapist directives, how to reduce their destructive battling behavior, and how to intervene so that marital therapy might proceed.

A promising model available in the social psychological literature is Tesser's (Tesser, 1988; Tesser, Pilkington, & McIntosh, in press) self evaluation maintenance (SEM) model. The SEM model assumes that persons are motivated to maintain a positive self-evaluation and that their self-evaluation is determined at least in part by two antagonistic social-psychological processes: reflection and comparison. The reflection process is one in which self-evaluation is bolstered by the outstanding accomplishments of a close other (Cialdini et al., 1976). The closer the connection with the other, the greater the potential positive reflection of the other's good performance. In the comparison process self-evaluation is threatened by the outstanding accomplishments of a close other (Wills, 1981). The closer the other, the greater the threat of comparison if the other's performance is better than one's own.

Because the better performance of a close other can bolster (via reflection) or threaten (via comparison) self-evaluation, a theoretical parameter regulating the relative activation of each of these processes is necessary. The *relevance* variable is such a parameter in the SEM model. According to the SEM model, although a person may recognize good performance on a variety of dimensions, he or she aspires to be good at only a few such dimensions. The relevance of another's performance is high if it is on a dimension for which the self has personal aspirations. The more relevant the other's performance to the self, the greater the importance of comparison processes. The less relevant the other's performance to the self, the greater the importance of the reflection process.

From an SEM perspective, power struggles can be understood as the operation of comparison processes in the context of decision making in an intimate relationship. The theoretical structure of the SEM model and related research combine to suggest four logical points of intervention that might be considered when a couple is noncompliant due to being locked in a power struggle: (a) reduce psychological closeness, (b) redefine the performance domain to alter perception of relative performance, (c) reduce the perceived relevance of power or particular areas of power to the self-definition, and (d) reduce or reattribute arousal.

Reduce psychological closeness. The SEM model states that the affective consequences of being outperformed by another on a relevant dimension should be stronger for someone who is psychologically closer than for someone who is less close. Psychological closeness refers to the extent to which the other is seen as part of the same unit. Thus, if a spouse thinks of his or her partner as being in a unit relationship with the self, there should be greater potential affective reaction than if he or she sees the partner as distinct. Because much of marital ritual and popular culture appears aimed at enhancing the view that the married couple is a single unit, psychological closeness is likely to be high in most married couples even when they are having marital difficulties. It should be noted, however, that when a clinician utilizes techniques to decrease psychological closeness an inescapable side effect predicted by the SEM model is that the magnitude of positive reflection experiences will be diminished as well. In the context of very destructive patterns of coercive interaction, this may appear to be a very reasonable trade-off. If successful, an intervention that reduces psychological closeness, while the couple remains physically proximate, should allow the spouses to suffer fewer disruptive emotional effects and to be more compliant with therapist directives.

How might one reduce psychological closeness in couples with power struggles? If spouses fail to view the partner as being psychologically independent, the therapist might provide the strong message that each spouse is an adult, a separate individual, responsible for himself or herself. The couple could also be given individual assignments to increase their separate outside interests, and lower their expectations of each other. The couple could be told that the intensity of their negative feelings is the result of too much concern and involvement with each other rather than too little. It should be noted that this is not a paradoxical intervention, but rather a genuine attempt by the therapist to help the spouses to understand their problems and to think of themselves as more independent. Although this intervention would not be expected to resolve the issue of who should make a particular decision, it might dissipate some of the affective "heat" associated with the decision-making process. If so, the couple should be better able to comply with subsequent therapist directives to reduce the frequency of extreme negative interactions and derive greater benefit from standard, problem-solving communication training. If later in therapy the comparison process was successfully deactivated, then the couple could safely begin to increase closeness once more.

It is important to note that the common suggestion of having a trial separation does not follow directly from an SEM perspective. Although this might seem to be a spontaneous attempt by the couple to reduce closeness as the SEM model suggests, it reduces only physical closeness, not psychological closeness. From an SEM perspective, a trial separation would be expected to be effective in reducing the intensity of affective responses to the spouse only in those cases where physical separation produced a subsequent reduction in psychological closeness as well. However, a marked reduction in psychological closeness in the context of having moved out of the house would appear to be a prescription for divorce. Thus, trial separations are not suggested by the SEM model.

Redefine the performance domain. According to the SEM model, if the spouse has not outperformed the self, then there is no possibility of comparison threat. If there is no comparison threat, there should be no negative arousal, and no rapidly escalating power struggle. Accordingly, any intervention that redefines performance in such a way that decision making no longer holds the threat of being outperformed by the spouse should be effective in reducing negative reactions during joint decision making with the spouse. For example, if the therapist can advance the position that agreement with the spouse requires active consideration of the issue, a consideration of all alternatives and the pros and cons of each, leading finally to agreement, then acquiescing to a spouse decision need not be viewed as being outperformed. To the extent that each spouse is able to redefine agreement in such a way that it no longer represents loss, this should be expected to do away with the comparison-induced negative arousal and the associated negative interaction.

A comprehensive approach to redefining performance in the decision-making domain might be to introduce a new set of criteria, which the spouses could use when evaluating their own performance. If the concern with controlling or dominating the decision-making process can be replaced with a more normative set of criteria for evaluating performance, the desire to do well could improve couple interaction rather than obstruct successful interaction. For example, a therapist might discuss the topic of power and differentiate between (a) legitimate power, which derives from laws or norms; (b) expert power, which derives from agreement that one person has greater skill; (c) referent power, which derives from a feeling of closeness and the resulting expectation of mutual influence; (d) coercive power, which derives from threats of punishment; and (e) reward power, which derives from anticipation of reward for compliance (Stuart, 1980). To the extent that the therapist was able to convince each spouse that only expert and referent forms of power constitute appropriate exercises of power, the domination of the spouse should lose its appeal. Dominating the decision-making process in a coercive manner would no longer be perceived as outperforming the spouse. Indeed, the therapist may suggest that, when one spouse exercises coercive power, whereas the other spouse exerts only expert or referent power, it is the noncoercive spouse who has demonstrated the better performance during the interaction. In this way the therapist may enlist the comparison process in the service of motivating positive changes in a couple's interactional style.

Alternatively, and perhaps more effectively, the therapist might attempt to enlist the spouses' desire for positive reflection. An interesting example of how this might be done is provided by Weiss and Heyman (1990). They suggested that in response to competitive battles the therapist should tell the couple, "There can be no winner in a marital fight, because if one is successful in beating the other down, one is left living with a loser." Again, it is clear that this systemic intervention, if successful, will redefine the nature of a successful performance such that winning an argument with the spouse is not perceived as a viable way to maintain or enhance self-esteem.

Although the strategy sketched above may persuade couples to adopt different patterns of interaction and decision making, the comparison processes that initially produced the dysfunctional pattern may not be completely eliminated. It is possible that partners would find additional overlapping performance-based dimensions that were relevant to both, and that placed them in jeopardy of continued comparison processes. Thus, couples could continue to suffer comparison threat and potentially show the resulting negative interactional style and distancing behavior in response to other behavioral domains, even if joint decision making no longer posed the threat of provoking a power struggle.

For the sake of maintaining a close relationship, it seems clear that spouses are better off engaging the reflection process rather than the comparison process when they feel they may be outperformed by their spouse. This implies the need for direct intervention concerning the partners' understanding of the relevance of each other's successful performances. For example, the couple could be encouraged to spend time discussing the ways in which they are complementary rather than similar to each other. By highlighting a large number of dimensions on which couples are complementary, the therapist may help each partner develop an elaborated and differentiated set of self-definitions. It is likely that such activity will bias the couple to respond in terms of complementarity rather than similarity in the performance domain. If successful, this type of intervention should replace the couple's tendency to attack each other, when the spouse performs well, with the disposition to bask in reflected glory.

Reduce or reattribute arousal.   The SEM model also suggests one additional point of possible intervention. Because the affective consequences of negative comparison appear to trigger the behavioral response (Tesser et al., in press), an alternative strategy for reducing destructive interactions that follow self-evaluation threat might be to help spouses learn to reduce their own arousal in such situations before interacting. The role of arousal suggests that events that heighten background arousal, such as multiple stressful life events or job loss, or perceived failure on some dimension of importance, are likely to intensify self evaluation maintenance processes. Accordingly, background stress may precipitate or intensify power struggles in couples, or increase the probability of relapse in couples who have gone through marital therapy successfully. Accordingly, relaxation training, stress management, and other forms of coping may be useful in decreasing the intensity of power struggles or preventing their recurrence.

The SEM model appears to be suited to enhancing the effectiveness of marital therapy with a particular set of clients who are currently difficult to handle: viz, couples locked in generalized power struggles, or couples who are noncompliant with therapist directives because of the potentially painful effects of increased closeness because of comparison threat. If compliance is found to be central to improvement on important mediating goals of therapy, and some SEM processes are found to predict noncompliance, this model has the potential for helping guide the integration of systemic and insight-oriented techniques with behavioral and cognitive techniques. Again, the goal would be increased efficacy in dealing with the problem of noncompliance, and the promise of increased overall effectiveness of marital therapy.

CONCLUSION

Reviews of the outcome literature show that there already exist some basic technologies that can influence discordant couples and produce reliable changes in relationship satisfaction. However, it also appears that about 30% of couples receiving standard marital therapies do not benefit at all and an additional number benefit only to a marginal degree. As noted earlier, this evidence should not lead us to reject proven technologies and continue building new schools of marital therapy. New schools of marital therapy tend to show broad areas of technical overlap with existing approaches and similar outcome success. Nor should we necessarily add new approaches as modules to marital therapy packages. Adding new modules either lengthens therapy or dilutes the presentation of other components of the treatment. In addition, combinations of modules have not shown the tendency to enhance outcome significantly. Rather, what is needed at present is research aimed at illuminating the process of change in therapy and the reasons for the lack of response to existing marital therapies.

In this chapter we argued that it is important to expand current hypotheses about the mediating goals of marital therapy and to explore common obstacles, that is, mediators of therapy's effect on goal attainment. The utility of this approach was illustrated by showing how elaborated change models and the social-psychological literature can help identify moderators of outcome. It was argued that process work of this type may guide the development of more effective interventions with discordant couples. The advantage of the type of process research outlined is that it is aimed explicitly at building on programs of marital therapy that have already shown considerable effectiveness. Accordingly, such process research offers the promise of systematic enhancement of the effectiveness of marital therapy and has the potential to more fully integrate clinical and social-psychological work.

REFERENCES

Ajzen, I. (1985). From intentions to actions: A theory of planned behavior. In J. Kuhl & J. Beckmann (Eds.), *Action control: From cognition to behavior* (pp. 11–39). Heidelberg: Springer.

Ajzen, I., & Holmes, W. H. (1976). Uniqueness of behavioral effects in causal attribution. *Journal of Personality, 44,* 98–108.

Ajzen, I., & Madden, T. (1986). Prediction of goal directed behavior: Attitudes, intentions, and perceived behavioral control. *Journal of Experimental Social Psychology, 22,* 453–474.

Baron, R. M., & Kenny, D. A. (1986). The moderator-mediator variable distinction in social psychological research: Conceptual, strategic, and statistical considerations. *Journal of Personality and Social Psychology, 51,* 1173–1182.

Baucom, D. H. (1989). The role of cognitions in behavioral marital therapy: Current status and future directions. *Behavior Therapist, 12,* 3–6.

Baucom, D. H., & Epstein, N. (1990). *Cognitive-behavioral marital therapy.* New York: Brunner/Mazel.

Baucom, D. H., & Hoffman, J. A. (1986). The effectiveness of marital therapy: Current status and application to the clinical setting. In N. S. Jacobson & A. S. Gurman (Eds.), *Clinical handbook of marital therapy* (pp. 597–620). New York: Guilford Press.

Baucom, D. H., Sayers, S. L., & Sher, T. G. (1990). Supplementing behavioral marital therapy with cognitive restructuring and emotional expressiveness training: An outcome investigation. *Journal of Consulting and Clinical Psychology 58,* 636–645.

Beach, S. R. H., Abramson, L. Y., & Levine, F. M. (1981). Attributional reformulation of learned helplessness and depression: Therapeutic implications. In J. F. Clarkin & H. I. Glazer (Eds.), *Depression: Behavioral and directive intervention strategies* (pp. 131–165). New York: Garland Press.

Beach, S. R. H., Arias, I., & O'Leary, K. D. (1987). The relationship of social support to depressive symptomatology. *Journal of Psychopathology and Behavioral Assessment, 8,* 305–316.

Beach, S. R. H., & Bauserman, S. A. K. (1990). Enhancing the effectiveness of marital therapy. In F. D. Fincham and T. N. Bradbury (Eds.), *The psychology of marriage* (pp. 349–374). New York: Guilford Press.

Beach, S. R. H., & O'Leary, K. D. (1985). Current status of outcome research in marital therapy. In L. L'Abate (Ed.), *The handbook of family psychology and therapy* (pp. 1035–1072). Homewood, IL: Dorsey Press.

Beach, S. R. H., Sandeen, E. E., & O'Leary, K. D. (1990). *Depression in marriage: A model for etiology and treatment.* New York: Guilford.

Birchler, G. R., Weiss, R. L., & Vincent, J. P. (1975). Multimethod analysis of social reinforcement exchange between maritally distressed and nondistressed spouse and stranger dyads. *Journal of Personality and Social Psychology, 31,* 349–360.

Bradbury, T. N., & Fincham, F. D. (1989). Behavior and satisfaction in marriage: Prospective mediating processes. *Review of Personality and Social Psychology, 10,* 119–143.

Cialdini, R. B., Borden, R. J., Thorne, A., Walker, M. R., Freeman, S., & Sloan, L. R. (1976). Basking in reflected glory: Three (football) field studies. *Journal of Personality and Social Psychology, 34,* 366–375.

Fincham, F. D. (1983). Clinical applications of attribution theory: Problems and prospects. In M. Hewstone (Ed.), *Attribution theory: Social and functional extensions* (pp. 187–203). Oxford: Blackwells.

Fincham, F. D., Beach, S. R. H., & Baucom, D. H. (1987). Attribution processes in distressed and nondistressed couples: 4. Self-partner attribution differences. *Journal of Personality and Social Psychology, 52,* 739–748.

Fincham, F. D., & Bradbury, T. N. (1987). Cognitive processes and conflict in close relationships: An attribution-efficacy model. *Journal of Personality and Social Psychology, 53,* 1106–1118.

Fincham, F. D., & Bradbury, T. N. (1991). Cognition in marriage: A program of research on attributions. In D. Perlman & W. Jones (Eds.), *Advances in personal relationships* (Vol. 2). Greenwich, CT: JAI Press.

Fincham, F. D., Bradbury, T. N., & Grych, J. H. (1990). Conflict in close relationships: The role of intrapersonal factors. In S. Graham & V. Folkes (Eds.), Attribution theory: Applications to achievement, mental health, and interpersonal conflict (pp. 118–149). New York: Guilford.

Glick, P. C. (1984). How American families are changing. *American Demographics, 6,* 20–27.

Gottman, J. M. (1979). *Marital interaction: Experimental investigations.* New York: Academic Press.

Guthrie, D. M., & Snyder, C. W. (1988). Spouses' self-evaluation for situations involving emotional communication. In P. Noller & M. A. Fitzpatrick (Eds.), *Perspectives on marital interaction* (pp. 153–181). Philadelphia: Multilingual Matters.

Hafner, R. J. (1986). *Marriage and mental illness.* New York: Guilford Press.

Hahlweg, K., & Markman, H. J. (1988). The effectiveness of behavioral marital therapy: Empirical status of behavioral techniques in preventing and alleviating marital distress. *Journal of Consulting and Clinical Psychology, 56,* 440–447.

Hart, H. L. A. (1968). *Punishment and responsibility.* New York: Oxford University Press.

Jacobson, N. S. (1989). The politics of intimacy. *Behavior Therapist, 12,* 29–32.

Jacobson, N. S., Follette, W. C., Revenstorf, D., Baucom, D. H., Hahlweg, K., & Margolin, G. (1984). Variability in outcome and clinical significance of behavioral marital therapy: A reanalysis of outcome data. *Journal of Consulting and Clinical Psychology, 52,* 497–504.

Jacobson, N. S., Holtzworth-Monroe, A., & Schmaling, K. B. (1989). Marital therapy and spouse involvement in the treatment of depression, agoraphobia, and alcoholism. *Journal of Consulting and Clinical Psychology, 57,* 5–10.

Jacobson, N. S., & Margolin, G. (1979). *Marital therapy: Strategies based on social learning and behavior exchange principles.* New York: Brunner/Mazel.

Kelley, H. H. (1972). Attribution in social interaction. In E. E. Jones, D. E. Kanouse, H. H. Kelley, R. E. Nisbett, S. Valins, & B. Weiner (Eds.), *Attribution: Perceiving the causes of behavior* (pp. 151–174). Morristown, NJ: General Learning Press.

Markman, H. J., & Kraft, S. A. (1989). Men and women in marriage: Dealing with gender differences in marital therapy. *Behavior Therapist, 12,* 51–56.

Noller, P. (1984). *Nonverbal communication and marital interaction.* Oxford: Pergamon Press.

Noller, P., & Vernardos, C. (1986). Communication awareness in married couples. *Journal of Social and Personal Relationships, 3,* 31–42.

O'Leary, K. D., & Arias, I. (1983). The influence of marital therapy on sexual satisfaction. *Journal of Sex and Marital Therapy, 9,* 171–181.

Ross, L. (1977). The intuitive psychologist and his shortcomings: Distortions in the attribution process. In L. Berkowitz (Ed.), *Advances in experimental social psychology* (Vol. 10, pp. 173–220). New York: Academic Press.

Stuart, R. B. (1980). *Helping couples change: A social learning approach to marital therapy.* New York: Guilford Press.

Tesser, A. (1988). Toward a self-evaluation maintenance model of social behavior. In L. Berkowitz (Ed.), *Advances in experimental social psychology* (Vol. 21, pp. 181–227). New York: Academic Press.

Tesser, A., Pilkington, C., & McIntosh, W. (1989). Self-evaluation maintenance and the mediational role of emotion: The perception of friends and strangers. *Journal of Personality and Social Psychology, 57,* 442–456.

Weiss, R. L. (1989, November). *Behavioral marital therapy faces the threat of a hostile takeover bid.* Paper presented to the 23rd Annual Convention of the Association for the Advancement of Behavior Therapy, Washington, DC.

Weiss, R. L., & Heyman, R. E. (1990). Marital distress and therapy. In A. S. Bellack, M. Hersen, & A. Kazdin (Eds.), *International handbook of behavior modification* (2nd ed., pp. 2–30). New York: Plenum Press.

Wills, A. (1981). Downward comparison principles in social psychology. *Psychological Bulletin, 90,* 245–271.

IV OVERVIEW

To provide a coda, Harvey and Orbuch critically review the chapters contained in this book. This chapter, *Cognition in Close Relationships: Overview and Integration,* also offers an integrative perspective on the role of cognition in close relationships and identifies avenues for further theorizing and research. We leave their review to speak for itself.

13

Cognition in Close Relationships: Overview and Integration

John H. Harvey
University of Iowa

Terri L. Orbuch
University of Michigan

INTRODUCTION

This book represents the melding of two vibrant domains of research in the 1980s: social cognition and close relationships. This melding has involved the integration of somewhat disparate methodologies and conceptual schools. Another characteristic has been the considerable borrowing back and forth between the two areas of work. As Fletcher and Kininmonth noted, a major part of this borrowing process has been the use of cognitive models in the explication of close relationship phenomena. Another direction of borrowing, however, has involved the relatively recent focus on relationship phenomena by social cognition scholars. Although the relationship field of work has often emphasized nonexperimental, survey, and interview methods, the social cognition field has emphasized almost exclusively experimental techniques. Thus, putting the two together has led to an interesting blending both of ideas and methods. In the following commentary, we discuss what seems to be the overarching theme of the book, namely, the importance of the integration of ideas and theoretical positions concerning the role of cognition in close relationships. Then we will discuss each of the papers with a special emphasis on what seem to be promising trends at this interface of scholarship, and directions for further work. Finally, we comment on some of the unanswered but vital questions that remain for this domain of scholarship.

AN EMPHASIS ON INTEGRATION AND ECLECTICISM

There are many themes in this volume. For example, several of the writers address the possibility that the operation of implicit theories or automatic processing occurs to a larger degree in relationships than previously has been recognized. However, the general theme that we wish to pinpoint is that of integration across ideas and theoretical systems and an accompanying focus on eclecticism in theory. In this vein, Sternberg and Beall explicitly call for approaches to cognition in close relationships that are eclectic in nature. We can easily resonate with this call given the natural breadth of this field—in fact, we believe that even more breadth of focus would have helped (see our final section on unaddressed issues). Essentially, many of the authors in this volume argue that no one approach, whether it emphasizes cognitive, social-psychological, personality, developmental, or psychophysiological processes, is sufficient to make sense of relationship phenomena. Further, they argue that the most compelling approaches will be integrative in nature (with the tacit point that it is likely that several fields of scholarship will have to come together to study these phenomena fully).

Why do we need such breadth in the study of close relationships? Simply put, people's close involvements with each other require that they, like we as scholar-scientists, exhibit emotional, cognitive, motivational, physiological, and sexual systems of activity at various points in their relationships. These systems often interact in their operation. There is even more complexity because people carry out such types of activity within dyads, larger groups, societies, and cultures, and they do so over time, personal stages of development, and over different historical eras. Truly, no other social phenomenon is more complex than are close relationships, and no simple theory will suffice to explain these intricacies of mind, body, heart, and social order (a position we have begun to increasingly appreciate as different perspectives are brought to bear on relationships, see Harvey, Weber, & Orbuch, 1990). Interestingly, given the title of this book, with its mention of cognition, it may be observed that in most of the chapters the authors are also advocating integrative positions that suggest we must necessarily examine other systems at the same time that we try to make sense out of cognitive processes in close relationships.

Instances of the advocacy of breadth and integration of ideas are found in all of the chapters. For example, Fletcher and Fincham develop a quite useful comparison of guiding metaphors in attribution theory versus mainstream social cognition approaches. Miller and Read synthesize several cognitive and interpersonal theoretical positions in presenting their ideas about mental models of persons and relationships. A focus on broad-gauged theory is found in the papers by Noller and Ruzzene, and Fletcher and Kininmonth, which speak to links among social interaction, cognition, and affect. Forgas, too, emphasizes breadth of analysis in his presentation of ideas about the role of affect in cognitive representations of social episodes in relationships. Cantor and Malley reflect further this integrative spirit in their analysis of one's quest for agency and communion within the context of close relationships, and how life goals serve as the motivational units for personality development. In the following commentary, we discuss some of the more salient and compelling ideas presented in the various chapters.

COMMENTARIES ON INDIVIDUAL CHAPTERS

Part 1: Conceptual Foundations

Part 1 represents well the breadth of theoretical approaches to the study of cognition in close relationships found in this volume. The first chapter, by Fletcher and Fincham, attempts to reconcile the so-called naive scientist and cognitive miser model-metaphors of attribution theory and mainstream social cognition work. Theirs is an ambitious piece filled with insights and refinements on the attributional approach to understanding psychological processes within close relationships. Because of its unique integrative quality, this chapter should be one of the most well-cited statements in the volume and possibly in the 1990s in this field. The analysis is made more powerful via the authors' reference to their own fertile programs of work in the area.

Specifically, we appreciate Fletcher and Fincham's suggestion of a naive lawyer metaphor to illustrate the pervasiveness of attributions of responsibility and blame in close relationships. Their discussion of automatic attributional processes complements the presentations in other chapters, such as the emphasis on implicit theory in Sternberg and Beall's chapter and much of Scott, Fuhrman, and Wyer's reasoning about how automatic processing frequently occurs in relationship events. Although we discuss below our reservation about an emphasis on automatic processing in dealing with relationship events, we strongly support Fletcher and Fincham's argument (attributed to Fletcher & Haig, in press) that attributional processes in relationships usually involve interactions between motivational and cognitive/rational systems; it is difficult to completely rule out the operation of either one of these systems in most relationship events. Such a conclusion was noted earlier by Bradley-Weary (1978) in addressing the dynamics of more general attributional processes.

Returning to our reservations about the automatic processing theme as applied to relationship events, in particular we believe that the dichotomous distinction of automatic versus controlled processing may not take into account very well the intricacies of relationships. We would find more cogent the idea of continua of *depth and nature* of processing, followed by the quest to understand different depths and types of processing in different social situations. We are less sanguine than Fletcher and Fincham appear to be regarding the interpretation of the work showing how automatic processing may occur in dispositional inferences. Moreover, we are hesitant about the extrapolation of these data to relationship events. The authors note the value of recent findings by Uleman and colleagues (e.g., Uleman, Winborne, Winter, & Shechter, 1986) in showing that trait inferences can be unintended and nonconscious. We agree that this work is important in questioning the extent to which trait information is processed in an in-depth fashion. But the case as yet is surely not strong enough to be extended to social interaction episodes or to relationship events in general. For example, consider the procedure used frequently in these studies: Research participants read the same kind of sentences as "distractors" in a study of "memory for digits." On each trial, participants read a digit series aloud, then read a distractor sentence, repeat it, and then recall the digits. After all trials and an intervening task, there was a surprise cued-recall test of memory for the sentences. Again, trait-cued recall exceeded semantic-cued recall and free recall, indicating presumably that the traits had been inferred at sentence encoding (see Newman & Uleman, 1989, for a fuller description of this line of work). In these studies, participants' thoughts about the last sentence were probed immediately after they had read it; again, there was no relationship between awareness of trait or personality inferences and traits' effectiveness in cued recall. Such evidence certainly suggests that people may process traits at a minimal depth of awareness on these rotelike tasks, but it does not necessarily indicate that in ongoing interaction they will exhibit such superficiality in processing.

Even if available research were supportive regarding the automatic processing of trait inferences, the logic of application to relationship events needs to be spelled out more convincingly than has been done to date. People, no doubt, sometimes think very little before jumping to conclusions about their relationship partners. Why might this be? One possibility is that the behavior of the partner may remind the perceiver of the behavior of his or her previous partners and personality factors assumed to be operating in producing that behavior. Or according to a principle of least effort, somewhat like that advanced in learning theory, it may be because a perceiver may be generally disposed to make trait ascriptions without much thought—at least until such a tendency becomes personally dysfunctional or punishing (Harvey, 1976). Or a perceiver may be in a relationship conflict situation and may attribute his or her partner's behavior to negative traits. Indeed, many possible explanations may account for knee-jerk trait attributions, without necessarily assuming that they are made in an unconscious or unintended manner. As many scholars (e.g., Harvey, Wells, & Alvarez, 1978; Weiss, 1975) have reported, people in troubled relationships often go to great lengths to analyze relationship events and possible personality dynamics associated with them. They may even be obsessive in such analyses. Further, in ongoing relationships that are harmonious, Fincham and Bradbury's (1987) work suggests that explanations even for negative events often do not directly implicate the partner's personality; rather, they are often dyadic—"We both were having a bad day and were tired as well. . . ." Our intention here has not been to provide a comprehensive account, but to illustrate the types of analyses that we see as necessary to address more carefully the concept of automatic processing as applied to close relationships.

In addition, we also have some trouble with the notion of controlled processing as it is being used in this and other chapters in this volume. Control of thought likely embraces varying degrees of retrospection, effortful thinking, intentional thinking, and implicit thinking; it is also likely to involve different thought foci and degrees of emotional intensities (as the work on rumination about major personal loss suggests). Further, and this point is relevant to the evidence reported by Uleman and others, people probably differ in their ability to articulate what they are or were thinking. In terms of research possibilities, Fletcher and Fincham's account suggests the great need for research aimed at providing a more comprehensive descriptive analysis of the thinking that occurs in different types of couples as they encounter a variety of social situations. Also, as the authors note, we need work on episodic sequences because attributions sometimes become part of well-practiced scripts that involve causal analysis early on, but that reduce over time.

In fairness, Fletcher and Fincham imply that there are conditions under which automatic processing in relationships may occur. Their examples (e.g., wondering about why one's wife is pounding weiner schnitzel) reflect the complexity of trying to understand or predict to what extent a perceiver will think in an in-depth fashion. So quickly what appears to be a fairly low-level processing event may become more involving, as when the husband infers that his wife is imagining himself as the weiner schnitzel as she pounds away during a heated debate concerning her statement that he is insensitive to her needs! Furthermore, we are not arguing that people typically engage in effortful, extensive cognitive-emotional work in understanding their relationships. Clearly, people cannot afford regular, great expenditures of such effort. But we are arguing for a continuum approach that recognizes rapid movement along the depth-of-processing dimension. Fletcher and Fincham's chapter not only stimulates a reconciled lawyerly conception for the naive scientist versus cognitive miser question, but it also stimulates deep and effortful thought concerning the extent of cognitive processing in different relationship situations.

Much of our foregoing reasoning about Fletcher and Fincham's analysis of the automatic-controlled processing dichotomy is applicable to the chapter contributed by Scott, Fuhrman, and Wyer. These authors also speculate about the possibility that people in relationships often operate on the basis of automatic-like event representations (see also Forgas' later chapter on social episode representations). Such representations are likely to be particularly potent when relationship events can be enacted in scripted ways—as Forgas later suggests—or when problems do not command greater attention and cognitive/affective work. Scott et al.'s presentation is especially valuable in noting the potential importance of many of the more molecular cognitive processes that may be relevant in relationships. We appreciated, for example, the concept of event representation in social memory as potentially highly relevant to relationship conflict situations. As these authors suggest, a person may have encoded elements of a conversation that indicate why he or she is experiencing anger regarding the partner's behavior. A husband may remember most saliently, for instance, the flirtatious behavior of his wife at a recent social occasion and experience anger about the implications of her behavior for the relationship and what it says about her loyalty to him. Research on vivid memories for relationship conflict and endings has pinpointed such event representations as one type of critical content of long-term retrospective memory for relationships (Harvey, Flanary, & Morgan, 1986).

Scott et al.'s analysis is also unique in its discussion of communication norms that frequently govern relationship events. We do not doubt that norms such as those of informativeness and politeness often operate in the unfolding of interactional sequences. Research clearly is needed to evaluate how such norms interact with more contemporary dynamics such as anger, jealousy, and passion in influencing the nature of the interaction and accompanying thought and feeling.

A different direction of analysis is taken in Miller and Read's formidable chapter on a knowledge structure approach to mental models of persons and relationships. Because of its scope, again we will give their ideas considerable attention. Miller and Read seem to believe that considerable processing is typically going on, even if implicitly, in relationship events. Their statement is quite remindful of the general ideas of Gestalt psychology. In suggesting that people form models of each other and relationship events, these authors emphasize the capacity of humans to develop holistic pictures and accounts from bits and pieces of raw data. Perceivers presumably find coherence among even discrete and conflicting strands of information. According to Miller and Read, people achieve such coherence with dispatch via mechanisms such as goals, plans, scripts, roles, and themes. Knowledge structures, in turn, are the composites of these mechanisms. Miller and Read's overarching conception is referred to as a theory of interpersonalism. This latter term perhaps needs a fuller definition but seems to refer to the meaning sub-stratum that permits interpersonal communications and relationships to develop and to be maintained.

Miller and Read's analysis is rich in implications for our understanding of close relationships. It elaborates on the logic that not only has been implicit in Gestalt psychology, but also the logic that has been explicitly described in the computer-like models of scholars such as Miller, Galanter, and Pribram (1960) in their acclaimed statement concerning plans and the structure of behavior. Beyond such elaboration, Miller and Read's argument links this cognitive school of thought with Heider's (1958) seminal work on interpersonal relations and attribution theory in general. A unique feature of their argument is the suggestion that knowledge-relationship structures (or models) may be examined in order to probe how people influence each other in developing relationships over time. One person's goals, plans, scripts, and so on may affect behavior, which in turn influences dyadic interaction and relationship development (e.g., a person's goal to be faithful in a close relationship may have such a rippling impact). These models presumably become quite complex over a long-term relationship. The authors' reference to Clark's (1985) point that people often utter words under the condition that the other possesses and makes an encyclopedia full of assumptions about them as they make the utterances reflects well the richness of knowledge structures. The same is true of their suggestion that novel reading also represents a good analogy for interpersonal understanding in daily interaction.

We also find interesting, although a bit cryptic, Miller and Read's use of

Thagard's (1989) model of explanatory coherence to characterize how people decide among alternate knowledge structures in understanding others' actions. This link represents probably the clearest case of interfacing between basic cognitive and social cognitive theory to be found in this volume. Implicitly, Miller and Read argue that the Thagard model helps us understand what the human mind can do in processing complex information such as that displayed in close relationships. For example, the model allows successful integration of multiple sources of information, when instances of presented information occur simultaneously. It also views the perceiver as unsatisfied if the application of a knowledge structure yields an incomplete understanding with many facts and events uninterpretable. Impressively, Miller and Read note evidence from their own program of work to support elements of this model.

Finally, Miller and Read provide a useful discussion of traits as knowledge structures, with the intriguing accompanying idea that traits often have embedded within them a story of the relationships an actor has with others. This reasoning coheres well with Sternberg and Beall's later emphasis on implicit theories that presumably include as key parts such implicative trait inferences.

Our major pause about Miller and Read's analysis is that, as yet, few of their ideas have been tested in the context of ongoing social relationships (although it could be argued that others can now take up that objective), and that little attention is given to the possible role of affect in knowledge structures. We assume that these two concepts can be fruitfully integrated in their application to relationship phenomena. But we do wish to praise Miller and Read's effort as one that is genuinely on the interface between important areas and, hence, is finely tuned to the integrative contribution of this volume.

Cantor and Malley take us in still another direction in their insightful analysis of self-goals in the context of close relationships. In this chapter, we do not read much about how mainstream cognitive ideas are relevant to understanding close relationships. We do read about what is probably a novel of line of reasoning within personality theory and its relevance to relationships. Following McAdams' (1989) well-received work on intimacy, power, and life stories, Cantor and Malley suggest that people have a need for balance between agency in achievement activities and communion in relationships. They point to Erikson's (1968) idea of a generative stage as an integrative device for these two often opposing needs. As an illustration, an individual's creativity in art may be of considerable value to his or her successors—and uplifting to his or her immediate loved ones even if the process of making art takes time and energy away from communal activity. Although Cantor and Malley's analysis follows a unique course in this volume, they implicitly address the volume's earlier focus on automatic processing. They note that the literature on cognition in close relationships is scant concerning how much of people's thoughts and attention serve to automatically confirm prior needs, goals, and expectancies, and how much deliberate cognitive effort is expended to shape new alternatives for intimacy.

We appreciate Cantor and Malley's emphasis on compatible life tasks within a close relationship as a way of linking agency and communal needs. A related point that is not explicit in their analysis is that, as a matter of timing of critical life endeavors, it may be essential for many people to establish warm, communal love relationships *first* in order for tranquility to be achieved and a high level of achievement to be possible. Indeed, we do know that achievement often suffers when such relationships are removed from people's lives (e.g., it is said that Elvis Presley completely lost his passion for singing and living when his "rudder"—his wife Priscilla—left him).

Cantor and Malley argue that the study of life tasks helps us understand key motivational units of personality and also may provide indirect evidence about the satisfying or dissatisfying features of a close relationship. For example, if a person's life tasks at a certain mature stage in a relationship involve little communal orientation, it may be a signal the relationship is not destined for a lengthy future. Or it could be that the relationship is scripted in a noncommunal fashion and that it can, thus, readily endure—many relationships appear to show such a landscape.

A final qualifying concern arose for us in reading some of the interesting excerpts of stories from talented persons with whom Cantor and Malley have worked as participants in their studies. It seemed obvious that these persons wanted it all, or quite a bit thereof, in their quest for balance between agency and communion in their lives. They no doubt represent well a large percentage of the people one encounters as they plug along in the system of higher education in most countries. But what about those millions who are not closely related to the role of higher education in terms of elevating and making more satisfying one's life? For this group, survival may be their goal rather than some more subtle form of conduct. Scholars focusing on impoverished, single, pregnant teenagers (e.g., Cutrona & Troutman, 1986) have provided useful evidence about the scope of this struggle to survive. These teenagers are a group for whom in the here and now, there may seem to be very little light at the end of the tunnel. They may survive and later adopt various goals for their lives, but they also may struggle along in a relatively aimless way for a lifetime.

Our concern is obviously speculation at best. Perhaps, Cantor and Malley would contend that most members of the Western culture at least dream about the balance between agency and communion—whether or not it ever will be their fate. In conclusion, Cantor and Malley have provided us with a stimulating set of ideas and research possibilities that speak convincingly to the value of integrating personality and close relationship foci.

In the final chapter in Part 1, Bradbury and Fincham present their contextual model of marriage and begin to provide some application of the model to recent developments in the study of marriage, such as longitudinal behavioral analyses of marital interaction. This model has merit not only because it was stimulated by these authors' systematic, pioneering work on cognitive-affective mediational factors in marital interaction, but also because it presents a host of directions for further inquiry. Their figure, which highlights key dimensions in the contextual model, reveals powerfully the intricacy of thought-interaction events and the numerous elements that go into even split-second judgments by persons regarding their spouses' behavior. Answers to how people weight and treat these proximal and distal features of their marital environment await such research. We have no doubt that Bradbury and Fincham are beginning a line of work that will bring close relationship, cognitive, and social cognitive domains of research into proximity and will lead to stimulating interconnections.

What this model does not do, as is usually true, is represent all of the complexity of the phenomenon. For example, not only can the wife's processing be stimulated by the husband's behavior, but also the husband's further behavior may be modified by his understanding that his wife is making some judgment about him—the renowned causal loop situation. Moreover, the wife's processing may bring to bear on the situation not only many contemporary thoughts and feelings about the husband, but also many memories—good and bad that color the thoughts and feelings—and interpretations provided by others (such as her mother) in her network of friends, relatives, and associates. Do these various inputs have differential impacts as a function of their saliency, valence, relevance, and so on, on the wife's judgment and subsequent behavior, as we would assume they would? At the minimum, though, Bradbury and Fincham's model helps us begin to understand the dynamics of marital interaction and satisfaction and ways of exploring these phenomena and their time line.

Bradbury and Fincham's chapter has a number of other strengths including discussion of work on personality and how personality processes may also enter into marital satisfaction and interaction. We certainly agree with one of their primary arguments that it is time to expand the behavioral formulation of marriage and that current work, such as their own, which has involved longitudinal analysis, creates a ready foundation for this expansion. We have a set of final questions about Bradbury and Fincham's work, especially as future research involving longitudinal designs is pursued. Do we know much about when negative reciprocal behavioral and/or attributional tendencies begin in close relationships? Do they follow any kind of normative patterns? How much negativity must be perceived by one party to set in motion intended reciprocal behavior? And what about personality traits such as self-esteem? Do they modify the course of such reciprocation—with, for example, a low self-esteem spouse being relatively reluctant to commence his or her role in the fated reciprocation dance? Even with some longitudinal evidence under our belts, we hunger for answers to a thousand questions like these.

Part 2: Cognition and Affect

Forgas' chapter represents an appropriate beginning piece for Part 2. Forgas argues convincingly from his own work and related reasoning that affect and cognition cannot be understood as separate, isolated domains, but must be studied as they interact in order to understand close relationships. A rich part of Forgas' presentation is the discussion of his own productive research about perceived social scripts or episodes and related cognition and affect. His work, for instance, suggests the importance of evaluative dimensions having to do with love and commitment in scripts about relationships. Forgas also finds that relationship cognition is closely related to a person's attitudes, personality, and heterosexual history. Their work is valuable because they have begun to examine how different groups exhibit different representations of social episodes.

Forgas also discusses his work on the role of affective states on how people perceive own and others' social behavior. In so doing, he invokes Bower's (1981) associative memory theory to suggest that transient processes such as current mood state may influence social perception. We certainly agree. We further concur with Forgas' conclusion that in ongoing relationships a number of factors such as history of conflict may overwhelm or modify the effect of induced mood on social perception and behavior. Research clearly is needed, as Forgas suggests, to understand the relation between transient mood and relationship events. This relationship is likely to be examined via nonexperimental techniques (in comparison to past work on mood and perception) in deference to ethical considerations about which moods can be justifiably induced in one or both members of an ongoing dyad. Nonetheless, Forgas and his colleagues' work establishes a strong foundation for this eventual extension.

We applaud Fitness and Strongman's analysis as another example of fine integrative analysis. In particular, we appreciate their incorporation of Berscheid's (1983) theoretical framework for understanding emotions in close relationships as a principal means for understanding the synergistic operation of affect and cognition. We agree with their argument that more fine-grained conceptual work is necessary on specific emotions within close relationships. Fitness and Strongman make a compelling case that there exists a wide berth for exploration of different facets of affect-cognition interactions within close relationships and that such interactions must represent a central focus for work in this area. Their statement includes useful discussion of several theoretical positions on emotions including Leventhal's (1982) perceptual-motor theory and Ellis' (1962) rational emotive theory. As with a theme in Forgas' analysis, it would be most helpful if an effort were made to empirically examine some of these prominent conceptions (e.g., Leventhal's) in the context of ongoing social relationships.

Noller and Ruzzene's chapter certainly involves relevant applications because it is based on findings drawn from Noller's influential program of work on marital communication and interaction. She and her colleagues have provided detailed information about many nonverbal aspects of marital interaction. In so doing, they have broadened our understanding greatly about possible gender differences in marital communication and about the interaction of thoughts, feelings, and subtle forms of behavior in marital relationships. Similar to Cantor and Malley, Noller and Ruzzene emphasize the centrality of interdependence in close relationships, with the implicit assumption that different systems will be involved in an interactive way in most relationship events. Their work speaks directly to this interdependence.

A major contribution of this chapter and Noller's program, in general, is the information provided about the role of communication and attribution in influencing spouses' beliefs about the quality of their marital relationship. They argue, for example, that the attributions of distressed spouses create a negative distal context (using Bradbury and Fincham's term) for marital communication, which then increases the probability that the spouses will misunderstand each other—or that negative reciprocal loops (not unlike the analysis so vividly described by Laing, 1970) will be established in the mutual understanding and reactions of spouses. This work is most impressive in its detail and focus on ongoing close relationships with dyads reacting to naturalistic stimulus situations. In general, it reveals much about the inaccuracy, negativism in attribution, and overall misunderstanding that delineate the phenomenology of distressed spouses vis à vis each other. Beyond these merits, this work speaks volumes to the concerns raised by Beach in his chapter in Part 3 regarding why marital therapy is not more effective. In addition to the type of work on mediational processes that Beach suggests is necessary, Noller and Ruzzene's chapter points to the importance of multivariate research on causal loop sequences over time (much as Fincham, Bradbury, and colleagues have begun to carry out). To reverse or modify these deleterious sequences requires a lot more understanding of the interrelated processes of thought, feeling, and behavior than presently exists.

A final salient aspect of Noller and Ruzzene's chapter to us was its emphasis on gender differences. Distressed wives, for example, appear to play an especially critical role in producing behavior that perpetuates negative feedback loops. We hesitate to advocate the use of psychophysiological techniques (e.g., Levenson and Gottman's, 1983, work) for *broad-scaled application* to relationship phenomena because of their intrusive and probably nonnaturalistic interplay with the dynamics under study. However, it would appear that Noller's rich research program, which already melds attribution, perception, and nonverbal behavior, might also have as an agenda the incorporation of some psychophysiological measurement in an effort to understand better the precise dynamics of distressed and nondistressed couples' interaction.

Fletcher and Kininmonth's chapter on interaction and social cognition complements well Noller and Ruzzene's. Fletcher and Kininmonth provide a useful discussion of major programs of work on interaction and cognition in couples, such as Fitzpatrick's (1988), Levenson and Gottman's (1983), and Bradbury and Fincham's research programs. This chapter is particularly valuable, and unique in the volume, in its contribution to assessment of methodological issues in studying how these systems interact. Many needs for further inquiry are ferreted out in this assessment. We learn, for example, there is a need for pre-interaction probing of cognition that then is related both to cognition and behavior that occurs during the interaction.

We also resonate with their concerns about the breadth of application of the so-called talk-table technique developed by Gottman for studying ongoing talk during interaction. This technique, while highly creative and helpful to a point, requires the complement of more traditional probes of cognition because it does involve a relatively unusual task for research participants and may intrude unduly on their natural thinking and behaving.

Fletcher and Kininmonth also address the importance of standardization in the techniques increasingly used in which couples review videotapes of their interaction and provide accounts of their own thinking and the thinking they impute to their partners. They urge standardization in obtaining the accounts—format, length, and so on—in the coding of the accounts; they also stress the value of employing instructions that ask respondents not to construct new thoughts or ideas as a function of viewing the videotape.

Their comments about how accuracy in perception is studied are persuasive regarding the need for refinement in relevant techniques. The attendant implication of their reasoning is that some of the conflicting data that exist in the literature may be understood better via such refinement.

Finally, Fletcher and Kininmonth describe a study by Fletcher and Fitness (1990) that developed and tested a method for accessing and recording social cognition in close relationship couples as that cognition occurs *in vivo*. Because of its naturalistic method and rich findings, this study promises to be one of the most influential studies in the literature concerned with how to measure ongoing cognition in couples and more specifically with the use of the video-reviewing technique. Overall, this chapter is a must read for scholars in this area because of its thoughtful treatment of methodological issues, including some on the philosophy of science that governs work in the area (e.g., whether a focus on theory testing permits greater latitude as to whether methods should have high ecological validity for relationship events).

The concluding chapter in Part 2 by Sternberg and Beall presents an interesting epistemological analysis of what love means to people. By strong implication, it fits under the "Cognition and Affect" heading for this section because these authors clearly are advocating a broad notion of love and the approach to studying it. We appreciate their focus on the value of implicit theories of love. This value must be compared against the frequent silence of such theories about specific hypotheses or the precise nature of expected relationships. As Sternberg and Beall suggest, this approach has received too little research to date.

We also agree with several of their arguments about more explicit approaches. For example, they suggest that learning theories probably help us understand attraction phenomena but not love and close relationship phenomena. Further, they contend that the currently prominent work on attachment (such as Hazan & Shaver's, 1987, analysis) are subject to methodological limitations such as the fraility of people's attempts to report on early attachment patterns with their parents. Continuing in this vein, Sternberg and Beall argue that the sociobiological approach is difficult to disconfirm and may even legitimize certain cultural values (e.g., that men are fundamentally polygynous) without adequate empirical analysis or attention to significant variance in behavior over persons, situation, time, and place.

As Sternberg and Beall note, each theoretical position has serious limitations. Thus, they opt for a general approach that involves eclecticism. As we have noted in the introduction to this chapter, that spirit permeates the entire volume. We very much would second a central implication of their analysis that suggests more attention should be given to the contents of folk psychology (e.g., Bruner, 1987) in order to provide a fuller understanding of how people think and feel about love and close relationships in their lives.

Part 3: Applications and Extensions

This part begins with a chapter by Surra and Bohman, which is concerned with cognitive interdependence and the development of close relationships and with how cognitive interdependence changes over broad spans of time. This latter concern focuses on Surra and her colleagues' impressive research on transition points in relationships and couples' attributions and accounts regarding the factors affecting those turning points. The chapter is highly relevant to earlier chapters by Miller and Read on knowledge structures and by Scott et al. on information processing. As emphasized by Kelley et al. (1983), the concept of interdependence has become central to the study of close relationships. Just what is meant by the term *interdependence* in close relationships? In its most elementary form, interdependence refers to reciprocal, causal influence between members of a relationship; it could also refer to such influence with persons in the couple's network, such as relatives or close friends. Using some of the current terminology of cognitive psychology, including ideas articulated by Scott et al., Surra and Bohman analyze cognitive interdependence and provide interesting commentary on its course over the development of a relationship.

This type of analysis is most complex because the investigator often is trying to understand thinking processes that occur simultaneously in two people, while also matching these thinking processes to ongoing behavioral interaction. This volume contains inviting discussion in several chapters about this type of imposing inquiry. But, in truth, we as investigators and scholars simply are not very sophisticated yet in the development of theory research techniques concerned with investigating what we will call *cognitive-behavioral interdependence* in couples, much less in the many other reciprocal, causal influences between couples and network members. So we applaud Surra and Bohman's effort and look forward to further inroads into these mysteries of relationship thought and action that approaches such as the turning-points technique may provide.

As compared to the final chapter on application by Beach, Surra and Bohman's chapter may be seen as relevant to an extension of theory on cognition in relationships. We would have liked to have seen interstimulation, or cross-referencing, between this chapter and the chapter by Miller and Read. Each is concerned with knowledge structures, albeit they have somewhat different perspectives (Miller and Read apparently emphasize ideas such as goals and scripts more than Surra and Bohman do; whereas, Surra and Bohman give comparatively more attention to affect and stress the particular knowledge structures of subjective conditions, relational schemas, and causal accounts). Each is committed to a focus on the meaning and experience of close relationships. Each is committed to analyzing mutual, causal influence and both explicit thinking and meta-thinking. Finally, each gives attention to stories or accounts as part of these knowledge structures. We find Surra and Bohman's treatment of accounts quite interesting and congenial to our own (e.g., Harvey et al., 1990) in its emphasis upon the empowering role of account making in defining relationships and giving individuals direction vis à vis relationship problems. We look forward to more detailed analysis and empirical evidence by Surra and Bohman and colleagues on the role of accounts in maintenance and change processes in close relationships.

In the concluding chapter in this volume, Beach provides a creative analysis of why marital therapy for distressed couples often flounders. We applaud his emphasis on well-researched social-psychological theory as a basis for the development of more effective implementation of such therapy (e.g., his discussion of Tesser's self-evaluation maintenance model and its applicability to marital satisfaction issues). We would hasten to add, however, that the present volume also suggests the potential value of other types of psychology (e.g., cognitive, developmental, personality, psychophysiological) as guides to application.

Overall, Beach's statement points to the need for outcome research in this area and, in particular, to the need for outcome research that examines more carefully the mediators of marital satisfaction and dissatisfaction. We need to know, for example, if enhancement of social skills on the part of the husband does indeed lead to the wife feeling more satisfied with the relationship. Along this line, we agree with Beach in praising the ground-breaking program of work by Fincham and Bradbury and in pinpointing the possible value of Ajzen and Fishbein's (1977) theory of planned behavior, with its emphasis on attitudes, intentions, and social norms, as having relevance for understanding whether marital therapy will be effective for distressed relationships.

In the end, we are struck too about the low success rate of marital therapy. But, as therapists frequently remind scholars in this area, the deterioration dynamics are likely to be well in place by the time intervention is sought and tried. So it is possible that therapy will often be confirmatory and uplifting. That is, therapy might be aimed at helping the couple develop an effective plan for their individual lives and a sense of personal control regarding some of the major subsequent events if separation becomes inevitable. As noted in previous comments, there is a growing body of evidence about the complex interactions among thought, feeling, and behavior in distressed and nondistressed couples. To begin to address the intervention dilemma requires both much more scholarly inquiry and more appreciation of this complexity on the part of therapists.

UNADDRESSED ISSUES

This final section of our commentary will focus briefly on relevant perspectives that are not well represented and perhaps should be in this volume. Clearly, the volume offers much valuable integration of work at the interfaces of cognition, social cognition, interpersonal relations, and close relationships. This was a feat. Further, one can only do so much with any one volume, and the editors deserve applause for serving the reader such a full plate of issues, ideas, findings, and perspectives.

One perspective that is not well represented in this volume is that of cross-cultural psychology and how different groups and cultures may differ in terms of close relationship dynamics. Admittedly, there has been little work on this topic. But there are germs of contribution available. For example, Fletcher and colleagues (e.g., Grigg, Fletcher, & Fitness, 1989) have studied spontaneous attributions in happy and unhappy dating relationships in New Zealand, and have usefully linked their findings to those emerging in the United States and Europe. In fact, quite a few of the research programs described in the present volume involved sampling from populations in different Western countries. It would help if more explicit attention were given to this topic, and if attention were directed to the study of relationships in non-Western cultures.

Hewstone's (see his 1989 book) work on cultural differences in attributional processes is exemplary and illustrates a possibly fertile direction for the relationship field. Some of us (e.g., discussions among the authors of this chapter and Bram Buunk and Steve Duck) have informally discussed the potential value of further international forums on relationships (not unlike the NATO series on various topics)—forums that would be specifically aimed at involving scholars from countries in which relationship work is just beginning. With the opening up of the European Eastern bloc nations, this type of forum in the near future appears even more timely. More generally, a logical question for cross-cultural work in this area concerns how political chaos or flux in many parts of the world (e.g., the Middle East) is related to changes in close relationship processes and structures. We very much need scholarship that addresses this possibility and that speaks in general to cross-cultural differences and similarities and the related theoretical dynamics of close relationships.

It also would have helped if the present volume had included more prominent perspectives such as the sociobiological perspective (e.g., Buss & Barnes, 1986) and relevant sociological perspectives such as that found in symbolic interaction theory (e.g., Crittenden, 1983; Stryker, 1977). These perspectives would provide not only breadth, but also quite different views of the role of cognition in close relationships. We interpret the sociobiological position to emphasize evolutionary processes and to downplay contemporaneous dynamics such as those involving thought and feeling. For example, from this perspective, a man should be attracted to physically attractive, intelligent women and want to date and mate with them in order to propagate more adaptive representatives of the species. However, notwithstanding considerable evidence in the literature (e.g., Byrne, 1971), the roles of consensual validation associated with attractive others or of mental stimulation associated with intelligent others would not be given much attention in this approach.

On the other hand, symbolic interaction theory has much to say about the role of thought in influencing social interaction (e.g., Mead, 1934). Related to writings in this volume, such as the Forgas analysis of social episodes, symbolic interaction theorists would be likely to emphasize the mental act involving a person's playing out of how his or her behavior would be received by the other and then how the other would respond to this behavior. Importantly, they also would emphasize the development of these symbolic "taking the role of other" types of activities in the young person. Such a developmental focus is sorely needed throughout the literature of close relationships. The symbolic interaction perspective certainly involves an integration of cognition and actual social interaction and would be likely to supplement many of the chapters in the present volume. Gladly, there are scholars who are pursuing this tradition in their study of close relationships (e.g., Orbuch, 1988).

In the end, we salute the editors and contributors to this volume for producing a work that captures well much of the diversity of the rapidly developing field of close relationships as it relates to social cognition. And, just as important, these writers celebrate diversity in ideas and methods—a most salutary direction.

ACKNOWLEDGMENTS

We thank Garth Fletcher and Frank Fincham for very helpful comments on an earlier draft of this chapter.

REFERENCES

Ajzen, I., & Fishbein, M. (1977). Attitude-behavior relations. A theoretical analysis and review of empirical research. *Psychological Bulletin, 84*, 888–918.

Berscheid, E. (1983). Emotion. In H. H. Kelley, E. Berscheid, A. Christensen, J. Harvey, T. Huston, G. Levinger, E. McClintock, A. Perlau, & D. Peterson (Eds.), *Close relationships* (pp. 110–168). San Francisco: Freeman.

Bower, E. H. (1981). Mood and memory. *American Psychologist, 36*, 129–148.

Bradley-Weary, G. (1978). Self-serving biases in the attribution processes: A re-examination of the fact or fiction question. *Journal of Personality and Social Psychology, 36*, 56–71.

Bruner, J. (1987). Life as narrative. *Social Research, 54*, 11–32.

Bryne, D. (1971). *The attraction paradigm*. New York: Academic Press.

Buss, D. M. & Barnes, M. (1986). Preferences in human mate selection. *Journal of Personality and Social Psychology, 50*, 559–570.

Clark, H. H. (1985). Language use and language users. In G. Lindzey & E. Aronson (Eds.), *The handbook of social psychology* (Vol. 2, pp. 179–231). New York: Random House.

Crittenden, K. S. (1983). Sociological aspects of attribution. *Annual Review of Sociology, 9*, 425–446.

Cutrona, C. E., & Troutman, B. R. (1986). Psychosocial outcomes of adolescent pregnancy: Maternal and child effects. *Seminars in Adolescent Medicine, 2*, 235–242.

Ellis, A. (1962). *Reason and emotion in psychotherapy*. New York: Lyle Stuart Press.

Erikson, E. H. (1968). *Identity: Youth and crisis*. New York: Norton.

Fincham, F. D., & Bradbury, T. N. (1987). Cognitive processes and conflict in close relationships: An attribution-efficacy model. *Journal of Personality and Social Psychology, 53*, 1106–1118.

Fitzpatrick, M. A. (1988). Approaches to marital interaction. In P. Noller & M. A. Fitzpatrick (Eds.), *Perspectives on marital interaction* (pp. 160–177). Cleredon, England: Multilingual Matters.

Fletcher, G. J. O., & Fitness, J. (1990). Occurent social cognition in close relationship interaction: The role of proximal and distal variables. *Journal of Personality and Social Psychology, 59*, 464–474.

Fletcher, G. J. O., & Haig, B. (in press). The layperson as "naive scientist": An appropriate model for social psychology? In R. Hogan, R. Wolfe, & K. Craik (Eds.), *Perspectives in personality* (Vol. 4). Greenwich, CT: JAI Press.

Grigg, F., Fletcher, G. J. O., & Fitness, J. (1989). Spontaneous attributions in happy and unhappy dating relationships. *Journal of Social and Personal Relationships, 6*, 61–68.

Hazan, C., & Shaver, P. (1987). Romantic love conceptualized as an attachment process. *Journal of Personality and Social Psychology, 52*, 511–524.

Harvey, J. H. (1976). *Dispositional attributions: A manifestation of the principle of least effort?* Paper presented at Midwestern Psychological Association meeting, Chicago.

Harvey, J. H., Flanary, F., & Morgan, M. (1986). Vivid memories of vivid loves gone by. *Journal of Social and Personal Relationships, 3*, 359–373.

Harvey, J. H., Weber, A. L., Orbuch, T. L. (1990). *Interpersonal accounts: A social psychological perspective*. Oxford: Basil Blackwell.

Harvey, J. H., Wells, G. L., & Alvarez, M. D. (1978). Attribution in the context of conflict and separation in close relationships. In J. Harvey, W. Ickes, & R. Kidd (Eds.), *New directions in attribution research* (Vol. 2, pp. 235–259). Hillsdale, NJ: Erlbaum.

Heider, F. (1958). *The psychology of interpersonal relations*. New York: Wiley.

Hewstone, M. (1989). *Causal attribution: From cognitive processes to collective beliefs*. Oxford: Basil Blackwell.

Kelley, H. H., Berscheid, E., Christensen, A., Harvey, J. H., Huston, T. L., Levinger, G., McClintock, E., Peplau, L. A., & Peterson, D. R. (1983). *Close relationships*. New York: Freeman.

Laing, R. D. (1970). *Knots*. New York: Pantheon.

Levenson, R. W. & Gottman, J. M. (1983). Marital interaction: Physiological linkage and affective exchange. *Journal of Personality and Social Psychology, 45*, 587–597.

Leventhal, H. (1982). The integration of emotion and cognition: A view from the perceptual-motor theory of emotion. In M. Clark & S. Fiske (Eds.), *Affect and cognition: The Seventeenth Annual Carnegie Symposium on Cognition* (pp. 121–156). Hillsdale, NJ: Lawrence Erlbaum Associates.

McAdams, D. P. (1989). *Intimacy*. New York: Doubleday.

Mead, G. H. (1934). *Mind, self, and society*. Chicago: University of Chicago Press.

Miller, G. A., Galanter, E., & Pribram, K. H. (1960). *Plans and the structure of behavior*. New York: Holt, Rinehart, & Winston.

Newman, L. S., & Uleman, J. S. (1989). Spontaneous trait inference. In J. S. Uleman & J. A. Bargh (Eds.), *Unintended thought* (pp. 155–188). New York: Guilford Press.

Orbuch, T. L. (1988). *Responses to and coping with nonmarital relationship terminations.* Unpublished doctoral dissertation, University of Wisconsin–Madison (related chapter by author in T. L. Orbuch [Ed.], in press, *Close relationship loss: Theoretical perspectives.* New York: Springer-Verlag).

Stryker, S. (1977). Developments in "two social psychologies": Toward an appreciation of mutual relevance. *Sociometry, 40,* 145–160.

Thagard, P. (1989). Explanatory coherence. *Behavioral and Brain Sciences, 12,* 435–467.

Uleman, J. S., Winborne, W. C., Winter, L., & Shechter, D. (1986). Personality differences in spontaneous personality inferences at encoding. *Journal of Personality and Social Psychology, 51,* 396–403.

Weiss, R. S. (1975). *Marital separation.* New York: Basic Books.

Author Index

Subject Index